Making Rights Real

THE CHICAGO SERIES IN LAW AND SOCIETY

Edited by John M. Conley and Lynn Mather

Also in the series:

Lawyers on the Right: Professionalizing the Conservative Coalition
by Ann Southworth

Arguing with Tradition: The Language of Law in Hopi Tribal Court
by Justin B. Richland

Speaking of Crime: The Language of Criminal Justice
by Lawrence M. Solan and Peter M. Tiersma

Human Rights and Gender Violence: Translating International Law into Social Justice
by Sally Engle Merry

Just Words, Second Edition: Law, Language, and Power
by John M. Conley and William M. O'Barr

Distorting the Law: Politics, Media, and the Litigation Crisis
by William Haltom and Michael McCann

Justice in the Balkans: Prosecuting War Crimes in the Hague Tribunal
by John Hagan

Rights of Inclusion: Law and Identity in the Life Stories of Americans with Disabilities
by David M. Engel and Frank W. Munger

The Internationalization of Palace Wars: Lawyers, Economists, and the Contest to Transform Latin American States
by Yves Dezalay and Bryant G. Garth

Free to Die for Their Country: The Story of the Japanese American Draft Resisters in World War II
by Eric L. Muller

Overseers of the Poor: Surveillance, Resistance, and the Limits of Privacy
by John Gilliom

Pronouncing and Persevering: Gender and the Discourses of Disputing in an African Islamic Court
by Susan F. Hirsch

Additional series titles follow index

CHARLES R. EPP

Making Rights Real

Activists, Bureaucrats, and the Creation of
the Legalistic State

The University of Chicago Press | Chicago & London

Charles R. Epp is associate professor in the Department of Public Administration at the University of Kansas. He is the author of *The Rights Revolution: Lawyers, Activists, and Supreme Courts in Comparative Perspective*, winner of the C. Herman Pritchett Award of the Law and Courts Section of the American Political Science Association.

The University of Chicago Press, Chicago 60637
The University of Chicago Press, Ltd., London
© 2009 by The University of Chicago
All rights reserved. Published 2009
Printed in the United States of America

18 17 16 15 14 13 12 11 10 09   1 2 3 4 5

Library of Congress Cataloging-in-Publication Data

Epp, Charles R.
Making rights real : activists, bureaucrats, and the creation of the legalistic state / Charles R. Epp.
    p. cm.
Includes bibliographical references and index.
  ISBN-13: 978-0-226-21164-0   (cloth : alk. paper)
  ISBN-13: 978-0-226-21165-7   (pbk. : alk. paper)
  ISBN-10: 0-226-21164-9   (cloth : alk. paper)
  ISBN-10: 0-226-21165-7   (pbk. : alk. paper)   1. Liability (Law)—United States.   2. Law reform—United States—Citizen participation.   3. Civil rights—United States—History—20th century.   4. Tort liability of police—United States. 5. Tort liability of police—Great Britain.   6. Liability for harassment—United States.   7. Playgrounds—Law and legislation—United States.   I. Title.
  KF1250 .E65 2009
  344.7305'2—dc22

2009020088

Contents

Acknowledgments   *vii*

1   Introduction   *1*

2   Theory: The Fertile Fear of Liability   *13*

3   The Problem with Policing   *31*

4   Liability's Triumph   *59*

5   Policing's Epiphany   *93*

6   Spreading the Word: Variations among Police Departments   *115*

7   Tort Liability and Police Reform in Britain   *139*

8   Sexual Harassment   *165*

9   Playground Safety   *197*

10   Conclusion   *215*

Methodological Appendix   *233*
Notes   *265*
Bibliography   *321*
Index   *345*

Acknowledgments

This book has been long in the making, and I owe a considerable debt to many supportive people and institutions. The research was made possible by generous grants from the National Science Foundation (Grant SES-9905189) and the University of Kansas General Research Fund (the usual disclaimers apply). I am grateful to a number of scholars for advice and comments at various stages in the book's development. I especially thank Bert Kritzer for very helpful conversations over the full course from planning to completion and for comments on several drafts. I am also especially grateful to Candace McCoy for several extremely helpful conversations, for helping me reach key sources, and for very thoughtful comments on a draft. With regard to my analysis of British policing, I am deeply indebted to Graham Smith for a number of valuable conversations and e-mail communications, for helping me to reach key sources, and for comments on an early draft. For helpful comments on drafts of the entire manuscript I thank Dick Brisbin, Lynda Dodd, Laura Jensen, Karen Orren, and Samuel Walker. I am especially indebted to Bill Haltom and Jon Gould, who reviewed and commented on the manuscript for the Press, offering thoughtful suggestions, and to series editors Lynn Mather and John Conley, who contributed equally valuable suggestions.

I am indebted to a number of other scholars for comments on parts of the book. For comments and suggestions on the survey instruments, I am grateful to Mia Cahill, Lauren Edelman, Lori Fridell, Bert Kritzer, and Samuel Walker. For comments and suggestions on conference papers or early parts of the manuscript, I thank Jeb Barnes, Tom Burke, Malcolm Feeley,

Marc Galanter, Joel Grossman, Simon Halliday, Christine Harrington, Bob Kagan, Stefanie Lindquist, Michael McCann, Marie Provine, Margo Schlanger, Susan Silbey, Mark Suchman, and Carroll Seron. I benefited from participants' comments on presentations at the political science departments of the University of Connecticut, Johns Hopkins University, Ohio University, and Wichita State University and at the Institute for Law and Society at New York University, the Law and Society Summer Institute at Oxford University, and the Conference on Culture and Tort Law organized by Michael McCann and David Engel at the University of Denver Law School. For their support, patience, and suggestions I am especially indebted to my colleagues at the University of Kansas, particularly Steven Maynard-Moody, John Nalbandian, George Frederickson, Marilu Goodyear, Justin Marlowe, and Charles Jones, and to my students Randy Davis, Solomon Woods, and Nathaniel Wright and my former student Shannon Portillo. For research assistance I thank Tori Barnes-Brus and Taehyun Nam; and for very helpful editorial comments on a final draft, I thank Paul Brandenburger and Emily Kennedy. Jamie Kratky provided helpful clerical assistance, and the staff of the Institute for Policy and Social Research at the University of Kansas, particularly Larry Hoyle and Xan Wedel, were unfailingly helpful.

I am especially grateful to the many activists, lawyers, and practitioners who gave generously of their time for interviews. Although it's risky to single out any particular sources, I feel compelled to especially thank Michael Avery, Constance Backhouse, Raju Bhatt, Tom Brady, Dick Chesney, Ann Fagan Ginger, David Hamilton, Candace McCoy, Patrick Murphy, David Rudovsky, Wayne Schmidt, and Graham Smith.

I am extremely grateful to the editorial staff at the University of Chicago Press. John Tryneski, as another university press editor told me, is "a prince among editors," and it's absolutely true: he offered extremely thoughtful comments and suggestions that improved the book in key ways. Thank you, John. I'm also indebted to Alice Bennett for superb copyediting and forbearance—in the extreme—toward my inability to let go, and to Rodney Powell for very helpful responses to my many questions.

Finally, I am deeply indebted to my parents, Robert O. and Amelia Epp, for their long support and to my wife Lora Jost for her help and thoughtful comments over many years. I dedicate the book to her and my son Nicholai (who at seven is already writing a book too—but he says his won't take ten years to finish!).

Introduction

1

We are being sued because we are not doing our job. The legal
system and its social engineering are combating our incompe-
tence in finding, selecting, hiring, and controlling our police
officers.
—Remarks of two police officials in a national
workshop on civil liability, 1983[1]

The past quarter-century has witnessed a sweeping, law-inspired
reform of American bureaucracy. The thesis of this book is that,
contrary to the widespread perception that this era was a time of
retreat from the pursuit of egalitarian reform through law, activists
and bureaucratic reformers pushed through law-modeled reforms
that radically reframed the core assumptions and tools of government administration. Police departments created strict policies on
the use of force and cracked down on abusive officers. Government
human relations departments created and strictly enforced policies
prohibiting sexual harassment. Parks administrators tore out and
replaced play equipment in tens of thousands of playgrounds, designing and managing the new installations to reduce the risk of injury. I argue that these developments, and many more, came about
because newly energized activist movements and liability lawyers
forced agencies to face up to long-ignored problems of abuse and
injury, and because managers came to recognize that these legal claims represented fundamental threats to their public and

professional legitimacy. In fact, as the chapter epigraph suggests, reform-oriented professional managers came to welcome the threat of lawsuits as an impetus for their campaign.

The bureaucratic transformation grew out of what Stuart Scheingold has called the "politics of rights." The rights revolution of the 1950s and 1960s promised many things, but the meaning of these promises depended on the course of conflict over how—or whether—to realize them. By the 1970s, as the civil rights movement collapsed, bureaucracies resisted reform, and conservatives came to power attacking judicial activism, the promise of rights seemed increasingly hollow. The problems of discrimination and arbitrary authority seemed more intractable than ever, more closely entwined with social and bureaucratic institutions, more impervious to court-led reform. The American state's decentralization and the bureaucratic insulation of its outer reaches especially seemed to conspire against reform. Rights announced by the Supreme Court awaited implementation in fifty states and tens of thousands of local governments, and officials in these places often evaded judicial mandates. "There is, these days, some ambivalence about litigation," Scheingold wrote in 1974. "The civil rights experience has made us all skeptics."[2] Gerald Rosenberg ultimately pronounced court-led reform a "hollow hope."[3] Activists and reformers, however, responded to these frustrations not by giving up the field but by regrouping and trying again in new ways.

Since the studies documenting the Warren Court's limited impact, there have been very few examinations of the effect of court-led reform on bureaucratic practices, even as the legal tools available to reformers have changed and our understanding of bureaucracies has improved. The main tool of reform has shifted from judicial orders ("reform this prison") to tort or tortlike lawsuits ("pay for this injury"). Likewise, our knowledge of bureaucracies has shifted from viewing individual organizations as separate entities to seeing them as parts of a web of interconnected networks. It is time for a fresh look, and this book is a first attempt. I will return to the significance of these two matters—the rise of legal liability under tort and civil rights law and improvements in our understanding of bureaucratic change—after a brief summary of the book's thesis and the evidence for it.

First, beginning in the late 1970s, reformers seeking to overcome bureaucratic intransigence in a number of policy fields carried out a flurry of law-inspired professional reforms. The reforms congealed into a common policy framework that I call *legalized accountability*, whose essence is a law-styled attempt to bring bureaucratic practice into line with emerging legal norms. In pursuit of that goal, reformers fine-tuned their efforts to address the common practice of bureaucratic "window dressing"—adopting policies on paper but doing little to implement them. The reformers' primary tools for bringing bureaucratic practice into line with legal norms were written rules, formal systems of training, and internal systems of oversight to assess compliance with the rules. While these rules and compliance systems were not required by specific laws or judicial decisions, they took on a lawlike form in the nature of their master norms ("sexual harassment is a form of sex discrimination and is illegal"), their reliance on clear, detailed rules, and their use of legalized procedures to implement these rules. Powered by professional networks, local agencies in many policy areas have adopted the key elements of this common framework; it has spread throughout all regions of the United States, all sizes of cities, all types of local political culture. By the 1990s the legalized accountability framework had taken on a life of its own, and it has proved remarkably effective and enduring. Reformers, in their increasingly fine-tuned efforts aimed at changing bureaucratic practices down to the front lines, created an institutional system that was lawlike in character: they were legalizing accountability.

Second, legalized accountability grew and spread from an interaction between activist pressure for law-based reform and conflict within the managerial professions over how to respond. This interaction reached a critical juncture in the late 1970s and early 1980s when activists' growing litigation threats against agencies and an emerging professional reform campaign within them fused, yielding an explosion in the fear of liability among professional practitioners. Both the external activists and the managerial practitioners were necessary to the development, but neither was sufficient. The activists supplied pressure for change in the form of lawsuit-generated publicity; the administrative professionals supplied practical tools—rules, training, and oversight mechanisms—to produce real, lasting change in bureaucratic practice. Although the threat of liability is a key factor in my analysis, this threat worked rather differently than is widely believed. Agency managers feared liability not primarily for its financial cost but for its risk to professional reputation: no city, for instance, wanted to be publicly exposed as employing abusive police officers or condoning sexual harassment among its employees. Similarly, bureaucratic reformers on the inside of the system—ostensibly the targets of liability—enthusiastically joined with external activists in using the threat of liability as a lever of reform. The interaction between these two forces—activist pressure from the outside and reform ideas from the inside—generated both enormous pressure for reform and a model of what to do. The result was a reform movement that, after a period when the defenders of the status quo fended off change, swept through fields of administrative policy in the 1980s and 1990s with surprising speed and thoroughness.

The resulting system of legalized accountability has spread widely, yet some agencies have adopted only its most visible elements, leaving internal practices unchanged. The conditions that contributed to the legal revolution also help to explain its varying depth from place to place: where there are vigorous activist groups and lawyers and where agencies are closely connected to professional networks, legalized accountability is adopted in depth. Where these conditions are absent, agencies honor the dominant model only in appearance.

Third, the character of legalized accountability reflects its twin sources: it contains elements of both popular accountability and managerial prerogative. It legally intrudes on bureaucratic prerogatives more than anyone in an earlier era might have imagined possible, yet it is also far more subject to managerial control than legal activists might prefer. Thus, key elements of legalized accountability—the requirement of detailed record keeping, for instance—open bureaucracies to the potential for intrusive legal oversight. At the same time, these internal legalistic controls are maintained and managed not by outside lawyers or citizen groups but by bureaucratic managers who have a powerful interest in avoiding embarrassing disclosures. Legalized accountability, in other words, is a hybrid that constrains and empowers both managerial practitioners and external activists.

The fear of liability and legalized accountability, in sum, are joined at the hip. They arose together in the late 1970s and 1980s through an interaction among activist pressure, media coverage of lawsuits, and professional practitioners' struggles to respond. The two ideas developed, in Max Weber's term, an "elective affinity."[4] Rather than causing the rise of legalized accountability, the fear of liability was a facilitating condition—and vice versa. As activists increasingly put liability pressure on agencies, practitioners' growing fear of liability—their diagnosis of the problem—led inexorably to a prescription shaped in part by activists' demands: adopt systems of legalized accountability. At the same time, as reformist practitioners became more certain that legalized accountability was a good idea they increasingly trumpeted the threat of liability to their fellow practitioners as a reason to accept that idea.

My evidence for this three-part thesis is based on a comparative study of local government reform efforts in three policy areas in the United States—

policing, sexual harassment in employment, and playground safety—and for policing, in Britain. I focus on local governments because their practices affect people almost every day and because, in the wake of the rights revolution of the 1960s, many of these practices seemed greatly in need of reform. There are, further, many local governments, making detailed comparisons of reforms possible across a wide range of local conditions.

I selected for investigation the areas of policing, sexual harassment, and playground safety because reform movements pressed for change in each of these areas but these movements differed in ways that make it possible to sort out the conditions supporting law-led bureaucratic reform. In both policing and sexual harassment, reformers used the language of constitutional and statutory rights and brought the problem under federal judicial control; in playground safety, they used more prosaic policy tools, and the issue remained a matter merely of state law. This crucial difference between rights-based and non-rights-based reform makes it possible to demonstrate that legalized accountability is not limited to areas covered by federal civil rights law. The difference between these areas, however, also enables me to demonstrate that the language of rights nonetheless supplied reformers in the first two areas with leverage that they lacked in the area of playground safety.

Beyond the rights-based difference, the three areas differ in other important ways. I selected policing as the lead case because the police have long been the flashpoint of controversy over racial discrimination and the subject of repeated efforts at reform. The civil rights movement faced repression at the hands of local police throughout the South, and northern outrage over such police abuse led to key advances in civil rights policy. By the mid-1960s, however, it was increasingly clear that police nationwide were in need of reform: studies documented widespread frustration and bitterness over police practices. In a controversial effort, the Supreme Court imposed new constitutional limits on the police in an attempt to induce reform, and some localities created citizen review boards to oversee them. Local police, however, resisted external control, and when riots swept through northern cities in the mid-1960s and crime rates began to increase in the late 1960s, public sympathy swung in favor of the police and against reform. Nearly every study of the implementation of the new constitutional limits on policing found widespread evasion and noncompliance. Still, a decentralized reform movement carried on in the 1970s and 1980s, employing a variety of tactics, among them litigation and local mass protest. By the 1990s it was clear that American police departments were increasingly accepting of law-based reforms. My analysis of the policing case fleshes out the character of these law-based reforms and shows why they made headway when so many earlier efforts did not.

I selected sexual harassment policy as my second case study because in this area, as in policing, reform advocates expressed deep frustration about organizational inertia but did not rely on mass protests to address the problem. Although the issue of sexual harassment is widely shared among all organizational employers, local governments are a useful site for investigating the sources and path of law-modeled sexual harassment policy. For one thing, local agencies, notably the blue-collar city departments of police, firefighting, and public works, have been key sites of controversy over female employment and sexual harassment. For another, government agencies, including local governments, have commonly led the private sector in adopting legalized personnel policies; these policies provided a model for later efforts in the private sector. More generally, the issue of sexual harassment as a matter of organizational reform shares some key characteristics with police reform. In both areas, reformers came to believe that the nature of the problem required an intervention reaching deeply into organizational cultures. Women had long pressed for an equal right to work, but when in the 1960s they won that right under Title 7 of the Civil Rights Act they found that getting the job was not enough. In many workplaces women faced harassment, and many quit jobs or changed positions to escape it. Complaints about sexual harassment, like complaints about police brutality, alleged that those in charge widely knew of the problem but looked the other way. The challenge, as in policing, was to change organizations down to the bottom, to address inner organizational cultures in their finest details. I demonstrate that reform of the sexual harassment problem ultimately came in a form (legalized accountability) and by a process (bottom-up pressure) very similar to those in policing.

Playground safety is significant beyond the fact that it is a "nonrights" policy area. Playground reformers in the 1970s complained that playground design and equipment had remained basically unchanged for decades and that many aspects of traditional playground design were grossly unsafe. Thus thousands of children were injured in falls onto asphalt, which until the 1980s was the standard surface on playgrounds. Reforming the playground, however, seemed a gargantuan task: tens of thousands of cities had playgrounds, and many cities had dozens upon dozens of them, virtually all designed according to an earlier framework that did not value safety. Nobody in positions of power seemed much concerned about the problem, and while some parents were concerned, it was difficult getting them organized to press for change. Yet since the 1980s, playgrounds have literally been remade according to a remarkably common model. I demonstrate that this common model and the process by which it spread share key elements with reform in the areas of policing and sexual harassment.

I have selected police reform in Britain as a comparison case because it is useful for clarifying whether a system—like Britain's—of managerial professionalism that is insulated from liability pressure nevertheless addresses abuse and injury more rapidly, comprehensively, and effectively than the more bottom-up, legalized American approach.[5] Many of the popular complaints about excessive legalism in the United States are based on the perception that other countries do things better, meaning less legalistically. Like the police in the United States, for over a generation the British police have been at the center of controversy over race relations. Unlike the United States, however, British policing reformers for a very long time avoided litigation and legalistic policies, relying instead on centrally directed managerial reform. In spite of sweeping managerial reforms, racial minority groups in Britain increasingly complained of racist police abuse, inaugurating in the 1980s a period of intense tort litigation against the police. As in the United States, liability pressure and the accompanying media attention forced the British police to pay attention for the first time to the problem of misconduct. Still, although liability pressure encouraged the British police to adopt some elements of legalized accountability, the British police remain less legalized than their American counterparts, for two reasons. The British courts capped liability payouts, cutting off media coverage of police misconduct; and British police professional associations, unlike their American counterparts, never fully endorsed the idea of legalized accountability. In comparison, American-style legalism has some clear benefits but also some limitations.

In each of these case studies, my analysis combines evidence of changes over time and data regarding variation from place to place. With regard to changes over time I trace, along the lines of studies of American political development, how Progressive Era institutions set the stage for legalized accountability. To this end I rely on archival records, interviews with key participants in past policy debates, and detailed content analyses of recommendations put forward by professional journals. With regard to variations from place to place, I rely on data on the adoption of a rich array of policies and practices in hundreds of United States cities in the year 2000, using data drawn from an original survey. In light of the widespread suspicion that liability pressure generates mainly window dressing, I sought to plumb not only agencies' formal policies but also their internal practices. My measures arguably reach more deeply into internal organizational processes than any previous study, starting from the obvious elements of the legalized accountability model—formal rules—and extending into the minutiae of internal training regimes, internal oversight regimes, and internal communications. The survey observations confirm that systems of legalized accountability have been widely adopted but also that the elements that intrude more deeply into organizational practices are less widely adopted than the model's less intrusive elements. These data also support a key element of my thesis, that agencies have adopted more intrusive elements of legalized accountability—for instance, detailed training and oversight systems—the more they have come under pressure to do so from external activists and internal reform-oriented professionals.

The Significance of This Study

I am not the first to claim that American society has become more legalized, and it will be helpful to clarify what is at stake in the debate over legal liability and how my analysis is distinctive. The spread of legalistic rules and procedures is controversial.[6] From one perspective, the phenomenon represents the successful use of law as an instrument of social reform. Even as progress on civil rights collapsed at the national level, local movements succeeded in getting police departments to adopt reforms aimed at reining in police shootings and brutality. This is, in the words of the eminent policing scholar Samuel Walker, a "great success story."[7] At about the same time, as corporate employers responded to the civil rights mandate by adopting symbolic equal employment opportunity policies that left in place business as usual, a movement to eradicate sexual harassment grew and successfully pressed for policies that would *change* business as usual. Like Walker, the feminist scholar Carrie Baker has called this "an incredible success story."[8] Viewed from this angle, the transformation is part of what David Rosenbloom and Rosemary O'Leary have called a broad judicial movement "to integrate large-scale administration into the nation's system of constitutional government."[9]

From the very different perspective of many policy studies, legalistic rules have spread widely not because they serve a valuable purpose but in order to appease courts and lawyers, and consequently they amount to red tape, a hindrance on responsible professional judgment.[10] Professionals, according to this perspective, can be counted on to do the right thing even in the absence of pressure from litigants and courts, and to do it more effectively and efficiently. Thus a *Newsweek* cover story in 2003 (titled "Lawsuit Hell: How Fear of Litigation Is Paralyzing Our Professions") claimed that in an attempt to avoid medical malpractice liability, "doctors waste $50 billion to $100 billion on 'defensive' medicine to prove that they left no stone unturned, no test untried, no medication unprescribed, no specialist unconsulted."[11] The critics of legalistic procedures, as the quotation suggests, characterize professionals' response to liability as almost a scattershot affair, leaving "no stone unturned" in the attempt to appease the courts. Although "defensive medicine" is the most prominent example, as the *Newsweek* cover story observed, similar complaints have been made about legalistic procedures that "confound common sense" in policing, education, recreational administration, and, across a host of fields, sexual harassment policy.[12] Many of these popular claims, as Tom Baker shows in his careful analysis of "the medical malpractice myth," are wildly exaggerated.[13] Still, serious and thoughtful scholars like Robert Kagan have argued that liability pressure does encourage practicing professionals to adopt law-modeled policies that serve no sensible purpose other than to satisfy the courts.[14]

From yet a third perspective, legalistic rules and procedures are mainly symbolic efforts to feign concern about such problems as police brutality and sexual harassment while allowing business to go on as usual.[15] There has been no litigation explosion, according to this perspective, and litigation rates and liability payouts remain very low relative to the number and cost of injuries.[16] Governments especially are shielded from liability pressure by the convoluted legal doctrine of sovereign immunity, which protects them from lawsuits over many of the injuries caused by their employees.[17]

Precisely because liability pressure (and judicial oversight) has little power, in this view defendant organizations are able to shape their response as they see fit.[18] Given wide choice on how to respond, they adopt merely symbolic policies masking underlying practices that depart sharply from their ostensible goal of respect for civil rights and safety.[19] At their worst, legalistic policies—according to this perspective—actually may facilitate such violations of legal norms by encouraging observers to believe that all is well. Thus the era I describe here also produced a policy of "governing through crime," as Jonathan Simon so compellingly shows and, as Doris Marie Provine poignantly observes, a "war on drugs" that filled America's prisons with African American men.[20] Legalistic policies, one might argue, have not stood in the way of these developments and may even have promoted them by making police practices appear to be professionally neutral. Similarly, some have argued that many employers' sexual harassment policies amount to little more than window dressing, "perhaps . . . of no more than ceremonial value."[21]

Finally, from the broadest perspective, associated with scholarship on American political development, the rise of rules may represent a shift in the structure of political authority. Legalistic rules addressing the issue of race and sex discrimination may be seen as a recent step in the long conflict between what Desmond King and Rogers Smith have called America's two contending political traditions, one favoring race- and gender-based hierarchies and the other egalitarian reform.[22] Or the rise of rules checking the authority of administrative officials may be seen, in Karen Orren's terms, as a significant erosion in the rights of the officers of government in favor of the rights of citizens.[23]

This study is framed in the light of these competing perspectives and seeks to address several questions. First, and most basic, What is the nature and character of the late twentieth-century efflorescence of legalistic rules and procedures? Are they, as some allege, scattershot affairs, efforts to "leave no stone unturned" in order to shield against liability? Do they instruct professionals to act against their professional judgment? Are they limited to symbolism, appearing to be doing something while leaving underlying practices unchanged? Or are they something else, or something more?

Second, What accounts for the rapid spread of these legalistic rules and procedures and for any continuing variations in their adoption from place to place? Why did they spread in the 1980s when, it seems, the window of opportunity opened in the 1960s had closed, the political environment had turned hostile to such reforms, and established ways of doing things seemed ever more impervious to change? Did this change reflect a sudden decision by judges to impose new rules on unwilling bureaucracies? Or did it move so swiftly because bureaucratic officials believed the new rules were empty symbols and posed no great threat to business as usual?

Third, To what extent have professionals responded innovatively to problems at the heart of the new legalistic rules—particularly police misconduct, employee sexual harassment, and playground injuries—independent of pressure from legal liability? Did professionals lead the charge against these problems, developing innovative, professionally guided solutions to which legal liability has served only as a diversion? Or did legal liability encourage these professions to attend to these problems?

Finally, What are the implications for American democracy, and particularly for struggles to make its institutions more responsive to excluded and subordinated groups? Law is notoriously the domain of the powerful and well-heeled, where "the haves come out ahead."[24] To what extent has the spread of legalistic policies reinforced or, alternatively, attenuated this bias?

I became interested in these topics more than a decade ago while interviewing local officials about the costs of tort liability. My interviews were with senior city administrators who had lived through the sea change documented in this book, and they had a long-term "before and after" perspective. To my great surprise, these officials typically emphasized liability's *benefits*.[25] Thus, after I had spent nearly an entire interview with one senior local official probing liability's costs and intrusions, he interrupted me and said, "I don't want this [interview] to end without emphasizing something that hasn't come up. I've talked a lot about the costs of litigation and the like, but I don't want you to get the impression that there are no benefits. In fact, I think the benefits far outweigh the costs. The rights of citizens and employees are far better protected as a result and only as a result of litigation, not other changes. And the safety of our citizens is far better protected. Remember all that training and inspection that I mentioned? It makes a difference . . . our whole operation is safer."

So I began asking questions about liability's benefits, and responses started pouring out. "You have no idea how bad the police were in this town," one official observed. "But pressure from lawsuits helped to bring about some needed changes. . . . They helped us get rid of some problem personnel, and this city is a lot better off for it." Another echoed: "Well, the police, of course. That's the area of biggest change. They're trained now, and we've gotten rid of problem officers, and people's rights are much, much better protected as a result." Another emphasized public safety more generally: "No question that this [the threat of liability] has raised the level of public safety. It's definitely a good thing, definitely. It raises our costs somewhat, I suppose, but it's cost well spent." Another went so far as to claim that "the biggest changes for the better in this city have come as a result of lawsuits or threatened lawsuits, not as a result of political changes in the council or anything else. The courts have done a far better job than politics of improving our policies."

This book, at base, is an effort to assess the hope expressed in these officials' claims against the pessimism expressed by the many academic studies noted above.

Outline of the Book

In chapter 2, against the backdrop of other scholarship on law and social change, I develop my thesis of legalized accountability as a broad, bottom-up development. Following chapter 2, the book is divided into two major sections. The first section presents my primary case study, police use-of-force reform in the United States, and, after a brief introduction to the case of policing, comprises four chapters. Chapter 3 surveys the historical development of two competing perspectives on the problem with policing: those of the professional movement and those of its activist critics. Chapter 4 analyzes the development of tort liability pressure on the police, its influence on media coverage, and the police response. Chapter 5 surveys the course of police acceptance of legalized accountability as a model of reform. Chapter 6 presents an analysis of data drawn from an original survey of 848 police departments conducted for this book.

Part 2 presents three comparative case studies of similar movements for legalized accountability in other policy areas. Chapter 7 presents my case study of the movement for legalized accountability in British policing. Chapter 8 examines the development of legalized accountability regarding workplace sexual harassment in the United States and is divided into two parts, the first analyzing the origins and development of the phenomenon and the second analyzing data drawn from an original survey of 454 city governments. Chapter 9 analyzes the growth of legalized accountability with regard to playground safety in the United States, and it too is divided into two parts, the first analyzing the origins and development of the movement and the second analyzing data obtained from an original survey of 233 parks and recreation departments in cities around the country.

In Chapter 10, the book's conclusion, I summarize my thesis and evidence and discuss the study's broader implications for theories of law and social change.

2

Theory:
The Fertile Fear of Liability

In 1980, as lawsuits multiplied and public outcry surged over police shootings of young unarmed African Americans, Patrick Murphy, a prominent former police chief, asked the International Association of Chiefs of Police (IACP) to adopt a resolution calling on all police departments to impose rules limiting police shootings. The prevailing common-law rule allowed officers to shoot at people fleeing arrest for a suspected felony, and it led, Murphy alleged, to tragedies like the killing of fifteen-year-old Edward Garner as he fled, unarmed, from the site of a ten-dollar home burglary. Murphy's proposed rule would allow officers to shoot only if necessary to defend a life. Police chiefs blasted Murphy as a traitor to their profession and voted down the idea four to one.[1]

At nearly the same time in the fields of personnel and parks administration, the other areas covered in this book, reform-oriented practitioners joined social activists in calling for sweeping organizational reforms aimed at addressing sexual harassment and playground injuries. Yet these reformers too faced limited support and even outright opposition from their peers.

Jump forward ten years. In a remarkable reversal in each of these fields, the administrative professions that once scorned the reformers' initiatives as virtual heresies now celebrated them as the professional state of the art. The reform initiatives had deepened, becoming models for comprehensive administrative systems. These systems aimed not only at addressing particular "bad apples" but at thoroughly changing organizational cultures and practices from top to bottom in the name of individual rights and safety. In policing, for instance, as Samuel Walker observes, reformers favored not only restrictive shooting rules but also rules governing all uses of force; training tailored to these rules; internal reporting and supervisory review of uses of force; complaint review systems; and comprehensive monitoring systems, called "early warning systems," for catching problems quickly.[2] In personnel management, the model likewise encompassed not only rules prohibiting sexual harassment but systems for communicating this norm to employees, grievance procedures for processing complaints, and even surveys for catching complaints not brought through the formal grievance procedure.[3] Parks management developed a similar model of rules, training, and organizational auditing.[4]

This book's central thesis is that these remarkable changes grew from an interaction between activist pressure for law-based reform and conflict within the managerial professions over how to respond. Both activist pressure and managerial conflicts were necessary to the development; neither was sufficient. Activists, with their demand for institutional reforms and their reliance on liability lawsuits as a lever, supplied an overarching motivating framework and steady, disruptive pressure on managerial institutions. Managerial practitioners supplied the administrative tools necessary to carry out the activists' goal of institutional reform. The idea for using these tools and the plan for how they could be turned from conventional bureaucratic purposes to the goal of institutional reform, however, came not from inside management but from policy experts at the border of the conflicts between activists and practitioners.

The dynamic among these groups grew out of "the politics of rights"— the ongoing conflict over the practical meaning of the civil rights revolution.[5] American law supported racial and gender hierarchies into the 1950s; by the 1970s it favored equality. This transformation contributed to spin-off rights in many areas, among them consumer protection (and thus playground safety). At the same time, Congress and judges expanded tortlike liability for violations of these new rights. While the legal revolution promised egalitarian transformation and checks on those in power, it left unclear what these aspirations might mean in practice. That practical meaning emerged in the dynamic of conflict among activists, managerial professionals, and policy experts at the borders of these groups. Its essence is legalized accountability, a policy framework that celebrates legal norms but applies them through managerial mechanisms.

My thesis may not surprise the activist lawyers, reform-oriented administrators, and judges who participated in the movement a generation ago, but it departs in key respects from leading theories of law and bureaucratic change. Policy-centered theories, among them Robert Kagan's "adversarial legalism" thesis, observe that activist litigation places intense pressure on agencies, forcing them to adopt policies that are contrary to their professional administrators' better judgment.[6] Media-focused theories, led by William Haltom and Michael McCann, show that distorted coverage of lawsuits in the mass media weakens liability-generated pressure for reform.[7] Lauren Edelman's "legal endogeneity" thesis argues that bureaucratic managers, responding to ambiguous liability messages, craft administrative policies that are little more than empty symbolism.[8] My analysis draws on each of these contributions.

Still, missing from these insightful theories is how activists' ideas shaped professional administrators' interpretations of and response to liability. In contrast to organization-centered theories, my research shows that legalized accountability's roots grew as much from activist ideas and pressure as from managerial ones. In contrast to policy-centered theories, however, I show that practicing professionals came to see these formerly radical reform initiatives as a valuable contribution to professionalism itself. My thesis is closest to the work of Malcolm Feeley and Edward Rubin, who have shown how judges and reformist administrators collaborated to reform prisons, often over the initial opposition of these agencies.[9] But even these scholars, in my view, have underestimated the contributions of external activists to the process of law-driven bureaucratic reform. This chapter will clarify my thesis, discuss how it grows from yet moves beyond other studies on law and social reform, and defend its plausibility in light of lines of research that might seem to call it into doubt.

Activists and Liability Campaigns

Half of the story is found in the growth of networks of civil rights lawyers, activists, and progressive policy reformers and in their use of legal liability as a lever for bureaucratic reform. They worked strategically for long-term legal change: many were "repeat players" in Marc Galanter's term or "cause lawyers" in Sarat and Scheingold's.[10] I will call these various groups "activists" for short. While it is useful to draw similarities and connections among the many kinds of activists, I should also note their diversity. In policing, the activist groups were the most varying and numerous, encompassing the civil rights movement, national civil rights and liberties organizations, and attorneys with national stature and extraordinary legal sophistication, as well as local ad hoc citizen groups, fringe movements, and run-of-the-mill local attorneys. In the area of sexual harassment, the movement was made up of a small number of national feminist organizations, a few sophisticated, nationally prominent attorneys, and local feminist groups. In the area of playground safety, by contrast, the cohort of activists was comparatively small. There was no meaningful grassroots movement, and the key activists were policy specialists and personal injury lawyers. Still, by generating liability-based pressure for reform, these playground safety activists played a role similar to their more numerous counterparts in the other policy areas.

My analysis of activists' contribution builds on three key observations made by scholars of social movements.[11] First, activist movements commonly have deep grievances against the status quo and frame problems differently from the way favored by dominant institutions. Second, the relative influence and longevity of activist movements depend in part on their ability to mobilize resources on behalf of sustained pressure, and this depends in turn on the presence or cultivation of a resource support structure. Third, their influence also depends on whether the mass media validate and amplify the movement's preferred framing of the problem.

Drawing on these ideas, I observe that in each of the policy areas studied here the reform agenda was shaped in part by activists' demands for deep institutional reform, but only as they were able to cultivate resources for sustained pressure and only as they attracted media coverage that favored their framing of the problem. At the level of problem framing, these activists wanted agencies to correct specific problems (in policing, for instance, they wanted departments to discipline or fire abusive officers; in the sexual harassment area, they wanted harassers disciplined or fired). The activists were under no illusion, however, that the problem was merely a matter of removing a few "bad apples," and therefore in each area they also consistently argued that individual problems were often fostered by organizational policies or cultures. Activists therefore consistently favored reforms aimed at changing these policies and cultures from top to bottom, to do more than simply adopt cosmetic reforms or pro forma rules that could be ignored in practice.

Activists' ability to get a hearing for their complaints depended to a considerable extent on their resources and organizational capacity to sustain pressure over time. Activists in each area initially depended on existing organizational support but were able to move beyond it as they began to obtain resources from liability litigation itself. Although activists have long used litigation as a lever of reform, they have turned to tortlike lawsuits only since the 1950s and increasingly after the 1960s. In the 1950s, state judges supported liberalizing tort liability under the common law.[12] In 1961 this legal movement spread to the federal courts with the Supreme Court's landmark decision in *Monroe v. Pape* reviving Section 1983 of the Civil Rights Act of 1871, a provision that authorized lawsuits seeking monetary damages from state and local officials for violations of federal rights.[13] In the Civil Rights Act of 1964, Congress extended the liability remedy to the area of employment discrimination, authorizing victims of discrimination to sue for financial compensation in federal court. In *Monell v. Department of Social Services* in 1978 the Supreme Court extended Section 1983 liability to municipalities, making them financially liable for some rights violations caused by their employees.[14] All of these remedies are tortlike in character: they provide financial compensation for violations of rights, and theoretically this compensation acts as an inducement to reduce such violations. In 1976, with the strong support of civil rights organizations, Congress adopted the Civil Rights Attorneys' Fees Award Act authorizing judges to require losing defendants to pay the attorneys' fees of winning plaintiffs, and these awards provided important support for activists' efforts.[15] In turn, lawyers' success in using liability lawsuits grew as they developed an infrastructure in support of it. As these lawyers learned how to sue government agencies and win, and as they spread that knowledge through "how-to" books, specialist casebooks, and formal conferences and training, the remedy gained teeth.

Liability litigation gave activists another unexpected resource—media coverage—and this helped them reframe public debate in favor of institutional reform.[16] As William Haltom and Michael McCann have observed, the popular media are drawn to litigation stories involving graphic or salacious evidence of individual wrongdoing.[17] Activists, not surprisingly, found that lawsuits alleging police abuse and employee sexual harassment made compelling news. But Haltom and McCann also observe that media stories tend to muffle evidence that individual problems are part of broader institutional failings. Activists struggled to overcome this tendency, and over the course of many stories the media began to frame individual abuses as part of institutional patterns. Activists supporting police misconduct litigation, for instance, eventually succeeded in reframing the problem of police abuse as the responsibility not merely of individual "bad apple" officers but of departments and, indeed, the broader profession. Similarly, the feminist movement against sexual harassment ultimately succeeded in reframing the debate as a problem not merely of individual harassers but of organizational cultures and policies. Liability litigation played no small part in these changes.

Although social movement scholarship helps in understanding the development of legalized accountability, studies of social movements generally stop at the organization's door. Very few examine whether and how movements in society extend inside bureaucratic institutions or how their demands are filtered into organizations' policies and practices. I turn next to research on organizations for help in addressing these questions.

Local Government Agencies as a Network Phenomenon

Another part of the story is found in the way bureaucratic institutions responded to growing activist pressure. While it is commonly believed that bureaucratic organizations respond to outside pressure mainly with shared, symbolic approaches that mimic responsiveness, I show that activists developed allies within the bureaucratic world and that these allies directly challenged bureaucratic traditionalists, leading to explosive conflict and sudden change. My analysis of these developments builds on several key insights of research on bureaucratic organizations.

First, bureaucracies are best understood not as fundamentally separate, isolated, individual entities but as the local instantiations of larger ideas about how best to organize and do things.[18] Thus, particular liberal arts colleges are expressions of broader ideas about how to organize such colleges; particular police departments are expressions of ideas about how to organize policing. These ideas are not free-floating, however, but grow from and are transmitted by webs or networks among administrative professionals. In what the eminent British administrative scholar Christopher Hood has called regulation by "mutuality," these networks foster shared pressure to follow dominant administrative models.[19]

Second, as a consequence of their network nature, bureaucratic organizations commonly respond as much to field-level ideas as to localized pressures and therefore (in the view of external proponents of change) often are intransigent, resistant to outside pressure, and mired in old ways of doing things. Put another way, existing bureaucratic models commonly take on the cast of orthodoxies, and administrative professionals who believe in the validity of the dominant orthodoxy can be vehement in defending it.

Third, although bureaucratic orthodoxies are undoubtedly powerful, they are almost never as monolithic as they may at first appear and often

contain dissenting perspectives favored by reformers—"institutional entrepreneurs" in the language of organization theorists—who seek to change
the orthodoxy from the inside.[20] Change in stable institutions commonly
emerges in part out of these clashes *within* administrative fields in the inevitable tensions between defenders of orthodoxy and proponents of reform.[21] Reformers gain allies among social movements, and these alliances
contribute both to a heightening of conflict within the profession and to
enormous pressure for change.

Building on these insights, I have focused my analysis especially on the
networks found in the administrative professions of personnel management, police management, and parks administration and on ideological
debates within these fields. Although these administrative professions
have never attained the status of the classic professions of law, medicine,
and engineering, they have assiduously developed shared professional
identities, and they connect widely scattered members by meetings, communications networks, publications, and, most basically, their shared
sense of mission.[22]

Facing liability pressure from activists in the 1970s, these administrative professions experienced growing tensions between defenders of a
traditional Progressive model of insulated bureaucracy and reformist
challengers who sought to impose law-based checks on bureaucracy. The
Progressive legacy grew from a reform movement that wrested control of
local government administration from the political machines, and even
fifty years later its defenders jealously guarded administrative insulation
from partisan political control, fearful that any compromise on these matters would place them on a slippery slope back to partisan domination of
government administration.

Even the "legalistic" departments in James Q. Wilson's famous description in 1968 used rules to serve nonpartisan professionalism, not control
abuses of force.[23] As late as 1980, the police chiefs who vehemently opposed Patrick Murphy's proposed rule-based restrictions on officers' discretion to shoot were, in their view, acting in *defense* of professional policing against the risk of external partisan control. To them, Murphy was a
heretic.

Heretics like Murphy played a key role in opening up the administrative
orthodoxy to the influence of outside activists. As I show, these administrative reformers largely accepted activists' claims that bureaucratic practices
commonly violated civil rights and liberties (in the case of policing and
personnel administration) or failed to protect the public's safety (in the
case of parks administration). They also accepted activists' demands for

bureaucratic change down to the front lines; they shared their view that these changes should encompass not only formal policies but also systems of administration aimed at giving life to these policies. Ultimately, they pressed for legalized checks on professional administration. Thus Murphy and his allies developed an innovative program of police reform encompassing sweeping law-styled change in police policies and practices.

Internal debates between defenders of the status quo and administrative reformers like Murphy set the stage for a sudden shift in the policy paradigm from a traditional orthodoxy to something new. Inflexible defense of the professional orthodoxy—common in fully-developed networks faced by activists' criticism—set the orthodoxy up for high-stakes symbolic tests with the potential for embarrassing failure. Defenders of the professional orthodoxy inadvertently established what Jeffrey Legro, in a persuasive discussion of the role of ideas in policy change, has called a crucial "social expectation"—a shared belief about "what should or should not" result from adherence to a dominant model—that is potentially subject to devastating refutation by events.[24] For instance, in the face of growing pressure for rights-based change, defenders of the status quo in both policing and personnel management claimed that administrative professionalism in their fields was already well up to the task of protecting rights in practice and that no additional legalized checks were needed. Such claims opened the defenders of orthodoxy to embarrassment as evidence mounted of the depth of the problem.

Interactions: The Fertile Fear of Liability

Growing professional dissent and activist pressure converged in the late 1970s, and a significant aspect of my analysis is focused on how these streams of development interacted in unexpected and fertile ways. The key dynamic was an eruption in the fear of liability and the emergence of a new shared model for how to respond to it: legalized accountability. These developments began first at the points of convergence between the separate channels of activist pressure and managerial practice. As scholars of institutional norms have long recognized, agents of change are commonly positioned at such borders, where they apply ideas drawn from one sphere to another or combine ideas from different spheres in new ways.[25]

A key condition for the explosion of fear of liability was the development of the legalized accountability idea. Proposals for legalizing accountability first grew at the points of convergence between the separate channels of activist pressure and managerial practice. In each policy area, the idea's creators had a foot in each of these channels. These key innovators had extensive practical experience inside managerial institutions but, by virtue of their legal training or connection to activist networks, they shared the activists' view that deep reforms were needed. In policing, for instance, in the mid-1960s Frank Remington and Herman Goldstein, law professors who had long studied or worked in police departments, proposed account-ability reforms that became the basis for later administrative innovations in United States policing. Their proposal relied on traditional manage-rial tools—rules, training, and oversight—but directed them toward the radical goal of controlling police discrimination and abuse. In the 1970s, similar experts in personnel management and playground administration likewise generated radically new accountability reforms for addressing sexual harassment and playground injuries. Later—as agencies came under growing activist pressure for reform—leading practitioners like Murphy in policing and others in the areas of personnel and playground management picked up these ideas, applied them in their own agencies, and tried to persuade other agencies to join the movement.

These developments in the managerial channel of change gave lever-age to the activists, and vice versa. For one thing, as managerial reformers adopted experimental administrative reforms in the 1970s, these first steps enhanced the leverage available to external activists when asking other agencies to follow suit.[26] In policing, for instance, liability pressure became more influential as dissident professionals like Patrick Murphy began assailing institutional orthodoxies from within, providing a profes-sional imprimatur to activists' claims that mainstream police departments were not doing enough to address abuse. A similar dynamic played out in the area of sexual harassment. Activist lawyers relied on dissident prac-titioners within each of the administrative fields as expert witnesses in court cases, in which capacity they testified regarding the inner workings of administrative agencies and emerging developments in professional standards. These experts helped fuel doubts about the status quo among juries, leading to major awards in a growing number of cases.

The growth of liability pressure by activists likewise enhanced the le-verage available to internal professional reformers. In debates within the practitioner professions, these reformers began to proffer liability as a key inducement for reform. They filled professional publications with articles reporting a litigation explosion, and they offered policy reforms as the antidote to this threat. As agencies began to adopt these reforms they became an evolving professional standard. The process contributed to a rapid, forced heightening of professional standards that fed back into pressure on agencies to do still more.

A central dynamic in the field-level interactive process described here was a great growth in the fear of liability. It emerged suddenly in the late 1970s from the interplay among activist pressure, managerial innovation, and conflict within professional fields, and it fueled the development and spread of legalized accountability as a shared policy model. By the early 1980s fear of liability filled the pages of professional magazines and formed the subject of a growing number of training sessions and conferences. My analysis of this fear of liability owes a considerable debt to the pioneering work of Lauren Edelman, Lynn Mather, William Haltom, and Michael McCann.[27] These scholars have observed that the mass media and practitioner journals typically exaggerate the threat of liability, at least from the standpoint of legal experts.[28] In the mass media, this exaggeration appears in the form of stories about sue-happy litigants and irrational juries.[29] Practitioner journals, too, exaggerate the threat of liability.[30] As Mather observes, practitioners focus less on the specific legal requirements of judicial decisions than on their direction—which side in a policy conflict the courts appear to be supporting.[31]

Building on these studies, I make two observations, the first being that what agency officials fear most about liability is the threat of public embarrassment and reputational damage. Although losing a costly case is undoubtedly embarrassing, lawsuits have the potential to erode an agency's legitimacy in the eyes of the public even if the agency wins. As one official observed to me, "Lawsuits bring publicity, and publicity alters the public perception of us, and for practical purposes, perception is reality. So that can be a big cost, and it can take a long time to overcome it." Another official observed that the publicity accompanying a lawsuit often transforms a "minor dispute" into a "public controversy." As my historical narratives will show, after the mid-1970s, as the popular media increasingly reported lawsuits over sexual harassment and police misconduct, the reputational damage arising from these stories increased.

Second, I find that while the popular media typically trace the liability problem to sue-happy individuals, this emphasis began to shift by the 1980s toward seeing harassment and abuse as an *organizational* responsibility. Professional publications especially began to point the finger at their own professions, characterizing *professional* irresponsibility as the problem. These publications played a crucial role in interpreting the threat of liability and its threat to professional reputations. Thus, the two police officials quoted in chapter 1's epigraph declared that "we are being sued because we are not doing our job"—a startling acknowledgment. But other practitioners soon echoed this admission in myriad articles in professional journals in each of the fields studied here. In keeping with this acknowledgment, professional publications recommended that to head off liability threats, agencies should carry out deep institutional reforms aimed at bringing their performance up to emerging professional standards and public expectations.

Although it is widely acknowledged that bureaucracies have evolved in response to liability pressure, some organizational sociologists have argued that these responses tend to be merely incremental evolutions of already dominant bureaucratic models.[32] Thus it is alleged that human resources managers responded to growing liability pressure regarding sexual harassment by adopting grievance procedures and training, things that were simply continuations of their profession's traditional tool kit and served mainly to muzzle employees' complaints rather than address the underlying problem.[33] In this perspective, bureaucratic responses to liability are merely "ceremonial."[34]

While I acknowledge organizational sociologists' observation that some of the specific recommendations found in practitioner journals (e.g., recommendations to adopt grievance procedures and training) might appear to grow from standard professional models (and thus might appear to be window dressing), my analyses suggest that even these professional recommendations amounted to more than mere ceremonialism. I find, as previously noted, that the practitioner journals' specific reform proposals initially came not from within the practicing professions but from policy specialists outside them who either were part of the activist coalition seeking fundamental organizational reform or were endorsing the views of that coalition. Second, I find that even such seemingly pat proposals as grievance procedures and training were typically presented not as stand-alone remedies but as elements of a more comprehensive organizational effort to address (or at least appear to address) the underlying problem. Third, most professional practitioners initially believed that the recommended policies violated professional norms of unfettered discretion and *were not* in their professional interest. They came to support these policies only after considerable resistance.

I find, in sum, that professional publications indeed do warn of the threat of liability and do proffer a standard prescription for protecting against liability. But I find that this standard prescription was shaped in part by activist demands and by the recommendations of policy experts who endorsed those demands. The professional prescription, in short, is to adopt legalized accountability to better protect individual rights and safety.

Consider one example. As activists increasingly mobilized against police shootings in the late 1970s, leaders of mainstream policing responded defensively, claiming that their traditional form of managerial professionalism was sufficient to protect individual dignity, civil rights, and safety. No legalistic checks, they said, were needed; if anything, these checks amounted to an illegitimate attempt at partisan meddling. Just as the defenders of mainstream police professionalism declared that the best way to ensure police respect for civil rights was a bigger dose of insulated police professionalism, James Fyfe, a police officer turned academic, carried out research aimed at testing whether discretionary professional judgment truly did the trick. Using data from the Memphis police department obtained through discovery during the early stages of litigating *Tennessee v. Garner*, Fyfe observed that the more police officers exercised discretionary judgment over whether to shoot at a suspect, the more the race of the suspect influenced their decision to shoot.[35] Put precisely, when officers confronted a suspect who was armed and threatening to shoot (a "nonelective" shooting scenario), for every white they shot, police officers shot two African Americans; by contrast, when officers confronted a suspect who was not armed and was merely fleeing arrest (an "elective" shooting scenario), for every white they shot, officers shot *eighteen* African Americans. Although a two-to-one racial disparity was troubling, an eighteen-to-one disparity was obviously outrageous and professionally embarrassing to the police. Fyfe favored imposing new shooting rules and training tailored to those rules. He served as an expert witness for plaintiffs in hundreds of liability lawsuits and advised an equally large number of police departments on developing internal administrative systems aimed at controlling officers' use of force. In the end, his and Murphy's favored reforms carried the day. They did so not because they fit the standard police tool kit but because both the threat of liability-induced professional embarrassment and departments' aspirations for professional legitimacy eventually made the choice obvious.

Legalized Accountability

I can now make clear the nature of the administrative model that I call legalized accountability. Its structure was framed by activists' demand to reform organizational policies and practices down to the front lines. Its key characteristic, as a consequence, is an aspiration to make legal rights real in the administrative state. It does so by means of administrative systems that are *legally framed* and *comprehensive*, encompassing a range of mechanisms for changing individual behavior and organizational culture in keeping with these norms. These mechanisms, while diverse in application, may be reduced to three key elements. The first is *administrative policies* that state an organizational commitment to legal norms (e.g., against excessive use of force, sexual harassment, or playground injuries). The second consists of *training and communication systems* intended to convey the importance of these policies and to change organizational culture in keeping with them. The third is *internal oversight* aimed at assessing progress in this endeavor and identifying violations of the policy. In drawing these categories, I build on Kenneth Culp Davis's and Samuel Walker's important distinction between "constraining" rules (which prescribe norms, set standards, define limits) and "checking" rules (which enforce the former).[36]

Legalized accountability, as Philip Selznick observed long ago, embodies a developmental dynamic: to more effectively bring hidden bureaucratic practices into compliance with public norms, reformers inside and outside agencies pursued an ever-deepening quest to control those practices through legalized rules and procedures.[37] Legalized accountability's more intrusive elements—its systems of training and internal oversight— were aimed at ensuring that organizational policies would be more than window dressing. General rules became over time ever more specific; departures from rules spawned efforts to change organizational cultures and routines through formal training; suspicion that training was not having the desired effect in practice spawned efforts to impose detailed oversight on actual practices. Selznick, however, underemphasized the conflictual nature of the process: the aggressiveness of the activist push, the bitterness of the practitioner reaction, the explosiveness of the critical juncture where these dynamics came to a head.

But the consensus that emerged at the end of that conflict-laden process, as Selznick emphasized, reflects a shared policy model. Legalized accountability is a "model," as I use the term here, in the sense that it is a norm or standard that provides guidance on how to understand a shared problem (in this case, activist pressure and legal liability to address abuses) and what to do in response to it. In making the claim that legalized accountability is a normative model, I mean to imply neither that I necessarily favor it nor that I believe it is an unalloyed force for good, whatever that term might mean. Instead, mine is an empirical claim: I *describe* a set of beliefs, structured in the form of a policy framework and held to be right and good by administrative professionals. Legalized accountability is such a normative model; it is a relatively stable structure of ideas, norms, and associated ways of doing things that is, in Peter Hall's influential formulation, a "policy paradigm."[38] It is, in Jeffrey Legro's terms, a "collective idea," something like a "dominant orthodoxy," or in the words of Lauren Edelman and her colleagues, an "ideolog[y] of rationality."[39] In simple terms, it has taken on a life of its own. In converging on a common form, legalized accountability has parallels in other developments, notably the common structure of judicially led prison reform, as observed by Malcolm Feeley and Edward Rubin, and the common structure of organizational Equal Employment Opportunity policies, as observed by Lauren Edelman.[40]

Although the legalized accountability model incorporates a big dose of standard bureaucratic tools inherited from the past, it uses them in radically new ways. Many of these tools, as illustrated by studies of the bureaucratizing of personnel administration, particularly Herbert Kaufman's classic study of the U.S. Forest Service and Samuel Walker's foundational study of police professionalism, grew from the Progressive impulse to insulate administrators from partisan influence and to enforce managerial control over employees.[41] Thus, in policing, prominent rules governed the use and upkeep of the official uniform, a primary instrument for ensuring consistency among officers.[42] By contrast, the rules associated with the legalized accountability model grew as a means of ensuring bureaucratic accountability to *external* legal norms. Thus, prominent rules now focus on treating members of the public fairly and equally. These newer rules, moreover, are not simply extensions of the old. While professional norms favored personnel rules, they *opposed* rules governing uses of force. Moreover, while bureaucratic rules in the past favored insulating internal administrative processes from external pressure (civil service rules being a prominent example), systems of legalized accountability ostensibly attempt to expose and thereby publicly regulate organizations' internal processes.

Variations from Place to Place

Although the legalized accountability model has spread widely among local governments and is not merely ceremonial, some agencies have adopted all or nearly all of its elements while others have adopted only its most visible symbols.[43] Formal rules are the centerpiece of the model and also the element most easily adopted without requiring deep changes in practice, and virtually all agencies have adopted such rules. Internal organizational practices and working cultures are quite another matter. Although in many places officials have used systems of training and oversight to bring organizational practices and internal culture closely into line with the organization's formal policies, in other places they have made only pro forma efforts at training and oversight, leaving the inner workings of their organizations largely unchanged. For instance, in the early 2000s, as the City of Denver faced enormous public controversy around a number of police shootings, the *Denver Post* reported that while the Denver police department's rules governing shootings were consistent with national standards, its internal training and oversight processes had been, in the testimony of a policing expert in one case, "grossly inadequate."[44] Similarly, although virtually all public agencies have adopted rules prohibiting sexual harassment by their employees, many of these agencies provide only pro forma training and rudimentary complaint procedures, and they do little at all to assess whether there is harassment among employees. Internal training and oversight are less visible to the public than an organization's formal rules, and agencies more commonly depart from dominant models in these less visible matters. Taking the step of discipline or dismissal is even more remote from public view, jealously guarded by rules of employee confidentiality.

These variations among agencies—full embrace of legalized accountability in some places, avoidance of all but lip service in others—arise from *local variations in legalized accountability's underlying conditions*. The activist infrastructure that fueled the model's development varies in strength from place to place. In some places there are many sophisticated lawyers willing to take on controversial cases against city governments and many vibrant citizen groups, among them local chapters of the American Civil Liberties Union and other civil liberties organizations. Other places have none of these lawyers and groups. Likewise, city governments vary considerably in the strength of their connections to professional networks. Some rely heavily on the recommendations of professional associations and employ professional administrators who are loyal to these associations; some do not. I find that the level of adoption of legalized accountability varies more in relation to these two things—activist infrastructures and professional connections—than to any other influence.

A Response to a Possible Objection

Scholars of particular policy areas and of the economics of tort liability may be skeptical of my thesis. Studies in these areas observe that tort lawsuits' financial penalties are too weak to deter negligence and abuse and therefore almost never generate meaningful reforms in practice.[45] Whether doctors or hospitals have been sued, for instance, allegedly has little effect on whether they improve their practices.[46] Lawsuits have so little effect, according to these policy specialists, because the tort sanction is very weak.[47] While many people believe, as a *Newsweek* report put it, that "Americans will sue each other at the drop of a hat," nearly every study of the matter finds that Americans are very hesitant to sue and that the vast majority of people—over 95 percent—who are injured through the negligence of another do not file a lawsuit to recover damages.[48] Even in the few cases where plaintiffs file a lawsuit and win, the monetary penalties typically are so small in relative terms that it is rational, one critic observes, for most potential targets of lawsuits to believe they have little incentive to reform.[49] Other factors, among them liability insurance, government immunity from liability, and lack of clarity in the law's recommendations, further lessen liability's weight.[50] These studies see judicial decisions and lawsuits, on the one hand, and their possible policy effects, on the other, as like weights on a scale: lawsuits or court decisions simply don't weigh enough to shift the balance.

Although these economic perspectives may accurately assess the effect of any *particular* lawsuit, they miss the impact of the rise of liability as a broader phenomenon in the hands of activist movements and of the development of practitioner networks committed to using liability as a lever of reform. These paired phenomena exert pressure less through the weight of monetary sanctions than through shared norms and through liability lawsuits' reputational sanctions. "Liability" and "reform," in other words, are not discrete weights but shared conceptual models connected by a persuasive logic and conveyed through networks of activists and professional practitioners. No accurate understanding of liability's meaning or impact is possible without consulting the messages and interpretations of the law developed and conveyed through these networks. This shared knowledge may counsel an agency to adopt particular reforms even if it has not been sued (because its policies have fallen below professional standards); it may counsel no changes even if the agency *has* been sued (because officials are confident the agency's policies satisfy the professional standard). What matters in these hypothetical scenarios is not liability's financial toll but managerial beliefs about the threat of being sued and of what should be done to minimize that threat, and these beliefs are shaped by activists' allegations and pressure.

Conclusion

The year 1980 marks a great divide in the world of professional government administration. Before that point, dominant norms in the administrative professions favored insulation from external legalized control, and legalized accountability was the pet project of marginalized reformers; after that point, legalized accountability became a nationwide administrative standard. Although not all agencies have adopted all of the model's elements, in many places legalized accountability extends deeply into agencies' internal processes, and seen as a whole the widespread adoption of such systems is a remarkable development. The United States has tens of thousands of local police departments that long resisted any form of national standards and emphasized the value of official discretion and insulation from external political meddling; for a similarly long time, the nature of interpersonal relationships in the workplace, from jokes to sex, was considered a "private" matter, not subject to public legal regulation. Systems of legalized accountability reversed these presumptions, calling to account many previously hidden discretionary practices and subjecting them to pervasive, comprehensive lawlike regulation.

This broad development is best understood as arising from an interaction between two institutional processes: emulation and conflict internal to professional institutions and legal leverage imposed on those institutions by activists from the outside. As dissenting professionals and social movement activists over time formed a new institutional orthodoxy that overturned traditional commitments to bureaucratic insulation, their networks spread far and wide among local governments, contributing to the widespread adoption of systems of legalized accountability. The rest of this book represents a sustained test of this thesis.

Although mine is an empirical claim, it has normative implications. They are divided, reflecting ongoing tensions between, on the one hand, activists and reformist professionals seeking greater bureaucratic fidelity to the norms of civil rights and safety and, on the other, administrative professionals seeking to ameliorate the administrative effects of these pressures. These very different processes contribute to what I will characterize as the divided character of legalized accountability. The phenomenon is at once a reform imposed by activists, generating often-painful changes in existing organizational routines, and at virtually the same time a managerial effort to shield against yet greater intrusion. The conflicting forces underlying these dynamics form the central dynamic of the story told here.

Once established, legalized accountability, like all institutions, has become a resource available to be used for different, even competing purposes. When, in Chicago, it was recently alleged that a unit of police officers had for years terrorized poor African Americans in one of the city's public housing projects and that the department's internal investigations of such allegations and its claimed "early warning system" were a sham, the two-sided character of legalized accountability was cast into sharp relief.[51] The Chicago department reportedly has claimed that its state-of-the-art early warning system demonstrates the department's goodwill in seeking to prevent such abuses. In official hands, legalized accountability thus was used in an attempt to shore up departmental legitimacy. But the activist lawyers and journalists who helped to expose the problem used the department's system of legalized accountability to call its legitimacy into question. They used data from the department's internal system to demonstrate that the department's monitoring process lived up to neither its promises nor the standard set by other police departments. Legalized accountability thus defines the field on which activists and managerial practitioners now joust. It is no magic solution to the problems of official intransigence and questionable policy. But few would now favor going back to the earlier era.

The Problem with Policing

End police brutality has become a battle cry ringing out from one end of the land to the other. It is repeated parrot-like by hundreds of thousands who have never had any personal experience which could remotely serve as a basis for the charge.... It has been used by supposedly responsible Negro leaders to whip up support among their followers.... And let us be mindful that these people—who are so ready to exaggerate and distort—are the same people who want to be given the power to review complaints against the police.
—Nelson A. Watson, project supervisor, International
Association of Chiefs of Police, in *Police Chief*, September 1964

I have witnesses who endured the brutality of the police many more times . . . but, of course, I cannot prove it. I cannot prove it because the Police Department investigates itself, quite as though it were answerable only to itself; it must be made to answer to the community which pays it, and which it is legally sworn to protect; and if American Negroes are not a part of the American community, then all of the American professions are a fraud.
James Baldwin, *Nation*, July 11, 1966

What is the problem to which legalized accountability became the answer? To what extent did professional policing, as suggested by recent critiques of liability, recognize this problem and address it with accepted "professional" solutions before being pressed by liability into adopting legalized solutions? To what extent did these legalized solutions, as suggested by some other perspectives, have their roots in mainstream professional techniques and procedures? In sum, is the character of legalized accountability, as some policy critiques would have it, a distortion of professional approaches or, as some studies in organizational sociology would claim, merely a ceremonial expression of pat professional answers?

To answer these questions I delve into the institutional history of policing in the United States. There we find the sources of two very different diagnoses of, and solutions to, the problem with policing. One, commonly called the "professional" model, characterized the problem as police corruption and partisan influence and the solution as insulation from partisan influence combined with managerial control over frontline officers. The professional model became institutionalized as the dominant approach to policing in the mid-twentieth century, represented by the International Association of Chiefs of Police. The other stream, which I will call the "activist" model, characterized the problem as racial discrimination and abuse by the police–encompassing harassment, excessive force, and unjustified shootings. Activists characterized the solution as systemic reform of policing aimed at changing police culture, policies, and practices and, specifically, at eliminating police abuse by disciplining or firing problem officers.

Ironically, as the institutions of professional policing gained ground and spread across the country after the 1920s, these successes helped intensify the activists' critique of American policing as racially discriminatory. In the hands of a group of scholars with extensive experience inside professional policing but with their feet planted firmly in legal academia, the clash between these alternative models in the 1960s yielded a third nascent model, the legalized accountability model. It was a hybrid, drawing key ideas from both the professional and the activist perspectives. Defenders of the professional model, however, greeted the first legalized accountability proposals in the 1960s with indignation and outright opposition, and though these proposals enjoyed considerable favor among legal elites, they initially made little progress within the police profession and fell into stagnation by the 1970s.

This chapter first situates debates over police accountability within their larger context and then outlines the development of the professional, activist, and legalized accountability perspectives, ending with the stalemate of the early 1970s.

Policing as a Bellwether Institution

Policing is the first case in this comparative study for simple reasons: the police affect people's lives almost daily like few other institutions, and police scandal and reform are key issues in the development of American public law, and particularly American law on racial equality.[1] The Supreme Court under the leadership of Chief Justice Earl Warren, for instance, focused much of its reformist judicial activism in the 1960s on police reform; and at virtually the same time, widespread frustration among African Americans over police harassment and abuse contributed directly to the wave of urban riots. White backlash against liberal judicial rulings and urban unrest helped lead to a conservative movement that still dominates American law. More broadly, police brutality and harassment and African Americans' movements against these things have shaped the histories and identities of both African Americans and the police. It is not an overstatement to say that police scandal and reform have shaped American culture as a whole.

Police reform is a vexing problem in part because it is so difficult to carry out in any coordinated way. Among the many decentralized elements of the American system of government, the police represent an extreme case of vesting powerful authority in a deeply decentralized system.[2] Unlike almost every other governing system in the world, the United States places police authority in tens of thousands of local police forces, and for a very long time neither the national government nor state governments made much effort to regulate these local forces. At the same time, local police forces exercise awesome powers, among them surveillance, arrest, incarceration, and the use of force up to and including the authority to kill. At various times in the past they used these powers on behalf of political party machines (against these machines' partisan opponents), white majorities (against racial minorities), and the established status quo (against its radical critics).

The reform efforts discussed in this book are among several relatively recent attempts to impose state and national standards and systems of external accountability on these local forces. Among these recent reform efforts, it is generally agreed that some, at least initially, did not live up to their promise. The most prominent was the Supreme Court's creation of new constitutional rights governing police procedures. Thus, among other important rulings, the Court held that evidence obtained in violation of the Fourth Amendment could not be used in court, that states were constitutionally required to provide defendants with legal counsel, and that before questioning an arrestee, the police must inform him or her of the right to counsel and the right to decline to answer questions.[3] Examining the impact of these rulings, a number of scholars observed that police practices remained surprisingly unchanged: police continued to obtain evidence without search warrants and to aggressively question arrestees in the absence of a defense attorney.[4] The studies, especially those of the late 1960s and 1970s, generally reached a common conclusion about why this was so: police responded less to externally imposed legal norms than to shared police values of restoring order in disrupted situations, getting bad guys off the street, and gaining useful information. In pursuit of these short-term goals, police often paid little attention to whether an arrest would be upheld in court weeks or months later. In short, the legal sanction carried little weight. Worse, police widely regarded the new constitutional rights as out of touch with realities on the street and as hindrances to professional police practices.

Another 1960s reform effort that initially fell short focused on subjecting police departments to civilian oversight, typically through citizen review boards. These boards were meant to provide an independent forum for the filing and review of citizen complaints about police abuses. Under intense pressure from popular movements, a number of major United States cities adopted citizen review boards in the 1960s. Generally these efforts met with frustration because police departments resisted external control and because the civilian amateurs on the boards lacked the expertise and access to perform an effective review function. By the early 1970s the widespread effort at civilian review was moribund, and the boards had been either neutralized or rescinded; New York City, for instance, rescinded its board after a hard-fought public vote.[5]

Those favoring greater police accountability have also tried criminal prosecution of abusive officers and high-level commissions, but, as Samuel Walker has observed, neither has been fully satisfactory.[6] Much police misconduct is not criminal in nature, and even when it is, prosecutors dislike bringing charges against officers and juries rarely convict them. High-level commissions have offered valuable suggestions and ideas but typically have no power to implement them.

It is my thesis that although the window of opportunity for police reform had seemed to close by the 1970s, resurgent reform movements among activists and police professionals contributed to a revolution in policing in the 1980s and 1990s. The federal courts supported these movements by exposing police departments to liability for some injuries caused by their officers. The combined and interacting pressure of these forces generated an explosion of liability pressure on policing; reframed the debate over police misconduct by fixing responsibility squarely on police departments; and produced a new administrative model for addressing the problem.[7]

In the changed legal context of the 1980s, as Myron Orfield and Samuel Walker have shown, the older reform initiatives of constitutional checks on the police and citizen review boards gained new vitality as key elements of legalized accountability.[8] In 1994 Congress authorized the Justice Department to bring lawsuits against police departments over patterns or practices that violate civil rights.[9] The Clinton Justice Department used this new authority to gain consent decrees requiring broad reforms in a number of large departments and, as Walker has observed, these decrees encapsulate many of the elements of legalized accountability.[10] I turn now to the institutional evolution of these debates over police accountability.

The Professional Channel: The Problem Is Political Control of Policing

The key commitment of the professional model grew from its roots in Progressive reforms aiming to insulate city services from partisan control. In the service of that goal, the Progressives "professionalized" policing by bureaucratically shielding departments from partisan control, upgrading the selection and training of officers, and subordinating them to the command of police chiefs. Even as Progressive-style professional policing triumphed by the 1950s and shaped police departments throughout the country, its leaders saw the risk of creeping partisan influence everywhere, and they were always on guard to defend "professionalism" against "partisan control." This commitment translated into a defensive reaction against growing complaints of police abuse of racial minorities (which I will survey in detail later in this chapter), so much so that leaders of professional policing in the 1960s came to label the complaints associated with the civil rights movement as nothing more than an old-style attempt to bring the police under partisan control. In the view of leaders of professional policing, abuses were perpetrated by isolated officers who deviated from professional standards; the solution was simply to apply well-known professional measures to root out these aberrant individuals. These measures were principally careful selection and training of officers.

For the Progressive urban reformers, reform of the police was a key to reforming America's corrupt cities. "Of all the institutions of city government in late-nineteenth-century America," observed Egon Bittner, a distinguished scholar of the American police, "none was as unanimously denounced as the urban police. According to every available account, they were, in every aspect of their existence, an unmixed, unmitigated, and unpardonable scandal."[11] For the reformers, the core problem was that police departments and their officers served particular private and partisan interests. Police departments, in Robert Fogelson's term, were an "adjunct" of urban political machines.[12] Departments were highly decentralized, with precinct captains appointed by ward politicians and serving at their beck and call. "The nineteenth-century patrolman," Samuel Walker similarly observed, "was essentially a political operative."[13] As such, he got his job by loyalty to the machine and lost it if the machine was thrown out of political power. In addition, police corruption was widespread, as officers and whole units accepted payoffs for not enforcing vice laws.[14] The position required no qualifications other than partisan loyalty. It was "a job for amateurs, requiring little more than common sense," and in most places there was no formal training.[15] As immigrants flooded the big cities around the turn of the century, police departments became a prime source of jobs handed out by the machines, cementing the relationship between them and their ethnic supporters.[16] As a consequence, policing lacked a formal professional identity: although some departments tried to require official uniforms, policemen resisted and generally wore civilian clothes, allowing them to blend in with the population (and resist oversight by superiors).[17] It is not surprising that the public seems to have widely disrespected and resisted police authority, so officers gained compliance with their orders primarily through power, often exercised through what Walker calls "the tradition of police brutality" and "curbside justice."[18]

To separate policing from partisan control, reformers drew on European models. European governing systems generally insulated the police from popular political influence and subordinated frontline officers to a centralized police command structure, and such an approach seemed very desirable to American reformers. The leading reformer Raymond Fosdick, for instance, in an extensive 1915 study of European police systems, celebrated their "unbroken record of rectitude," their status as a "profession," "the infinite pains with which police administrators are trained and chosen, and the care with which the forces are shielded from political influence."[19] Fosdick particularly admired the London police force, which was managed by the national government, as professional, efficient, and insulated from meddling by local political officials.[20] Although Fosdick expressed concern about the London force's wide range of arbitrary power and "a certain air of aloofness" in its operations, he concluded that these characteristics were "justified by their outcome," particularly the force's efficiency and independence from partisan pressure.[21]

Based on European models, Progressive reformers imported the idea of police professionalism, or what became, essentially, bureaucratization.[22] Reform meant strict separation of the police from partisan control; consolidation of authority under a strong centralized administration headed by a single executive; a narrowing of the police function from the catchall social welfare duties assigned by machines to a focus on crime fighting; systematic selection and training of officers; granting the police generous resources to do the job; and instilling within the rank and file a professional identity symbolized by the uniform. Reformers argued that these reforms were necessary for achieving professionalism in the public interest. As the model came to shape policing reforms in a number of cities, the changes represented a dramatic institutional shift at the level of ideas, norms, and organizational structures.[23] Reform-oriented police chiefs raised selection standards for officers, imposed the first systems of formal training, and adopted increasingly elaborate and detailed rules governing officers' bearing, equipment, and conduct. Thus, detailed rules required officers to wear uniforms, specified the condition of those uniforms, and governed the upkeep of service pistols and vehicles.[24] Increasingly, in order to evaluate officers' service to the public interest, departments began to require the keeping and reporting of detailed internal records on officers' patterns of work. The institutional model that emerged out of these reforms emphasized nonpartisan professional service. Its symbol, the immaculately maintained (and proudly worn) police uniform, became recognized nationwide.

By the 1950s, the professional model had triumphed as the dominant institutional form in American policing, and police departments in most major metropolitan areas had adopted key elements of it. The definitive statement of that model appeared in the widely used text *Police Administration*, by O. W. Wilson, dean of the School of Criminology at the University of California–Berkeley (formerly chief of police in Wichita, Kansas, and subsequently superintendent of police in Chicago), first published in 1950.[25] In that book, Wilson summarized "the main features of a sound police administrative program." Among other things, they included professionally selected, trained, and disciplined officers; efficient organization aimed at ensuring "effective direction, coordination, and control"; thorough written policies and procedures covering "every police operation"; and inculcation of a mission of nonpartisan public service.[26] Further, Wilson emphasized that these features followed the esteemed British policing model.[27] Although by the 1950s the reform campaign had triumphed, its progress over the previous decades had been unsteady as many major police departments suffered periodic corruption scandals, and leaders of professional policing remained ever watchful for evidence of encroaching political control.[28]

From the 1940s through the 1960s, as I will describe in the next section, activists mounted increasingly prominent campaigns alleging police harassment and abuse of African Americans. Leaders of professional policing responded to these complaints by arguing that professional reform was already addressing the problem and that if any reforms were needed they amounted to simply more of the same, meaning improved selection and training. Professionalism, in this view, had already solved policing's worst problems. Thus the International City Management Association's (ICMA) reformist text *Municipal Police Administration* (to which O. W. Wilson, the dean of the professional reform movement, was a major contributor) proudly declared in its 1954 edition that "a complete change has been made in the nature of police administration during the present century."[29]

As criticisms of police brutality mounted, some professional leaders occasionally acknowledged that a few isolated problems might remain, even in professionalized departments. Thus O. W. Wilson, writing in 1954, acknowledged that police officers sometimes violated individuals' civil rights and even occasionally engaged in "sadistic brutality."[30] By 1963 he acknowledged that "training should also emphasize that the police must scrupulously avoid petty graft, corruption, brutality, and prejudice."[31] But this sort of acknowledgment came extremely rarely, and even in Wilson's case it represented only the briefest of nods to the growing storm around policing. Further, Wilson punctuated his claim that the problem was isolated by prescribing merely a bigger dose of bureaucratic professionalism: better training, better supervision, more secure insulation from "unwholesome outside influences," and better leadership.[32] Similarly, the ICMA's reformist text in 1954 suggested that if any additional reforms might be needed, they should come in the form of more of the same: better planning, organization, and leadership in police departments.[33] In its 1961 edition, the ICMA text gave a brief nod to growing racial tensions, calling on departments to put in place a system for objectively processing complaints against officers in order to enhance "public relations with minority groups."[34] But these suggestions appeared almost as afterthoughts.

Further, professional leaders began to characterize the criticisms as simply another illegitimate attempt at imposing partisan control. When the *Harvard Law Review* published a note in 1964 favoring the adoption of civilian review boards, *Police Chief* magazine, the official voice of the International Association of Chiefs of Police (IACP), responded that "we cannot tolerate the partisan manipulation of public safety."[35] Police professionalism, not legalistic oversight, was the solution: "The problems of law enforcement manifested by citizens' complaints will not be cured or even revealed by a rigid legalistic hearing procedure. . . . Those persons who share in the dreams of a police profession dedicated to public service" will see success only "if they are willing to insist upon the highest possible standards for selection and education."[36]

Rules restricting police use of force, a key demand of policing's activist critics, as we shall see, never featured prominently on the professional agenda. Thus the ICMA's five-hundred-page *Municipal Police Administration*, a leading statement of the professional model, in its 1954 and 1961 editions contained roughly three pages of guidance on appropriate types of police firearms ("The caliber should not be less than a .38 special . . . shocking power remains essential in a gun battle") but did not address the question of when to shoot at members of the public or use other forms of force.[37] In 1967 Samuel Chapman, a political scientist, conducted a study of police department policies on the use of deadly force (mainly shootings) and observed that most departments made no real effort to regulate officers' use of deadly force.[38] Thus, as Chapman observed, the policy in one department consisted solely of the following admonition regarding the service pistol: "Never take me out in anger; never put me back in disgrace." Another department's policy required merely that "officers shall not intentionally fire their gun except as authorized by law," and a third declared, "It is left to the discretion of each individual officer when and how to shoot."

In the 1960s, as criticisms of the police grew intense, the leaders of professional policing became increasingly embattled and indignant. In the face of great social upheaval, observed a writer in 1963 in *Police Chief*, "Never have we [the police] been so alone."[39] Quinn Tamm, the IACP's executive director and a long-standing leader of professionalism, similarly declared in 1964, "Never before in the history of the police service have we been singled out so mercilessly and so wrongfully as the whipping boys by demonstrators."[40] Claims of police brutality particularly rankled with professional policing's leaders. Thus Tamm declared, "I know of no period in recent history when the police have been the subject of so many unjustified charges of brutality, harassment and ineptness."[41] He went on to echo a *Police Chief* editorial from the previous year claiming that many allegations of police brutality were a "smokescreen" intended to draw public attention away from the "excesses and illegal conduct" of demonstrators.[42] Another writer too characterized "the cry 'police brutality'" as "a handy smokescreen."[43] As journalists in the mid-1960s began reporting that police brutality had sparked some of the urban riots, professional policing leaders responded with cries of outrage. The IACP's president, Daniel Liu, labeled these "despicable charges" "completely false."[44] "The news media . . . appears to believe that it is a better story to play up allegations of police brutality," a leading speaker declared at a national IACP conference, "than it is to place the emphasis on who started the riot."[45] Tamm, the IACP's executive director, responded equally bitterly, excoriating such claims and the "false criers of police brutality."[46] All of these writers acknowledged that sometimes, in some places, police officers engaged in brutality. But such incidents were, Tamm declared, remarkably rare, and the United States had the world's best systems for ferreting out and punishing police misconduct. That in 1963 there had been only twenty-five indictments of police officers on charges of civil rights violations demonstrated, he suggested, the rarity of the problem.[47]

The Activist Channel: The Problem Is Police Abuse of African Americans

The observation that only a few police officers were charged with civil rights violations demonstrated to civil rights activists and lawyers not the rarity of the problem but the failure of professional policing's system of self-regulation. These activists were from a diverse collection of local grassroots groups and national civil rights and civil liberties organizations. In their view, police officers often abused or harassed African Americans and other marginalized groups, and the abuse was so widespread that departments must be condoning or even fostering it. Activists and their academic allies consistently argued that the problem in policing went beyond abuses by individual officers, though these were serious enough. The problem was institutional: police departments were more interested in maintaining police solidarity and loyalty to the organization than in minimizing abuses. Commanding officers therefore were unwilling to carry out meaningful investigations into allegations of abuse and were unwilling to discipline officers except in the most egregious cases. In the 1950s the activist critics gained support from a growing number of academics whose systematic research confirmed the activists' claims. By the 1960s, in the context of flagrant abuses of civil rights activists by southern police, the mainstream media began to echo these claims. Just as popular pressure seemed to be growing to address the policing problem, however, the northern public's sympathies swung strongly in favor of the police in reaction to urban riots and street disorder. In this section I fill out these points. Although a growing number of studies address issues of race and policing, there is no comprehensive history of activist campaigns against police brutality, so my evidence in support of these claims is necessarily drawn from a wide variety of sources and remains more fragmentary than would be ideal.[48]

Activists' campaigns for root-and-branch police reform dated to the 1920s and grew in several waves, ironically gaining vigor as policing came under the sway of the professional model. Although police in the South played a key role in controlling the black population dating to the era of slavery, in the nineteenth-century North the police served to control subordinate racial and immigrant groups generally.[49] Moreover, when officers rarely wore uniforms, made no pretense of enforcing the law in the public interest, and retained intense ethnic loyalties, they abused many members of the lower classes. When abuse was widespread, racial harassment and abuse, to the extent it existed—and it surely did—appeared to be part of the problem of *unprofessional* policing, and not a special problem in itself. Marilynn Johnson, in a significant history of police abuse in New York City, found that before the efforts at Progressive reform the victims of police brutality were a diverse lot.[50]

In the early twentieth century the migration of African Americans to cities contributed to the growth of specifically race-based police abuse. The pattern is not surprising in the South, of course, where police officers sometimes even frankly declared that their role was to defend the "southern way of life."[51] But police played a key role in enforcing racial lines in the North as African Americans migrated to cities and were increasingly confined in black ghettoes. As urban areas descended into racial conflict between whites and growing black populations, the police increasingly used surveillance and violence on behalf of white majorities.[52] In New York City, Chicago, and Detroit, for instance, the police, acting as agents of urban white supremacy, vigorously and brutally enforced a color line.[53] In the early decades of the twentieth century, a number of northern cities experienced "race riots" in the form of rampages by mobs of whites attacking blacks, and in these conflicts the police commonly joined the whites.[54] A writer in 1914 observed that in Chicago, "the police department is especially filled with the wicked and unlawful determination to degrade Afro-Americans and fix upon them the badge of inferiority."[55] William

Tuttle, a distinguished historian of American race relations, observed that by World War I, Chicago's black population had come to view the police "as the armed representative of white hostility."[56]

Police professionalism ironically increased the level of police conflict with minority communities.[57] Civil service reforms limited access by African Americans to the ranks of the police (because few fared well on the required exams); the professional commitment to "preventive patrol" placed squads of white officers in black ghettoes, cruising and carrying out surveillance over the minority population; and bureaucratic insulation kept departments aloof from a rising chorus of complaints.[58] Moreover, as police departments increasingly focused on crime control and began gathering crime and arrest statistics, they began to see street crime in racial terms, as a problem predominantly of minorities. In Los Angeles, for instance, the police department's increasing professionalization and focus on crime control "coincided with the department's linking of race and criminality."[59] Although many of these trends were not fully manifested until consolidation of the professional model in the 1940s and 1950s, their roots lay earlier.

From roughly the turn of the century onward, activists carried out sporadic campaigns against police brutality. Local African American activists mounted grassroots campaigns in several big cities and, in the context of a spectacular growth in racial tensions following World War I, the National Association for the Advancement of Colored People (NAACP) mounted a campaign against both lynching and police brutality.[60] Still, as Dan Carter has observed, the NAACP was "jealous of its reputation" and careful not to become too associated with campaigns against police brutality, since in the white public's perceptions the issue was closely linked with black criminality.[61]

World War II, it is well known, jump-started more broad-scale organizing around civil rights.[62] To mobilize support, the Roosevelt administration characterized the war as a fight for freedom and against a race-based totalitarianism, and civil rights organizers successfully used the new rhetoric of rights to build a broader popular base and to achieve new civil rights policies. The first federal efforts to address police abuses date to the period, among them the Justice Department's prosecution of several police brutality cases.[63] In one of these cases, *Screws v. U.S.* (1945), the Supreme Court revived federal authority to prosecute official violations of civil rights but limited it to instances in which officials "specifically intended" to violate federal rights, a high standard.[64]

Many observers began to see in American police policies something akin to the abuses perpetrated by authoritarian states. As early as 1940, Justice Hugo Black had cryptically compared police brutality to the police practices of the Nazis.[65] That comparison became more explicit in later years. In 1946 an author characterized "official homicide" by the police as "startlingly similar to terroristic practices which obtain in authoritarian police states of the world."[66] A widely cited law review article from 1953, claiming that American police carried out millions of illegal arrests annually, observed that "there is hardly a single physical brutality inflicted by the Gestapo and the NKVD which American policemen have not at some time perpetrated. Certainly the torture of Negroes by the police in some communities rivals the barbarism of the Gestapo and NKVD."[67] Equally significantly, African Americans in northern cities had started calling police brutality "lynching, northern style."[68]

Concerns about internal subversion during the war increased the level of police repression, and this too contributed to heightened complaints of brutality. In the South, police repression undoubtedly increased during the war years.[69] In Georgia at the height of the war, for instance, the commissioner of the Georgia Highway Patrol issued a directive "to stop and search all colored persons found on the road after 9 p.m." and to "use your black jack on them when you can."[70] In the North, growing racial tensions around access to jobs and police repression of African Americans exploded in 1943 in "race riots" in Detroit, New York, and Los Angeles.[71] As tensions rose, the FBI carried out a yearlong investigation of black communities throughout the country, culminating in a massive report sent to the White House, which observed that African Americans were intensely frustrated with police brutality and recommended that security forces prepare for black-led internal subversion.[72]

The NAACP, the American Civil Liberties Union, and the National Lawyers Guild began broad campaigns against police brutality during the war years and ratcheted up their efforts in the late 1940s and 1950s. Responding to appeals from its chapters in several southern states, the NAACP (and its offshoot the Legal Defense Fund) began campaigning forcefully against police brutality during the war years, and its membership surged, drawn in part by the widespread appeal of that campaign in black communities.[73] After the war the NAACP, with the support of the actor Orson Welles, mounted a prominent campaign to prosecute police officers who brutally killed an African American soldier returning from service.[74] In 1948 local branches of the NAACP resolved to make police brutality their top priority in the coming years, and the New York branch formed the Committee for Action against Police Brutality, which ran a storefront office to receive complaints, provide legal assistance and representation, and help in organizing street demonstrations.[75]

Likewise, the National Lawyers Guild began a broad campaign against police harassment and abuse in the 1940s and increased its efforts in later years. The Guild was an unusual association of elite lawyers associated with the Roosevelt administration (who formed the organization in 1936 as an alternative to the American Bar Association over the latter group's opposition to the New Deal and exclusion of Jews and blacks from membership) and many marginalized radical, ethnic, Jewish, and black lawyers.[76] These marginalized lawyers brought to the association a wealth of experience representing people at the lower rungs of society where police abuses were most prevalent; the elite attorneys brought contacts with the highest levels of the Roosevelt administration. This combination helped to bring police abuses to the attention of administration leaders.[77] After the war, the Guild increased its efforts on the issue, adopting resolutions condemning police brutality and holding a series of national conferences, with "standing room only" attendance, on "Police Treatment of Negroes," as one was titled, with a specific focus on developing practical legal strategies to check police abuses.[78]

The third organization to begin working concertedly on problems of police abuse was the American Civil Liberties Union (ACLU). Several of its leaders contributed directly in the early 1930s to the Wickersham Commission's report on police abuses in the prosecution of Prohibition, and in 1937 the ACLU carried out a concerted campaign against abuses by Jersey City Mayor Frank Hague's political machine, among them police harassment of labor organizers.[79] As tensions between the police and African Americans heated up during the war years, local ACLU affiliates in Chicago, Los Angeles, and St. Louis began focusing increasingly on police misconduct.[80] In 1948 the ACLU established a national Committee on Police Practices aimed at addressing police abuses, and a number of local ACLU affiliates formed similar committees.[81] The New York ACLU affiliate's efforts led in 1955 to the publication of a booklet titled *If You Are Arrested*, aimed at informing ordinary Americans of their rights in relation to the police, which was soon reprinted widely throughout the country.[82]

Each of these groups alleged that the problem with policing was both individual, in the form of egregious abuses by particular officers, and institutional, in the form of widespread patterns of abuse and departments' unwillingness to address these issues with real reforms. Thus, in the wake of the 1943 Detroit riot, Thurgood Marshall and the NAACP's Walter White condemned the Detroit police for widespread racism and brutality and failing to address the problem institutionally.[83] The National Lawyers Guild similarly alleged that police brutality against African Americans and the poor was widespread, so much so that it was "unhealthy for Negro men to walk the streets at late hours of the night," and alleged that departments lacked the will to address the problem.[84] In the late 1950s The Illinois affiliate of the ACLU carried out a systematic study of police practices in Chicago and published the results in a 1959 report titled *Secret Detention by the Chicago Police,* documenting an extremely widespread practice of illegal arrest and detention in that city.[85] A number of major newspapers praised the report, and at least two Supreme Court justices (William O. Douglas and Tom C. Clark) asked for copies.[86] For a final example, the National Lawyers Guild held a national conference in 1959 on police reform, and the president of the Los Angeles chapter of the NAACP issued a dire and prescient warning in his keynote address.[87] Reporting wanton police harassment, brutality, and killings of minority residents in Los Angeles, he observed a "general consensus among minority leaders that our police department is doing more harm to good race relations than any half dozen groups of professional hate mongers."[88] He concluded, "The tides of protest against this type of police procedure are mounting in Negro and Mexican communities, and we are urging the support of every right thinking person in the community to support us in an effort to stop this lawless conduct before the waves of resentment come tumbling down to our total demoralization."[89]

Beginning in the early 1950s, academic researchers began confirming the activists' complaints with systematic research. Sociologist William Westley conducted a pioneering observational study of the police in Gary, Indiana, in the early 1950s, riding and walking along with police officers.[90] In 1953 his initial report from the study observed that police commonly acted without regard for even the semblance of the rule of law and often treated citizens brutally, especially when they were disrespectful toward an officer. "The police believe," he observed, "that certain groups of persons will respond only to fear and rough treatment . . . [and] they defined both Negroes and slum dwellers in this category."[91] A study of Philadelphia police practices published in 1952 similarly reported that the police were commonly abusive, carrying out random frisks of people on the street, wholesale roundups of young black men for questioning about crimes, and general harassment of African Americans and the poor.[92] Another study observed that among people killed in shootings by the Philadelphia police from 1950 to 1960, 88 percent were black.[93] The Ford Foundation and American Bar Foundation (ABF), acting in 1956 on a suggestion of Supreme Court Justice Robert Jackson, sponsored a four-year observational study of police practices in a number of cities.[94] The ABF researchers, as Samuel Walker observes, were "stunned by their observations."[95] "Team members were struck by the rampant lawlessness of official behavior, the disregard for legal norms in decision making, and the extent to which decisions such as arrest were routinely made for reasons unrelated to arrest."[96] Thus some researchers observed police breaking into buildings, harassing gays and African Americans, and conducting massive "sweep" arrests in urban ghettoes.[97] With regard to officers' discretion to shoot at fleeing felons, in one instance an ABF observer watched as a police officer on foot tried to flag down a speeding motorist and, when the driver did not stop, fired his pistol at the car five times.[98] Further, "the willful mistreatment of black citizens," as Walker observes, "was pervasive."[99] Thus one researcher observed police in Milwaukee engaging in "unrestrained frisking" of black residents, and another observed police in Pontiac, Michigan, severely beating a black citizen for photographing officers as part of a local campaign to identify officers accused of brutality.[100]

By the 1960s, as the civil rights movement grew and riots engulfed many Northern cities, the trickle of studies documenting widespread police discrimination and abuse of racial minorities became a torrent. The evidence went far beyond the well-known brutality of southern police toward civil rights activists. The first report issued by the then new Commission on Civil Rights in 1961, for instance, observed that "police brutality—the unnecessary use of violence to enforce the mores of segregation, to punish, and to coerce confessions—is a serious problem in the United States."[101] Documenting a large number of cases of police brutality, the Commission reported that "Negroes are the victims with disproportionate frequency," because they either were deliberately targeted in order to quell civil rights activism or simply were poor and vulnerable.[102] Studies conducted in the wake of the urban riots revealed that police widely employed stops and frisks in black ghettoes.[103] The San Diego police, for instance, in the mid-1960s were conducting at least 20,000—and possibly as many as 40,000—stops and frisks *per month*.[104] This practice, as Hahn and Jeffries observe, was widespread in northern cities, "produced a strong legacy of public grievances" in African American communities, and often provoked violent confrontations between the police and the people subjected to search.[105] In 1967, after three summers of riots, President Lyndon Johnson appointed the National Advisory Commission on Civil Disorders, which in 1968 reported that the riots grew out of conditions of intense urban poverty and growing resentment against police harassment and abuse.[106] Roughly half of the riots were triggered by an incident with the police, and in many more of the riot-torn cities African Americans expressed deep frustration and resentment against police practices. A survey of citizens in fifteen cities conducted as part of the research for the Commission, for instance, found that 6 percent of whites but 22 percent of blacks reported that police had frisked or searched them without a good reason, 9 percent of whites but 20 percent of blacks reported that the police had verbally harassed them, and 2 percent of whites but 7 percent of blacks reported that the police had physically abused them.[107] Similarly, Bayley and Mendelsohn surveyed 806 residents of Denver in 1968 and found that while 4 percent of whites reported that they had personally experienced police brutality, this was true of 9 percent of African Americans and 15 percent of Hispanics.[108] A study of Newark residents' perceptions showed that while only 5 percent of whites viewed the police as "too brutal," 49 percent of African Americans held this view; a study of Detroit residents found that 81 percent of African Americans believed the police treated some groups better than others; and a study of the Watts neighborhood in Los Angeles found that 72 percent of African Americans believed the police frisked or searched blacks without good reason.[109] *Justice without Trial*, Jerome Skolnick's influential observational study of police practices in two West Coast cities, published in 1966, observed that police rarely observed legal procedures and viewed African American men and other marginal groups as "symbolic assailants" to be treated with suspicion.[110]

Emergence of the Legalized Accountability Model

As complaints against American policing grew in the 1960s, a group of scholars proposed a law-based model for dealing with the problem. Their proposal became the basis for the legalized accountability model that grew to dominate law-based reform of policing in the 1980s. In light of scholarly debates over the character of bureaucratic "legalization," particularly competing claims that legalization is either forced on professional practitioners from the outside or simply an extension of these practitioners' preferred models, it will be useful to plumb the origins and character of the legalized accountability model. It is my central claim that this model drew key elements from both the professional and activist perspectives and thus represented a hybrid. But its central characteristic was an emphasis on legal norms.

The leaders of this third group occupied positions at the border between professional policing and academia, but with their feet firmly planted on the academic side of the line. The intellectual leaders were Frank Remington, a law professor at the University of Wisconsin–Madison and one of the leaders of the research team that conducted the American Bar Foundation's late-1950s study of American policing, and Herman Goldstein, a staff member of that research team who became special assistant to O. W. Wilson when he was chief of police in Chicago and still later a law professor at the University of Wisconsin–Madison. The ABF study, as we saw, had systematically documented that police officers exercised wide discretion in carrying out their duties and, in doing so, often acted in highly abusive ways, particularly toward African Americans.[111] In other words, as we have seen, Remington and Goldstein had confirmed complaints made for years by the activist critics of the police.

Remington and Goldstein wrote key portions of the 1967 *Task Force Report: The Police*, the report of the professional staff to the President's Commission on Law Enforcement and the Administration of Justice.[112] As Walker has observed, the *Task Force Report* entirely reframed the agenda of police reform. It did two things. First, the *Task Force Report* endorsed activists' allegations that American police were widely abusive, particularly toward African Americans and the poor, and urged police departments to face frankly the seriousness of the crisis. "A community's attitude toward the police," it observed, "is influenced most by the action of individual officers on the street."[113] Summarizing recent studies, the report observed that there was widespread evidence of verbal abuse and harassment by police, particularly against African Americans.[114] While speculating that physical abuse, common in an earlier era, had declined, the report acknowledged that brutality remained a significant problem.[115] Surveys of African Americans in Los Angeles, for instance, showed that almost 50 percent of respondents had seen the police act disrespectfully or use insulting language, and equal proportions had seen the police stop and frisk people without good reason and use unnecessary force in making arrests.[116] These were stunning levels of police harassment, illegality, and abuse, the report observed, and to correct them would require deep institutional reforms.

Second, the *Task Force Report* proposed institutional reforms in the shape of rule-based regulation of officers' conduct, training around the rules, and internal oversight over officers' behavior. The report observed that no department currently did these things with regard to the sorts of abuses that gave rise to complaints, and it declared that professional policing faced a fork in the road.[117] Policing could continue its practice of "unarticulated improvisation," or it could engage in systematic "administrative policymaking."[118] The former was more "comfortable": "Direct confrontation of policy issues would ... require recognition that many practices are not legal or constitutional," and most departments had concluded implicitly that it is better to "let sleeping dogs lie."[119] Although improvisation by individual officers on the street undoubtedly often produces "surprisingly good" results, the report acknowledged, officers' ad hoc improvisations too often were infected by racial bias, resulting in a catastrophic breakdown of relations with minority communities:

> Proper and consistent exercise of discretion in a large organization, like a police department, will not result from the individual judgment of individual police officers in individual cases. Whatever the need for the exercise of judgment by an individual officer may be, certainly the development of overall law enforcement policies must be made at the departmental level and communicated to individual officers. This is necessary if the issues are to be adequately defined and adequately researched and if discretion is to be exercised consistently throughout the department.[120]

The *Task Force Report* then laid out the essential elements of what became the legalized accountability model. Rules: Departments, relying on careful internal research into "problem areas," should systematically develop clear internal administrative rules governing officer discretion. Departments, the report urged, should employ internal legal advisers to aid in developing and implementing such policies. Training: After adopting such rules, departments should systematically disseminate them so that all officers are well aware of them, and should provide ongoing training so that officers know how to follow the policies in practice. Oversight: After such implementation, departments should carry out ongoing review of the policies' effectiveness and should devise appropriate methods of "internal control" over officers' actions.

Among these elements of legalized accountability, the *Report* devoted most of its attention to oversight or internal control aimed at addressing the problem of abusive police behavior. Reform, the *Report* argued, required significant improvements in this area, particularly "'good administration,' that is, the use of the whole array of devices commonly employed in public administration to achieve conformity. These include, but are not limited to, the setting of individual responsibility, the establishment of systems of accountability, the designing of procedures for checking and reporting on performance, and the establishment of methods for taking corrective action."[121]

Among the 1967 *Task Force Report*'s most specific recommendations was a detailed proposed rule governing the discharge of weapons. The common-law "fleeing felon" rule had long authorized the use of deadly force to stop fleeing persons suspected of having committed a felony. As reforms over time eliminated the death penalty for all but a few felonies, however, the fleeing felon rule had become an anachronism, and reformers increasingly called for replacing it with a "defense of life" rule that allowed officers to shoot only to defend against an imminent threat of substantial harm to the officer or a third party. The *Task Force Report* joined the call for reform, observing that the shooting of unarmed individuals fleeing the scenes of crimes had often provoked extreme community outrage and that unfettered police discretion to shoot had become intolerable.[122] "It is essential," the *Report* declared, "that all departments formulate written firearms policies which clearly limit their use to situations of strong and compelling need."[123] Further, the *Report* proposed a detailed shooting rule that would prohibit officers from firing weapons except to defend their own lives or the life of a third party.[124]

Getting police departments to accept such a radical reform would be difficult, and the *Task Force Report* anticipated this problem by suggesting that professional policing should see legalized accountability not as a departure from the professional ideal but as its fulfillment.[125] Professionalism, the *Report* suggested, should be understood as committed to systematic development of police expertise, with an emphasis on *systematic*. Legalized accountability would serve this ideal by allowing departments "to systematize experience so that it can be effectively communicated through police training,"[126] to systematically inform officers of "what is expected of them," to systematize training, and to provide supervisors with a systematic basis for disciplining officers when they acted improperly.[127] Professional policing already was committed to this sort of agenda, at least in general terms, the report suggested, and it was only a small step toward applying it to police abuses. As the Kerner Commission observed, echoing the *Task Force Report*'s argument, "There are guidelines for the wearing of uniforms—but not for how to intervene in a domestic dispute. There are guidelines for the cleaning of a revolver—but not for when to fire it. There are guidelines for the use of departmental property—but not for whether to break up a sidewalk gathering. There are guidelines for handling stray dogs—but not for handling field interrogations."[128]

The *Task Force Report*, as Walker has observed, proved exceptionally influential in elite circles. The report of the Kerner Commission on the mid-1960s riots echoed the *Task Force Report*'s recommendations, calling for police departments to adopt internal guidelines governing the use of force (among other things, including "the proper manner of address for contacts with any citizen") and to implement these guidelines through systematic training and internal oversight.[129] Similarly, the preeminent administrative law scholar Kenneth Culp Davis (like Frank Remington, a law professor at the University of Wisconsin) crystallized the growing consensus in a pair of books in 1969 and 1975, arguing that while *externally* imposed legal rules are usually ineffective in regulating administrative action (and may be very counterproductive), *internally developed* rules are more likely to be professionally accepted and influential.[130] Davis observed that externally crafted rules typically are developed without sufficient understanding of the nature of the administrative process and of workable solutions, and administrative officials often resent such rules and seek to escape their control. But when administrators develop rules to channel their own discretion, Davis argued, the rules can be highly relevant to the nature of the problem and are not so commonly resented and evaded. By the mid-1970s, as Samuel Walker has observed, Davis's argument "met little dissent."[131] The emerging elite consensus on internal police rules appeared in a number of other high-level reports as well, among them the American Bar Association's *Standards relating to the Urban Police Function*[132] and the National Advisory Commission on Criminal Justice Standards and Goals.[133] On the matter of police shootings, the American Law Institute's Model Penal Code of 1962 had proposed a similar rule restricting police discretion in shootings,[134] and the National Commission on Reform of Federal Criminal Laws of 1970 joined the *Task Force Report* in recommending rules restricting shootings.[135]

There were signs that professional policing too might be open to the idea. In 1966 Nelson A. Watson, director of research at the IACP, called for departmental action against police abuses.[136] Grand talk about police professionalism, he argued, would no longer suffice. "It is going to take action—action which demonstrates we mean it when we say we will not tolerate brutality."[137]

Still, although advocates within professional policing pressed their case, it was clear that they were on the defensive. In 1967, although Watson frankly proposed adopting the "defense of life" rule in *Police Chief*, the magazine soft-pedaled the proposal as merely "a 'think' piece" and not a recommendation for all departments.[138] An accompanying article by a political scientist also favored legalizing accountability with regard to police shootings but acknowledged that "public definitions of 'proper' police conduct reflect wide variations geographically.... Reputedly 'tough' communities or cities in frontier-like settings may tolerate more aggressive police behavior than the more sedate, sophisticated college town.[139] The call for reform of shootings policies was out of step with police norms in 1967, and nothing so clearly illustrates that fact as an advertisement accompanying these articles (both of which opposed shots fired from or at vehicles). It was a full-page ad from a gun manufacturer for a shotgun described as ideal for shooting at fleeing vehicles during police chases: "12 GAUGE FIREPOWER WITH PISTOL CONTROL"—"THE IDEAL POLICE CAR GUN! . . . Only the Model Ten can be aimed to deliver five shots directly ahead of a speeding patrol car."[140]

Legalized Reform in Stagnation

The *Task Force Report*'s proposal for legalizing accountability took ideas from both the activist critics of the police and the professional policing model. From the activists, it took the idea that policing was in need of fundamental reform with regard to police abuses. From the professional model, it took the standard administrative tools of rules, training around the rules, and oversight aimed at assessing and encouraging adherence to these controls. Professional policing, of course, was quite comfortable with these rules when applied, as a general matter, to the problem of individual conformity to centralized command. There had even been an earlier proposal to extend the rule-based model to relations with minority groups, in the form of a 1944 report by the reformist ICMA, favoring departmental rules and training for dealing with riots and other "incidents" involving minority groups, and the professional text *Municipal Police Administration* had incorporated that report verbatim.[141]

But professional policing had never applied these tools in any systematic way to the problem of police abuses, and therein lay the difficulty. Taking such a step would require, as the activist critics declared, a thoroughgoing, institutional reform of American policing, and the *Task Force Report* frankly acknowledged this and favored it. After 1967, in sum, professional policing faced a choice between adhering to its by then traditional commitment to insulation and professional discretion or embarking on fundamental institutional reform in the name of systematic policymaking to eliminate abuse.

Then, at the end of August 1968, radical demonstrators clashed with the Chicago police outside the Democratic Party convention and the police, in full view of a national television audience, "unleashed physical force that was described by most press observers . . . as far in excess of what was required."[142] The national television networks were flooded with letters condemning their criticism of the Chicago police; a survey conducted immediately afterward by the *New York Times* revealed overwhelming public support for the police, and this was later confirmed by systematic surveys showing that only 25 percent of respondents believed the police had used too much force.[143]

Quinn Tamm, the IACP's leader, after years of complaining about unjustified criticism of the police, observed "a turning point," to be seen not only in "spiritual support" for the police but also in "material assistance."[144] Buoyed by resounding support among the white majority, leaders of professional policing reasserted their profession's central commitment as insulation from external control. In response to the *Task Force Report*, the International Association of Chiefs of Police expressed indignation. The *Report*, as the IACP's Quinn Tamm put it, "contains some broad, sweeping generalizations which cause concern to the police."[145] Foremost, he declared, it couldn't possibly be true that police harassment and abuse of minority groups is widespread. But even if so, "we must be practical. . . . There is an axiom in law enforcement that the successful policeman is the one who 'dominates the situation'—and he is also likely to be the one who lives the longest." Certainly, Tamm emphasized, he was not condoning "nasty" behavior. Still, "It's about time that wrongdoers, thugs and criminals learn that the police have a job to do; it's a dirty, tough and dangerous task . . . and they should not be expected to be timid exemplars of personality and courtesy."[146]

In subsequent years the movement in favor of legalized accountability stagnated. Only a handful of articles in *Police Chief* favored legalizing accountability,[147] and those that did avoided any discussion of national standards or explicitly condemned them in favor of exclusive local control.[148] "The all too frequent and common reference to these standards and goals as *national* standards for state and local law enforcement agencies," one police leader argued, for instance, "is a *myth* that is repugnant to local and state law enforcement executives."[149] Although some states adopted legislative restrictions on officers' discretion to shoot at fleeing felons, in the absence of *departmental* restrictions, the police disregarded the legislative reforms.[150] In two cases in 1977, the Supreme Court declined to address whether officers' unrestricted discretion to shoot at fleeing felons violated the Constitution.[151]

At the level of practice, two studies of police policymaking in the late 1970s found that police departments exercised little administrative control over officers' uses of force. The first, published by the Police Foundation in 1977 as part of a research program in favor of legalizing accountability, focused specifically on police shooting policies in seven major police departments.[152] Although the report declared optimistically in its executive summary that "there is a clear national trend in police departments toward enactment of written policies governing the use of firearms," the substance of its findings demonstrated that "many police chiefs . . . are unwilling to adopt strict internal regulations governing the use of deadly force."[153] All of the departments observed in the study had adopted some form of written policy or policies governing deadly force, but their substance and restrictiveness varied widely, and most "*appear to be more restrictive than they really are.*"[154] With regard to shooting fleeing felons, the wedge issue that would soon become the focus of attention and conflict within professional policing, all seven cities authorized shots at fleeing felons in many circumstances.[155] More generally, "many police firearms policies seem poorly organized, badly worded, or both," the report observed, and "in some cities, it is difficult even to locate a complete copy of the firearms policy, which may be split among several department orders issued over a period of years."[156] If formal policies remained haphazard, the report observed an even greater degree of informality, variation, and disjuncture between appearance and reality in police departments' training and internal oversight regarding use of deadly force.[157]

The second late-1970s study was equally bleak in its assessment, observing that most police departments had not adopted internal policies governing officers' behavior on the street, and in the few instances where they had done so, the policies were pro forma and could not function as effective constraints on officers' discretion.[158] As the authors pessimistically observed, "Despite over ten years of discussion on the advantages of police agencies engaging in policymaking to structure the discretion of their officers, very few police departments report having developed written policies for this purpose," and most lacked the capacity to develop such rules and internal mechanisms for overseeing frontline officers' actions.[159] As the authors observed, "Few departments reported any mechanism to determine compliance with their policies or any attempt to discipline or commend officers with regard to these policies."[160] The report concluded that there was "a major need" for "mechanisms for knowing and reviewing what officers are doing."[161]

Resistance by frontline officers and police unions contributed to the reform movement's difficulties. Although reformist police chiefs in several cities tried to push through new policies restricting use of deadly force, frontline officers fought them tooth and nail.[162] In Montgomery County, Maryland, resistance by frontline officers resulted in a watered-down policy. In San Jose, California, the department's police union sued the police chief over a new defense of life shooting rule and gained a temporary restraining order blocking enforcement of the rule.

By the late 1970s, as we saw in chapter 2's opening example, a very large swath of the country's police chiefs had joined in the reaction against rule-based reforms. In response to Patrick Murphy's campaign to reduce police shootings by new rules and training, IACP president Joseph Dominelli wrote a series of editorials in 1980 in *Police Chief* attacking the idea and, as the Association's annual conference in September approached, Dominelli sent members a twenty-one-page mailing denouncing Murphy, the proposal to impose new shooting rules on the police, and more specifically a joint Police Foundation–NAACP project to develop grassroots support in a number of cities for restrictions on police shootings.[163] The police, the IACP leader wrote, were fed up with constant criticism and "were rapidly approaching the point of rebellion."[164] Quoting the police chief of Syracuse, New York, Dominelli declared, "*Enough* is *enough* is *enough.*"[165]

At the Association's annual convention in St. Louis in September 1980, the issue came to a head. The leadership, after attempting to close off a public debate on the issue, allowed Murphy's proposal to go to a vote of the membership. As the *St. Louis Post-Dispatch* reported, "Brief but bitter infighting on police use of 'deadly force' issues erupted."[166] The membership, as we saw, defeated the proposal four to one and then adopted, by a similar margin, a resolution opposing any restrictions on police authority to shoot at fleeing felons.[167] The proposed reforms, according to the *Post-Dispatch*, were pushing "issues unpopular with many police chiefs and officers," and most IACP members "consider their colleagues in the Foundation disloyal to the police fraternity."[168] In 1980 the International Union of Police Associations, a new police union associated with the AFL-CIO, adopted a resolution calling for removal of Patrick Murphy as head of the Police Foundation and urging members "to boycott any organization or foundation that supports the Police Foundation."[169]

Conclusion

The solutions that policing professionals and their external critics offered to the problem of police abuse differed considerably, and this chapter has traced the early development of these alternative reform ideas and their fundamental collision in the 1970s. Mainstream police leaders hewed closely to the well-established Progressive ideology that the problem was partisan control and the solution was bureaucratic insulation. In response to a growing chorus of external criticism of police abuses, these professional leaders argued that the critics were attempting to impose illegitimate partisan control and that established professional tools—careful selection, training, and discipline—could adequately address what they characterized as rare cases of abuse. Activist critics, by contrast, argued that the problem was not creeping partisan influence but widespread police harassment and abuse of racial minorities and the poor. They demanded sweeping institutional reforms aimed at weeding out problem officers and changing the culture of policing.

As clashes between these competing perspectives reached a high point in the wake of the mid-1960s urban riots, a third group, composed of law scholars with extensive experience inside professional policing, proposed an alternative reform model. They agreed with policing's activist critics that abuse was widespread and required institutional reforms; but they agreed with defenders of professional policing that some of its administrative tools were up to the task of carrying out such reforms. Professional policing, however, had never systematically applied these tools—administrative rules and training and internal oversight tailored to the rules—to the problem of police abuses of force, the key issue in dispute, and thus the proposal represented a significant departure from standard professional approaches. Although a handful of reform-oriented police chiefs experimented with the proposal, the broader profession rejected the idea.

In answer to the questions posed at the outset of this chapter, then, legalized accountability as a policy model grew from both activist demands and professional ideas, but the activist demands were the driving force. Contrary to the claims of the policy studies critics of liability, there is no evidence that the policing profession was adequately addressing the problem of misconduct. Undoubtedly the professional movement had improved policing, but it remained deaf to the problem of racial discrimination, harassment and abuse even as complaints about these problems increased considerably after the 1940s. Nor is it accurate to characterize legalized accountability as simply a profession-driven ceremonial refashioning of standard techniques in response to outside pressure. It was something new, with a potential to thoroughly refashion the institutions of policing, and the leaders of professional policing immediately recognized this. They reacted strongly against the proposal, condemning it in the 1970s to a period of stagnation.

4

Liability's Triumph

Although the police turned against legalized accountability after
the late 1960s, pressure to adopt legal checks on the police grew in
the 1970s, and by the early 1980s the idea gained widespread support. This growing pressure reflected the emergence, evolution,
and increasingly widespread acceptance of a norm—a value, an
ethic, a profound "thou shall not"—opposing abusive uses of force
by the police and favoring legalized checks on them. Police ended
the 1960s, as we have seen, confident of public support for vigorous
action up to and including extravagant uses of force to quell disorder and control crime. Well over 70 percent of the public thought
the police were justified in their use of force against radicals at the
1968 Democratic Convention in Chicago, and basking in this public support, police leaders proudly reaffirmed their commitment to
officers' right to use force as they saw fit, free from intrusive legal
oversight. But by the 1980s, as this chapter will show, police were
on the defensive, reeling from rapidly growing public concern over
police abuses and a newfound support for legalized checks.

This chapter traces the development of the norm favoring legal
checks on the police. Traditionally, abrupt changes in legal norms
are thought to grow mainly from new official pronouncements:
new statutes, landmark judicial decisions, and the like. Revisionist
theories have replied that in a bureaucratic society these official
pronouncements often follow what the (ostensibly) regulated organizations are already doing. If so, we might expect to find that in

the case of legal checks on the police, police departments themselves led in creating the norm against excessive force and a police-friendly version of what counts as compliance with that norm. Although I find some evidence in favor of this view—a handful of leading police departments did indeed develop new restrictions on use of force in the 1970s, and these innovations did indeed become the basis for the spread of legalized accountability and for subsequent judicial landmarks—I also find that focusing only on what was happening among police departments would miss a fundamental element of the process. What is missing is the activist half of the story. As I show, focused pressure by activists in the form of liability lawsuits contributed directly to conflict among police leaders, leading to shifts in professional norms and the innovations that eventually became the legalized accountability model.

In the chapter's first section, I summarize developments in the activist channel, where police misconduct litigators developed an infrastructure of support for sustained tort litigation against police departments and, in order to encourage systemic reform, pursued a long-term campaign to make departments liable for the actions of their officers. The growth of activist litigation, I suggest, was critical to the developmental dynamic just noted, since it framed the debate and set the process in motion. In the chapter's second section, I examine developments among professional practitioners, where a handful of reformers and policy experts, acting over the vehement objections of mainstream police leaders, implemented legalized accountability reforms and demonstrated their effectiveness. Both police misconduct litigators and reformist police professionals pressed their campaigns before the bar of public opinion, and in the third section I show that media coverage shifted over the course of the 1970s in favor of legalized accountability. Finally, in the fourth section, I show that the convergence of these developments generated a cascade of interactions that fueled the spread of legalized accountability among departments.

The Growth of Activists' Litigation Campaigns and Shifts in Media Coverage

A Growing Infrastructure Of Support for Litigation

The challenge, in the eyes of the activist critics of the police, was to devise a lever that would force departments to take abuse seriously and to impose meaningful controls on their officers. The activist critics mounted increasingly prominent campaigns to document and publicize public abuses, and they called for broad-scale police reforms aimed at disciplining or firing abusive officers and reforming police culture from top to bottom. By the early 1970s there were growing doubts that the exclusionary rule would do the trick. It was increasingly clear that this rule, which allows judges to exclude from trial any evidence obtained in violation of law, was effective only with regard to arrests that actually led to trial, and even then only to the extent that officers cared what happened in trial. But mounting evidence showed that very few police actions led to trial and that in all but "big busts" officers were far more concerned about maintaining order on the street than about what might happen in court months later.[1] Although later studies qualified these stark conclusions, it was clear by the early 1970s that the exclusionary rule would be no magic lever of reform.[2]

The activists cast about for an alternative lever, ultimately rejecting most available remedies and settling on liability lawsuits. The roots of this turn to liability lay in the 1950s, and it is useful to briefly consider these origins, since they exerted a long-term influence on the movement. In that conservative decade, tort law began to take on the cachet of a weapon of the weak that was useful in extracting justice from big business and unresponsive government alike. Supporters of tort law saw themselves as engaged in a popular movement, in the words of attorney Stuart Speiser, a tort lawyer who later reflected on tort law's rise to prominence in the 1950s, "to equalize the positions of the great and the small."[3] Tort liability, declared Thomas Lambert, an early leader of the tort bar, was "the jurisprudence of hope."[4] Tort lawyers became increasingly organized and sophisticated as firms retained by labor unions branched out into personal injury claims and as auto-related injuries soared.[5] The National Association of Claims Compensation Attorneys (NACCA), which later became the formidable Association of Trial Lawyers of America (ATLA), was organized in 1946 and worked to improve tort law's image.[6] The organization's founder, Sam Horovitz, a Boston attorney associated with the National Lawyers Guild, traveled around the country recruiting members and supporters, among them the prominent attorney Melvin Belli and the eminent former Harvard Law School dean Roscoe Pound.[7] Belli campaigned energetically to increase awards in tort cases and to make plaintiffs' arguments more "scientific" by using such evidence as photographs, models, and economic figures.[8] He eventually wrote *Modern Trials*, a six-volume practical guide to "scientific" tort lawyering.[9] NACCA's mailing list, files on cases, lists of expert witnesses, index of winning techniques, and Belli's famous seminars at NACCA conventions coordinated the tort bar's growing knowledge base and networks.[10] NACCA "went way beyond the normal functions of a bar association," Speiser observed. "It became the command-post of the entrepreneur-lawyers' revolution, by teaching techniques as well as law, and by organizing lawyers into action groups to cooperate in pending cases."[11]

Just as the legal landscape seemed increasingly friendly to tort lawsuits, McCarthyism ironically contributed to turning torts against the police. "You can't understand the growth of police misconduct litigation," observed Ann Fagan Ginger, one of the Guild's early leaders, "without understanding the impact of McCarthyism."[12] By the late 1940s, National Lawyers Guild members included a Who's Who of prominent liberal and progressive lawyers, many of whom relied on retainers from the country's major labor unions. In 1953, as the McCarthy scare mounted, Attorney General Herbert Brownell issued a letter of intent to declare the Guild a "subversive organization," an action that would have opened the organization and its leaders to criminal prosecution.[13] The attack decimated the Guild's membership, and unions throughout the country dropped their retainers with Guild-affiliated law firms.

As the Guild-affiliated firms cast about for work, they increasingly focused on tort cases, and the Guild itself began advocating torts as a lever of reform.[14] The shift was easily made, since the firms' retainers with major unions had required them to represent union members in routine individual cases, a growing proportion of which had involved torts, and so Guild-affiliated firms had already developed a growing expertise in tort law. Beginning in 1953, annual Guild conventions commonly had panels on personal injury litigation, and the Guild held workshops on the topic around the country.[15] In 1956 the Guild's journal published an extended, glowing review of the first installments of Melvin Belli's multivolume guide to tort litigation, calling it "the most exciting and stimulating work in recent years on trial practice" and urging readers to "RUN—DON'T WALK" to get a copy.[16] The Guild's growing support for tort litigation quickly spilled over into tort litigation against the police. The Guild, as we saw in the previous chapter, had long documented police abuses and called for policing reform. In the 1950s, Guild lawyers' economic interests and political principles with regard to policing reform increasingly coincided as, inevitably, a portion of the new tort cases involved claims against the police. "The Guild attracted liberal and progressive lawyers," observed Doris Brin Walker, a Guild member since the 1940s, "and those sorts of lawyers were among the few willing to take cases against the police in those years."[17]

McCarthyism also ironically contributed to documentation of those cases. In 1954 Harvard University demanded that Ray Ginger, a young assistant professor, and his wife, Ann Fagan Ginger (who was not affiliated with the university), sign oaths stating that they were not members of the Communist Party. The Gingers refused to comply, Ray Ginger resigned, and the couple moved to New York City, where Ann Fagan Ginger gained work as an assistant in the National Lawyers Guild's main office. There, in 1955, she created the Civil Liberties Docket, which became for a time the leading national case reporter on civil liberties and civil rights. The Docket "had a wide circulation among lawyers handling civil liberties cases," observed Victor Rabinowitz. "It put us in contact with hundreds of lawyers, many in the South."[18] As police misconduct litigation developed, Ginger became a point of contact among police misconduct attorneys scattered around the country.[19]

McCarthyism pushed the NAACP, too, toward litigation against the police, but for different reasons. By the 1930s, NAACP attorneys recognized that police brutality cases would take up much of their time, and they developed a three-pronged strategy: press for discipline or dismissal of problem officers; sue for civil damages; and, in extreme cases, demand criminal charges. Among these tactics, the most commonly used was tort litigation.[20] By the late 1940s, with frustration growing over the limits of the tort litigation strategy,[21] the NAACP had turned toward supporting street-level demonstrations and organizing against police misconduct.[22] But in the early 1950s, as McCarthyism grew and as the NAACP famously attempted to cut its ties to the American left, the organization shifted its tactics away from street organizing (which was, its leaders thought, too closely associated with the Communist Party) and primarily toward civil lawsuits against the police under state tort laws.[23] The New York chapter, in particular, "filed a steady stream of civil suits" against the police, winning a number with significant damage judgments.[24]

Still, as the legal scholar Caleb Foote argued in a prominent article in the mid-1950s, ordinary tort lawsuits had two key limitations that fatally handicapped them as a meaningful inducement for reform: juries remained wholly unsympathetic to complaints by African American plaintiffs, and police officers were judgment proof.[25] Lawsuits against the police therefore were not financially viable, and police departments felt no incentive to carry out reforms. He also disparaged criminal prosecution of police officers and policing's system of internal accountability, mocking each as wholly ineffective in controlling abuses.

Foote expressed hope, however, for an emerging remedy that later became known as "constitutional torts."[26] This remedy dated to the Civil Rights Act of 1871 (specifically its Section 1983) and allowed monetary damages in federal court for official violations of federal rights. Although moribund for decades, the remedy was being revived in the 1950s, mainly in litigation against the police. Foote suggested that, by allowing lawsuits in federal court and authorizing monetary damages, this remedy might succeed where common-law torts lawsuits had failed in placing the police under real pressure for reform—but only if police *departments* were made subject to liability. By the late 1950s, however, even this newly revived federal civil remedy seemed a failure. In the two-year period from 1957 through 1959, plaintiffs filed forty-two civil suits against the police in federal court and lost every one.[27] Federal courts had come to interpret Section 1983 very restrictively, requiring proof of specific intent to violate constitutional rights (the same strict requirement imposed by *Screws* in criminal prosecutions);[28] narrowly interpreting "color of law" to mean acting within the purview of an official's statutory authority (thus when officials acted outside their lawful authority they could not be sued under the federal statute);[29] or narrowly construing the nature of the federal rights protected by Section 1983.[30] Just as tort law's egalitarian potential seemed on the march in so many areas of the common law, by 1960 the federal courts had cut short its early prospects as a remedy for violations of civil rights.

Police misconduct litigators in the late 1950s repeatedly petitioned the Supreme Court to resolve the impasse and open the doors to federal civil lawsuits against the police. In late 1960 the Court finally agreed to hear the issue, taking up *Monroe v. Pape*, a case brought by Donald Page Moore, a member of a group of active police misconduct attorneys in Chicago. The case involved a claim by plaintiffs James and Flossie Monroe against a number of Chicago police officers who, seeking evidence against Mr. Monroe in a murder case, allegedly had ransacked their home in the middle of the night, pulled the Monroe family out of bed, and interrogated Mr. Monroe for hours at a police station, all without a warrant and without bringing any formal charges. The complaint, relying on the Chicago ACLU's report *Secret Detention by the Chicago Police*, further alleged that the police in that city had a custom, indeed a de facto policy, of arresting suspects and holding them for up to several days while carrying on interrogations to induce them to make incriminating statements or simply to punish them. As the brief for the plaintiffs alleged, "The most frightening thing about what happened to the Monroe family is not that they were terrorized by bad men who bore ill will against them. The sobering truth of the matter is precisely that what was done to the Monroes was done almost casually—as part of a routine investigation. This case portrays a standard police procedure—whose victims are often innocent."[31]

The plaintiffs' brief written by Morris Ernst, the leading ACLU attorney, asked the Supreme Court to authorize lawsuits for monetary damages in federal court against both the individual officers and the police department. The Monroes, their attorney Donald Moore observed, had no hope of gaining a fair hearing in a city or state court. "I suspect that any realistic trial lawyer with experience in this kind of litigation anywhere in the country," Moore observed in a newspaper interview, "would tend to agree with me that when a penniless Negro family attempts to sue a politically potent high ranking police officer who is white, he is more likely to obtain a fair and impartial trial of his case from a federal judge."[32] Moreover, as an inducement to real reform of these "routine" practices, the brief argued, damages against the department were necessary.

The Supreme Court, in a landmark decision written by Justice William O. Douglas, authorized civil suits against state and local officials but not against police departments or city governments.[33] The new federal remedy, the Court declared, "should be read against the background of tort liability that makes a man responsible for the natural consequences of his actions," thereby making state and local officials financially liable for violations of constitutional rights.[34] But the Court declined to endorse departmental liability, observing (contrary to historical evidence) that Congress in 1868 had rejected municipal liability for the actions of employees.[35] *Monroe*, in sum, was a double-edged landmark. By declining to extend liability to police departments, the Court had given the plaintiffs only part of their request. To observers in 1961, however, it was not what the Court withheld but what it granted that mattered. In the decision, "the Court swept away an accumulation of lower court decisions that over the years had almost entirely emasculated that [civil rights] law."[36] The result was, in the words of the editors of the ATLA's journal, "the emancipation proclamation for the full and effective utilization of the Civil Rights Acts."[37]

Still, there were few attorneys willing to sue the police over misconduct and little shared knowledge about how to do it. The National Lawyers Guild had been decimated by McCarthy-era attacks, and its few remaining members remained preoccupied with Cold War ideological battles. The Mississippi Freedom Summer project in 1964 jump-started police misconduct litigation, as it did for sixties activism in general, bringing the Guild out of its political exile, introducing aggressive lawyering into the movement's tactics, and generating a broader support structure for litigation against the police.[38] The Student Nonviolent Coordinating Committee (SNCC), the organizer of Freedom Summer, turned for legal defense to National Lawyers Guild attorneys and more mainstream civil rights lawyers.[39] The experience proved transformative for Guild attorneys, generating a renewed commitment to the rising cause of civil rights and, in light of widespread police abuse, a commitment to police accountability.[40] Freedom Summer also radicalized many of the more mainstream lawyers who had volunteered for the cause, contributing particularly to their growing disillusion with the police.[41] Attorneys returning north after Freedom Summer were newly attuned to the problem of police abuse and committed to doing something about it.

In this context, the longtime Guild organizer Ann Fagan Ginger and a colleague published the first legal guide to police misconduct litigation, with an emphasis on the remedies available to plaintiffs under Section 1983.[42] The authors provided model interrogatories and mapped a number of practical strategies for building successful police misconduct cases. Equally significant, they summarized more than fifty successful Section 1983 claims against police officers, aiming to demonstrate to plaintiffs' attorneys that lawsuits against the police *could* be won. Although in retrospect the guide is brief and rudimentary, it represented a substantial advance in existing knowledge about police misconduct litigation. With that guide, observed Wayne Schmidt, legal director of Americans for Effective Law Enforcement (AELE), an organization formed to coordinate legal defense of the police, "Ann Fagan Ginger practically invented the field of police misconduct litigation."[43] He continued:

> That manual made a huge difference as an impetus to litigation against the police. Frankly, your ordinary lawyer doesn't want to reinvent the wheel in an area of law. If he doesn't know how to bring a lawsuit in an area, he won't put in the work to learn. But if he has a manual that provides a step-by-step guide to all of the parts of the process in an area of the law, then he's much more likely to bring cases in that area. And that is exactly what that National Lawyers Guild manual did: it provided a step-by-step guide that was extremely careful and well done, and suddenly individual attorneys all over the country could simply pick it up and begin suing the police without having much background at all in that area of law.

Police misconduct lawyering soon expanded beyond the networks around Ginger and the older National Lawyers Guild cohort. At the 1971 Guild convention in Boulder, Colorado, David Rudovsky, a young Philadelphia attorney, organized the first national seminar on police misconduct litigation. As Bill Goodman, a pioneering police misconduct attorney in Detroit recalled, that seminar "brought together people from all over the country to share notes."[44] Rudovsky had been suing the Philadelphia police, at the time among the most notorious in the country. "We started to bring selected cases against Frank Rizzo's police department," he recalled, "and began to share our ideas and pleadings with other lawyers across the country, and I think that sort of thing was happening in other cities too."[45] Many of these widely scattered lawyers were associated with the Guild and came together to share information and ideas at the annual conventions. "When I started," Rudovsky observed, "most of the support and reference group and ideas were circulated among National Lawyers Guild members. At national Guild conventions we would share ideas, share pleadings, and so forth."[46]

While Rudovsky in Philadelphia was a center of these growing networks, another was Michael Avery, a young attorney in New Haven, Connecticut. At Yale in the early 1970s, the eminent constitutional law scholar Thomas Emerson (long associated with the Guild) taught a seminar called the Political Justice Workshop, and, Avery recalls, one of the participants wrote a paper arguing that the police would be brought to accountability only by concerted litigation campaigns targeting individual departments but aimed at getting the attention of the profession as a whole.[47] But it would have to be big: to get the police profession's attention, lawyers would need to flood a particular department with cases. "And so," Avery recalls, "that's what my partner, John Williams, and I decided to do." They filed a lawsuit against the New Haven police department in every meritorious case that came through their office door. At the height of the campaign, Avery and Williams sometimes had as many as forty-five cases pending against the New Haven department. "We were sort of experimenting with this idea of a litigation barrage. And, you know, it went pretty well. We achieved some reforms, and it certainly put the police on notice that we were out there and were looking for cases and weren't afraid to file as many cases as they generated."[48]

Avery and Rudovsky met in the early 1970s and began conducting joint seminars for lawyers on how to sue the police. After the pivotal 1971 conference in Boulder, the two conducted seminars at nearly every National Lawyers Guild conference, bringing together attorneys from around the country to share ideas on litigating against the police. In addition to the Guild conferences, they began leading sessions on police misconduct litigation at a number of continuing legal education seminars.[49]

In 1978 Avery and Rudovsky published a comprehensive guide to litigation against the police titled *Police Misconduct Litigation Manual*.[50] It was based on several years of work and the contributions of some twenty-five other attorneys around the country, and the manual represented a substantial advance in legal strategies beyond those mapped in Ann Fagan Ginger's 1968 guide.[51] Since 1978, a handful of other texts on police civil liability have been published.[52]

After the mid-1970s, the support structure for police misconduct litigation grew beyond the National Lawyers Guild networks. Although the American Civil Liberties Union never created a police reform project comparable in scope to its Prison Reform Project, the organization supported a test-case strategy in the mid-1970s against the fleeing felon rule.[53] The NAACP Legal Defense Fund, too, supported cases challenging the fleeing felon rule. Additionally, prominent individual attorneys in many major cities developed reputations for suing the police. For instance, Johnnie Cochran gained his reputation with lawsuits against the Los Angeles police department. The networks of police misconduct litigators also began to expand beyond such prominent attorneys and public interest groups as lawsuits against the police began to pay off financially. As Sean Farhang has shown, the Civil Rights Attorneys Fees Awards Act of 1976, which authorizes judges to award attorneys' fees to plaintiffs who prevailed on the merits of their claims, contributed significantly to plaintiffs' attorneys' monetary incentive.[54] With the Fees Act, even if the award in a case of police abuse reached only a few thousand dollars, the attorney's time in developing the case—often amounting to tens of thousands of dollars—might be compensated. Every police misconduct attorney interviewed for this study reported that fees are commonly awarded in police misconduct cases where the plaintiff prevails, and that the 1976 act marked a watershed in the development of support for such cases. As Michael Avery observed, after passage of the 1976 act, ordinary tort lawyers increasingly joined principled civil rights and liberties lawyers in bringing police misconduct cases.[55]

By the late 1970s, litigation against the police began to consolidate into two prominent "case congregations," in Marc Galanter's[56] term, one seeking to strike down the fleeing felon rule as unconstitutional (or merely contrary to law) and the other seeking to establish departmental liability for the actions of officers. In 1977, in a case supported by the ACLU, the California Court of Appeals ruled that the use of deadly force was excessive as a matter of California law unless there was reason to believe that the person shot at posed a threat of "death or serious bodily harm" to the officer or to another.[57] Other litigation pursued the matter in federal court. In *Mattis v. Schnarr* (1976), a case supported by the ACLU involving the shooting of an eighteen-year-old fleeing the site of a burglary, the Eighth

Circuit Court of Appeals struck down Missouri's fleeing felon rule.[58] By contrast, in *Wiley v. Memphis Police Department*, the Sixth Circuit Court of appeals upheld a rule allowing the shooting of unarmed fleeing felons.[59] The U.S. Supreme Court overturned the *Mattis* decision on narrow procedural grounds, holding, essentially, that the victim's parents had no standing to sue with regard to the statute's constitutionality.[60] Shortly thereafter, in another case of a shooting of a young unarmed burglar (this time in Omaha, Nebraska), the Eighth Circuit reaffirmed its ruling that statutes authorizing shots at unarmed fleeing felons are unconstitutional.[61] Whether the fleeing felon rule would stand or fall nationwide increasingly depended on the Supreme Court, and I examine its decision in the final section of this chapter.

In addition to attacking the fleeing felon rule, police misconduct litigators sought to establish departmental liability for injuries. In light of the *Monroe* ruling against municipal liability, plaintiffs' attorneys sought judicial injunctions requiring reform, a tool widely used in suits to desegregate schools and reform mental institutions and prisons.[62] After extensive lower court litigation, the Supreme Court in 1974 upheld an injunction against several Texas law enforcement agencies requiring them to cease harassing and brutalizing union organizers, inspiring hope that injunctions might be a useful tool for achieving police reform.[63] But the Court quickly dashed these hopes in a second case, *Rizzo v. Goode* (1976), which authorized injunctive reform of police departments only based on extensive evidence of widespread, deliberate departmental support for abuses by frontline officers. The decision effectively ended the use of the judicial injunction in policing cases.[64]

With the collapse of injunctive relief, police misconduct attorneys actively sought to extend constitutional tort liability to departments. Tort lawsuits alleging departmental negligence in failing to take appropriate steps to regulate officers' behavior, as Wayne Schmidt of the AELE observed in 1976, were "increasingly successful" in state courts.[65]

But success in federal court was the ultimate goal, and *Monroe v. Pape* seemed to block it. "Getting to the department, of course, was the big strategy," as David Rudovsky observed. "We tried a number of different legal theories . . . to get to municipalities as opposed to the individual officer."[66] The *Bivens* strategy seemed to offer the greatest hope. In *Bivens*, the Supreme Court in 1971 had created constitutional tort liability for federal officials based on the Constitution itself, because no statute authorized this liability.[67] Litigators seeking to expand municipal liability for constitutional torts saw in *Bivens* a hopeful precedent and sought to use it as a foundation for municipal liability—because doing so would bypass the convoluted interpretation of Section 1983 dating to *Monroe* that had limited municipal liability for the actions of officers.

In 1978 Avery was advancing such an argument in *Turpin v. Mailet*, and on June 5, 1978, the Second Circuit Court of Appeals, sitting en banc, agreed, creating a significant precedent in favor of municipal liability.[68] But to have broader impact, Avery and Rudovsky and their network would have to extend the *Turpin* precedent to other federal appellate circuits and ultimately the Supreme Court, an arduous, time-consuming, and highly uncertain process.

"But then," Rudovsky observed, on the very next day, June 6, 1978, "*Monell* sort of fortuitously opened the door."[69] The Supreme Court's decision in *Monell v. New York Department of Social Services* (1978) exposed cities to liability for violations of civil rights by their employees in at least some circumstances. *Monell* was an "accidental landmark" that initially had nothing to do with policing; the case grew out of a dispute over mandatory pregnancy-leave policies in the New York City Department of Social Services.[70] It was brought by Jane Monell, a social worker, represented by her husband, Oscar Chase, a law professor at New York University, and Nancy Stearns, a litigator at the Center for Constitutional Rights. After the New York Department of Social Services, under litigation pressure, had dropped its mandatory pregnancy-leave policy, Monell filed suit for back pay, on behalf of herself and other women who had been affected by the policy. But under the *Monroe* doctrine, the *city* could not be held liable to pay financial compensation—even though it could be found liable for other kinds of relief (e.g., dropping an unconstitutional policy). Chase and Stearns exploited this "crack . . . in the foundation of . . . *Monroe*" to ask the Supreme Court to allow awarding back pay.[71] With the assistance of an experienced school desegregation litigator from the NAACP Legal Defense Fund (which was interested in the case as a possible mechanism for defeating *Monroe*'s exclusion of municipal financial liability), and with help in the form of a careful supporting amicus brief (on the crucial issue of the legislative history of the relevant civil rights act) from the National Education Association and the Lawyers' Committee for Civil Rights under Law, the plaintiffs gained a seven-to-two decision from the Court extending financial liability to municipalities.[72]

Monell was an especially opaque decision—but it fundamentally changed the game. The Court specifically rejected "respondeat superior" liability, or making cities automatically liable for injuries caused by their employees; instead, cities would be liable only where it could be shown that a municipal "policy or custom" had caused a violation of federal rights. Thus, simply because it could be shown that a police officer had used excessive force against a person did not necessarily mean that the officer had been acting pursuant to a municipal policy or custom. Proving that misconduct resulted from "policy or custom" turned out to be rather difficult. Still, the decision authorized plaintiffs' attorneys to try to show that the actions of individual officers reflected broader organizational policies or cultures, and this changed the rules of the game. Which police policies contribute directly to patterns of discrimination or abuse? At what point does a pattern of police abuse become so commonplace that it must be viewed as condoned by the department even if not authorized by formal policy? What preventive steps must departments take to demonstrate that any subsequent abuse resulted from individual officers' aberrant actions as opposed to an implicitly accepted departmental custom? Plaintiffs' lawyers had been aching to get evidence on these sorts of questions into court, but *Monroe* had stifled them. Now they could. Roger Wilkins reported in the *New York Times* that "civil rights and civil liberties lawyers were jubilant."[73]

David Rudovsky and Michael Avery immediately recognized the decision's potential for establishing the liability of police departments for abuses by their officers. In the months after *Monell* came down, Avery and Rudovsky traveled around the country giving seminars on how *Monell* could be used to establish departmental liability. "We did an awful lot of seminars around the country for a lot of different audiences," Michael Avery observed. "We tried to popularize how you could use that decision."[74] They had "a traveling road show," observed Candace McCoy, at the time a young Guild-affiliated attorney. "They were on it, man."[75]

The growing support structure for police misconduct litigation generated a rising number of police misconduct cases in the 1970s, a point that may be illustrated in several ways. The AELE surveyed police departments in the early 1970s, and the results, covering 1967 to 1971, "confirmed what had only been a suspicion until then—the number of civil suits alleging police misconduct . . . was taking a dramatic upsurge."[76] The report observed that the total number of suits in 1971 had increased by 446 percent over the number in 1967 and concluded that "the threat of civil liability hangs over the head of every police officer," constituting "a demoralizing and disruptive influence."[77] In the survey, seven departments reported what the AELE called "catastrophic" awards above $100,000 in 1967–71; the

AELE reported at least eleven more of these large damage judgments in 1972 and 1973, including two above $1 million, suggesting an upward trend.[78] The organization began publishing a regular report on liability decisions against the police in 1973 and, a year later, began providing regular seminars on police liability, aiming to educate police managers in how to defend against liability lawsuits.[79] The group reported that by 1976 some 13,000 lawsuits a year were filed against the police, and by 1985 the number had risen to more than 20,000.[80]

Police Misconduct Litigation and Media Coverage

Police misconduct attorneys learned early that high-profile lawsuits against police departments, even if legally unsuccessful, could draw and frame media coverage and galvanize public opinion in favor of police reform. Johnnie Cochran's first major case, for instance, was a lawsuit over a police shooting that, although unsuccessful, generated immense publicity. The case, as Cochran later observed, "confirmed for me ... that this issue of police abuse really galvanized the minority community. It taught me that these cases could really get attention."[81]

That dynamic eventually shifted public opinion—even *white* opinion—in favor of systemic police reform. In this section I trace the path of media coverage of police abuse over the course of the 1970s and early 1980s. Although the police ended the turbulent 1960s with wide support from the white public, by the mid-1970s, in the context of growing litigation against the police, this support began to erode. The news media increasingly covered high-profile lawsuits dramatizing police shootings and other abuses, and as a consequence the public climate began to change in favor of heightened police accountability. Sometime in the mid-1970s, media coverage and public sympathy reached a "tipping point" after which the police were increasingly on the defensive. Although my evidence in favor of these claims is necessarily somewhat impressionistic, it is drawn from a variety of sources and comprises several indicators of growing concern about police accountability.

One factor in the erosion of support was growing publicity in the early 1970s about heavy-handed police tactics against radicals. Although vast majorities of the public initially sided with the police in their confrontations with radicals, the long-term dynamic was less favorable to them. For instance, as we saw in the last chapter, although the Chicago police enjoyed wide public support for their actions in suppressing radical demonstrations at the 1968 Democratic National Convention in Chicago, the incident undoubtedly made policy elites and reporters more skeptical of the police. An official investigation, appointed by the National Commission on the Causes and Prevention of Violence, issued a report condemning the police response to the demonstrators and characterizing the situation as an uncontrolled "police riot."[82] The incident likewise contributed to growing media skepticism about the police, since it was clear that many officers had singled out reporters and beaten them.[83] Although national television networks were flooded with letters condemning their criticism of the police actions and a nationwide survey showed that only 25 percent of respondents believed the police had used too much force, the survey also revealed a sharp polarization along lines that portended eventual trouble for the police.[84] On one side were whites with little education and supporters of right-wing candidate George Wallace, of whom only 6 percent thought the police had used too much force; on the other side were African Americans, people with graduate degrees, and people under age thirty with college degrees, of whom solid majorities believed the police had used too much force.[85] Skepticism about the police was, of course, highest among young radicals, who, as Todd Gitlin observed, "thought Chicago was Mississippi—or the early days of Nazi Germany."[86] Like Gitlin himself, these groups—young, liberal or radical, and well educated—moved into positions of influence in the 1970s.

After the 1968 Democratic Convention riot, the media covered a growing number of cases of police harassment or shootings of radicals in cities throughout the country.[87] In my interviews for this book, attorneys for both the police and plaintiffs observed that these cases increasingly led the public, and especially juries, to distrust the police in cases of alleged abuse.[88] Several attorneys, for instance, mentioned the police shooting of Chicago Black Panther leader Fred Hampton as a critical episode. Hampton was killed in December 1969 by Cook County deputies and FBI agents in a predawn raid on the headquarters of the Chicago Black Panthers. Although the initial police investigation exonerated officers of any wrongdoing, subsequent independent investigations portrayed the Chicago police as corrupt and abusive and the official investigation as a cover-up.[89] For one thing, these later investigations reported that in the neighborhood where the Hampton shooting had occurred, the police had killed eleven young black men in the months before Hampton's killing; that African American members of the police department had formed an organization to press for reform of police treatment of blacks; that virtually all significant black organizations in Chicago, including one calling itself the Committee to End the Murder of Black People, favored sweeping police reforms; and that many residents characterized conditions in black neighborhoods as "life under a military regime."[90] Additionally, later investigations revealed that the Hampton shooting arose out of a massive spying and disruption campaign mounted by the FBI and local police departments against radical black groups.[91] In 1982 the federal government, Cook County, and the City of Chicago settled a civil suit over the shooting for $1.85 million.[92]

The *Washington Post*, in a lead editorial accompanying its publication of excerpts of a 1970 grand jury report in the case, called it "a stunning document," observing that the grand jury had declared the police actions "unprofessional," the coroner's autopsy "incompetent," and the internal police investigation into the shootings "a whitewash."[93] The grand jury had concluded that Fred Hampton had been shot while in bed, that only one shot could be attributed to a Panther weapon while some one hundred came from police weapons, and that the official internal investigation was "so seriously deficient that it suggests purposeful malfeasance."[94]

The editorial observed that the grand jury report "demonstrates, in the most vivid terms, why some Negroes in this country regard the police as their natural enemy and demand that the entire system of American government be changed. . . . One cannot read the entire report . . . without being appalled at the conduct of law enforcement agencies in Chicago."

Media coverage of police abuses expanded well beyond cases involving radicals. By the mid-1970s, civil liberties groups and plaintiffs' lawyers had filed lawsuits alleging police harassment or brutality in localities around the country, sometimes winning large damage awards.[95] For instance, a New York jury in 1978 awarded $3.3 million to the widow and children of a man beaten to death by police officers.[96] As police misconduct litigation became more widespread and prominent, the tone of media coverage began shifting against the police. Newspapers widely covered stories arising out of litigation and protests over violent rampages by drunken policemen,[97] brutal beatings of African Americans,[98] and police killings.[99] The Los Angeles police department, for instance, in the context of prominent shooting scandals like that of Eula Love, an African American mother shot to death by officers in 1979, found its image of "efficiency" replaced, in the words of a journalist, by one of "alleged 'spying' on citizens, brutality and other abuses."[100] The New York City police department too faced a growing outcry over police shootings and unflattering media coverage.[101] Indianapolis was torn by controversy in 1980 over five police shootings, in particular that of a young unarmed African American fleeing the scene of a burglary.[102] New Orleans, under pressure from lawsuits over allegations of racial abuse and brutality, in 1981 fired an officer named in five lawsuits.[103] Bessemer, Alabama, faced a highly publicized lawsuit in 1981 alleging that its police used electric cattle prods—originally employed against civil rights protesters in the 1960s—to extract confessions.[104] In Boston the police department faced a growing controversy over a court judgment arising out of the 1975 police killing of an African American man.[105]

As media coverage grew, prominent stories began echoing the claim of activists that police abuses were widespread, were institutionalized, and required institutional reforms. The Chicago police in 1975, for instance, faced federal lawsuits filed by some sixty individuals and organizations after a grand jury report declared that police surveillance of political activities in that city had "all the earmarks of a police state."[106] A *New York Times* reporter similarly observed, "Unkempt officers, some fresh from stops at local bars, ransacking homes, breaking furniture and shouting obscenities while holding terrified families at gunpoint. Germany in the 1930's? No, the United States in the 1970s."[107] In a prominent Miami case, the victims' lawyer declared that "these policemen conducted themselves like the Gestapo," and the chairperson of the local Community Relations Board observed that the case was part of a broad pattern "that is causing our communities to be at a flash point, ready to blow."[108]

By the mid-1970s the Vietnam War, evidence of corporate malfeasance, the growing fiscal crisis in the cities, and, especially, the Watergate scandal contributed to a massive erosion of public confidence in government and other institutions, and this extended to the police. Trust in government, declining since 1964, plummeted by seventeen percentage points from 1972 to 1974, going well below the 50 percent mark for the first time.[109] Police legitimacy in the eyes of federal juries also collapsed. "I call that the Watergate effect," observed Michael Avery.[110] Similarly, Wayne Schmidt, director of the pro-police Americans for Effective Law Enforcement, observed that "the Chicago killing and cover-up of Fred Hampton destroyed police legitimacy in the eyes of white juries. Suddenly downstate jurors started wondering whether they could trust the police."[111]

The issue of police abuses eventually reached the highest levels of public debate. In 1978 Attorney General Griffin Bell, under pressure from Hispanic members of Congress, ordered the Justice Department to investigate police brutality against Hispanics.[112] Shortly thereafter President Jimmy Carter in a news conference addressed what he called a "particularly disturbing case" in Texas involving the police shooting of a twelve-year-old Mexican American boy while he was handcuffed in the back of a police car.[113] In 1979, in a pathbreaking action that made front-page news around the country, the Justice Department filed a major civil rights law-suit against the Philadelphia police department alleging a pattern of systematic brutality.[114] Although a federal court eventually dismissed the suit on the grounds that the Justice Department had no statutory authority to sue a department itself, the agency's action generated a raft of unflattering media coverage of Philadelphia police policies. As the *New York Times* reported, in spite of widespread reports of abuses, among them "people being pulled from cars and beaten unconscious; of unarmed teen-agers being fatally shot in the back as they fled from police officers; of a man being shot to death while handcuffed; of policemen being found guilty of criminal assault, then being cleared by the department and permitted to remain on active duty," nonetheless "there has seldom been any response from the department, whose practices and policies are often kept secret."[115] Even in Philadelphia, where the mayor, Frank Rizzo, had long been able to count on support from white ethnic voters, "public opinion slowly shifted" against the mayor over media coverage of "incident after incident of police brutality."[116] Although a federal court threw out the Justice Department's lawsuit, the mayor elected in 1980 instituted most of the police reforms demanded by the Department.[117] In early 1980, after an eighteen-month investigation into allegations of police brutality against the African American residents of Memphis, the Justice Department obtained an agreement from the Memphis police department restricting officers' authority to shoot and requiring the department to improve its training in alternatives to the use of force.[118]

By 1983 journalists were reporting that police departments were increasingly concerned about liability, were under increasing pressure to tighten their policies and oversight of officers' behavior, and were taking steps to do so.[119] Juries and judges were regularly handing down massive damage awards in cases of police shootings. Troy, Michigan, faced a $5.7 million judgment over the killing of a young man mistaken for a burglar; Richmond, California, was hit with a $3 million judgment; Saugus, Massachusetts, with a $1.6 million judgment, and Concordia Parish, Louisiana, with a $1 million judgment.[120] "Juries," observed the finance director of Troy, Michigan, "seem to be bidding against one another to raise these awards."[121] In the face of increasingly distrustful juries, cities began settling cases for large sums. Savannah, Georgia, settled a case for $700,000; South Tucson, Arizona, settled one for $3 million; and New Orleans, Louisiana, settled thirteen claims arising out of a series of connected incidents for $2.8 million.[122] In response to growing demand, the Justice Department's Community Relations Service (CRS) began offering seminars for cities on how to regulate and limit their police officers' use of force, and in the mid-1980s the number of cities signing up for these seminars grew dramatically.[123] In a major article in 1985 summarizing growing controversy over police use of force, the *New York Times* observed that "many of the nation's cities, large and not so large, are having serious problems involving complaints of police use of excessive force, an emotional issue that appears to be taking a mounting toll on municipal finances and civic harmony."[124] The article documented growing awareness of the problem in the "White Community," largely as a result of growing numbers of police brutality cases. "Frequently," the article observed, "cities wind up defending against multimillion-dollar lawsuits."[125] A notorious case in New Orleans, in the view of a civil rights lawyer interviewed for the article, "had a profound effect on the way people think about the Police Department."[126]

Police Reformers and Their Campaign to Legalize Accountability

As police misconduct lawyers brought increasing liability pressure to bear on police departments, a network of dissident reformers within policing began pressing the wider profession to adopt systems of legalized accountability. Two leaders stand out: Patrick V. Murphy and James J. Fyfe, both products of the New York City police department. Murphy, the son of a New York City police officer, joined that department and moved up through the ranks to become deputy chief, then moved on to head the police departments in Syracuse, New York, Washington, DC, and Detroit. He headed the Justice Department's Law Enforcement Assistance Administration from 1968 to 1969 and then the New York City police department from 1970 to 1973. Throughout this illustrious career in policing, Murphy earned a reputation as a fierce advocate of reform, particularly with regard to police corruption and race relations. Fyfe, too, began his career as a frontline New York City police officer, rising to become a lieutenant in 1979 when, after earning a PhD in criminal justice, he left the force to become a university professor.[127] In 1972, while serving as one of Murphy's principal deputies, Fyfe revamped the department's policy, training, and oversight regarding use of deadly force, and later, in his PhD dissertation, he examined the effectiveness of the new policy.[128] Building on earlier efforts at legalizing police accountability that I surveyed in the previous chapter, Murphy and Fyfe pursued a broad-ranging agenda for legalized control of police use of force. I focus here on their campaign to regulate police shootings, since it became the opening wedge that led to all later efforts at legalizing police accountability.

In 1973 Murphy became director of the new Police Foundation, a Ford Foundation–funded think tank focused on police practices and reform.[129] Murphy's philosophy at the Police Foundation is summed up in his autobiography: "The underlying thought for everything it does rests not on the proposition that American policing, with minor modifications, is in good shape *but precisely the opposite*."[130] Under Murphy's leadership, the Police Foundation in the late 1970s supported a wide-ranging research program on police use of deadly force, much of it focused specifically on the reform of police administrative policies governing shootings. Murphy also coordinated a broader effort among other police professional associations—notably the Police Executive Research Forum (PERF) and the National Organization of Black Law Enforcement Executives (NOBLE)—to reform policing via legalized accountability. As this coordinated professional campaign gained strength in the late 1970s and early 1980s, professional police networks increasingly divided between the Police Foundation, PERF, and NOBLE—the voices of legalized reform—and the IACP, the voice of traditional policing.[131] By the early 1980s, even the professional staff of the IACP had joined the reform movement.

The Foundation's first major project on the use of force, a study of departmental policies on police shootings (published in 1977 and introduced briefly in the previous chapter), formed the basis for this campaign.[132] That study, as we saw, observed that although some police departments were adopting written rules governing the use of deadly force, most of these policies were extremely disorganized, poorly written, hard to find, and far less restrictive than they first appeared. In particular, every police department examined in the Police Foundation study authorized the shooting of unarmed fleeing felons in some circumstances.

In the context of that bleak assessment, the study issued a ringing call for adoption of restrictive shooting policies, arguing that such reforms were necessary in response to rising pressure from legal liability.[133] In making this argument, it pioneered a legal liability rationale for police reform that would soon become the centerpiece of the reform movement. The American Law Institute's Model Penal Code, the report observed, had long called for legal restrictions on police authority to shoot, and some states were beginning to impose such restrictions.[134] More specifically, the report declared, "The number of civil suits filed against police departments and individual officers rises each year," with the likelihood of "more decisions refining and extending tort liability for the unjustified use of deadly force."[135] "Police departments," the report declared, "should carefully note this trend," because "a collective judgment is emerging through the resolution of lawsuits that accuse the police of using too much or the wrong kind of force."[136] Citizens are more aware of their rights and more willing to sue, and "judges and juries . . . seem to be placing greater emphasis on the individual's right to life and physical integrity."[137] The effect of these developments, the report observed, "is to place a greater degree of responsibility on departments, as well as officers, in their use of deadly weapons."[138]

Moreover, the Police Foundation report observed, courts increasingly were demanding that police departments adopt internal rules to guide their officers' discretionary decisions. Although police chiefs commonly feared that adopting internal rules governing the use of force would increase the likelihood of civil liability for officers' actions, the report observed, it was wiser to adopt such rules, because doing so would diminish the number of shootings and, furthermore, courts were beginning to find departments negligent for failing to provide any meaningful rule-based direction for their officers.[139] But written rules, the report observed, are not enough: "Some policies are so routine that officers follow them unthinkingly; others are so obscure that few know of their existence. Some policies are widely interpreted to mean something very different from what they say; others are generally ignored except when some particularly egregious violations prompts a temporary crackdown. *Enforcement is the ultimate test.*"[140]

The Police Foundation report therefore recommended, in addition to rules governing the use of deadly force, careful training and internal oversight with regard to those rules.[141] Training in rules limiting deadly force, it declared, should be conducted in realistic, hands-on scenarios, and in light of real incidents in the past; this training should be incorporated into many phases of each department's overall training program; and each officer should be required to undergo annual recertification of competence in the rules and training limiting shootings. Officers' understanding of their department's shooting policies and their record of conformity to these policies, the report recommended, should be incorporated into every phase of the evaluation, discipline, and promotion process. Further, there should be careful, rule-governing internal investigations of shootings and meaningful discipline and retraining where policies are violated. Finally, the Police Foundation report declared, departments should implement systems of data gathering and analysis that allow command-level officers to identify and monitor "violence-prone" officers.[142]

All in all, the 1977 Police Foundation report provided a road map for the development and rhetorical defense of the legalized accountability model in policing. It provided a model of rules governing deadly force, training based on those rules, and internal oversight aimed at enforcing them. And, crucially, the report pioneered the idea that legal liability is a powerful inducement for departments to adopt these elements of legalized accountability.

A nagging question in the policing field, however, was whether restrictive shooting policies would "work" to reduce shootings—and whether they would increase the risk of death for officers who, when faced with a choice of whether or not to shoot, might hesitate or decline to shoot until too late. Fyfe examined the effect of the shooting rules adopted in 1972 by the New York City police department under Murphy's leadership and, in results that were widely reported, found that New York's rules and oversight contributed to a significant, substantial decline in the number of police shootings, and that the decline was greatest "among the most controversial shooting incidents," particularly those involving unarmed fleeing felons.[143] Equally important, Fyfe found that the restrictive shooting rule did not lead to more injuries to officers but instead contributed to a *decline* in officer injuries and death. In 1980 Albert J. Reiss Jr., citing an internal Los Angeles police department analysis, confirmed that that department's restrictive shooting rule, adopted in 1977, appeared to have a similar effect in reducing shootings in that city.[144]

In 1979, in the *FBI Law Enforcement Bulletin*, a publication widely read in police departments around the country, Fyfe summarized the results of his research and presented practical administrative suggestions for controlling shootings.[145] He reported "compelling evidence that civilian injuries and deaths can be reduced" if police departments impose clear restrictions on officers' authority to shoot, and that these restrictions did not increase injuries to officers. He then went on to suggest the following components of an effective administrative program aimed at restricting shootings: providing a clear statement of policy restricting authority to shoot; enforcing this policy through high-level review of every shot fired; tailoring training to the department's policy; and evaluating supervising officers with regard to how carefully they oversee subordinate officers' uses of force.[146] Fyfe's suggestions provided the foundation for nearly everything that followed in the development of the legalized accountability model.

In the late 1970s and early 1980s, Fyfe and Murphy carried out a remarkable blitz of professional consultation and media interviews supporting their campaign to get departments to regulate police shootings. Fyfe alone provided professional consultation on deadly force policies to several hundred police agencies at the federal, state, and local levels and was interviewed for the *New York Times, Washington Post, U.S. News and World Report, Newsweek, Chicago Tribune, Wall Street Journal, Los Angeles Times, TV Guide,* NBC's *Nightline,* NBC's *First Camera,* NPR's *All Things Considered* and *Morning Edition,* and the evening news programs of ABC, NBC, and CBS.[147] Murphy focused on high-profile appearances that gained national attention. In congressional testimony in 1980 in the wake of the Miami riot, for instance, he warned against forgetting the lessons of the 1960s riots and declared that "it is time to get tough with police departments which—inadvertently or deliberately—have not adopted clear-cut, restrictive, humane policies on when police officers may use their weapons or force against citizens."[148]

In this context, Murphy asked the IACP membership at their annual conference in 1980 to adopt a resolution favoring departmental restrictions on the use of deadly force; as we have seen, the gathered delegates rejected the resolution four to one and immediately adopted an affirmation of the fleeing felon rule by a similar margin. As Murphy continued his campaign, the IACP leadership censured him in 1982 for his ongoing criticism of traditional police policies.

But the leaders of professional policing, clustered around the old-line IACP leadership, were losing the public relations battle. The 1980 vote was reported only in the *St. Louis Post-Dispatch,* the local newspaper covering the IACP convention. In 1982, however, as the association moved to censure Murphy, the issue was widely covered in terms highly unfavorable to the IACP. The *New York Times* gave front-page coverage to the story on July 8, 1982, accompanied its primary article on the matter with a flattering profile of Patrick Murphy as an "idea man," and the next day published a lead editorial declaring that the IACP's action "only confirms that the IACP is out of touch with reality . . . [and] makes the IACP fair game—beyond criticism—for ridicule."[149] Similar stories, all unflattering to the IACP, appeared in other newspapers and magazines.[150] A number of large-city police chiefs issued letters opposing the IACP's action, and the executive directors of the National League of Cities, the International City Management Association, and the U.S. Conference of Mayors issued a joint letter expressing "distress" over the IACP's action.[151]

Synergies between Legal Mobilization and Professional Reform

As litigation against the police and the Police Foundation's campaign converged in the late 1970s, they interacted in complex and fertile ways that contributed to a rapid legitimation of legalized accountability and its spread among police departments. In the next chapter I analyze the course of these interactions in the channel of professional reform; here I sketch their course in the channel of legal mobilization.

Litigation over police shootings grew dramatically in the late 1970s and early 1980s, becoming a highly public embarrassment for police departments around the country. For instance, in 1980 the city of South Tucson, Arizona, faced possible bankruptcy over $3.5 million in liability judgments in two police shootings;[152] the New Orleans police chief resigned over controversy about the recent police shootings of four black men whose relatives were represented by prominent San Francisco attorney Mark Lane;[153] and a federal judge ordered the Prince Georges County police department, in a suburb of Washington, DC, in a case involving a $12 million lawsuit over the police shooting of a firefighter, to turn over to plaintiffs' attorneys all its internal reports on citizen complaints of police brutality.[154]

High-profile cases led to reform of police shooting rules and training in a number of prominent police departments. The New York City police department's 1972 shooting rules—the foundation for all subsequent reforms—were adopted in the midst of an intense scandal over the police shooting of an unarmed ten-year-old African American boy fleeing from a vehicle taken for joyriding.[155] The Los Angeles police department in 1977 adopted a policy restricting shootings in the midst of a scandal over the police shooting of an unarmed chemist.[156] The Houston police department similarly changed its policy on deadly force in the wake of a scandal in 1978 over the beating death of a young Hispanic man.[157]

Police misconduct lawyers began using administrative reforms in these leading departments as a means of winning cases against other departments and pressing them to reform their policies. Departmental restrictions on shootings appeared to be taking on the cachet of a professional state of the art. In tort law, "industry standards" have great weight in assessing whether an injury resulted from "negligence." If it can be shown that a person acted negligently in causing an injury, then he or she may be required to pay the costs of the injury. Negligence is a relative standard: what is negligent depends on what a "reasonable person" would do (and would take care not to do). What reasonable people do, however, is shaped by evolving standards, *particularly in areas of activity where human understanding and technologies of safety are advancing*. Armed with *Monell*'s permission to examine departmental "policy or custom," police misconduct litigators jumped on the fact that some leading police departments had successfully reduced shootings by their officers. This, these litigators argued, amounted to an emerging professional standard against which all departments and their officers should be judged.

These synergies between police misconduct litigation and the legalized accountability model emerged especially strongly in key legal developments in the areas of rules regarding the use of deadly force, protocols regarding training, and mechanisms of internal oversight. With regard to standards for deadly force, the litigation leading to the Supreme Court's landmark decision *Tennessee vs. Garner* (1985) built a powerful case in favor of departmental restrictions on shootings. The case was brought by the father of a fifteen-year-old boy shot by a Memphis police officer while fleeing the scene of a burglary. Common law and a Tennessee statute had authorized the officer to shoot a fleeing person suspected of a felony, but black communities had long complained that officers were much more likely to shoot at black suspects than white ones. The NAACP Legal Defense Fund supported a lawsuit filed by the victim's father, but the district court dismissed the complaint, holding that the police officer had acted lawfully within his authority under Tennessee law and City of Memphis policy and that the fleeing felon rule was constitutional. The Court of Appeals for the Sixth Circuit reversed, holding that Tennessee law and Memphis policy were unconstitutional to the extent that they authorized shots at any fleeing felon.[158] The state of Tennessee and the City of Memphis asked the Supreme Court to overturn the appellate court's ruling, and the Court agreed to take up the issue, setting the stage for a major ruling.

In pretrial discovery, the plaintiffs had obtained from the Memphis department its records on police shootings from 1969 to 1976.[159] They played a key role in the ongoing debate over police shootings. James Fyfe analyzed the data and observed that "although black Memphians were about twice as likely as whites to be killed when using guns . . . they were 18 times as likely as whites to die from police bullets when unarmed, not assaultive, and generally running away."[160] Fyfe concluded that the data "suggest that Memphis police used their broad authority to shoot in elective situations"—that is, when not necessary to defend the life of the officer or another person—"when their targets were black, and that typically they refrained from doing so when white subjects were involved."[161] Although the courts never endorsed an equal protection claim based on these data, the striking racial disparities had a profound impact on policing research and professional discussions regarding police shooting policies.

By 1984, when *Tennessee v. Garner* reached the Supreme Court, growing pressure had led many big-city police departments to adopt rules limiting their officers' authority to shoot, and most of these rules were considerably more restrictive than the fleeing felon rule.[162] The Police Foundation filed an amicus curiae brief in *Garner*—written by Fyfe—calling on the Supreme Court to overturn the fleeing felon rule and to authorize officers to shoot only when necessary to defend the life of the officer or another person. The Foundation sought to persuade the Court that professional police officials overwhelmingly opposed the fleeing felon rule. To this end, the organization marshaled an impressive list of cosigners to the brief: nine national or international police professional associations, the heads of the professional police associations of two states, and thirty-one prominent police chiefs. Further, the Foundation's brief reported that almost half of the states had adopted legislation restricting shots at fleeing felons, and the brief summarized a number of research studies demonstrating that the vast majority of police departments surveyed had adopted similar administrative rules. The brief did not acknowledge that at least some, and perhaps many, of these departmental rules were not as restrictive as the proposed defense-of-life rule and that the surveys of police departments had generally focused on bigger cities where reform had been most prevalent. The brief also understandably did not mention that the IACP, amid its internal battle over the reform effort, had not joined the list of amici. The Supreme Court, apparently heavily influenced by the Foundation's evidence (the Court's opinion specifically cited the trend among police departments toward restrictive rules) struck down the fleeing felon rule as unconstitutional, holding that "where the suspect poses no immediate threat to the officer and no threat to others, the harm resulting from failing to apprehend him does not justify the use of deadly force to do so."[163] The reform coalition greeted the decision with surprised relief. Steven L. Winter, the NAACP-Legal Defense Fund attorney who had argued the case, said he was "stunned" by the decision: "we couldn't have asked for more."[164]

The *Garner* decision, in the context of a growing infrastructure of support for police misconduct litigation, placed intense pressure on laggard police departments to adopt rules sharply limiting officers' discretion to shoot. Some police chiefs vigorously objected. "The real impact will be felt when extra police officers are needed for manhunts," declared John Whetsel, chief of police in Choctaw, Oklahoma. "The real impact will be felt when the lives of police officers and bystanders are in jeopardy when a felon attempts to escape."[165] But the logic was now clear, and it pointed powerfully in the direction of tighter shooting rules. "A department that does not immediately review—and, if necessary, rewrite—its policy on the use of deadly force to conform with *Garner*," observed a legal adviser to the police, "is potentially playing with a firestorm of legal liability."[166]

By the mid-1980s, as the vast majority of major police departments had begun rapidly developing formal rules regulating their officers' use of force, litigators' pressure shifted toward how departments implemented those rules. The key question increasingly was not whether departments had adopted professionally acceptable rules, but whether they condoned or supported a custom or practice that led to officers' violations of federal rights. Addressing this question required going below the surface of written policy and procedure: it was a matter of assessing the department's working culture and the implicit signals sent by commanders to subordinates. "Proving the policy was a bit of an art," observed Candace McCoy. "It involved looking very closely at the department's written policies and formal training procedures, but it also involved a bit of reading between the lines to get at what the department's working policy actually was."[167]

To get at those subtle matters, plaintiffs' attorneys increasingly turned to expert witnesses. "Relying on an expert witness," McCoy observed, "was how plaintiffs proved the nature of the department's policy."[168] "Experts," Avery concurred, "were essential to proving a *Monell* claim, because you had to talk about what the municipality should have done to have discovered the misconduct, how they should have supervised their officers, how they should have monitored their officers, and so on, and those things were the domain of the experts."[169] Beginning in the late 1970s, the use of experts by police misconduct attorneys grew significantly. George Kirkham, the first widely used policing expert, was employed regularly after 1975. By 1979 one other expert (William Bopp) began advertising regularly in the Association of Trial Lawyers of America's magazine *Trial*; after that the number of experts advertising in the magazine increased to three in 1981, seven in 1983, eight in 1984, ten in 1986, and twelve in 1989, a number that has since remained roughly constant.

The most persuasive expert police witnesses were former police officers (particularly commanding officers), who knew policing intimately and had credibility with a jury. Plaintiffs found such experts among the newly developing criminal justice professoriat, itself a product of the federal government's major push in the 1970s to support research and education in the area of policing. The dean of expert police witnesses in the 1980s and

1990s was James Fyfe, who by the early 1980s was widely known as "Dr. Deadly Force."[170] Fyfe began serving as an expert witness in police misconduct cases in 1980, observing later that he had not sought the work and "was surprised when I began to receive calls requesting my services."[171]

In the mid-1980s Fyfe outlined the types of evidence he used to evaluate the sufficiency of departmental policies, procedures, training, and supervision.[172] It is a road map to the police reform in the late 1980s and 1990s on training and internal oversight. Cases against departments increasingly turned on the adequacy of their policies, procedures, and training in equipping officers for predictable difficulties. "One very predictable characteristic of policing," Fyfe observed, "is that officers will occasionally encounter situations that, if poorly handled, may escalate to violence that is otherwise easily avoided."[173] The key variable in determining whether such situations were resolved safely or fatally, he said, was the adequacy of departmental policies and training: "Excessive force cases often involve well-meaning and courageous officers who were inadequately prepared by their employers to deal with very predictable police field situations, and who subsequently converted relatively minor incidents into disasters."[174] How such tragedies may be minimized by systematic departmental policies, procedures, training, and supervision became the key question in expert testimony. Obviously, answering that question requires something of a baseline, a standard against which to judge the practice of a particular defendant department. The standard, as Fyfe observed, was "generally accepted custom and practice . . . , the best professional thinking about the manner in which field problems should be resolved."[175] As a preliminary step, departmental policies should be compared with professional standards. But most cases hung on more complex matters, particularly departmental practices and departments' failure to act. Departure from professional norms might be found in departmental failure to take corrective action; overlooking evidence of a problem; failure to discipline or retrain an officer with a history or pattern of citizen complaints; failure to send clear signals to officers that abuse will not be tolerated; and failure to continue training of officers even after they have gained considerable experience.[176] Sources on that "best professional thinking" were found in professional policing studies and training materials.[177] As the IACP joined the reform bandwagon in the mid-1980s—a development to be explored in the next chapter—its recommendations increasingly carried weight. "My experts," observed Michael Avery, the police misconduct litigator, for instance, "typically relied on the IACP's training materials and recommendations as one indicator of the professional standard."[178]

To get information on departments' track records on these topics, plaintiffs' attorneys quickly began seeking extensive discovery of internal departmental records. Because the question increasingly was framed as whether cities have adequately kept up not only with professional police policies but also with professional *practices*, plaintiffs must be allowed to find out what a department's practices *are*. That implication allowed litigators to demand evidence of internal police department procedures and training. In many police misconduct cases, the discovery process generated enormous amounts of previously hidden information about police departments' internal workings. "The advent of computerization changed a lot of this," Rudovsky observed, "by increasing the sorts of data available on what police departments were doing, and how they were tracking things like what sorts of data departments were keeping or should keep, and on uses of force or racial profiling. In some ways it made things easier in litigation, or at least more data were available on what departments were doing."[179] A self-feeding dynamic developed. As internal records became increasingly central to establishing whether a department was engaging in professionally sufficient oversight over its officers' practices, plaintiffs' attorneys succeeded in establishing that failure to keep records, particularly on the types of force that could lead to death, amounted to a failure to meet the bare minimum of professional standards.[180] In turn, as departments kept increasingly detailed records, these records became the basis for claims that particular practices (or failures to engage in a particular practice) amounted to a failure to meet professional standards.

By the mid-1980s, police misconduct litigators also strategically sought to establish departmental liability for *failure to adequately train or manage their frontline officers*. Immediately in the wake of *Garner*, the International Association of Chiefs of Police had convened a blue-ribbon panel of police chiefs from major cities around the country, along with other experts, among them Michael Avery, to develop a "best practices" training protocol with regard to use of deadly force.[181] The IACP then conducted training sessions around the country to disseminate this training protocol. It became a professional baseline.

The litigation effort to establish liability for failure to train began very shortly after *Monell*, and, in contrast to that fortuitous decision, the litigation strategy was very deliberate.[182] Avery and Rudovsky, in their seminars and their manual, began arguing shortly after *Garner* that "policy or custom" should encompass "failure to train," and they encouraged lawyers to bring cases advancing that theory.[183] "As we began pushing that issue early on," Rudovsky recalled, "a number of district courts got on board with it, and then the Supreme Court ducked the issue a couple of times. It was kind of a typical development. The idea was out there, plaintiffs started pushing it, defendants resisted it, lower courts were split on both can you do it and what's the legal standard."[184]

Indeed, by the mid-1980s lower courts had decided a number of cases involving allegations that cities had failed to adequately train their police officers. Some courts had concluded that a single egregious rights violation by a police officer, in conjunction with a failure to train on the topic of that rights violation, could provide a basis for municipal liability. The Supreme Court in 1985 ruled that, in the absence of a clearly unconstitutional departmental policy, a single incident could not ordinarily provide the basis for municipal liability: something more, such as a pattern of rights violations, or a clearly obvious risk of rights violations, was needed.[185]

As the law on failure to train developed, some federal appellate courts had applied a standard of "gross negligence," meaning that a city could be found liable for failure to train only if the jury decided that the absence of training was due to "an intentional failure to perform a manifest duty in reckless disregard of the consequences."[186] Other federal appellate courts had applied a standard of "deliberate indifference," meaning that a city could be found liable for a failure to train only if there was a clear need for more training and the failure to provide it was in effect a deliberate decision not to meet the clear need.[187] Although the line between the two standards was not entirely clear in practice, there was little doubt that the "deliberate indifference" standard would be more difficult for plaintiffs to meet. The year after the Supreme Court decided *Tennessee v. Garner*, the Court agreed to hear a case involving city liability for failure to adequately train officers, apparently aiming to resolve the circuit conflict. But after oral argument a slim majority of the Court voted not to decide the case on the grounds that the defendant city had agreed at trial to the lower "gross negligence" standard.[188] Failure to train remained alive in the lower courts.

Two years later, the Court agreed to hear *City of Canton v. Harris*, which became the landmark decision on failure to train. The legal and professional climate had so changed by 1989 that police misconduct litigators were concerned not that the Court would reject failure to train but that it would set the negligence standard too high. After the Court agreed to hear the case, Rudovsky observed, "It was clear to me that the Court was going to allow liability for failure to train, and the only question was what would be the culpability standard. We were fighting over negligence, gross negligence, deliberate indifference, recklessness. It was clear that the Court was going to go with failure to train, the only issue was what would be the standard."[189] The Court, indeed, did allow municipalities to be found liable for failure to train, but it set the negligence standard at the relatively conservative level of "deliberate indifference"—requiring evidence of a *deliberate* departure from professional norms. The practical meaning of deliberate indifference has been subject to extensive litigation since 1989.

Although the standard is conservative, protecting cities from liability for any but "deliberate" negligence in failing to follow professional standards and then allowing liability only if the departure "causes" a violation of rights, it has nonetheless offered plaintiffs' lawyers additional leverage in gaining admission of expert testimony on departmental practices. The standard of "deliberate indifference" is relative to what is considered to be responsible professional police management. Not everything that departs from responsible management is an instance of "deliberate indifference," but at some point a departmental policy, procedure, or training protocol varies so substantially from professional norms that it can only be characterized as deliberately indifferent to known risks and known solutions to those risks. That is a question of fact, and it is properly left to juries. But it is a question of fact relative to professional standards, and police misconduct litigators increasingly have used experts to provide evidence of the state of these standards. And indeed, in the wake of *Canton v. Harris* the use of expert witnesses exploded. "After Canton, with the theory solid," Rudovsky observed, summarizing these developments, "we started to see a lot more use of experts, a lot more sophisticated discovery to try to get the data to demonstrate that the department had a problematic practice or so forth.[190]

The synergies between police misconduct litigation and the legalized accountability model fed back after the early 1980s into a richer infrastructure of support among the litigators. Rudovsky recalled that "by the mid-1980s, late 1980s, into the 1990s, there were some substantial verdicts and significant successes, and I started seeing more lawyers starting to take these cases. . . . The law was starting to fill out and there were materials available to help them develop cases."[191] By the 1990s, the networks that grew up around the National Lawyers Guild had generated a formal organization, the National Police Accountability Project, which provides a forum for training and information sharing about police misconduct litigation.

Well into the interactive process described above, James Fyfe, in a memo to Patrick Murphy, summarized progress on the campaign to reform police deadly force policies, observing that "we got the police and public thinking and talking about it."[192] "At first," he acknowledged, "much of the talk from the police was in the form of shouting, condemnations and denials of the validity of what we had to say." But the climate had changed: most police departments in major cities had adopted restrictive shooting rules, the IACP's professional staff had shifted from opposing restrictive shooting rules to supporting them, the Commission on Law Enforcement Accreditation had adopted a recommendation that all departments issue restrictive shooting rules, and—the icing on the cake—the Police Foundation had obtained wide professional police association support for its amicus brief in the pending Supreme Court case *Tennessee v. Garner* and had succeeded in keeping any professional police association from filing an opposition brief. Policing was in the midst of a legalized accountability revolution.

Conclusion

In this chapter I have traced the development of a legal norm favoring legalized accountability in policing and have argued that this norm's development grew less from police departments' innovations than from two other sources—activist pressure and a reform campaign among policy experts on the border of policing and academia. Activist police misconduct attorneys and professional experts together transformed the legal climate around policing in the 1970s, generating conditions that increasingly favored opening the police up to legalized accountability. Activist attorneys built an infrastructure of support for widespread litigation against the police, cultivating constitutional torts as a key regulatory tool.

Further, over the course of the 1970s litigation against the police increasingly shaped media's framing of the problem of police abuses. By the late 1970s, the news media were regularly reporting not only high-profile litigation alleging police harassment of radicals but also litigation over police shootings of ordinary citizens. Litigation over shootings of unarmed young African Americans fleeing sites of small-time burglaries generated particularly unflattering media coverage of the police. By the early 1980s, media coverage commonly reflected activists' call for institutional reform of police departments on the use of force.

Reform-oriented police experts, led by James Fyfe and Patrick Murphy, developed practical administrative ideas for how to regulate police uses of force, implemented those ideas in a handful of major police departments, and then, through careful empirical research, showed that those programs worked in practice to reduce police shootings. As these separate developments converged in the mid- and late 1970s, they interacted in ways that further empowered the movement for legalizing accountability. Litigation spurred leading departments to do more, and their adoption of administrative innovations gave activist litigators a foothold for pressing other police departments to follow suit. Some police "insiders" agreed to serve as expert witnesses in lawsuits, further spurring police innovation and the spread of innovations to laggard departments.

The growing wave of police reform in turn provided the pragmatic foundation for the Supreme Court's key intervention in the area, its decision in *Tennessee v. Garner* (1985) striking down the fleeing felon shooting rule as unconstitutional. By 1989 a far more conservative Court was drawn deeper into support for legalizing accountability when its majority, in *Canton v. Harris*, endorsed the idea that police departments may be financially liable for injuries caused by their failure to adequately train their officers. The norm requiring legalized accountability of policing, growing through decentralized channels of popular and professional pressure, had gained the highest court's imprimatur.

5

Policing's Epiphany

The legal environment around policing, as we saw in the previous chapter, changed dramatically in the late 1970s. How did police leaders respond? American policing experienced an epiphany. Although many scholars characterize liability's sanction as weak, its message as ambiguous, and organizations' responses as superficial, the police increasingly portrayed the liability sanction as shockingly powerful, its message as very clear and precise, and the appropriate organizational response as comprehensive systemic reform. Professional policing publications reported that to avoid liability police departments should adopt lawlike internal controls over police misconduct. By the 1990s these messages—that liability was exploding and that departments should adopt deep institutional reforms—had melded into a new policy model focused on legalizing accountability. In the process, legalized accountability was transformed from a virtual heresy into a new professional orthodoxy, the badge of honor for a new legally oriented version of police professionalism.

My evidence in support of these propositions consists of two bodies of observations: historical evidence of changes over time in professional recommendations for reform (covered in this chapter) and a comparison of police departments' adoption of the elements of legalized accountability (covered in the next). My historical tracing of professional recommendations relies primarily on changes over time in recommendations appearing in the IACP's official voice, *Police Chief*, a monthly magazine published continuously since 1934, supplemented by other publications (particularly management texts, described below) that indicate developments in professional norms. My examination focuses particularly on police use of force and civil liability from 1960 to 2000, when police exposure to liability grew dramatically. During this period, each month's *Police Chief* consisted of roughly one hundred pages and reached some twenty thousand subscribers. I examined every issue from 1960 to 2000 and identified every article that discussed either the use of force or legal liability (or both). *Police Chief* coverage provides an institutional history of police accounts of legal liability. I have supplemented and confirmed the *Police Chief* observations with a similar historical analysis of changes over time in the professional recommendations made by police management texts; legal guides for police officers and departments; and the official position of the U.S. Department of Justice.

My analysis reveals that professional concern about liability exploded in the late 1970s and early 1980s *before* professional publications began favoring systemic, legalized reforms in the area of police misconduct. As concern about liability approached panic, professional publications began recommending such reforms as the answer. Professional publications came to accept and favor the recommendations long pushed by dissident reformers associated with the Police Foundation.

Policing in these years, of course, was buffeted by other momentous changes, particularly a widespread push for "community policing," generally understood as a return to a less insulated structure more engaged with the community.[1] Even so, liability represented a distinct pressure, and it unleashed especially powerful institutional dynamics within policing.

Police Chief Magazine

In the 1960s and 1970s, legal liability was simply a nonissue in the pages of *Police Chief*. Until 1978, when the issue exploded on the pages of the magazine, *Police Chief* published only four articles that even *mentioned* legal liability, and two of these mentioned it only in passing.[2] None drew from legal liability anything more than a vague lesson. For instance, one of these articles, from 1967, warned that police shootings "may well" give rise to liability lawsuits, but in support of this proposition the author cited only one case in state court decided eight years earlier; the other article observed merely that in formulating gun policies, "a review of pertinent court decisions would be much worthwhile."[3] Further, to the extent that the IACP acknowledged any growth in civil litigation against the police, the association favored policies to discourage lawsuits and curb the courts.[4] Although *Police Chief* authors began advising departments to get better legal advice and defense, they acknowledged that this was a tough sell, since police officers commonly felt a natural animosity toward lawyers.[5] In other words, well into the 1970s, professional policing had no institutionalized understanding of the liability issue and could draw no clear message from legal liability.

But this soon changed dramatically. "November 1, 1977," *Police Chief* reported, "was a day of reckoning for a substantial number of law enforcement agencies around the country which suddenly found themselves without police professional liability insurance coverage."[6] The primary police liability insurance company, pointing to concerns about rising legal liability, had pulled out of the market. As early as 1976, municipalities in general had been increasingly concerned about a looming liability insurance crisis.[7] In retrospect, it is clear that the 1977 crisis in liability insurance reflected a now predictable "insurance cycle" characterized by dramatic increases in premiums followed by equally dramatic declines.[8] In 1975–77, the rate of growth in liability insurance premiums increased to 30 percent annually.[9] Although scholars disagree over whether liability lawsuits contribute marginally to rapid increases in premiums during the "hard" phase of the cycle, it is clear that the cycle itself is generated by competition among insurers. Still, when the cyclical increases hit, they commonly draw attention to liability lawsuits.

In rapid succession, the IACP began holding training sessions on liability at its annual conferences, and *Police Chief* began publishing a growing stream of articles expressing dismay about legal liability. "During the 1970s, the law enforcement community has experienced a rapid rise in the number of lawsuits," observed an article appearing in *Police Chief* in 1978, predicting that the Supreme Court's *Monell* decision that year would increase litigation pressure even more.[10] Soon leaders of professional policing were making sky is falling speculations about the future. "The potential for loss is staggering," a writer reported in 1981, as "an act which will result in a million dollar judgment [in your jurisdiction] could be occurring as you read this article, or it may never happen. The risk is your risk."[11] Another writer observed that "the past two decades have seen a ballooning in civil liability litigation of police misconduct claims."[12] "There is every indication that during the 1980s," another observed, "civil action against police chiefs will increase."[13] "Federal litigation," another said, "has become a fact of life," an "epidemic . . . infecting the present legal system."[14] "In the first 42 years of the Ohio Highway Patrol's existence," a representative of that agency reported, "there was approximately one law suit filed against our officers every two years. Since 1975, however, there has been an average of forty such suits filed every year," a "very pronounced upward trend" that was likely to "worsen."[15] "Will we see the day," another lamented, "when an injured victim holds an officer negligent for dallying over a doughnut after receiving a call for assistance? . . . And on and on, ad infinitum?"[16]

Writers in *Police Chief* began claiming that virtually *every* department in every region of the country faced the threat of litigation. "Where in the past such litigation was limited almost exclusively to larger departments in major metropolitan areas," one writer observed in 1983, "today any area of the country, and even smaller, rural communities, are now learning firsthand the hard facts of legal life and civil liability."[17] A proliferation of attorneys willing to bring lawsuits against the police contributed to the increasingly widespread nature of the threat. As one writer observed, "In many instances, the modern radical group has at least one attorney minutes away from its public activity," compounding the potential for lawsuits.[18]

Remarkably few authors referred specifically to the Supreme Court as a source for the new threat of legal liability, attributing the sea change instead to larger numbers of plaintiffs' attorneys and civil liberties groups.[19] Thus one writer (a lawyer commonly used by *Police Chief* for legal commentary), observing that litigation against the police had "reached epidemic" levels, succinctly summarized many of the developments reported in the previous chapter:

> There are books and articles published regularly that explain to a potential litigant in almost blueprint-like fashion how to file and successfully prosecute civil actions against law enforcement officers and agencies. There are seminars routinely conducted that teach attorneys how to tactically and strategically bring a civil action to successful conclusion at trial. There are expert witnesses—many of them former police officers or college professors at law enforcement or criminal justice programs in universities across the country—who will testify for healthy fees against law enforcement officers and departments in civil actions. . . . Having tried over 350 police misconduct cases [as defense counsel], I . . . can only observe the problem gets worse rather than better as time passes.[20]

These themes—litigation against the police has reached epidemic proportions and every department is threatened—continued virtually unchanged from the 1980s to the 2000s. Writers complained that lawsuits
took a "heavy toll on police morale";[21] that "almost any" of the "thousands
of interactions between police officers and citizens" in a jurisdiction "could
result in litigation;"[22] that "numerous lawsuits" generated "high-figure
judgments;"[23] that we live in a "litigious society;"[24] that liability for excessive use of force was becoming "the primary liability drain on taxpayer
funds;"[25] that "many of the daily activities of police officers have led to
the filing of a wide variety of lawsuits;"[26] that there was an "onslaught of
litigation;"[27] that "a chief should not go to work without his attorney;"[28]
and so on. If there was any appreciable change over time, it was that by the
1990s, articles on the liability threat had begun to summarize liability law
in greater specificity, detail, and nuance, focusing on such issues as negligent failure to prevent suicide,[29] the use of force,[30] and failure to train.[31] In
the 1980s, the more general discussions of liability had tended to emphasize *exposure* of departments or officials to liability. The more specific articles of the 1990s, by contrast, began to focus not only on exposure to
liability but also on identifying the areas in which police officers or departments were protected from liability.[32]

What, precisely, did professional policing fear in legal liability? Although
financial costs appear prominently in many discussions,[33] the more significant penalty, in the eyes of many *Police Chief* writers, was the risk of public
and professional embarrassment. "The results [of a lawsuit] can be disas-
trous," an author observed. "In fact, the fallout from a major lawsuit can be
damaging even if the lawsuit is won."[34] A key risk, another article declared,
was to "maintaining departmental credibility" in the public eye.[35] Another
article concurred that in liability lawsuits what is at stake is "departmental
credibility."[36]

My survey of police departments in 2000 confirmed that police chiefs
widely share the view that liability's greatest threat is to their agencies'
public legitimacy and credibility. I asked respondents to rate the impact
of a lawsuit on a scale from one, "virtually no impact," to ten, "major long-
term damage," with regard to media coverage of the department, the
public's image of the department, the department's budget, employee morale, and their own job security. Chiefs widely reported that lawsuits have
a very significant negative impact on employee morale, media coverage,
and the public image of the police—and that these impacts are substantially greater than a lawsuit's impact on the budget or the job security of

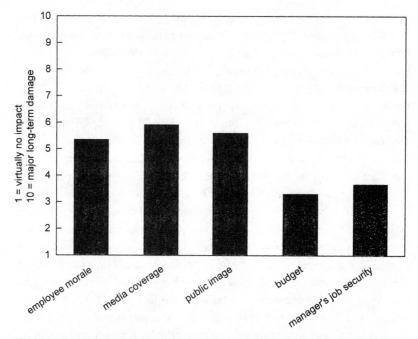

Figure 5.1. Perceived impact of a lawsuit on police department, by nature of impact. N = 817–25. All differences between variables in the first category (morale, media coverage, and public image) and those in the second (budget and job security) are significant below the .001 level (t > 17.00).

commanding officers (see fig. 5.1). In other words, liability lawsuits' reputational sanction is significantly greater than their financial sanction.

The fear of reputational sanctions suggests the emergence of a public standard or norm requiring police departments to regulate their officers' use of force. In the late 1960s, as we have seen in earlier chapters, public opinion solidly supported extravagant uses of force by the police against disorderly people, and leaders of professional policing proudly defended aggressive uses of force. As we have seen, in 1967 Quinn Tamm, the IACP executive director, had responded to critics of police brutality by celebrating "the successful policeman" who "dominates the situation."[37] By the early 1980s a very different public and professional norm in favor of careful regulation of force was emerging, and by the early 1990s professional police leaders commonly articulated it. Thus IACP president Lee Brown observed in 1991 that police administrators must "recognize that excessive use of force *is* an issue, and one which we ... must deal with immediately and effectively."[38] An article in 1992 observed that "society does not accept the use of *excessive force*" and urged police chiefs to create policies of "zero tolerance" for it.[39]

The new norm required concrete administrative reforms. This came to mean, specifically, that departments should bring officers' use of force under internal legalized control. If departments fail to meet the standard, *Police Chief* began to declare, they risk financial losses and public and professional embarrassment. Since 1982 this twin theme—liability threats are everywhere and, as a consequence, departments should adopt systems of legalized accountability—has been among *Police Chief*'s primary messages to the profession. This message, with its focus on the responsibility of police to engage in reform, represented a dramatic reversal of the previous effort to blame sue-happy litigants and irresponsible judges. As the police officers quoted in the epigraph to chapter 1 put it in 1983, "we are being sued because we are not doing our job." They went on,

> Through the use of intentional torts, negligence, and constitutional torts, we are paying a tremendous price for the incompetent people which we hire and allow to continue to work in our system. Until we, as managers, become competent in handling the conflicting needs of our individual officers, union leadership, and yet satisfying the need to preserve the fundamental rights of citizens, we will continue to pay a tremendous prices [*sic*] because of the wrongs committed by the officers on the streets.[40]

Article after article in *Police Chief* made such a remarkable admission. "The signal is a clear one," declared another author, writing in 1983: "You, as chief, must discharge your duty to guide and direct the men under your command in all aspects of their work. Any failure to do so, which proximately causes a plaintiff's injury, will likely result in personal or municipal liability, or both."[41]

Another, again writing in 1983, succinctly observed:

> One frequently encounters the phrase the "Seven Deadly Sins" . . . commonly enumerated as follows:
>   1. Negligent appointment.
>   2. Negligent retention.
>   3. Negligent assignment.
>   4. Negligent entrustment.
>   5. Lack of training.
>   6. Failure to supervise.
>   7. Failure to direct.

None of these "Seven Deadly Sins" speaks to the patrol officer negligently performing his job or intentionally committing a tort against a citizen! All of these negligent sins have to do with the police administrator and his role in the department.[42]

Technology in the twentieth century, as the eminent legal historian Lawrence Friedman has argued, transformed assumptions about responsibility.[43] With the growing sense that humans can solve problems—in engineering, medicine, abuses by those in power, and the like—we have come to believe that officials and organizations who do not take widely known steps to address acknowledged problems are morally and legally responsible for any resulting injuries. Precisely such a recognition permeated the pages of *Police Chief* in the 1980s and 1990s. In article after article, leaders of professional policing observed that professionalism had increased their departments' capacity to regulate the actions of their frontline officers—and that legal liability, in light of this increased managerial capacity, imposed an obligation on departments to plan for and regulate officers' use of force. In 1984—the year Friedman published his compelling analysis—a police officer writing in *Police Chief* adopted precisely such an argument for why police departments were compelled to engage in legal reform:

> Whenever a dangerous, armed individual resists arrest, a potential danger exists and force, including the use of firearms, may be necessary. It is the agency's duty to minimize the danger, within the limitations of the available equipment, tactics, and techniques. An analogy would be in the area of motor vehicles used by officers.
>
> In the early days of automotive design, all vehicles were equipped with mechanical brakes. When the mechanical brake was the standard of the industry, an agency or its chief would not automatically be liable for an injury that occurred due to short stopping distance. . . .
>
> With the introduction of hydraulic brakes, however, the effective braking distances of automobiles was significantly reduced. If a police agency continued to use cars equipped with mechanical brakes, it would expose itself to liability if an officer or citizen were injured in a collision under circumstances similar to the previous example. If the available equipment would have permitted a stop without collision, the failure to equip could become the legal cause of the injury. Those responsible for the failure to equip safely might become liable for monetary damages.

The management of any organization that is involved in dangerous activities has a duty to upgrade the equipment whenever improved versions are widely available. The same duty applies to the upgrading of training and supervision. Failure to implement safety improvements would expose the agency and management to civil liability. . . .

A growing number of individuals across the country are now aware of the past failures regarding tactics and techniques. These experts are familiar with the newer standards and their value in minimizing injury. . . . This will make it easier for the plaintiffs to show the wide gap between the high level of training and supervision that is possible . . . and that which existed at the time of the injury.

Police managers will not succeed by simply showing that *some* training occurred and that *some* supervision existed. *If they cannot show that they discharged their duty responsibly, they will lose these suits. They must show that they provided training at the new levels of competency. They must prove that they were indeed in the world of hydraulic brakes rather than that of mechanical brakes. They must show that their departments were safe.*[44]

Police Chief's specific prescriptions for reform focused on rules governing the use of force, training framed around those rules, and internal oversight aimed at assessing adherence to the rules. At the same time, the publication began favoring departmental accreditation, a new initiative requiring review and certification that departments were adhering to the recommendations above.[45] I turn now to *Police Chief* recommendations in each of these key areas.

Rules

The first element of the IACP's reform prescription was rules, specifically detailed departmental policies regulating officers' uses of force. This recommendation amounted to an abrupt reversal of the IACP's previous posture, which, as we have seen, opposed rules limiting police shootings, labeling the idea virtually a heresy. As late as 1982 a policing leader suggested that detailed departmental rules might actually *increase* the threat of liability (by making it easier for plaintiffs to establish that conduct failed to conform to the rule of law).[46] But in the new liability environment, the pro-rules faction gained ground, and administrative rules soon emerged as the centerpiece of *Police Chief*'s reform message. As early as 1980, an author in *Police Chief* forcefully urged departments to adopt a comprehensive policy manual for the purpose of saving lives and preventing lawsuits. Such a manual, the author declared, "serves to protect the police officer and the agency from accusations of mismanagement, inconsistent policies, and lack of standard operating procedures."[47]

A near consensus, framed in light of judicial decisions in liability cases, coalesced around the pro-rules position by about 1982 or 1983. In 1982 the IACP published a report by Kenneth Matulia, the association's director of research, on police shootings.[48] After an extensive (fourteen-page) discussion of police liability arising out of shootings, Matulia recommended that departments adopt a rule allowing the use of deadly force only when necessary to protect the officer or another person from "an immediate threat of death or (near death) critical bodily harm."[49] This was the defense of life rule, long favored by legalized accountability reformers, and its publication represented a significant reversal for the IACP. Hedging its bets, the Association published the report with a disclaimer that it represented the views of the author alone and was not the official position of the IACP; indeed, the report contained a statement of the Association's official position on the issue of deadly force, and this, of course, was an affirmation of the old fleeing felon rule.[50] Still, there could be little doubt that change was in the air. The following year *Police Chief* published an article by Matulia on the subject, forcefully favoring departmental adoption of restrictive shooting rules. Acknowledging that although some departments had failed to adopt written shootings policies for fear they would increase their liability exposure, the opposite was true: "A greater liability exists where the issue has been avoided or left to the total discretion of individual officers."[51] Matulia's article was accompanied by an advertisement by the IACP for Matulia's report; the advertisement prominently proclaimed that the report contained a model deadly force policy and procedure.[52] At the same time (1983), in the context of a new Supreme Court decision on constitutional tort liability, *Police Chief* finally reported a several-year-old Supreme Court decision, *Owen v. City of Independence* (1980), that had explicitly endorsed adoption of formal administrative rules "to minimize the likelihood of unintentional infringements on constitutional rights."[53] It was a belated discovery, made possible by the emerging professional consensus around rules.

Then, in 1985, the Supreme Court handed down its decision in *Tennessee v. Garner*, striking down the fleeing felon shooting rule and providing qualified endorsement for rule-based restrictions like those contained in the "defense of life" rule. Although the IACP, as we saw in the previous chapter, did not sign on to the Police Foundation's amicus brief in the case, the Court's decision strengthened the hand of the reformers within the IACP, and the IACP's official spokesman quickly announced the association's support for the new policy.[54] In the wake of the decision and in the midst of a flood of requests from police departments, the IACP began publishing "Models for Management," containing specific model policies, and by spring of 1988 the column had become a regular feature.[55] Among the first of the regular columns was a model policy on the use of deadly force.[56] From that point to the present, the IACP has published a continuing stream of specific model policies covering a wide range of issues. The threat of legal liability was never far in the background as an impetus to such models. Thus, in March 1989 *Police Chief* carried a model policy on departmental response to the risk of civil litigation.[57]

With the advent of "Models for Management" and its proposed training protocol, the IACP effectively abandoned its long-standing opposition to national policies governing policing. To be sure, the IACP presented its model policies as voluntary guides. Thus "the term 'model policy,'" the manager of the IACP's new National Law Enforcement Policy Center averred, "is not meant to imply that the . . . policy is completely suitable for . . . all agencies."[58] Still, the Policy Center's director observed that the typical department would benefit from following the models, since most departmental policies were ad hoc, poorly written, and subject to "incompleteness," "out-of-date information," and "ambiguity."[59] Few could doubt that in the hands of police misconduct attorneys the voluntary guidelines would impose enormous pressure to follow the IACP's suggestions. As we saw in the previous chapter, that is precisely what happened. It was a new era.

One of the era's key attributes was the publication of increasingly detailed and specific policies on the use of force.[60] By the 1990s the dominant recommendation was for a "graduated use of force" policy, outlining different levels of force from deadly force at the highest to officer presence at the lowest. The idea for such a force continuum had been first proposed in 1984 by John Desmedt, a special agent in the Secret Service's office of training.[61] At the time, Desmedt observed that while police agencies were increasingly imposing clear rules on officers' use of deadly force, "when the use of *less*-than-deadly force is involved, however, everything is left to the judgment of the officer. He is given no guidelines about how much force to use; he is given no specifics."[62] Desmedt proposed a "use of force model" based on a "confrontational continuum" that claimed to identify precisely how much force is appropriate in light of the amount of resistance to police authority, and other writers soon supported the concept.[63] Some type of use of force continuum was widely seen as an appropriate response to the Supreme Court's 1989 decision in *Graham v. Connor* (1989), which held that uses of nonlethal force should be judged by an "objective reasonableness" standard in light of the level of resistance offered by a suspect.[64] In recent years, however, a debate has grown over whether use of force continua are more restrictive than required by that decision.[65] Still, as a command-level officer who is director of training for a large Midwestern police department told me, as a guide to police training "the use of the force continuum is the only thing that matters."[66]

Training

In addition to formal policies, as a response to growing liability threats, in the early 1980s *Police Chief* began endorsing better training of officers in relation to the new rules. Thus a president's editorial from 1981, titled "Training: A Critical Requirement," argued that adequate officer training is among the key reforms necessary to minimize the growing liability threat.[67] Similarly, a leading article from 1981 argued that "the importance of training cannot be overemphasized in light of the trends toward suing individual officers, supervisory personnel, and chiefs of police."[68] It went on, "Adequate training will minimize the potential liability that each of us in the law enforcement community faces."[69] Articles on searches and seizures—an area of police practice already subject to the exclusionary rule as a deterrent force—soon began to refer to liability for failure to train. Thus in 1981 a report of a just-decided search warrant case by the Supreme Court concluded that civil liability greatly increased the need to gain proper warrants.[70] A final example comes from *Police Chief*'s report on the decision in *Harlow v. Fitzgerald* (1982), which observed that "*Harlow* states a powerful case for increased and improved training for police officers and other public officials."[71] "For departments that learn this lesson and implement effective training programs," the article continued, "*Harlow* may prove to be a great blessing. For the departments that do not, it may prove to be a curse."[72]

Training may be done pro forma or in a more searching attempt to change organizational culture and officer behavior. As the legalized accountability agenda emerged, *Police Chief* authors began frankly favoring efforts to go beyond pro forma training. Thus a 1981 article argued that police training must take into account and overcome officers' cynicism about legal procedures and individual rights.[73] A similar, more extensive article from 1986 tackled officers' resistance to legal training forthrightly and extensively, observing that officers' "negative impressions of the law" arose in part because of the "flood of lawsuits against police officers," and proposed that departments should address the problem with "a system of legal instruction that commences early in recruit training and continues throughout the officer's career."[74] Law, the writer proposed, should be taught not as an abstract set of rules but rather as an essential aspect of *"proper police procedure"*—which is to say, as an element of police professionalism.[75]

In the wake of the Supreme Court's *Garner* decision, the IACP immediately convened a meeting of professional leaders and police misconduct litigators—among them Michael Avery—to develop a model for police training with regard to deadly force.[76] The federal Bureau of Justice Assistance provided funding for the program, and it was carried out over the following two years.[77] *Police Chief* in this context began devoting greater attention to training in avoiding illegal uses of force, and these discussions became increasingly detailed and legally oriented.[78] Thus, in 1987 the magazine provided a detailed report of the presentations in a national symposium on training.[79] In 1990 a writer declared that "adequate police training is even more important now than it was in the past" because of the growing threat of liability. "Good police training," the article observed, "helps to reduce liable incidents for the officer, the chief and the municipality."[80]

Other indicators abound of a professional consensus that the risk of liability requires departments to carry out training in the use of force. Thus the legal adviser for a California department declared:

> Training, training, training is the key. Remember, a "policy" . . . is the moving force behind the training; but it is the training which establishes the "actual policy." While a policy statement such as this may accurately reflect the legal limits on use of force established by law (statutes and precedent decisions of the courts), training (or lack of it) will establish how the policy of the Department is executed and carried out. Where the policy and training are integrated, training defines the actual or "real policy," and runs with it. Where there is a lack of essential training or inadequate training, the void or inadequacy also establishes a "policy": it is a policy of "deliberate indifference" to the potential injurious consequences of having a non-existent or inadequate training program. Not surprisingly, it leads to liability for the administrator who is also the policymaker, when an untrained or under-trained officer uses excessive or unauthorized force, causing injury which is unnecessary or unreasonable.[81]

Internal Oversight

Police Chief authors quickly added to rules and training the third element of the legalized accountability model, internal oversight. Critics of the police had long claimed that lofty pronouncements by police officials often were not matched by the actions of frontline officers, and bringing practice in line with pronouncement remained the key challenge. They demanded that police chiefs exercise greater internal oversight over frontline officers.

Police Chief first addressed internal oversight in a 1983 article reporting the decision *Webster v. City of Houston* (1982),[82] which had found the Houston department liable for condoning a custom among officers of carrying "throw-down" guns for use in building a defense if they shot a person who had no weapon. The article forcefully argued that "*Webster* means that attention to official written policy is only part of the answer.... The larger and more difficult job is the constant scrutiny of every phase of the department's work and the eradication of any notion that 'ignorance is bliss.'"[83] Indeed, "courts are now willing to find the required 'custom,' making a city liable, in even those situations where the misconduct is not condoned, but simply occurs with some regularity.... General supervision will seemingly not suffice; *only supervision close enough to detect and curb pervasive practices will protect the department*" from liability.[84]

By the 1990s, much of the discussion of internal oversight in *Police Chief* reflected a growing sophistication regarding the complexity of modern police bureaucracies and the need for proactive control over departmental culture. Thus an article appearing in 1992 urged departments to come into line with the reform program of written policy and improved training and oversight, but it went further by observing that police chiefs "set the tone" for their departments and that chiefs' "tone" may be a more significant influence than even policy and training; the article then called on chiefs to set a tone of "zero tolerance" for excessive force.[85] Similarly, an article in 1993 called on chiefs to examine two aspects of their agencies, "what is the written standard, and what is the actual practice," and take steps to reform both.[86] To tackle "the actual practice," the article urged departments to institute "tracking systems" aimed at identifying officers who use force substantially more often than other officers, or generate more complaints, and to use the information as a means to change the culture of the agency via retraining, discipline, or dismissal.[87]

The proposal for such tracking systems was part of a growing movement in favor of early warning systems. These administrative programs, as observed by Walker, Alpert, and Kenney, are aimed at tracking the performance of officers, identifying officers who exhibit problem behavior, and intervening to correct such behavior through training, counseling, and ultimately discipline.[88] "An EW [early warning] system is 'early,'" these scholars observe, "in the sense that it attempts to identify officers before their performance results in more serious problems" such as a lawsuit or a public controversy.[89] Although a handful of departments experimented with ad hoc tracking systems in the late 1970s, the first well-developed system was instituted by the Miami police department as public controversy in that city grew in the wake of the 1979 killing of a black motorist.[90] The U.S. Commission on Civil Rights endorsed early warning systems in a 1981 report observing that a small proportion of officers typically incur a very large proportion of a department's citizen complaints and that correcting these officers' behavior may significantly address the overall problem.[91] The Christopher Commission's report on the Rodney King beating case made a similar observation.[92] Although early warning systems primarily aim to monitor the conduct of frontline officers, a secondary effect (or goal), as Walker, Alpert, and Kenney observe, is "holding supervisors accountable for their behavior" by requiring these officers to evaluate the performance of their subordinates with regard to citizen complaints.[93] By the late 1990s, writers were describing early warning systems as necessary to minimize departmental liability. Thus a 1998 column in *Police Chief* observed that "employment files can be a ticking bomb" of liability, and therefore the reasonable supervisor must review all files for evidence of misconduct and follow up with any necessary retraining, discipline, or dismissal.[94]

Finally, *Police Chief* writers began pressing departments to hire in-house legal counsel and carry out ongoing internal legal review of police policies and procedures. Although writers had favored hiring police "legal advisers" intermittently since the early 1970s, by the 1980s this recommendation took on a more urgent tone and favored not only legal defense but also internal legal oversight. As one article (a report of remarks at the 1981 annual IACP conference) put it, "The notion that police lawyers unnecessarily and unduly complicate matters is archaic and shortsighted. . . . Since law is the rule, arm yourself with a lawyer."[95] Another declared that in-house counsel contributes not only to defense against civil suits but also to better internal policies, improved design of training programs, and better internal oversight. "The benefits," the writer argued, "are unending."[96]

A Comprehensive Policy Model of Legalized Accountability

After the mid-1980s, writers in *Police Chief* began to characterize rules, training, and oversight as parts of a comprehensive, proactive program. An article on physical restraints concluded, for instance: "Restraint liability *can* be minimized. Through knowledge, proper guidance, competent training and supervision, the various risks associated with restraints can be controlled and virtually eliminated. After all, none of us want to be reading about our agency's having spent millions of dollars to compensate a victim of improper handcuffing, when it is so easily avoidable."[97]

Similarly, an article from 1985 by the noted policing expert William Geller outlined fifteen "shooting reduction techniques," described as a comprehensive "package" of "administrative innovations" (among them a clear policy, focused training, "strong and effective supervision," "a proactive field investigations and inspections unit," a fair administrative review system, and the like).[98] An article from 1990, for another example, described "the six-layered liability protection system" as composed of "policies and procedures, training, supervision, discipline, review and revision, and legal support and services," encompassing the main elements of the legalized accountability model.[99]

In the wake of the Rodney King incident in March 1991, *Police Chief* simply amplified the now institutionalized themes of liability as a threat and legalized accountability as the answer. Thus, in 1991 IACP president Lee Brown observed that police administrators must "recognize that excessive use of force *is* an issue, and one which we . . . must deal with immediately and effectively."[100] Another article observed that the King incident emphasized the need for formal policies, training, and oversight regarding uses of force.[101] The IACP established a new Center on Police Use of Force and Misconduct, whose main task would be to develop a national database on police misconduct.[102]

By the late 1980s the fear of liability and the legalized accountability model had become institutionalized, and from then to the present, representations of that model in professional policing publications have continued relatively unchanged. As the model gained legitimacy, the number of articles on civil liability and police reform in *Police Chief* became so large that no summary here can do them justice.

Liability pressure and the Police Foundation reform campaign ultimately transformed mainstream policing's professional identity. Before 1980 policing's dominant professional ideology resisted external legal accountability; by the 1990s it was that legalized accountability not only protected departments from liability but also enhanced safety and protection for individual rights—and ultimately enhanced police professionalism itself. Sociologists Frank Sutton and John Dobbin have observed that an indication of the institutionalizing of legalized reforms is that their rationale shifts subtly from law-related incentives to efficiency or simply good management practice.[103] After about 1990, precisely such a shift is observable in *Police Chief*'s coverage of legalized accountability. An article on risk management from 1990, for instance, argued that "risk management and excellent administration have complementary objectives."[104] The article contained a "personal risk management checklist for the Police Chief"; number four on the nine-item list is this question: "Have I recognized that good supervision and good management are synonymous with liability management at its highest level?"[105] A similar article by the same author argued: "There is a link between the management of liability and police professionalism. Factors that decrease the chance of liability ultimately increase the agency's overall professionalism. Even the busiest executive, then, will benefit from establishing the most comprehensive, systemic approach to managing liability, realizing that the level of professionalism in the department will be simultaneously improved."[106]

Another article, titled "Protecting Your Community from Lawsuits," declared that comprehensive legalized accountability reforms would generate sweeping benefits, among them increased administrative efficiency, reduced "overall costs," less time spent in court, "improved public relations" owing to reduced "losses to the community," improved officer morale and productivity, and "sharpen[ed] . . . management skills."[107] Similarly, an article on training argued that "not only does a good training program increase the effectiveness and safety of police officers, it may also reduce the potential for liability of the officers, supervisors and the agency."[108] In all these ways, legalizing accountability came to be seen as synonymous with police professionalism.

Supplementary Evidence of the Change in Police Norms

To demonstrate the liability-induced institutional sea change in policing, I have focused here especially on articles and opinion pieces in the IACP's official magazine *Police Chief*. Other sources confirm that police norms shifted dramatically in the period after 1980.

A simple illustration is the nature of advertisements in *Police Chief*. In some respects advertisements, responsive as they are to the market, illustrate better than articles the implicit norms of the profession. Thus, recall that in 1967 two prominent articles in *Police Chief* had condemned the "fleeing felon" rule—and, along with it, the then common practice of shooting at fleeing vehicles. But accompanying those articles, ironically, was a full-page advertisement for a shotgun described as ideal for shooting at fleeing vehicles during police chases. After 1980, however, commercial advertisements increasingly marketed very specific programs associated with the legalized accountability model. The September 1985 issue, for instance, carried an advertisement for a training film on the use of deadly force (graphically depicting a hooded skeleton aiming a pistol at the reader and asking, "Is your Department prepared for the proper use of . . . DEADLY FORCE?"). A 1991 two-page advertisement—touting a private firm's "comprehensive and professional" training program as a means to minimize liability—featured on the first page a scowling judge with gavel in hand, and, on the other, the headline "Do You Have Any Idea How Much a Suit Costs These Days?"[109] Markel Service, a liability insurance carrier, ran numerous advertisements in *Police Chief* during the 1980s and 1990s. An ad from 1991, for instance, focused on the firm's "loss control" efforts, consisting of training programs and consultation aimed at minimizing liability.[110] I cannot do justice here to the growing number of advertisements in the 1980s and 1990s on the subject of liability and preventive programs.

Additionally, after 1980 police management texts changed considerably, in keeping with the patterns described above. O. W. Wilson's foundational text *Police Administration*, as Walker has noted, dramatically shifted its emphasis.[111] Throughout all its editions through the fourth, published in 1977 (with the addition of a second author, Roy McLaren, a former professional staffer at the IACP), this classic text reflected the traditional professional agenda.[112] Although the fourth edition recommended that larger departments employ a legal adviser, there was no discussion of the threat of legal liability.[113] Further, although it emphasized that police abuses must be checked to prevent riots, it provided no specific guidance on how to do so.[114] Moreover, the 1977 edition repeated Wilson's detailed description of ideal police firearms but, like earlier editions, contained no discussion of appropriate limits on when to shoot or on other uses of force.[115] By contrast, the fifth edition, thoroughly rewritten by a team of scholars led by James Fyfe and published in 1997, gave pride of place to the new norm of legalized accountability.[116] Unlike earlier editions, it contained a new opening chapter frankly describing the "storm of change" around policing in the 1960s and 1970s and new chapters on discipline, police misconduct, and standards and accountability, with a specific focus on law and legal controls over the police.[117] Unlike earlier editions, the fifth contained discussions of police policies for regulating the use of force; moreover, these were extensive and detailed.[118] And, unlike earlier editions (which contained no discussions of judicial decisions or legal controls on the police), the fifth contained extensive discussions of legal liability and the consequent need for clear, detailed rules, training, and internal oversight governing uses of force.[119] Thus the authors observed that "jurors in civil suits invariably ask: Why even have a policy on use of deadly force (or any other sensitive police problem), if it is not put to use or enforced when officers use deadly force?"[120] The authors recommended that departments do the following, and they followed this summary with a detailed discussion of each area:

1. Establish policies that guide the most critical decisions made by . . . personnel.
2. Make sure that personnel are trained in what these policies mean and how to apply them.
3. Hold personnel accountable for abiding by policy.
4. Continually review policies to ensure that they are responsive to community needs and that they hold personnel properly accountable.[121]

Swanson, Territo, and Taylor's *Police Administration*, first published in 1983, devoted an entire chapter to legal liability from its first edition onward, and the tenor became increasingly concerned about liability and increasingly specific in its recommendations for departmental reforms.[122] In the first edition, the authors reported that police concern with liability was widespread, but they judged it to be somewhat exaggerated; still, they acknowledged a significant growth in lawsuits in federal court, particularly seeking to establish departmental liability.[123] They thus recommended adopting departmental regulations governing discharge of weapons, but they hedged, declaring that it would be "difficult" to write and apply these with "precision."[124] By the 1990s the authors, reporting a "major trend" (third edition, 1993) and "enormous increase" (fourth edition, 1998) in constitutional tort litigation, recommended clear policies governing uses of force, training in these policies, and forceful supervision and discipline the ensure compliance.[125]

Thibault, Lynch, and McBride's *Proactive Police Management*, first published in 1985, incorporated discussions of civil liability from its inception, but these became more detailed and focused over subsequent editions.[126] In the first edition, the authors referred to civil liability in recommending that departments hire legal advisers and devote considerable attention to officer training; introducing the section on officer training, they observed that failure to adequately train officers could lead to incidents resulting in "bad publicity" and lawsuits.[127] Subsequent editions repeated these themes but with greater emphasis and detail. Thus these editions summarized a number of cases in which courts held departments liable for training deficiencies that contributed to misconduct and injuries or death, observing that "*proactive police managers need to realize that their police agencies, municipalities, and even individual employees may be sued and that issues in relation to training may very well be raised.*"[128] They offered specific recommendations, among them tailoring training to departmental policies and continually updating these in light of liability decisions ("a saying for instructors that comes especially true in tort cases is: 'Do not laminate your lesson plans, for they will probably become obsolete next year!'").[129]

Finally, Whisenand and Ferguson's *Managing of Police Organizations*, an introductory text, underwent a similar transition. While its first edition in 1973 devoted no attention to the issues of police misconduct and excessive use of force, beginning with its second edition (1978) the text has devoted an entire chapter to the issue, and the discussion has become more legally informed over time.[130]

Additionally, legal guides written for the police began appearing in the mid-1970s, and these provide another indicator of the transformation in professional norms. Apart from the guides and training offered by Americans for Effective Law Enforcement, which I have already referred to, the earliest legal guide for the police was written by trainers for the state of North Carolina's police training academy and published in 1978.[131] The authors observed that "until recent years law enforcement officials had little reason for concern" about liability, but that the number of lawsuits against the police "has increased to an alarming figure" and "the threat of liability hangs over the head of every law enforcement officer."[132] The guide surveyed a range of causes of action against police officers and departments, providing a brief summary of case law in each area and assessing the areas of greatest liability concern. Thus the authors identified particular problem areas as lawsuits alleging brutality (resulting in awards as high as $3 million) and wrongful death (resulting in no fewer than ten settlements over $1 million in 1973 alone).[133] Additionally, the guide reported that for commanding officers "the most serious recent trend . . . has been the successful attempts of plaintiffs to tie in police chiefs and administrators" for liability over the actions of subordinates, and the authors summarized growing threats in the areas of negligent employment of an unfit officer, negligent retention, failure to properly train, and failure to give proper directives, among others.[134] Liability lawsuits, the authors reported, were sending an increasingly clear message: departments must reform their policies, training, and internal oversight. Thus clear written policies are "imperative," and "the best, and perhaps only, prevention of vicarious liability is to prevent misconduct on the bottom levels, which . . . entails conscientious and careful selection, training, retention and appointment of all subordinate officers."[135] In short, "almost like the owner of a bad dog, a police chief retains a known unfit officer at his peril."[136]

Similarly, a police legal guide published in 1982 by Northwestern University's Traffic Institute, a research institute serving police agencies, provided a detailed summary of case law on police civil liability and concluded that "the key to success in avoiding civil liability is training, guidance, supervision and discipline."[137] Further, the guide warned that police civil liabilities were "in a state of expansion . . . as they have been for the past decade" and that departments should keep abreast of these changes.[138]

Victor E. Kappeler's more recent, sophisticated text is equally forceful in describing an "explosion" of lawsuits against the police and in recommending clear policies regulating uses of force and training and oversight tailored to those policies.[139] Thus, in his first edition he observed that "innovative police executives will have a substantial advantage over those who are less inclined toward change. As the courts recognize the necessity for change, those agencies who do not conform will find themselves in a liability quandary" generated by the heightened professional standards adopted by more "innovative" departments as "policy and procedures that were acceptable in the past will become legally obsolete."[140]

Finally, as Samuel Walker has observed, by the mid-1990s the Justice Department, in "pattern or practice" lawsuits against several scandal-ridden police departments and consent agreements obtained in those cases, was officially favoring systemic departmental reforms in the form of rules governing uses of force, training tailored to these rules, and systematic internal oversight focusing on use of force reporting, supervisory review, and early warning systems.[141] Walker labeled the Justice Department's position "the new paradigm of police accountability."[142]

Conclusion

In the 1980s law-based reform in the form of legalized accountability swept American policing. At the outset of the period the International Association of Chiefs of Police resoundingly rejected a principal element of the reform proposal, rule-based restrictions on police shootings. In 1985, in an abrupt reversal, the Association supported and celebrated the Supreme Court's decision in *Tennessee v. Garner* favoring such reforms. By the early 1990s, legalized accountability had become a badge of honor, the symbol of police professionalism.

Those favoring a profession-centered understanding of the history told here might argue that *Police Chief*'s reform proposals amounted to little more than old, pat professional techniques, and perhaps even that liability was little more than a trumped-up rationale for these ideas. The evidence that, relative to their overall budgets, cities never really lost significant amounts of money in legal damages might seem to support such an interpretation.[143]

But the idea that liability is merely a post hoc rationalization for what professionals wanted from the start ultimately is unsustainable. Between 1978 and 1982, the legal liability message in *Police Chief* reached full volume, and writers seemed genuinely alarmed by the shift in the liability climate. Moreover, *Police Chief*'s growing attention to legal liability *preceded* the IACP leadership's conversion to the administrative legalization reform agenda by at least four years. Not only did the IACP not officially support any aspect of that reform agenda until at least 1982, its leaders actively *opposed* it for much of that period. As late as 1984, the organization did not join the Police Foundation's amicus brief favoring the reform agenda in *Tennessee v. Garner*.

The Police Foundation, of course, had long argued in favor of legalizing accountability. By the early 1980s these two versions of police professionalism—the Police Foundation's legalized version and the IACP's traditional one—vied to represent and control the police mainstream. By the late 1980s the legalized version of police professionalism had won. Even the IACP's *Police Chief* begin to express pride in the new police professionalism—the "advances in training, management and administration" celebrated by an author in 1993—emerging out of the Police Foundation campaign and in response to legal liability.[144] "Seldom is change accepted quietly, however, especially in law enforcement," that author reflected, where reforms "unfortunately" result only from judicial mandates or "the looming threat of liability."[145]

6

Spreading the Word:
Variations among Police Departments

If legalized accountability has become the new professional standard, to what extent have police departments followed this norm? Is it followed by only a few—in the big or liberal cities—or by many? If many follow it, are they doing so merely with fine-sounding policies or with a deeper, searching effort to change their working cultures and practices? Are legalized policies and procedures substitutes for concrete efforts at controlling abuses, or do they contribute to such efforts? If departments vary in their commitment to legalized accountability, what explains these differences? Why are some departments more than others committed to addressing abuses with legalized checks?

Using an original survey of United States police departments, this chapter addresses these questions in two ways. One is by examining how widely departments have adopted the various elements of legalized accountability and have taken steps to retrain, discipline, or dismiss officers who engage in problem behavior. I pay particular attention to variations in policy adoption ranging from the model's most visible or surface elements (like official rules) down to its more intrusive and costly elements, among them diverse methods of training and searching systems of internal oversight, as well as variations in disciplinary actions ranging from doing nothing, at one extreme, to dismissing problem officers at the other.

Second, this chapter examines the underlying conditions that contribute to differences among departments. My analyses sort out the independent impact of a range of factors, among them local infrastructures of support for police misconduct litigation, departmental connections to professional networks, the formal law, and a host of organizational and demographic variables.

My analyses yield three general observations. First, virtually all police departments have adopted elements of legalized accountability, particularly its most visible (and potentially symbolic) aspects, supporting my contention that this model is the new administrative standard and that few departments are willing to appear out of step with it. Second, however, police departments vary considerably in how fully they have adopted the model's elements. While virtually all have adopted its most visible elements, some go no further than this. Others, however, have adopted all or virtually all of the model's elements down to its most intrusive and searching components. Similarly, while some departments have taken no steps to require retraining, to discipline, or to dismiss officers over misconduct, others have taken all these steps. I find, further, that systems of legalized accountability contribute to rather than detract from ongoing departmental efforts to correct officers' misconduct. Third, variations in departments' commitment to legalized accountability are best explained by variations in the presence of local infrastructures of support for police misconduct litigation (activists and lawyers) and in the strength of departments' connections to professional networks.

As far as possible, I have tried to make this chapter accessible to general readers; those interested in more detail on the survey and my statistical methodology may turn to the book's methodological appendix.

The basis for my analysis is a survey conducted in 2000 of 838 police departments drawn from a stratified random sample of United States cities, supplemented by data taken from a variety of other sources. I asked detailed questions about departments' internal policies, procedures, and practices and about their organizational characteristics and local environments. Although there have been several surveys of police departments regarding their policies and procedures, none before mine has covered all the elements of the legalized accountability model; assessed variations in the depth of its adoption ranging from its more visible, surface elements to its more searching, hidden elements; and tested alternative explanations for these variations.[1] My survey questions focused on critical indicators of the depth of departmental policy and procedure, perceptions of the local legal environment, and the strength of connection to professional networks, among other things to be reported below.

My research design for this chapter is cross-sectional rather than diachronic; it does not make use of event history analysis, as is now common in studies of policy diffusion. I adopted this cross-sectional design because data for the three concepts that are central to my theory—how far departments have adopted the elements of the legalized accountability model, the extent of local support structures for litigation, and the extent of agency connections to professional networks—are for the most part impossible to gather for periods in the past. The resulting cross-sectional design obviously represents a trade-off: it cannot capture the dynamics of policy diffusion over time, but it can assess the depth of legalized accountability procedures and the possible influence of factors for which time-based data cannot be gathered and thus that event history analysis cannot assess. I believe the trade-off is merited by the richness of the resulting data: my data on the three key factors are arguably richer than those obtained by any previous study.

How Departments Vary in Commitment to Legalizing Accountability

How widely have police departments adopted key elements of the legalized accountability model, and how much do they vary in their level of commitment to this model? The basic answer is that departments have widely adopted especially visible policies but have less widely adopted internal or hidden procedures and practices, particularly those that intrude significantly on police discretion. Thus, virtually all departments have adopted written rules regulating most types of the use of force, but departments less commonly have incorporated ongoing internal legal consultation. I will shortly summarize the data on each dimension of legalized accountability. First, however, the basic pattern may be illustrated by transposing the various elements of the legalized accountability model to be reported below onto a ten-point scale and arranging them in order from those most widely adopted or used to those least widely adopted or used (see fig. 6.1).[2] The least widely adopted innovation, as the figure illustrates, is the citizen review board; as I noted above, it is the only component that remains widely opposed in professional police circles. Nonetheless, citizen review boards are equally widely favored by external activists, and Samuel Walker characterizes citizen review as part of a comprehensive approach to police accountability.[3]

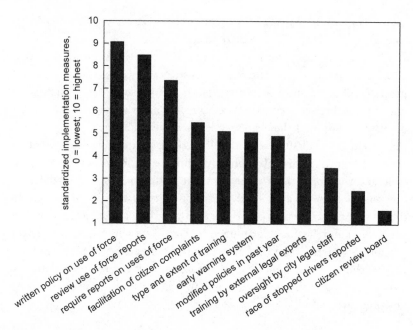

Figure 6.1. Police use of force policies and procedures, extent of adoption by city.
$N = 796$–835. See accompanying text and methodological appendix for discussion.

These patterns in figure 6.1 may be illustrated with examples of representative police departments drawn from my survey. The cities of Tradition, Middling, and Legality (not their real names, of course) have much in common except for sharp differences in their police departments' levels of commitment to legalized accountability. None is in the South, each is relatively close to an urban area but is an independent city of some tens of thousands. But the Tradition police department has adopted relatively few elements of legalized accountability, the Middling department has adopted about the average (mean) number, and the Legality department has adopted relatively many.[4] Specifically, all three, not surprisingly, have written policies regulating the use of less than lethal force; such policies are so common that they no longer mark significant distinctions among departments. But with regard to more demanding elements of the legalized accountability model, the departments differ significantly. The Tradition department provides training on key issues to experienced officers only at intervals of thirteen months or more; the Middling department provides training on some issues at relatively long intervals and for other key issues at shorter intervals; and the Legality department, the one most committed to legalized accountability, provides training on most key issues at intervals of less than a year. Similarly, on the crucial issue of internal oversight, Tradition, the least committed to legalized accountability, requires officers to report uses of nonlethal force only when injuries result, while the other two departments require officers to report all uses of force even if no injury occurs. Likewise, Tradition does not generally conduct internal reviews of officers' use of force reports, while both other departments conduct such reviews of all use of force reports. Punctuating these differences at the most general level, the Tradition and Middling departments neither have an early warning system nor plan to adopt one, while the Legality department employs such a system.

These differences among police departments matter. Critics of the police have long claimed that departments tend to adopt fine-sounding policies regulating the use of force but do little to implement and enforce them. It is no great stretch to observe that the Tradition department may well fit that characterization: it has specific policies governing less than lethal force yet requires officers to report only some such uses of force; further, the department reviews only some of these reported instances. The Legality department, by contrast, seems to fit the model of legalized accountability: it has policies governing less than lethal force, conducts regular in-service training in those policies for experienced officers, requires reports on all uses of force and reviews all of those incidents, and has implemented an early warning system for identifying problem patterns in officer behavior. This last department seems to closely follow professional recommendations regarding appropriate administrative systems for controlling officers' uses of force.

Rules

How widely have police departments adopted specific rules governing different types of force? As we have seen, the dominant professional model by 2000 favored specific rules addressing different levels of force, ranging from very low levels up to lethal force, rather than a single general policy covering all such types. But as we have also seen, several studies in the late 1970s reported that some departments had taken tentative steps to formalize rules governing the use of deadly force, but most had not done so, and in those that had, the rules remained haphazard, disorganized, and ambiguous. Since then, scholars generally agree that most departments have adopted some types of rules (particularly rules governing the use of deadly force), and studies have documented that some big-city departments have adopted comprehensive use of force rules.[5] Phoenix, for instance, has a rule governing uses of force that includes six steps, particularly No Force; Police Presence; Verbal Commands; Control and Restraint (handcuffs); Chemical Agents; Tactics and Weapons (other than chemical agents and firearms); and Firearms/Deadly Force.[6]

My survey of police departments revealed that by 2000 the vast majority had adopted written policies governing specific types of nondeadly force by their officers. Since there is little doubt that virtually all departments have policies governing the use of deadly force, my survey did not address deadly force policies but focused instead on rules governing nonlethal force. As we have seen, by 2000 the dominant professional model favored specific rules addressing different levels of nonlethal force rather than a single general policy covering all such types of force. Among 837 police departments responding to a question on whether the department had adopted specific rules governing different types of nonlethal force, only three reported that they had no written policy governing its use. And 147 departments, or just under 18 percent, reported having a written policy that provides only general rules on the proper use of force. By contrast, 686 departments (82 percent), reported having a written policy that specifically discusses particular types of nondeadly force—in other words, some sort of continuum of force policy. These observations document that by 2000 there had been a remarkable reversal of formal police policy governing the use of force: whereas in 1980 few departments had clear rules governing the use of deadly force and virtually none regulated the use of nondeadly force, by 2000 most had specific rules governing various types of nondeadly force.

Training

How extensively do departments train officers in the proper use of force and related issues? Very few systematic studies address this crucial question. In the 1960s, according to a survey by the IACP, most police officers were given no training before entering service, but by the 1990s state statutes typically required hundreds of hours of preservice training, often provided by a centralized state training academy.[7] The type of training has also changed. An old study compared training of new recruits in several cities in 1982 with the results of a 1952 study, observing that the hours of training had almost doubled over the course of those thirty years and that, though the hours devoted to firearms training had not changed, the *subject* matter of that training had changed dramatically from target practice to "decision making as to the legal circumstances of when using deadly force was justified."[8] "The most striking change in firearms training," the authors observed, "has been the concern for the moral and legal consequences of the use of deadly force."[9] Still, most policing scholars agree that on-the-job training, both formal and informal, may more greatly shape officers' behavior than preservice training, yet there is very little research on how extensively departments carry out continuing training for experienced officers and how these in-service training programs vary.

My survey aimed to assess how fully, by the year 2000, police departments carry out ongoing training of experienced officers in relation to departmental rules. The question is crucial, since formal policies may be little more than window dressing unless implemented through training that emphasizes their importance. Although state statutes generally require some training for officers, the level of ongoing training still varies considerably among departments. The survey focused on several training-related issues that may be seen as key indicators of how comprehensive a department's training regime is. These questions focus on training of experienced officers in several areas, specifically the use of a baton (a common less than lethal weapon), cultural sensitivity, and legal liability issues as well as a particular type of training technique, hands-on role-playing, that is generally regarded as more intensive and effective than more traditional training techniques.

The survey revealed significant commonalities among departments as well as some variations (see fig. 6.2). Most police departments provided training to experienced officers in the use of a baton, cultural sensitivity, and legal liability, and the majority provided role-play training; only 8 percent of departments, for instance, reported no continuing training in the use of a baton. Still, departments vary widely in *how often* they provide these types of training to experienced officers. The vast majority of departments do not provide frequent retraining in these things, measured by intervals of six months or less between training sessions; and most departments offer training in legal liability issues at longer intervals than for training in use of a baton. With regard to use of a baton, for instance, almost a third of departments reported providing such training to every experienced officer at intervals of thirteen months or more; only 108 departments, or just over 13 percent, reported providing such training to every experienced officer at least every six months. Similarly, although only 13 percent of departments reported providing no role-play training in the proper use of force to experienced officers, about a third provided such training only at intervals of thirteen months or more, and only 16 percent provided such training to experienced officers at least every six months.

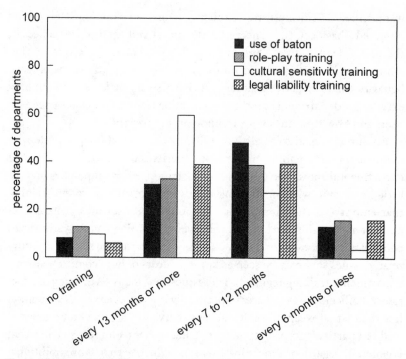

Figure 6.2. How often police departments provide key types of training to experienced officers. *N* = use of baton, 820; role-play training, 832; cultural sensitivity training, 832; legal liability training, 830.

Generally, departments seem to provide cultural sensitivity training significantly less frequently than the other types of training.

Additionally, I sought in the survey to assess how far departments provided training by external experts in legal norms. This is a crucial question: how legal norms are interpreted may vary considerably, and external legal experts may be more likely than sworn officers to emphasize the constraints imposed by law. My survey reveals considerable variation among departments in how far they provide officers with training by outside (nonpolice) legal experts. The majority (62.8 percent) provide training by a local prosecutor; less than half (42.2 percent) provide training by a member of the city's legal staff; and a much smaller proportion (20.1 percent) provide training by a law professor.[10]

These survey observations of departmental training, taken as a whole, suggest that police departments have widely implemented the professional recommendation to train, but also that commitment to training varies considerably from department to department.

Internal Oversight

As we have seen, the IACP and other professional police groups recommend a number of mechanisms of internal oversight. To what extent do police departments carry out proactive oversight over officers' actions in light of their rules and training? This is important, since oversight is arguably the bellwether of a department's commitment to restraining police misconduct. Few studies have assessed how widely police departments have adopted different kinds of internal oversight. One leading study examined adoption of early warning and intervention systems and found that by 1999 only 27 percent of police agencies in jurisdictions with over 50,000 residents had adopted this key mechanism of oversight, while another 12 percent were planning to do so.[11] Another observed that few police departments have adopted formal risk management systems.[12] How far departments carry out other kinds of internal oversight, however, has not been studied.

My survey of police departments plumbed several indicators of internal oversight within police departments to assess how widely departments have adopted *Police Chief*'s professional recommendations for searching systems of internal oversight. My survey used several measures of internal oversight: how far departments require officers to report uses of force, carry out internal reviews of these use of force reports, require officers to report the race of the driver in traffic stops, facilitate citizen complaints, and have instituted an early warning system.

One of these indicators is when departments require officers to report certain uses of force. This is a basic issue; there can be no internal oversight if officers are not required to report when they have used force against a person. A previous survey assessed departmental variations in such reporting requirements, finding that departments vary considerably in whether they require reporting of different types of force, and my survey built on this earlier observation.[13] Since virtually all departments require officers to report the use of deadly force, my survey did not ask whether departments required such reports. By contrast, whether departments require reports on lesser uses of force varies widely, and so my survey inquired about requirements to report three uses of nondeadly force, selected because they vary considerably in the likelihood of injury or pain. A high level of force is using a baton against a member of the public; it typically produces injury, ranging from a bruise to broken bones or, in extreme cases, head injuries. A medium level of force is the wristlock, a compliance technique that generates pain but typically no injuries. A lower level of force is a "firm grip,"

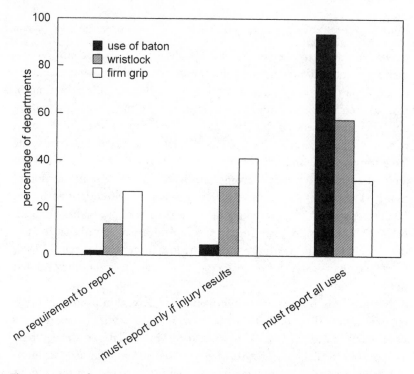

Figure 6.3. How far departments require officers to report the use of different types of force. N = use of baton, 826; wrist lock, 814; firm grip, 824.

a compliance technique that involves grasping someone's arm to gain attention but typically produces neither injuries nor pain. Departments vary considerably in how far they require officers to report these uses of force (see fig. 6.3). Almost all (94 percent) require officers to report any use of a high-level force technique, the baton; by contrast, only 58 percent require officers to report any use of a medium-level force technique, the wristlock, and an even smaller proportion, 32 percent, require them to report any use of a lower-level force technique, the firm grip. Further, how far officers are required to report uses of force and the extent of supervisory review are *positively* rather than inversely correlated: departments that require more thorough reporting also tend to carry out more extensive supervisory review of these reports.[14] These observations confirm that, while most departments carry out internal oversight over high-level uses of force, fewer departments do so over lower-level uses of force.

Additionally, in the context of growing concern over racial disparities in traffic stops, my survey assessed whether police departments require officers to report the race of the driver in all vehicle stops. Many departments have policies prohibiting "racial profiling," but such policies may be merely symbolic if not backed up by efforts to compare the records of individual officers to identify whether any are stopping racial minorities at exceptional rates. My survey reveals that police departments in 2000 varied considerably in whether they require their officers to report the race of the driver in vehicle stops. Only a small proportion of departments (18.9 percent) required such reports, and an additional 12.4 percent reported that such a policy was in the planning stages; but a majority, 68.8, reported that they neither required such reports nor planned to do so.[15]

My survey also plumbed how widely departments review officers' uses of force. In systems of legalized accountability, officers' reports of the use of force are theoretically only the start of a process of internal review in which superior officers evaluate uses of force to assess whether frontline officers are abiding by departmental policies.[16] Yet departments vary in whether superior officers review their subordinates' use of force reports. Virtually all can be expected to review a use of force report if a complaint or lawsuit is filed over the incident, and so my survey inquired how widely departments regularly review reports even if no complaint or lawsuit is filed. While most (76.9 report) report that they review all such reports, significant proportions acknowledge that they review only selected use of force reports (16.3 percent of departments) or generally do not review such reports (6.8 percent).[17]

In addition to officers' reports on uses of force, citizen complaints are a useful indicator to police supervisors of whether an officer or a unit is abusive; these complaints may be crucial if an officer is falsifying his or her reports. Yet departments vary widely in how far they facilitate citizen complaints, and my survey sought to assess these variations as an indicator of departments' commitment to using complaints as a means of internal oversight. Undoubtedly the demeanor of the official who initially receives complaints is among the most important influences on whether members of the public feel comfortable filing a complaint; unfortunately it cannot be measured with a survey method. But departments also widely adopt formal requirements for filing complaints that may signal their openness to receiving them. The majority of departments (64.7 percent) require a person filing a complaint at least to sign it; a very substantial proportion (25.8 percent) go further, requiring a person to certify, notarize, or swear to the complaint—steps that may discourage some people.[18]

Departments also vary considerably in whether they have a formal early warning system for identifying officers who may be in need of retraining, counseling, or discipline. By the time of my survey, in late 2000, almost half of departments (46.2 percent) reported having such a system in place, and an additional 9.1 percent reported that one was in the planning stages; but almost as large a proportion (44.8 percent), reported that they neither had such a system nor planned to institute one.[19] Still, this level of adoption is considerably higher than the 27 percent of departments that reported adopting such systems in 1999.[20]

Departments also vary considerably in how far they are subject to ongoing external oversight, and my survey sought to examine several forms of this oversight. A crucial form of external oversight is ongoing communication between police departments and city legal staff outside the department (other than prosecutors); legal staff offer perspectives on the law that are independent of the police view of things. My survey revealed wide variation in the extent of these communications: only a very small proportion of departments communicate with city legal staff daily or weekly, while at the other extreme a small but significant proportion (17.2 percent) never or almost never do so; the bulk of departments engage in such communications only occasionally over the course of a year or more (see fig. 6.4).

Finally, critics of the police have long favored citizen oversight of the police, principally in the form of citizen review boards or, at the least, involvement of persons other than sworn officers in reviewing citizen complaints, and my survey assessed how widely departments are subjected to some form of citizen review. Police departments have generally resisted citizen review, and therefore it is not an element of the well-institutionalized legalized accountability model. Still, since external activists continue to press for it, and since other elements of legalized accountability were favored by external activists long before being adopted by police departments, we should view citizen review as an adjunct to legalized accountability, neither fully part of the model nor wholly separate.[21] My survey confirms earlier reports that only a small proportion of departments are subject to citizen oversight: 14.5 percent are subject to citizen review boards, while 17.9 percent involve nonsworn officers in the review process.[22]

How widely do departments impose discipline or retraining to address the problems of abuse and excessive use of force? Although some leading scholars have argued that the accountability mechanisms discussed above are in fact elements of a comprehensive program to do just that, skeptics might reasonably ask, But are these policies a substitute for action? For activist critics of the police and police reformers alike, a key measure of

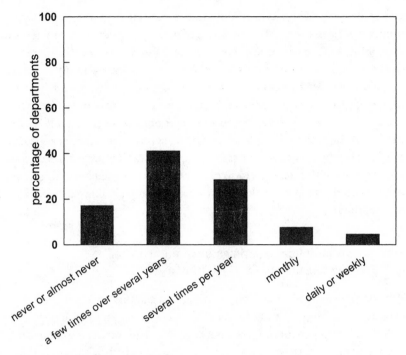

Figure 6.4. Frequency of communication between police departments and city legal staff (other than prosecutors). $N = 830$.

doing something is how far departments take steps to retrain, discipline, or dismiss officers with questionable records. My survey asked departments whether they had taken any of a number of such steps in cases of excessive use of force in the past year. On a scale of increasing intervention, 27 percent had given an officer an oral reprimand; 35 percent had given a written reprimand; 44 percent had required an officer to undergo counseling or retraining; and 13 percent had fired an officer. Almost half of the departments (49 percent), however, had done none of these things in the previous year. Obviously, whether any of these steps are taken depends to some extent on whether there is a problem; but it is hard to believe that half of police departments truly have experienced no problem with excessive use of force over the course of a year.

In sum, with regard to adoption of legalized accountability and corrective steps with regard to individual officers, my survey reveals both substantial commonalities among police departments and significant variations. Virtually all departments have adopted the most prominent and visible elements of legalized accountability, particularly written rules governing the use of force and some forms of internal reporting and review of uses of force. As mechanisms of legalized accountability become more intrusive or hidden (or both), however, they are less widely adopted. Thus, relatively few departments engage in ongoing communication with city legal staff, carry out frequent and ongoing hands-on training of experienced officers in how to avoid improper uses of force, or have a full-blown early warning system. Even fewer are overseen by a citizen review board. Finally, although half of departments reported taking some sorts of corrective steps with regard to individual officers over the course of a year, half reported taking no such steps, even the relatively limited step of an oral reprimand.

Why Are Some Police Departments More Committed to Legalizing Accountability Than Others?

Why do police departments vary so greatly in their commitment to legalizing accountability? Why have some taken corrective steps with regard to individual officers while others have not? Are these variations haphazard and random, or do they grow systematically from identifiable conditions? If they grow from particular conditions, what are these conditions, and are they open to deliberate influence, particularly from outside police departments?

It is my thesis that variations among police departments are shaped, especially, by the relative strength of the local infrastructure of support for rights—the civil liberties bar and activist groups—and of departmental connections to professional policing networks. Activist pressure from the outside and reformist professionals from the inside—the two factors that initially combined to generate the revolution in policing—continue to drive the diffusion of legalized accountability among individual departments. In this section I provide support for this claim through statistical analyses of variations among police departments.

My analysis takes into account both my own thesis and several possible alternative explanations suggested by past research. Here I briefly summarize my measures of the dependent variables and the alternative explanations. A more complete discussion of these hypotheses and measures may be found in the methodological appendix. Throughout, I rely on ordinary least squares regression with robust standard errors (clustered by state), a simple and acceptable method for assessing these alternative hypotheses.

The Dependent Variables: Legalized Accountability and Corrective Actions

My measure of departments' adoption of legalized accountability is an additive index of the elements of legalized accountability illustrated in figure 6.1 and described in more detail in the pages following that figure. Factor analysis of the components of the index (using the principal factors method) confirms that it consists of a single primary factor, providing statistical support for my claim that this is a common policy model.[23] My measure of departments' corrective actions with regard to individual officers consists of an additive index of the steps described above (oral reprimand, written reprimand, requiring retraining or counseling, and dismissal).[24]

The Independent Variables

The Local Support Structure for Litigation on Police Misconduct

I expect that the stronger the local support structure for litigation, the more extensively departments will have adopted the elements of legalized accountability. These local support structures are instances of the spread throughout the country of police misconduct attorneys and citizens' groups working against police brutality, as documented in the previous chapters. Their strength varies considerably from place to place. I rely on two measures of the local support structure: a report by the police chief of the number of citizen groups working on police brutality issues and the number of local attorneys willing to bring lawsuits against the police (combined into a single index); and an independent, objective measure of the number of government liability attorneys in the local jurisdiction, obtained from the Martindale-Hubbell database of lawyers at the time of the survey.[25]

Police Department Connections to Professional Networks

I expect that the stronger a department's professional connections, the greater will be its adoption of elements of legalized accountability. I measured these connections with two survey questions. The first is an assessment by each department's police chief of how far departmental policy changes are influenced by professional guidance provided by the IACP. The second is the chief's report of whether the department employs a sworn officer who is a lawyer; these officers are typically the department's legal advisers.

Organizational Characteristics

Following a long line of research on bureaucratic organizations, we might expect that particular organizational characteristics will affect how widely police departments have adopted elements of legalized accountability. Among these, *size* is the most prominent. In keeping with the dominant line of research on bureaucratic organizations, I expect that the larger a police department, the greater will be its adoption of elements of legalized accountability.[26] Larger organizations are thought to need more rules to function than smaller organizations and to be more exposed to pressure from their environments, and therefore larger police departments might be expected to have adopted more of the elements of legalized accountability than smaller departments. I measure size by the population of the jurisdiction and the police chief's report of the number of sworn officers in the department; since these are closely correlated and the population data are independent of the survey, my analyses rely on the independent population data. Additionally, I expect that police departments in city governments with *reformed* (council-manager) administrative structures that place administrative responsibilities in a professional manager will have adopted more elements of legalized accountability than those with unreformed structures (which give administrative control to a popularly elected mayor). My measure of whether cities have a reformed structure is drawn from the ICMA database on cities. Additionally, I expect that the greater the presence of a police *union* in a department, the less it will have adopted elements of legalized accountability (since these unions are known to oppose legalized checks). My measure of unionization is drawn from a survey question. Additionally, I expect that *liability insurance coverage* will be associated with higher levels of adopting legalized accountability. Insurance companies are known to press their organizational clients to adopt policies aimed at reducing their exposure to legal liability. I measure insurance coverage by a survey question. Finally, I expect that the more adequate the department's *budget* to its needs, the more it will adopt elements of legalized accountability. This is so because budgetary slack makes adopting costly policies possible. My measure of relative budget adequacy is a survey question.

The Formal Legal Environment

I expect that the more liberal the laws and judges in a jurisdiction, the greater will be departments' adoption of elements of legalized accountability. I measure the formal legal environment in three ways: the relative liberalism of the appellate circuit courts on the issue of government immunity from lawsuits, by appellate circuit (using a measure drawn from Donald Songer's U.S. Courts of Appeals Data Base); the relative liberalism of the state supreme courts, by state (using Brace, Langer, and Hall's measure of state supreme court liberalism);[27] and the relative liberalism of the government immunity laws of the states, by state, which I coded from the fifty states' statutes.

Political Culture

State political culture is generally found to influence state policies, and accordingly some might expect local bureaucratic policies to be influenced by the surrounding political culture. Thus we might expect that the more liberal the political culture around a department, the more it will adopt elements of legalized accountability. I rely here on Erikson, Wright, and McIver's measure of state political preferences; as alternatives to this valuable measure, I substituted, but do not report here, models including other well-known measures, among them those of Putnam.[28]

Experience with Litigation

In addition to local support structures, particular lawsuits against cities, of course, are perhaps the most visible sort of localized liability pressure, but it is important not to overstate their significance. Even if a city has never been sued over excessive use of force by the police, for instance, its officials may justifiably perceive that such a suit is a real possibility (especially if they fall far below professional norms). Moreover, not all lawsuits are equal—some are justifiably regarded as either frivolous or lacking in sufficient backing to be carried far—and forms of liability pressure such as a lawsuit threat from a city's leading civil rights litigator probably outweigh ordinary lawsuits. In other words, we might expect that how widely agencies have adopted the legalized accountability model is shaped more by the relative availability of a local support structure than by whether the city has been sued or has lost a suit. Nonetheless, experience with being sued seems so closely associated with liability pressure that it obviously should be measured and tested. With regard to the number of lawsuits filed against each department, my survey pretests indicated that respondents were unable or unwilling to report the precise number of such suits per year. Thus I adopted a set of simpler indicators of organizational experience with litigation, summed to form an "organizational experience with litigation index":

- Whether any lawsuits over police misconduct have ever been filed against the city
- Whether the city settled any such lawsuit in the previous five years
- Whether the city lost any such lawsuit in court in the previous five years

The Demographic Context

In addition to the factors above, I controlled for a variety of demographic factors: crime rates, the wealth, racial composition, and education level of the local population, and proximity to a major city. More detailed discussion of these variables is found in the appendix.

Results

Among these various factors, how widely departments have adopted the legalized accountability model is associated most powerfully with two forces—the relative vibrancy of local support structures for police misconduct litigation, and how closely departments are connected to broader professional police networks (and employ internal legal advisers). The stronger local support structures for police misconduct litigation, the more extensively police departments have adopted elements of the legalized accountability model. Likewise, the more closely connected departments are to broader professional networks in policing, the more extensively have they adopted elements of that model. Among the hundreds of cities in my database, these two factors—support structures and professional networks—remain significant even when controlling for every other plausible influence. Additionally, these two factors are more influential than any of the other possible factors. In particular, how widely police departments have adopted the legalized accountability model is *wholly unrelated* to whether they have been sued. It is not *being* sued that matters as much as the messages and knowledge conveyed by networks of plaintiffs' attorneys and administrative professionals.

These observations are illustrated by figure 6.5, which reports the extent of departmental adoption of the legalized accountability model to be expected for cities with weak and strong local support structures for police misconduct litigation, weak and strong connections to broader professional networks, and other significant factors. (The statistical technique

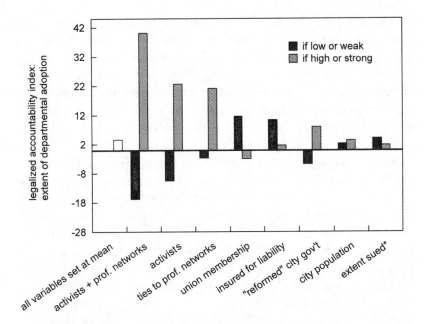

Figure 6.5. Factors explaining police departments' adoption of the legalized account-ability model. *Indicates that relationship is not statistically significant. The figure's y-axis runs from the twenty-fifth to the seventy-fifth percentile on the dependent variable, the legalized accountability index. Results obtained using Monte Carlo simulations derived with the Clarify application in Stata.

used here is Monte Carlo simulation, based on estimates derived from multivariate analysis of the data. The full results of the multivariate model are reported in the methodological appendix.) The legalized accountability index, as noted above, runs from −1.59 to 1.20; the range reported in the figure runs from the twenty-fifth to the seventy-fifth percentile on that scale (thus from −.28 to .45). Holding all independent variables at their mean would result in a policy score slightly above the mean of the index. A shift in the local infrastructure of support for rights litigation from non-existent (the most common situation) to strong (e.g., the seventy-fifth percentile on my measures of the support structure), holding all other factors equal at their means, results in a substantial shift on the policy index from roughly −.10 to .23.[29] Similarly, a shift in the strength of police departments' professional connections from weak to strong (twenty-fifth to seventy-fifth percentile on my professional connections measures, a range that is substantially similar to the range reported above for the support structure) results in a substantial shift on the policy index from

−.03 to .21.[30] A similar shift on both factors together has an even greater impact. In addition to these two primary influences, departments are likely to adopt more elements of the legalized accountability model the less their officers are unionized; if their city self-insures for police liability (rather than carrying insurance); if their city government has a "reformed" structure (a professional manager rather than a powerful mayor); and the larger the city's population (the figure illustrates the impact of a shift from the twenty-fifth to the seventy-fifth percentile on population).

These results support my thesis that legalized accountability grew from two forces: pressure from a support structure for police misconduct litigation, and reform ideas conveyed by professional policing networks. Secondarily, they support the common claims that police unionization has slowed the pace of police accountability reform, that city managerial reform contributes to these reforms, that liability insurance blunts the impact of liability pressure, and that being sued is not on its own a powerful inducer of organizational change. (These results are not necessarily the final word on the influence of liability insurance, at least during the formative period of the 1980s; in a new analysis Candace McCoy has persuasively argued that insurance companies at that time placed pressure on police departments to improve their systems of control over officers' uses of force.)[31]

Additionally, these results indicate that variations in adoption of legalized accountability are unrelated to variations in jurisdictions' level of legal liberalism (measured by statutory provisions and judicial preferences), political culture, wealth, education level, or racial demographics.

Very large police departments may be less affected by liability pressure than smaller ones. In the multivariate equations summarized here, if a dummy variable representing large departments (coded as 1 for departments in cities with populations over either 750,000 or one million) is introduced, it is negatively associated with adoption of legalized accountability (the association only approaches the conventional level of statistical significance—$p < .10$ but not $<.05$).[32] This pattern is consistent with Samuel Walker's observation that the effect of liability may be muffled in cities where there is little coordination between the department committing misconduct, the one handling legal defense, and the one paying the check—a situation especially prevalent in very large city governments.[33] In other cities, there is less fragmentation among these functions.

What factors influence departments to take corrective actions in the cases of individual officers? Further, do systems of legalized accountability contribute to, or detract from, taking these actions? Substituting my index of corrective actions as the dependent variable in the model described above, I find that, controlling for all relevant factors including city size, the extent of corrective actions is significantly greater the greater the department's experience with litigation; the stronger the local support structure for misconduct litigation; among cities in the South; among cities that do not carry liability insurance; and the weaker the presence of police unions (the latter influence approaches statistical significance only below the 0.1 level).[34] Adding the legalized accountability index as an independent variable to this equation demonstrates that *systems of legalized accountability contribute to, rather than detract from, corrective actions* (the association is below the .1 significance level, however, and thus only approaches statistical significance). The full results are reported in the appendix.

Conclusion

This chapter is the final piece in my analysis of the development and spread of legalized accountability among police departments in the United States, and I am now in a position to provide an overview of my evidence and its significance. Legalized accountability is a hybrid—at once legal and managerial—reflecting its sources in both activist and professional reformist campaigns.

At the initial level of *problem definition,* the key innovations were driven not by practicing professionals but by outside activists. Activist complaints characterized police misconduct as systemic, requiring institutional reforms, and this definition of the problem shaped all subsequent developments. As activists cultivated the right to sue police departments in federal court, their demand for institutional reforms began to influence the course of public debate, ultimately shaping news media coverage of the issue in the 1970s and 1980s to the point where the media assumed that excessive use of force was a serious problem, amenable to reform by police departments, but that departments were not fulfilling their responsibility to carry out such reforms. But long into the 1960s, practicing police professionals were deaf to the problem of police abuse.

At the level of *concrete proposals for reform,* innovations again came mainly from outside the professional mainstream. Activists defined the need—systemic, institutional reform—but lacked specific proposals for how to achieve this goal. Policing experts with extensive experience inside policing but with their feet firmly planted in legal academia provided the key policy innovations, proposing specific administrative reforms: systematic departmental policies and training and internal oversight tailored to those policies. These administrative reforms, while built on the legacy of

Progressive police professionalism, represented a sharp departure from the past. Although many departments had used rules, training, and internal oversight to bring officers into conformity with a departmental image of professionalism (embodied in the uniform), none had used these mechanisms as the reformers recommended, to control and limit uses of force. To confirm the point, mainstream police leaders initially opposed the idea.

In the *spread or diffusion* of these reforms among police departments, both activists and reformist professionals played key roles. The first major reform directed at police uses of force, as we have seen, was made in New York City in 1972 under the leadership of then police commissioner Patrick V. Murphy, a leading police accountability reformer. But before Murphy acted, he had been police commissioner for several years, and his 1972 reform was made under intense pressure from local civil rights activists in the midst of a scandal over police shootings (particularly the killing of an unarmed ten-year-old African American boy fleeing from a vehicle taken for joyriding).[35] The next major reforms, Los Angeles (in 1977) and Houston (in 1978), were made in a similar context as local activists pressed departments to reform use of force in the wake of scandals.[36] These three initiatives provided the foundation for all later use of force reforms in other cities.

In the late 1970s and early 1980s, activist campaigns ratcheted up liability pressure on police departments, and reformist professionals demonstrated, through adoption of experimental policies and research on their effects, that legalized accountability reforms worked and, further, that these reforms might enhance policing's professional legitimacy. These activist and professional influences interacted, generating further refinements in the mechanisms of legalized accountability and ever-increasing pressure on departments to keep up with what had become an evolving professional standard. Expert witnesses who had extensive background within policing provided courts and juries an unprecedented window into a previously hidden world. Police departments found themselves exposed to sharp, sustained investigation and critique, all before the eyes of the media and the public and conducted by experts with impeccable professional police credentials. As momentum tipped in favor of reform, professional leaders began frankly using the threat of liability as a justification for systemic reform. "We are being sued," as one put it, "because we are not doing our jobs." Litigation by Avery, Rudovsky, and allied attorneys alleging a departmental failure to adequately train and oversee officers became an acute threat by the early 1980s. Departments, in response, scrambled to ramp up their rule-based regulation of officers, their training, and their internal oversight. The Supreme Court, in the context of sustained litigation campaigns, contributed landmark decisions affirming rules limiting uses of force and holding that failure to adequately train could give rise to departmental liability. Under these influences American policing underwent a fundamental revolution.

Both activist pressure and professional reform networks continue to shape variations among police departments. Indeed, how widely departments have adopted legalized accountability, as my statistical analyses demonstrate, grows more from these two factors than from any other, including the provisions of the law and the preferences of judges.

The threat of legal liability (as a threat to police legitimacy) and the legalized accountability model are now joined at the hip. As a writer in the IACP publication *Police Chief* put it in 1993,

> We must ensure that all force issues are clearly defined by policy, that our personnel have been thoroughly trained in the proper use of force, that they are constantly supervised in their use of force and, lastly, that they are consistently disciplined when force is misused.
>
> The cost of failure to properly implement just one of these four key areas is certain to be expensive, entailing a loss of public faith in your department, lower morale among your people, monetary losses through lawsuits and civil claims and—most importantly—the pain and suffering that comes from the abuse of the use of force and the subsequent legal proceedings.[37]

Tort Liability and Police Reform in Britain

7

"A High Court jury yesterday awarded record damages of £100,000 to a man who had cannabis planted on him by a police officer," a London newspaper reported in 1989.

> The sum is nearly eight times the previous highest award in a case of this kind, and highest ever against the police. Mr. Rupert Taylor, aged 30, a BBC motor engineer, lay preacher, teetotaler and non-smoker, was arrested and planted with the drug by PC David Judd on his way to play dominos with a friend at a community centre in Notting Hill, west London. He told the court PC Judd had radically [*sic*] abused him saying, "You had to open your fucking black mouth."[1]

Although such a report might seem unremarkable in an American city, in Britain in the 1980s it was stunning. It was centered in a poor London ghetto long the subject of lurid press reports of "black" muggings and riots, often portrayed as contained only by heroic police action. Yet in contrast to earlier depictions, the black man entangled in the criminal justice system in this story is portrayed as innocent, the police as abusive, vulgar, and racist. The difference—and, as we shall see, it was part of a radical shift in the legal terrain—lay in the endorsement of the man's story by a jury of ordinary Britons. For virtually the first time, a jury threw its sympathies wholeheartedly behind the black victim and expressed outrage against the police, punctuated by its award of £70,000 in exemplary (punitive) damages.[2] The 1989 case opened a decade of dramatically rising liability pressure on the British police.

This chapter describes the growth of tort litigation against the British police and shows that it contributed directly to two unexpected and surprising developments: media coverage calling for legalized accountability and major policy initiatives to do just that. The chapter also suggests, however, that in Britain, unlike the United States, tort litigation did not—at least not yet—contribute to full institutionalizing of these reforms. The explanation for that difference lies in two things: the British courts cut off liability pressure, and professional associations of the police never unanimously endorsed legalized accountability as did their American counterparts.

Britain provides a useful comparative perspective on law-based reform in the United States. As we saw in earlier chapters, Progressive police reformers in the United States looked wistfully to Britain for a model of police professionalism, where they saw in contrast to the partisan, corrupt, poorly managed, untrained, sometimes nonuniformed American police well-trained, smartly uniformed, efficiently managed, scrupulous, politically neutral police forces. The contrasts between the two country's police still captivate American observers.[3] In contrast to the fundamental decentralization and fragmentation of the United States policing system (into tens of thousands of local police forces), the British policing system underwent considerable consolidation and nationalization. In contrast to the United States penchant for exposing police expertise to aggressive second-guessing by lawyers and judges, the British legal community and judiciary long followed a tradition of respectful deference to the police, virtually never meddling in the decisions of police leaders or frontline officers. In all these ways, some American observers have seen an admirable model in Britain's professionally managed bobby and the deference accorded to him (and her) by that country's courts and lawyers.

But Britain is increasingly a multiracial society, and the British police have been very slow to catch up to that reality. Their model of insulated managerial professionalism showed considerable strain and gave way, albeit incompletely, to legalized accountability.

My analysis in this chapter is based on extensive interviews and documentary evidence. The centerpiece is a litigation campaign against the Metropolitan (London) Police Force in the 1980s and 1990s and its effects. I interviewed the key participants in that campaign on both the plaintiff and defense sides. These interviews, in turn, guided me to key government documents, court cases, and other documentary evidence.

My analysis also focuses on newspaper coverage, because the struggle over police reform played itself out as much in the news media as in the courtroom.

Race and the Crisis in British Policing

According to Robert Reiner, a leading scholar of British policing, since the 1950s the British police have suffered a "repeated cycle of scandal and reform" and a "permanent crisis."[4] "From a position of almost complete invincibility as a political issue," Reiner observed, "after 1959 policing became a babble of scandalous revelation, controversy and competing agendas for reform. . . . Evidence mounted of an increasing haemorrhage of public confidence in the police."[5] Although part of the problem has always been garden variety corruption, the key source of the current crisis is pervasive race discrimination by the police, resulting, as Reiner observed, in a "catastrophic deterioration of relations with the black community."[6]

In the wake of World War II, race became a significant polarizing factor in Britain, as in the United States. In both places black immigration into the cities generated increasing urban conflict; in Britain the immigrants came mainly from former British colonies, particularly the countries of South Asia and the Caribbean. Although the racial minority proportion of the British population remains small compared with that of the United States, the growth has been significant, from only 0.4 percent of the overall population in 1951 to 7.6 percent in 2001, typically growing by more than 50 percent per decade.[7] But at the same time, the British police and much of the British government remained virtually entirely white—even in communities with large minority populations—setting the stage for terrible tensions between minorities and the police.[8]

In the 1950s conservative parliamentarians began a bitter debate over the threat to British culture of "black" immigrants, setting the tone for a racially polarizing politics of immigration.[9] Whites attacked West Indian and South Asian immigrants in the Notting Hill section of London and in Nottingham in 1958, provoking a firestorm of controversy over racial minorities and "race riots." Conservative parliamentarians seized on the riots to issue dire warnings of the dangers of "undesirable immigrants."[10] Enoch Powell, a prominent Tory member of Parliament and a member of that party's shadow cabinet, in 1968 delivered a major speech warning that immigration by racial minorities threatened "a total transformation" of British society and that soon Britain would face American-style racial tensions. To head off such a future, Powell proposed restricting minority immigration and expelling many minority immigrants already in the country.[11] Although controversy forced Powell out of Tory Party leadership, other leaders and the media increasingly portrayed racial minorities as causing a host of mounting social problems.

By the 1970s Britain's racial minority populations were increasingly concentrated in urban ghettos in the major cities, where they were seen as foreigners.[12] In the deepening economic crisis of that decade, urban racial minority ghettos became, in the view of the broader culture, virtually synonymous with poverty, unemployment, disaffected youth, and street crime. Tensions between the police and black youths escalated to the point of "open 'warfare,'" according to an observer at the time, signaling "a massive breakdown in relations between the police and the black community."[13] In a foundational book titled *Policing the Crisis*, Stuart Hall and his colleagues observed that portrayals of blacks and street crime reflected an affinity in policing and the media for stories of individual irresponsibility—the black mugger attacking an elderly white widow—rather than stories of structural or systemic problems.[14] By focusing on "black muggings," Hall and his colleagues argued, the police and media created a "moral panic" about street crime as much as they reflected it. The British police, the authors demonstrated, had "structured" and "amplified" the panic by deliberately targeting areas frequented by minority youths for increased surveillance and arrest. The media further amplified and refined the image of young black men as inherently criminal.

The British police have considerably broader powers than their United States counterparts to stop and search people on the street, and in the 1970s blacks in Britain increasingly complained that they were being subjected to discriminatory and harassing searches.[15] Careful research eventually confirmed these complaints.[16] Resentment against police searches boiled over in a series of major urban riots in British cities in the late 1970s and 1980s. In 1978 an Afro-Caribbean carnival in Notting Hill, west London (the site of the 1958 "race riot"), erupted in a riot between black residents and the police, leaving ninety-five policemen injured.[17] More famously, the south London borough of Brixton, a very poor, mostly black section of London plagued by inadequate housing, high unemployment, and crime, exploded in successive days of rioting in 1981. The police had turned increasingly to heavy-handed tactics in the area, among them "Operation Swamp," which inundated the area with constables who employed street sweeps in which everybody on the street was stopped and searched. Residents' resentment erupted on the afternoon of April 13, 1981, beginning several days of disorder in which rioters engaged in running battles with the police, smashed and burned shops, and burned police vehicles, shocking the British public and the government. Similar riots exploded in 1985.

Scandals arising out of prosecutions of high-profile crimes, among them IRA bombings, also plagued the police into the 1980s. In that decade the courts released a number of people convicted of participation in IRA terrorist violence in the 1970s after public inquiries or appeals revealed their innocence.[18] The improper convictions generally were traced to police abuses, among them perjury, fabricating evidence, and extracting false confessions. In 1989 the West Midlands Serious Crime Squad, a specialist unit, was disbanded amid irrefutable evidence that its constables had engaged in an ongoing pattern of serious abuse involving perjury, physical abuse, and fabrication of evidence.[19] By the late 1980s, in sum, the British police, like their American counterparts a generation before, had compiled a record of scandal and discrimination.

The British Police System

Unlike the United States, the British system until recently has favored broad, programmatic policy reforms to the virtual exclusion of responsiveness to individual complaints. Those complaining of police insensitivity and abuse theoretically had several options for checking and reforming the police, none very attractive or effective. *No* elected body directly controls the country's police forces. In formal, legal terms, chief constables—and indeed constables in general—are "officers of the Crown" and thus have legal independence from direct control by any external agency; the common-law doctrine of "constabulary independence" declares that constables are answerable only to "the law."[20] Although "answerable to the law" might seem to imply that a primary check on police authority is judicial, traditionally even that check was largely unavailable. Until quite recently, the British courts gave the police unusually broad discretion in gathering evidence of criminality. For decades the courts' policy toward suspects' rights was captured by the "Judges' Rules," dating to 1906 and formalized in a 1964 judicial announcement.[21] Commentators widely agree that courts never applied the Judges' Rules and that the police virtually ignored them in practice.[22] Similarly, criminal prosecutions of police officers were rare, even in cases of egregious misconduct.[23] Another option, filing complaints in the official complaints process, was equally without teeth.[24]

The British government, instead, has relied on broad-based legislative reform and managerial control.[25] Instead of the judicial check used heavily in the United States, the British governing system has traditionally relied on high-level official inquiries based on research and expert consultation, and on national legislative reforms.[26] The 1960 Royal Commission on the Police, for instance, led to legislative reforms that consolidated and partially nationalized the country's police forces.[27] Under this and other nationalizing reforms, the balance of administrative power within policing, according to Reiner, has swung increasingly toward the national government in the form of the Home Office.[28]

After the Brixton riots, the government responded characteristically to the crisis by appointing a prominent retired judge, Lord Scarman, to conduct an official inquiry. He reported his conclusions in late 1981 in what is known as the Scarman Report, concluding that the riots grew out of a confluence of poor economic opportunities and poverty, on the one hand, and, on the other, growing popular resentment against heavy-handed policing techniques, particularly the excessive use of stop and search powers.[29] Significantly, he also concluded that British policing was increasingly insensitive to the effects of its policies on racial minority communities and that there was a dire need for policing reform aimed at improving relations with those communities. Scarman characterized the problem, however, primarily as a matter of controlling the behavior of a few individual police officers.[30] Although many prominent officials greeted the report warmly, scholarly observers and members of minority communities were less enthusiastic; they argued that Scarman, by characterizing the problem as one of a few "bad apples," had failed to recognize the depth of the policing problem and the extent of reforms needed to correct it.[31]

The Scarman Report, as Reiner observes, dominated the British policing agenda of the 1980s and contributed to a further nationalizing of control over policing.[32] The report led to a comprehensive legislative reform, called the Police and Criminal Evidence Act of 1984 (PACE), that enhanced national administrative oversight over the police and, for the first time in British history, seriously attempted to bring police practices under a comprehensive legal code governing police conduct.[33] The code is comparable to American court-led reforms symbolized by *Mapp*, *Gideon*, *Miranda*, and their progeny (although less defendant-friendly). PACE also created new police oversight agencies: the Police Complaints Authority had a mandate to supervise investigations into police abuses, and the Crown Prosecution Service (CPS) had a mandate to oversee police decisions to prosecute crimes.[34] PACE gave the Home Office, the Cabinet agency in charge of policing, the authority to establish Codes of Practice, among them detailed regulations of police conduct.[35] The pressures for reform in the 1980s also strengthened centralized oversight of the police, as several agencies—Her Majesty's Inspectorate of the Constabulary, an agency under the Home Secretary, the Audit Commission (an agency created in 1982), and the Association of Chief Police Officers (ACPO)—began exercising increasingly aggressive oversight of police forces.[36] For instance, in recent years ACPO has developed a number of policy guidelines that the country's forty-three police forces generally follow quite precisely.[37]

After Legislative Reform: Continuing Crisis

Although the 1980s reforms enhanced centralized managerial control over the police, at the same time they increased officers' discretionary authority to stop and search people on the street, and complaints of racially discriminatory policing increased dramatically. Police use of their stop and search powers has increased radically, from 109,800 recorded instances in 1986 to almost 750,000 in the early years of the new century.[38] As we have seen, a similarly widespread use of stops and frisks in American cities in the 1960s undoubtedly contributed to that era's urban riots. Currently, the most careful studies of racial disparities of traffic stops in the United States find that African American drivers are stopped at roughly 1.5 to 2 times (or slightly more) the rate at which white drivers are stopped.[39] In Britain, by contrast, blacks are stopped and searched fully *eight times* as often as whites, a disparity that has been increasing over time and that almost certainly is an underestimate.[40]

By the mid-1990s many observers characterized the centralized reforms of British policing in the 1980s as a failure: managerial reform had no bite.[41] Thus Philip Scraton, summarizing the numerous official reports and social scientific studies, observed that "the police habitually break the rules, commit unlawful acts before, during, and after questioning, and fabricate evidence."[42] Andrew Sanders observed that the police treatment of suspects who are poor, members of racial minorities, and young "is frequently humiliating—and deliberately so."[43] And Reiner noted that after the 1980s reforms "the socially discriminatory pattern of use of police powers remains as marked as before."[44] In frustration, many observers began calling for more litigious and judicial checks on the police. "The system is failing," as one put it, "because it is insufficiently adversarial."[45]

Litigation against the Police

Activist lawyers began supporting civil liabilities lawsuits against the police in the 1980s, and juries began responding with outrage over the abuses they revealed and handing down increasingly large damage judgments, fueling growing media attention to the issue of police misconduct.

Several features of British law facilitated lawsuits against the police. Chief constables are vicariously liable for injuries caused by their officers, something that American plaintiffs' lawyers can hope for only in their wildest dreams.[46] Additionally, although plaintiffs have no right to demand a jury trial in most types of civil cases in Britain (a fact to which some observers attribute a less adversarial mode of adjudication in Britain), through a quirk in British statutory law, plaintiffs have a right to a jury trial in the most common types of civil claims against the police.[47] This fact, as we shall see, made it possible to use the civil lawsuit as a mechanism for bringing popular outrage to bear on the police. In the story told below, organizers against police abuses typically sought to get cases before juries on the expectation that they were more likely than judges to find the police liable.[48] Additionally, until very recently the complaints and disciplinary processes of the British police were extremely inefficient and insulated from external oversight, encouraging injured individuals to pursue redress in the courts instead. Nonetheless, vicarious liability, the availability of the jury in claims against the police, and a hidebound official complaints process existed for years before litigation against the police developed much momentum.

In the 1980s, however, activist lawyers began building an infrastructure of support for such cases. Well-established solicitors' firms, particularly the noted civil liberties firm Birnberg's, provided space and resources to begin researching and bringing civil lawsuits against the police. "It wasn't a business proposition," observed Raju Bhatt, one of the pioneers, "because at the outset these cases weren't paying. . . . Without Birnberg's, this area of the law would not have gotten off the ground."[49] Additionally, in virtually every civil case brought against the police in the events described below, plaintiffs relied for financial support on legal aid. It was especially critical both because plaintiffs typically were very poor and because cases supported by legal aid are not subject to fee shifting or to the common judicial order requiring a losing party to pay the winning party's legal fees.[50]

In addition to support from solicitors' firms and legal aid, organizers against police abuses could rely on a growing body of shared knowledge about litigation against the police. Perhaps the key contribution was the publication, beginning in 1987, of several legal guides to such litigation (the first—a how-to guide for suing the police—was financed by the Greater London Council, and its publication helped to jump-start the development of a legal knowledge base for police plaintiffs).[51] In the early 1990s Graham Smith, a police accountability campaigner, and Russell Miller, a solicitor with Birnberg's, developed a database containing the names of police officers who had been implicated in civil lawsuits or whose testimony had been found by a court to be faulty.[52] As the number of lawyers bringing actions against the police increased, several joined together to form the Police Action Lawyers Group (PALG), an organization that expanded networks among police misconduct litigators and other civil liberties groups.[53]

As these resources developed, victims of police abuse increasingly turned to litigation as an accountability mechanism. A major lawsuit brought by the National Union of Miners over police misconduct at a 1984 strike (and resulting in an unprecedented judgment of £425,000 plus the plaintiffs' legal costs) jump-started the process.[54] Lawyers who worked on that case went on to apply their experience in supporting lawsuits against the police arising out of abuses in inner-city London neighborhoods.

London residents complained increasingly of police abuses by officers stationed at the Stoke Newington police station, which had a troubled history dating to the 1950s. By the late 1980s, residents of the Stoke Newington neighborhood had formed two grassroots organizations, the Roach Family Support Committee and the Trevor Monerville Campaign, calling for investigations into allegations of police abuse in two prominent incidents. In one, Colin Roach, a young black man, was found dead of a shotgun blast in the foyer of the Stoke Newington police station in January 1983.[55] In the other, police reported discovering Trevor Monerville, also a young black man, in the back seat of a car unconscious from an apparent beating.[56] In both cases, residents of the neighborhood deeply distrusted the police version of events.[57] Journalists' reports and an unofficial inquiry painted a picture of an urban area "close to [the] racial boiling point"[58] over "police harassment, wrongful arrest, uncivil conduct during home raids, misuse of stop and search powers and other abuses of Stoke Newington's residents."[59]

In 1988 the organizers of the Trevor Monerville Campaign joined with other local groups to form the Hackney Community Defence Association. The group worked closely with a number of solicitors, including Raju Bhatt, an attorney on the miners' team, who were finding "a striking similarity between cases."[60] Bhatt began to pursue civil lawsuits, he said, after representing criminal defendants in "case after case" and developing a sense of outrage "when it was clear to all that the police had abused the defendant" but nothing was done to correct the problem beyond an occasional dismissal of charges.[61] The turn to litigation, Smith concurred, was motivated by the failure of traditional mechanisms of accountability.[62] "We faced a situation in which there were literally two cases of police beatings per week in a small section of east London" and neither the police, nor the courts, nor agencies overseeing the police were doing anything to address the problem.[63]

In the late 1980s and early 1990s, damage awards and settlements in lawsuits against the police began increasing. Among the earliest significant awards was the case of Ace Kelly, a black man who alleged that he had been unjustifiably arrested and charged five times in eighteen months in 1983 and 1984, including two arrests arising out of demonstrations over the death of Colin Roach and one while he was attending the trial of another protester.[64] The Metropolitan (London) Police Force settled Kelly's civil action over false arrest in late 1988 for a reported £20,000. The next year a Stoke Newington officer, by then fired from the force, was held liable for £8,000 for extorting sexual favors from a Nigerian immigrant in exchange for not reporting her to immigration authorities.[65] In early December 1989, in the case discussed at the outset of this chapter, a jury gave a record damage award of £100,000 to a man who had been falsely arrested and charged with marijuana possession after the police had planted the drug on him.[66] By the spring of 1990, the new Hackney Community Defence Association reported that it was supporting at least six lawsuits against the police over allegations of assault and abuse, among them a case brought by Trevor Monerville's elderly grandparents alleging police harassment.[67] A journalist observed, "The incidents have aggravated already tense relations between police and the local community."[68]

In May 1990 the *Independent* newspaper published a letter from Graham Smith and Martin Walker, organizers of the Hackney Community Defence Association, arguing that the problems in policing were systemic, requiring institutional solutions. The letter was the first in a series of strategic efforts by the Association to reframe the growing public debate. Smith and Walker argued that the police were "stereotyping whole sections of society," and they called for "a complete reappraisal of the criminal justice system, most particularly the role of the police."[69]

As the Stoke Newington controversy slowly grew, a criminal case dating to the notorious killing of a policeman, Police Constable Keith

Blakelock, during the 1985 "Broadwater Farm" riot seriously undermined police credibility. The three defendants in the killing had long maintained their innocence, and an official inquiry and a BBC documentary in 1991 had supported that claim.[70] On appeal to the Court of Appeal in November 1991, the prosecution case fell apart as it became clear that police investigators' notes of alleged confessions, the sole basis for the convictions, were, as the barrister for the defense in one of the cases declared, "fabricated."[71] The Court of Appeal immediately overturned the convictions, and "in an unprecedented admission of failure, apologized" to the three falsely convicted men.[72] The case dealt a heavy blow to police legitimacy, and some observed that juries increasingly doubted the honesty of the police to the point that "it has now become difficult to secure a conviction on police evidence alone."[73]

Ongoing complaints about the Stoke Newington station expanded into a major scandal in 1992 after a drug dealer alleged that officers had accepted bribes.[74] Soon other defendants alleged that Stoke Newington officers had planted drugs on them, and, under mounting pressure from an increasingly coordinated group of defense attorneys, judges began to doubt police testimony.[75] The allegations formed the basis for Operation Jackpot, a secret internal police investigation begun in April 1991, which grew over the following year into what senior Met officers eventually called the most serious allegations of police corruption in Britain in twenty years.[76] The *Guardian* broke the story in late January 1992, reporting that the Metropolitan Police Force had transferred eight officers from the Stoke Newington station in the midst of the investigation, and observed that "a shake-up of the station is now underway."[77] The revelations rocked the police station and the neighborhood, an area, as another newspaper observed, "already boiling with anti-police sentiment and where they stage annual torch-lit marches to commemorate the deaths of alleged victims of police violence."[78]

In the wake of the revelations, the Hackney Community Defence Association reasserted its demand for institutional reform.[79] "The situation in Hackney," stated Martin Walker, a leader of the Association, "is completely and utterly out of control."[80] Graham Smith, another representative of the group, warned, "It is not good enough for Scotland Yard to move police officers to another division. There should be a full, independent public inquiry."[81] The Hackney group reported that the number of lawsuits it was supporting had grown to twenty-five.[82] At the end of March, in one such case, Marie Burke, the grandmother of Trevor Monerville, won a £50,000 damage award, marking a major victory for the group.[83] A number of lawyers who were members of the Hackney group, in coordination with their local member of Parliament, suggested that the published allegations might be only the "tip of the iceberg" and called on the government to bring in outside investigators.[84]

As public attention to the scandal increased, the Metropolitan Police suspended three Stoke Newington officers over allegations arising out of the investigation,[85] and by early July the Crown Prosecution Service was reexamining pending cases in which implicated officers had participated—but was refusing to reopen cases already resulting in convictions.[86] Ultimately it was learned that the station had secretly disbanded its entire drug investigation unit and reconstituted it with different officers.[87] The scandal reverberated through the criminal courts as well, where judges began overturning drug convictions coming out of the Stoke Newington station.[88] Then the Crown Prosecution Service offered no evidence in seventeen pending cases, effectively admitting they were tainted, and an additional seventeen cases resulted in acquittals,[89] "specifically because Stoke Newington police witnesses were found to be not credible."[90] "Something of a siege mentality has descended" on the Stoke Newington station, a journalist observed, and its chief superintendent declined requests for further interviews.[91]

As the official internal investigation dragged on through 1993, activists and even judges began to express frustration. A leak of the internal investigation's preliminary report in September 1993 revealed that criminal prosecution would be recommended against a small number of officers but that the Stoke Newington command structure would be cleared of responsibility.[92] Graham Smith, of the Hackney Community Defence Association, declared that the official investigations "have been found wanting time and time again. Maybe now there will be a judicial inquiry."[93] Similarly, Lord Taylor of the Court of Appeal complained that "'dynamite' should be put under the Police Complaints Authority" in order to induce speedier action.[94]

When the Met's investigators released a statement in early 1994 announcing the end of the inquiry and recommending prosecution of only ten officers, the Hackney group replied that this number paled in comparison with the 381 complaints it had received and the 83 lawsuits it was supporting against the police.[95] "Operation Jackpot," Graham Smith said, "has been unsatisfactory on all levels. Its terms of reference were too limited and it has taken far too long. The inquiry raises serious questions about police complaints investigations."[96] Seemingly confirming Smith's pessimistic assessment, the Crown Prosecution Service, after a delay of nearly six months, announced criminal charges against only two officers. Smith declared, "This is an insult to the community."[97]

As jury awards and settlements in cases against the police continued to grow in number and size, media coverage increasingly reflected activists' call for institutional reforms. In June 1992 the widely read London entertainment magazine *Time Out* had published a weekly article on the "Stoke Newington Scandal."[98] Mainstream newspapers soon followed with similarly critical accounts. "The illusion of a regulated, user-friendly law enforcement vanishes," a journalist for the *Independent* put it after talking with neighborhood residents.[99] "There are sullen reminders of 'bent' cops and disgruntled observations that nobody seems in a great hurry to do much about them. The allegations against the police include gratuitous violence, fabricated evidence, perjury, racism, racketeering, conspiracy, fraternizing with criminals, trafficking in drugs."[100] The day after the Crown Prosecution Service's announced prosecution of only two officers in the scandal, the *Guardian* published an extensive summary of prominent cases in which the police force had settled civil claims alleging police abuse but had taken no disciplinary action.[101] In reporting another case, brought by a bystander at a demonstration falsely arrested and assaulted by the police, the *Guardian* quoted Raju Bhatt, the man's solicitor, condemning the Met's decision to give only an informal admonishment to one of the officers and apply no discipline to the others.[102] "The way in which the authority has chosen to exercise its judgment, discretion and powers in this matter," Bhatt declared, "has done nothing to inspire any confidence."[103] The article concluded by reporting that "in 58 cases where the Metropolitan Police paid out £10,000 or more in damages, 46 resulted in no disciplinary action being taken against any officer."[104] In yet another story, the *Independent* reported "what could be one of the most embarrassing civil actions mounted against the Metropolitan Police," a case in which the police planted a weapon to justify shooting an unarmed, innocent jogger.[105] In the months following the report of the jogger lawsuit, newspapers published a growing cascade of stories about lawsuits against the police,[106] with the increasingly familiar refrain "no officers had been disciplined over the incident, no CID [internal] inquiry would be held and no apology offered."[107]

Tort lawyers won two key procedural victories in the early 1990s that contributed to the shift in media coverage. Bhatt had long sought to dignify and publicize his clients' complaints, and beginning in the late 1980s he began using a procedure drawn from libel law in which victorious libel plaintiffs issue a "statement in open court" vindicating their reputation. In

1990, in an unreported decision, a judge granted victorious police plaintiffs the right to present statements summarizing their stories of abuse.[108] Newspapers publicized such statements until the Court of Appeal in 1997 sharply limited them.[109] Additionally, in mid-July 1994 the Appellate Committee of the House of Lords issued a landmark decision (*R v Chief Constable ex parte Wiley* [1995]) granting plaintiffs access to the official evidence in internal police investigations. "Once we had access to the record," Bhatt observed, "we saw how weak was the whole investigatory process. We could show to juries [in tort cases] that the investigations were, in fact, efforts at *mitigation*, not investigation. There were instances where investigators effectively told officers how they should answer questions in order not to substantiate the complaint."[110]

In September 1995 the *Independent* published a highly unflattering portrait of the Met's responsiveness to complaints of police abuse, observing in its lead that "Scotland Yard has paid out nearly £1.5 million to settle 48 substantial court claims for assault or false imprisonment over the past two years—but has taken disciplinary action against only four officers as a result."[111] "Although dozens of police were involved in the civil actions which resulted in payments ranging from £10,000 to £550,000," the paper reported, "only one officer was cautioned, another fined and two 'given words of advice.'"[112]

In response, members of Parliament voiced concern. "It is quite remarkable that, despite these enormous payments," observed Chris Mullin, a Labour MP (a former investigative journalist and campaigner against corrupt police tactics in a prominent bombing case), "So little appears to happen to those responsible for the payout. I really think it is about time that the officers who are costing millions of pounds of taxpayers' money for their actions are called to account."[113]

During the late spring and summer of 1995, the news media heavily reported the case of an illegal Jamaican immigrant, Joy Gardner, who had died during a struggle with Metropolitan Police officers arresting her for deportation. It was revealed that, after restraining Gardner, the officers, apparently in response to her verbal abuse and biting, had wrapped her head with thirteen feet of tape and left her lying face down on the floor for several minutes, killing her.[114] In mid-June, after a four-week trial, the officers were cleared of manslaughter charges, and a solicitor for Gardner's mother condemned the lack of any official inquiry into the case.[115] A month later the Police Complaints Authority confirmed that the three officers involved in the case would face no disciplinary action, in part because discipline was not authorized in cases in which the allegations were tried and an acquittal reached in court.[116] The member of Parliament for the neighborhood where Gardner lived condemned the failure of the Met leadership to act and called on black community leaders to protest.[117]

As frustration with internal police discipline mounted, juries increasingly turned against the police. The year 1995 ended with two rare occurrences in legal challenges against the police, portending things to come. In the first, a jury in an inquest into the death of a man after a police officer restrained him with a neck hold returned an extremely rare verdict of "unlawful killing" on learning that the coroner had condemned the police training process for an "appalling lack of instruction" in proper restraint techniques.[118] Ironically, the Crown Prosecution Service had declined to prosecute, on the grounds of insufficient evidence.[119] A month later the Met settled yet another case arising out of the Operation Jackpot inquiry, this time for £76,000, for fabrication of drug evidence against a longtime respected community volunteer on homeless issues.[120] The man's solicitor, Russell Miller, declared, "The significance of this case is that it is another example of victims of police abuse of power having to seek redress through the civil courts in the absence of satisfactory action being taken through the complaints procedure."[121]

Sir Paul Condon, the commissioner of the Metropolitan Police, on releasing the force's annual report in 1994, had complained that solicitors were beginning to see the police as a "soft option" and "soft target" willing to easily settle lawsuits, and he declared that the Met would begin fighting more such suits in court.[122] As the *Independent* observed, "the comments follow the disclosure that the Metropolitan Police paid what is believed to be a record" in damages over the previous year.[123] Raju Bhatt retorted, "It's disgraceful for the Commissioner to suggest that the problem is with solicitors rather than with any misconduct in his police force and the machinery to deal with that misconduct."[124]

As more cases proceeded to court, jury outrage produced a series of stunning verdicts. At the end of January 1996, a "day of shame for Scotland Yard," an inquest jury turned in another verdict of unlawful killing in a case involving a neck hold (a case in which the CPS had yet again declined to prosecute), and the Met settled a separate case alleging malicious prosecution, assault, and false imprisonment for £90,000.[125] The following day the political fallout began. Chris Mullin, the prominent Labour MP, declared: "The Metropolitan Police are paying millions each year in damages and lawyers' fees, yet the Commissioner is flatly refusing to take any action against officers whose misbehaviour is responsible for this cost to the taxpayer. The longer this goes on, the more that public confidence will be undermined."[126]

Mullin's critique proved to be only the beginning of a venting of public indignation against the police. Following Condon's direction, the Met had begun fighting more lawsuits before juries, and the juries responded. On March 28 a jury handed down an award of £64,000 involving a claim of false arrest, assault, and malicious prosecution.[127] On the same day, a different jury handed down a record-breaking £220,000 award to Kenneth Hsu in his case alleging that police had falsely arrested him and then, after putting him in a police van, had kicked and punched him and jabbed him with keys.[128] The jury awarded Hsu £200,000 in exemplary damages after Hsu's barrister urged,

> Send a clear message to the Commissioner that the public will no longer tolerate lying, bullying, perjury and racism by officers of the Metropolitan Police. In this case a small award of damages would be greeted as a victory by the officers involved. Even a moderately large award would be greeted with relief at Streatham police station. It is only if you award damages on an unprecedented scale that you can be sure the commissioner will be told of your award, will take note of it and will act on it.[129]

"But yesterday Scotland Yard was defiant," reported the *Independent*, "saying that none of the officers would be disciplined—and that in both cases there would be an appeal against the amount of damages."[130] A flurry of newspaper articles followed on the theme, as one headline put it, that "anger grows at soaring cost of police assaults."[131] "MPs and lawyers are concerned," the article observed, "that awards and settlements are now so frequent that urgent action is needed. Their greatest anxiety is that officers are rarely the subject of criminal charges or disciplinary action."[132] Sadiq Khan, Hsu's solicitor, argued that "it is because the Police Complaints Authority is so impotent that more people are resorting to remedies offered under civil law to seek out some sort of justice."[133] The *Independent* published a scathing commentary on "thuggery in uniform," comparing the Hsu case with the murder convictions of three British soldiers stationed in Cyprus, declaring that neither was "an isolated incident."[134] Labour MPs were reported to be planning to press the Government to open an official inquiry into the Streatham police station, where the Hsu case originated.[135]

An embattled Metropolitan Police leadership maintained its defiance. Brian Hayes, deputy commissioner of the Met, declared that the agency would "'keep its nerve' in the face of civil actions by people complaining about officers' conduct."[136] "Despite the growing fear of litigation in almost every profession which comes into contact with the personal aspects of peoples' lives," he said, "we must keep our nerve and not allow ourselves to be deflected from our job. We must do what we believe to be right, we must not become paralysed through fear of litigation."[137]

Three days later, in another case of police brutality, the Met was hit with yet another record jury award. A London jury awarded a man, who had been handcuffed by two officers and then hit over the head with a police truncheon by another officer, a record £302,000, including £170,000 in exemplary damages.[138] The officer who hit the man had been dismissed by the Met's commissioner but was reinstated on appeal by the Tory home secretary; his colleagues were not disciplined. "What is particularly chilling," observed Jane Deighton, the man's solicitor, "is that [the constable] told the jury that he would do it all over again."[139] The Met stated that the officers involved in the case would face no further disciplinary action.[140] Four days later a London jury awarded another man £108,000, including £45,000 in exemplary damages, over allegations of false imprisonment and malicious prosecution for drug offenses by London officers.[141]

Jane Deighton and Sadiq Khan, solicitors for several people who had sued the police, published a commentary in the *Guardian* arguing that the rising toll in damage awards, and particularly the increase in exemplary damages, reflected a growing desire by Londoners to "send a message."[142] The people, they said, were demanding fundamental police reform. Deighton and Khan also criticized the Police Complaints Authority for declining to pursue investigations and discipline in many cases where juries had found official liability. Khan observed in a similar commentary in the *Times*, "I believe that the way allegations of misconduct against police officers are investigated is flawed and inadequate, and that complainants will continue to seek recourse to the civil courts as long as the complaints system remains unsatisfactory."[143]

As spring turned into summer of 1996, the big damage awards kept coming, many above the previous symbolic ceiling of £100,000.[144] At the same time, public debate was renewed over the controversy of deaths in police custody.[145] The *Independent* reported that over the previous ten years, 576 people had died in police custody, "an average of more than one a week."[146] Inquest juries had returned verdicts of "unlawful killing" in six cases, "yet no police officer has been prosecuted."[147] A representative of a local citizen group in east London declared, "when police officers kill, they do so with impunity."[148] The article observed that "the discontent of the public in the way that the criminal justice system is failing to deal adequately with errant police officers is manifesting itself " in civil disobedience and "spiraling compensation awards."[149]

Condon ordered the Met's solicitors to prepare an appeal against the size of jury awards, which he said had gone "stratospheric."[150] "Senior police sources" soon reportedly told the *Guardian* that the rising cost of damage awards could force the Met to take up to one hundred officers off the street within a year to cut costs.[151] "I find his [Condon's] attitude scandalous and chilling," declared Jane Deighton. "He is shooting the messengers instead of listening to what they are saying—that some of his officers are out of control."[152]

The Court of Appeal heard the Met's appeal in two companion test cases, *Thompson and Hsu v. Commissioner of Police*, in December 1996 and issued a landmark decision on February 19, 1997.[153] The Met asked for caps on damages, and the most noted aspect of the decision was its rate structure, which capped exemplary damages at £50,000 and suggested appropriate rates for typical kinds of claims, many of which amounted to suggested reductions in the awards given by London juries in recent cases. On this basis, London newspapers widely reported the decision as an outright victory for the Met.[154] Ironically, the damages framework also *increased* the size of awards in many outlying jurisdictions where jury norms had not reached the levels found in London and other major cities.[155] But on other key issues the decision rejected the Met's appeal.[156] The Met had asked the Court of Appeal to discourage exemplary damages, at least in cases where plaintiffs had opted to sue rather than pursuing an official internal complaint, by requiring judges to notify juries of plaintiffs' decisions to bypass the complaints process. The court declined, ruling that judges should mention the possibility of internal discipline and prosecution only when those alternatives are likely to be pursued in a case. Since discipline and prosecution, as we have seen, are extremely rare, the decision on this matter amounted to a direct repudiation of Condon's position. Condon also asked for a ban on exemplary damages against chief officers in cases where the allegation attributed misconduct to a lower officer and the chief officer was not implicated in the complaint. But Lord Woolf, writing for the court, strongly supported exemplary damages against chief officers "to demonstrate publicly the strongest disapproval of what occurred and make it clear to the Commissioner and his force that conduct of this nature will not be tolerated by the courts."[157]

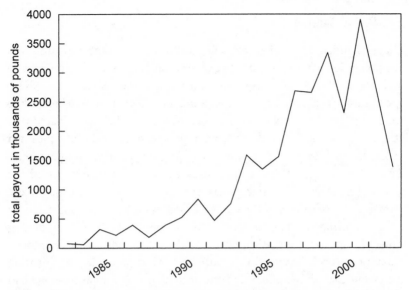

Figure 7.1. Total payouts in lawsuits alleging police misconduct, Metropolitan (London) Police Force, over time. Source: Metropolitan Police Force.

Many plaintiffs' attorneys took the new rate structure and the damages cap as a death knell for litigation against the police. "The Court condemned the police behaviour as 'outrageous,'" Jane Deighton declared, "but those words are wasted without the sting of a hefty penalty. The Court's words will be ignored by the police even as they consider this judgment."[158] Indeed, after dramatic growth in damage awards for a number of years, the size of awards in individual cases against the police plummeted (from nearly £50,000 a year to below £15,000 on average) and eventually the Met's total annual payouts began to decline as well (see fig. 7.1).[159] Although isolated cases still draw attention in the media, the wave of media coverage associated with the litigation campaign declined along with the damage awards.[160]

Policy Reform in the Wake of the Litigation Campaign

To what extent did the Stoke Newington litigation campaign contribute to legalizing accountability in British policing? The evidence is mixed. As I will show here, although the campaign undoubtedly contributed to the adoption of several national policy reforms, these reforms have been only partially absorbed into police practice.

The Policy Agenda

On one hand, the litigation campaign contributed to a substantial shift in the policy agenda on policing. The older agenda is concisely expressed in *Winning the Race*, the first in a series of major inquiries by Her Majesty's Inspectorate of the Constabulary into police and race relations, which, while reporting "pockets of wholly unacceptable racist policing," declared that "these comments . . . should be kept in perspective" since the police had "done as much as any other public organization" in addressing racism.[161] By 1997, however, as litigation pressure and media coverage increased, the policy climate changed. In the summer, activist lawyers succeeded in destroying the legitimacy of the Crown Prosecution Service's long-standing refusal to bring criminal charges in cases of police abuse, leading, among other things, to an investigation of deaths in custody by the European Committee for the Prevention of Torture.[162] More generally, the litigation campaign against the police and the accompanying media coverage had thoroughly changed the terms of political debate. It was no longer possible to claim that the problem in policing was limited to a few aberrant individuals; by widespread acknowledgment the problem lay deeper in police culture and policy. And if the problem lay in these areas, it was widely agreed that any solution would need to be systemic or institutional in nature. In May 1997 the Labour Party returned to power and placed police reform high on its domestic agenda. Chris Mullin, the longtime critic of the police, was selected as chair of Parliament's Home Affairs Committee with jurisdiction over domestic policy, including policing. Under Mullin's leadership, the Committee conducted hearings on the problem of police misconduct, recommending sweeping reforms.[163]

The Labour government also appointed Sir William MacPherson to head an official inquiry into the 1993 murder of Stephen Lawrence, a young black man, by white racist youths, and MacPherson issued a stunning report that largely endorsed the Hackney activists' long-standing call for institutional reform of policing.[164] He concluded that British policing was shot through with "institutional racism," which he defined as "the collective failure of an organization to provide an appropriate and professional service to people because of their colour, culture, or ethnic origin. It can be seen or detected in processes, attitudes and behaviour which amount to discrimination through unwitting prejudice, ignorance, thoughtlessness and racist stereotyping."[165]

In a sharp departure from the tenor of the Scarman report, MacPherson recommended a number of broad reforms aimed at making policing "as open and accountable as possible."[166] He dismissed the view that reform need focus only on removing a few "bad apples" or making incremental improvements in policies and training. Police leadership, MacPherson observed, had already attempted such limited reforms but, as evinced by statistics and the perceptions of minority residents, little had changed. Residents' "collective experience," MacPherson observed, "was of senior officers adopting fine policies and using fine words, but of indifference on the ground at the junior officer level."[167] In presenting his argument for institutional reform, MacPherson approvingly quoted the pastor of a Baptist church in one of London's troubled minority communities: "I have now been forced to the conclusion, by this and other cases, that the problem is much, much deeper than that [individual bad apples]. I believe that the procedures and management systems of the police are at fault. . . . Simply tinkering with the police system and putting in a bit of extra racial awareness training will not address this: *a radical transformation is needed.*"[168]

MacPherson recommended a number of accountability reforms, particularly better internal training, oversight, and discipline of frontline officers.[169] He called for the Home Office to establish uniform police policies and procedures; training on these policies; internal oversight, using performance indicators to monitor compliance; strategies for preventing and controlling racist incidents; recruitment programs to attract racial minorities into the police service; and a freedom of information act aimed at exposing police policies and procedures to public review.

The government quickly adopted legislation and national policies aimed at implementing a number of MacPherson's recommendations. In 2000 the government adopted the Race Relations (Amendment) Act, imposing on all government authorities a duty to promote racial equality by adopting policies to this end and monitoring their implementation, and the Freedom of Information Act. Additionally, the home secretary established a new "Ministerial Priority" of increasing the level of trust of the police among minority communities; performance indicators measuring progress in this direction; new Codes of Practice governing police recording and reporting of racist incidents; and new police training regarding race relations and cultural awareness. And so on.[170]

The Institutions of Policing

The government's legalized accountability reforms, however, have made only mixed progress within policing.[171] Although this is due in part to the relaxation of liability and media pressure after the Court of Appeal capped damages, it is also due to the bifurcated structure of British policing's professional institutions.

In the United States, as we have seen, the agenda of police professionalism is dominated by the voice of the International Association of Chiefs of Police, which is now controlled by reformist police chiefs. By contrast, in Britain there are two police professional associations: one speaks for "management" (chief constables and their lieutenants), while a separate association speaks for "labor" (lower-ranking constables). The former, the Association of Chief Police Officers (ACPO), moreover, is in large part a creature of the Home Office and serves to develop official policing policies. Unsurprisingly, ACPO has generally supported the Home Office's recent initiatives in favor of systemic reforms related to the treatment of racial minority groups. The organization has also increased the level of legalized accountability within British policing. In September 2006, for instance, ACPO published official "guidances" on the use of handcuffs and limb restraints, each of which embodies rulelike constraints on these types of use of force, along with suggestions for appropriate training and oversight.[172]

British police forces at their higher management levels have begun to develop internal managerial systems, many paralleling key innovations in the United States, aimed at addressing problems in police practices. For instance, some British forces are developing programs similar to early warning systems that collate quantitative indicators of individual officers' performance on key matters (such as racial patterns in stops and searches) and thus allow for comparisons among officers and managerial supervision and intervention aimed at correcting questionable patterns. Such programs are effective only to the extent that police supervisors actively monitor officers' self-reports and then actively analyze the data and use them for oversight and frontline management. A recent study conducted under the auspices of the Home Office observed that some British forces are developing several such internal management reforms and concluded that they were having a desired impact.[173] Similarly, by 2001 all but one of the forty-three forces had developed a community race-relations strategy, and focus groups among minority residents revealed "a renewal, or, in some cases, a birth, of confidence in their police."[174]

Additionally, the liability campaign itself contributed to some changes in police practices. In the midst of the litigation against Stoke Newington officers, the station's drugs squad, as we have seen, was disbanded and reconstituted with different officers, and the station's management structure was reorganized and several officers were either fired or encouraged to resign.[175] In late December 1992 Peter Hall, a barrister who had represented a defendant arrested by Stoke Newington police, observed: "The only reason that the police finally took the action that they did is the pressure placed on them by the community, in particular the Hackney Community Defence Association."[176] A journalist later observed that the Association challenged the Stoke Newington police "with striking success."[177] More generally, as the pressure from tort litigation increased, British police forces became increasingly attentive to legal norms. John Beggs, a leading barrister who has primarily represented the police in tort cases, began offering training sessions for police leaders regarding the new legal environment.[178]

Further, several local forces have developed internal reforms aimed at adjusting police practices to the requirements of the law.[179] Chief among these internal reforms are systematic legal analysis and systematic feedback from the legal analysis to policy development and officer training. Remarkably, until very recently most British police forces either did not have internal legal departments or had very small departments focused mainly on employment issues. Although the Met has had an internal legal department for many years, its activities and internal influence have increased markedly since the rise of litigation against the force and involve developing a system for analyzing the lessons of losses in court and informing the force's policy development and training sections regarding those lessons.[180] Based in part on the Met's pioneering efforts in legal analysis, other forces have developed similar internal legal feedback loops. The Thames Valley Police, for instance, instituted a similar system of legal analysis and policy correction in the late 1990s. Other forces have recently consulted with the Met and with the Thames Valley Police in developing similar systems in their jurisdictions. Beginning in the late 1990s, the internal legal departments in British police forces developed a communications network for sharing information about legal defense strategies as well as how best to reform policy and training to stay abreast of legal changes.

Although senior officers and their professional association have provided some support for the accountability agenda, however, the Police Federation, the professional association for frontline constables through midranking officers, is somewhat less supportive. To be sure, the Police Federation has called for more training in matters of safety and the use of force.[181] On the other hand, some of its official pronouncements seem to voice resentment at the widespread calls for systemic police reform regarding the treatment of racial minorities. Thus, just as public controversy over alleged police racism was reaching fever pitch in the early 2000s, an editorial in *Police*, the official voice of the Federation, fretted that "almost overnight, we became a multi-racial, multi-cultural society" and that "a new generation of senior officers," drawn from professional training and not the rank and file, speaking "the same language as the social scientists, liberals, and civil libertarians," were discarding policing's traditional "basic tenets."[182]

Several major reports have castigated the police for continued race-relations problems, particularly in the area of stop and search. The Home Office reported in 2004 that blacks in Britain were eight times as likely to be stopped and searched as whites.[183] In the Metropolitan Police Force, by far the country's largest, the number of stops and searches continued to increase (by 18 percent annually for the most recently available data). More troubling, the extent of racial disparity increased even more dramatically. Between 1997 and 2003, the stops and searches of blacks increased from 75,583 to 89,916, while those of whites dramatically declined, from 187,105 to 130,645.[184] Perhaps more troubling yet, the arrest rates in stops and searches in the Met are remarkably low: 10 percent overall, and only 7 percent in searches for drugs.[185] It is no wonder, then, that the Metropolitan Police Authority's (MPA) inquiry into the Met's stop and search practice observed that wide racial disparities in searches grow from institutional failings and that "stop and search practice is the flashpoint of police-community relations."[186] Similarly, in June 2004 the Commission for Racial Equality, Britain's enforcement agency at the time on matters of race discrimination, released a major report concluding that although British policing is starting to address persistent problems of race discrimination in its ranks, the response remains only weakly institutionalized.[187]

In this context, while the National Black Police Association consistently has called for the police to address the deep racial disparities in stops and searches on the street, spokespeople for the Police Federation have defended the use of stop and search powers and have argued that the problem is largely one of perceptions built by publication of the statistics themselves.[188] In response, Ray Powell, president of the National Black Police Association, observed that on the subject of racial disparities in stops and searches, "the police service is still in a state of denial."[189]

Conclusion

At first the story told above may seem very *English*. English courts and law have long been famous for preferring order, stability, and respect for authority. By American standards the damage awards and settlements in the London cases of police abuse were really rather small, yet the British press and governing officials responded as if stunned by a massive onslaught. Thus the commissioner of the Metropolitan Police said the awards had "gone stratospheric." Ultimately, after only a few years of rising damage awards, the Court of Appeals, at the request of the commissioner, placed caps on awards, undercutting tort-based challenge to police authority.

The American and British experiences with tort litigation, however, also have much in common. In both settings, activists pressed the message that police abuses were the product not of individual bad apples but of systemic failings, particularly improper policies; inadequate training, supervision, and discipline of officers; and inadequate systems of oversight and accountability. In both settings, as jury awards increased, media coverage came to reflect the activists' message. In both settings, mainstream professional policing remained deaf to complaints of racial harassment and abuse until prodded by tort liability into addressing the problem. In both settings, tort liability's sanction was reputational rather than monetary: a powerful synergy developed between tort lawsuits, the institution of the jury, and news media coverage. As William Haltom and Michael McCann show, the popular news media have an affinity for tort litigation, since an individual plaintiff, graphic complaints, and money awards make compelling news.[190] Finally, in both settings, lawsuits and damage awards carry a disruptive potential widely perceived to threaten the stability of institutionalized power by reframing the key issues in the media. What mattered to police officials, it seems clear from a distance, was not the size of jury awards but their significance in the battle over how to frame the issue of police accountability.

The rise of the £100,000 award thus indicated that the terrain had shifted, that policing was entering a new era whose defining feature was a collapse of public faith in the integrity of police treatment of racial minorities and the managerial system of police accountability. The clearest indicators of that collapse were the decisions by juries, in cases pitting the word of blacks against that of police officers, to believe the former and to characterize them as innocent victims of racist police abuse. In case after case, juries of ordinary Britons sided with blacks complaining of police abuse, and as time went on juries' frustrations with a perceived lack of police responsiveness increased, resulting in rising damage awards. Litigation against the police thus achieved something unprecedented: it brought to full public view the long-held complaints by minority communities of discriminatory and abusive police action and, through detailed examination of the experiences of particular individuals, legitimated those complaints.

Tort litigation, in sum, threatened the legitimacy of police authorities by a simple mechanism: routinely exposing them to public embarrassment. That general assessment is almost certainly true of the United States as well. Although financial damages in policing cases in the United States are generally higher than in the United Kingdom, even relatively higher damages impose little financial pain on large police departments. As in the United States, lawsuits hit agencies where it matters—in adverse publicity—and this publicity helped redefine the problem from a conception of individual police officer responsibility (the "bad apple" syndrome) to institutional responsibility.

Although British policing remains far from fully reformed on the matters of racial discrimination and use of force, the problem is now openly recognized, discussed, and framed as a matter requiring systemic reform rather than merely rooting out a few errant officers. That shift in the agenda may be attributed, at least in part, to a tort litigation campaign and media coverage of it.

8

Sexual Harassment

American employment is in the middle of . . . the "second civil
rights revolution."
—Martha I. Finney, quoting an unnamed Washington, DC,
labor lawyer (*Personnel Administrator,* March 1988)

If legalized accountability has overtaken policing in the United
States—a field exposed to intense street-level activism and widespread claims that police brutality violates fundamental rights—has
it been adopted equally widely and in a similarly searching form
in fields less subject to such pressure and less amenable to rights
claims? To address these questions I have traced the development of liability pressure and adoption of legalistic policies in two
other policy areas: employment sexual harassment and playground
safety. Both have been subject to liability pressure, but unlike policing neither has experienced much street-level activist pressure.
The problem of sexual harassment, like policing, has been brought
under federal law and is widely understood as a violation of important rights. Playground safety, by contrast, is neither regulated by
federal law nor widely understood as a "rights issue." This chapter
focuses on sexual harassment, the next on playground safety.

No reader would be surprised by a claim that sexual harassment
policies have swept through local governments and that liability
pressure contributed.[1] Some writers claim that these policies are a
classic example of legalism run amok, of procedures adopted at the

behest of courts against the better judgment of practicing professionals.[2] Others doubt that these policies really changed anything, claiming that organizational sexual harassment policies are shaped primarily by personnel administrators' standard "tool-kit" and are therefore extremely limited in scope (e.g., grievance procedures), representing "ceremonial" alternatives to steps that might better address the underlying problem.[3] This chapter shows that each of these perspectives is partly right but incomplete. Practicing professionals—the administrators in charge of personnel policies—indeed were pressed by liability into addressing sexual harassment. After initial panic over this new threat of liability, however, these practitioners quickly came to acknowledge the significance of the sexual harassment problem and came to endorse a common administrative response to it. This common administrative model incorporates standard managerial practices like grievance procedures. Still, the model grew not only from personnel administrators' familiar repertoire but also from activists' reform proposals that were aimed at achieving deep organizational change. Consequently, the model was (at least for a time) richer, more diverse, and arguably more effective than sometimes reported. As in policing, the combination of liability pressure, media coverage, and ideological conflict within professional networks led to a transformation: a legalized accountability model that incorporated both activist ideas and managerial tools.

My analysis thus begins with what activists wanted. They argued that it was employers' responsibility to eradicate sexual harassment. Several activists proposed administrative steps to accomplish this goal. As I show, professional journals accepted and repeated these recommendations, which in time consolidated into a shared model consisting of the following elements: a written policy prohibiting sexual harassment and clearly defining it; communication of this policy to employees by diverse methods of training and other types of messages; and diverse methods of internal oversight that included grievance procedures but extended beyond them to include employee surveys. I acknowledge that this model may be applied only ceremonially in practice, but I show, as I have done in the policing chapters, that whether agencies have gone beyond pro forma steps depends on how much they face activist pressure and professional guidance to do more. Further, I show that the more thoroughly agencies have adopted these diverse policies, the more steps they have taken to retrain, counsel, discipline, or fire people who engage in harassment. Administrative sexual harassment policies, in other words, *contribute to rather than distract from* concrete steps to address harassment.

I support these claims with two types of evidence. First I trace the development of activists' complaints, their proposals for reform, and practitioners' reception of these ideas. For data on these things I rely on activists' publications, histories of the feminist movement against sexual harassment, and articles in practitioner journals. Then I analyze original survey data regarding city governments' adoption of practitioners' professional recommendations and the forces contributing to this adoption.

The Development of a Model Administrative System for Addressing Sexual Harassment

The Movement against Sexual Harassment

The movement against sexual harassment grew in the 1970s from the feminist movement's "second wave," which characterized sexual discrimination as more than an issue of economics. It was, these feminists argued, an almost elemental aspect of culture in which men used a multitude of everyday devices, from housework to pressure for sex, to subordinate women. Thus feminists identified unwanted sexual attention from men at work and hostility toward women in nontraditional jobs as widespread, deeply offensive elements of a larger problem.

The issue of sexual harassment burst into public consciousness and, once defined, spread rapidly.[4] The term "sexual harassment" was first used in 1975 by a group at Cornell University that grew out of a course on women and work taught by Lin Farley.[5] The group was diverse—black and white, blue-collar and white-collar, poor and affluent—but "there was an unmistakable pattern" to the stories that emerged: "Each one of us had already quit or been fired from a job at least once because we had been made too uncomfortable by the behavior of men."[6] Specifically, women often experienced offensive behavior ranging from sexual joking to pressure for sex. The women were surprised by how many shared such experiences. Farley and several others then organized a more public "speak-out" on the Cornell campus to give wider voice to women's outrage. In planning publicity for the speak-out, the organizers selected "sexual harassment" as the problem's name. It was the term's first appearance. The speak-out brought out intense emotions and widespread participation, suggesting that the organizers were tapping into a very widespread concern. At about the same time, Lin Farley testified on sexual harassment at a hearing held by the New York City Human Rights Commission, chaired by Eleanor Holmes Norton.[7] It was the first connection between Farley and Norton, who later, as head of the U.S. Equal Employment Opportunity Commission, would issue guidelines that institutionalized a common model for addressing the issue.

Feminists quickly formed organizations against sexual harassment. In 1975 the Cornell women formed Working Women United. In 1977 the organization relocated to New York City and there became a hub of nationwide organizing on the issue; as publicity about the group expanded, it began receiving, as Carrie Baker reports, hundreds of requests a week for information and counseling and soon formed a referral service to connect women with sympathetic attorneys throughout the country.[8] In the meantime, similar groups sprouted in many other places. In 1975, for instance, a group of students at Yale University organized and gathered extensive data in support of a class action sexual harassment lawsuit against Yale professors, and the University of Delaware Commission on the Status of Women began organizing efforts against sexual harassment.[9] The most important of these early organizations was the Alliance Against Sexual Coercion (AASC), formed in 1976 by a group of women in Cambridge, Massachusetts.[10] Their efforts, focused initially on rape, quickly expanded to include counseling and referral services for women experiencing sexual harassment on the job. Women from the Cornell group Working Women United and the Cambridge-based AASC met for the first time in the spring of 1978 and engaged in a valuable exchange of ideas.[11] Other groups grew up around the country.[12]

Within a short time, leaders of the new movement published sophisticated scholarly analyses as well as advocacy guidebooks on the issue, consistently arguing that they wanted harassment to stop and organizations reformed so as to prevent it. Catharine MacKinnon, associated with the organizing at Yale, began circulating drafts of her influential scholarly treatise *Sexual Harassment of Working Women* in 1975 (it was ultimately published in 1979). By 1978 Deirdre Silverman and Lin Farley, two of the leaders of Working Women United, had published extended analyses of the issue.[13] Constance Backhouse and Leah Cohen, two of the organizers of the Alliance Against Sexual Coercion, similarly published a book-length analysis in 1978,[14] and that organization published an advocacy guidebook in 1979.[15]

In the mid-1970s the issue took off in the popular media too.[16] In 1975, based on the speak-out at Cornell, the *New York Times* published the first prominent report of the growing chorus of women's complaints.[17] In 1976 *Viva* ran a brief article on sexual harassment, and *Redbook* ran an extensive, widely cited article reporting the results of an informal survey of some nine thousand women, which revealed that a stunning 90 percent of these self-selected respondents reported experiencing unwanted sexual pressure at work.[18] In the following years, popular magazines, newspapers, and book publishers released a stream of articles and books providing informal documentation of the problem and suggesting remedies. In 1977, for instance, *Ms.* magazine, *Ladies' Home Journal*, and *Glamour* ran prominent stories on sexual harassment (three in *Ms.* alone), and management consultant Betty Harragan published *Games Mother Never Taught You*, claiming that "more women are refused employment, fired or forced to quit salaried jobs as a result of sexual demands and ramifications than for any other single cause."[19] The outpouring continued over the next several years.[20]

By the early 1980s, a number of surveys confirmed the widespread nature of the problem. Definitions of harassment varied from survey to survey, as did estimates of its prevalence, but no results published during those years found that less than 20 percent of working women had experienced harassment on the job.[21] The most careful of the early surveys, conducted by the U.S. Merit Systems Protection Board and published in 1981, estimated that 40 percent of female federal employees had been sexually harassed on the job.[22]

In the late 1970s, agencies of the federal government began giving the issue attention. The first significant federal developments occurred in the courts. Several women initiated lawsuits against their former employers, alleging that at work they had been subjected to pressure for sex and that this constituted a violation of the civil rights laws' prohibition on employment discrimination. Although most lost their cases in the trial courts, several of the plaintiffs appealed, and in 1976 a federal appellate court, in *Williams v. Saxbe*, ruled that at least some forms of sexual harassment at work constituted violations of Title 7 of the Civil Rights Act of 1964. Other favorable decisions soon followed,[23] and the number of federal cases began growing significantly. Between 1974 and 1981, the years when the concept of sexual harassment began to crystallize, there were at least fifty-two federal district court and appellate court decisions on the matter.[24] Although these decisions were notoriously ambiguous about when employers were liable for harassment by their employees, many favored women's claims, giving the impression that legal liability for sexual harassment was expanding. Congress too turned its attention to the issue, holding major hearings on sexual harassment in 1979, 1980, and 1981.[25] Perhaps the most important of these was the first, chaired by Congressman James Hanley, chair of the House Post Office and Civil Service Committee's Subcommittee on Investigations, along with an investigation of sexual harassment in federal employment conducted by Hanley's subcommittee.[26] Hanley called on the Equal Employment Opportunity Commission to issue guidelines addressing sexual harassment.

By the late 1970s these forces—popular organizing, civil lawsuits, media coverage, and federal investigations—had converged into a rapidly growing policy agenda on sexual harassment. The 1976 sex scandals in Washington, in which it was revealed that a number of members of Congress pressured their staff members for sexual favors, contributed to the issue's growing momentum.[27]

Proposing a Solution: The Origins of Legalized Accountability

In the period before 1980, although activists against sexual harassment advocated a wide range of alternative remedies, two eventually converged and formed what became, by the late 1980s, the dominant model in the field. The more famous of the two roots of that model was Catharine MacKinnon's proposal to interpret the Civil Rights Act as prohibiting sexual harassment.[28] MacKinnon's analysis, published in 1979 but circulated among feminist networks over the preceding four years, remains by far the most significant and influential legal analysis of the problem of sexual harassment and what to do about it. MacKinnon pioneered an influential distinction between "quid pro quo" harassment, consisting of exerting pressure or offering rewards in exchange for sexual favors, and "hostile environment" harassment, encompassing a wide range of comments and actions indicating that women are unwelcome, less respected, or considered objects of sexual domination in the workplace. Crucially, MacKinnon offered a powerful legal analysis demonstrating that both quid pro quo and hostile environment harassment are prohibited by Title 7 of the Civil Rights Act of 1964 because they constitute employment discrimination based on sex. Tying sexual harassment to federal civil rights law was a brilliant strategic move, for it opened the possibility of drawing on the sophisticated legal knowledge and networks in the broader employment civil rights bar. Equally important, higher damage awards were available under civil rights law than under most other legal remedies. For all its comprehensiveness and legal sophistication, however, MacKinnon's analysis offered little in the way of a proposal for what employers should *do*, in concrete administrative policy, to end harassment.

The second key ideological source of the sexual harassment policy model was a proposal from two Canadian feminists, Constance Backhouse and Leah Cohen, for what employers should do *administratively* to stop harassment and change workplace culture. Both Backhouse and Cohen had extensive experience in administrative and managerial settings.[29] Backhouse had worked in Canada's Ministry of Labour, learning much about the practical administrative details necessary for successful pro-labor policy.[30] Cohen had worked for the business corporation IBM, where she gained experience in implementing management policies. Specifically, she observed how IBM, in the context of the mid-1970s controversy over sexual harassment, had developed a formal policy against sex at work that remained "solely symbolic" and had no impact on managerial practices or IBM's organizational culture.[31]

Backhouse and Cohen's managerial experiences led to a productive cross-fertilization of ideas with the feminist AASC in Cambridge.[32] When Backhouse moved there to attend law school at Harvard, she joined the rich network of feminists centered on AASC and its coordinator, Freada Klein. For a book project, Backhouse and Cohen began carrying out interviews with administrative managers on the topic of sexual harassment. At the time, AASC was being approached by business corporations and personnel associations for advice on how to respond to the sexual harassment issue. Because of their experience in organizational administration, Backhouse and Cohen became increasingly central to AASC's response to these requests. In putting together seminars on the issue, the two began to develop specific ideas for how to change the organizational cultures they were documenting in their interviews with managers. The problem, as they saw it, was increasingly clear: to reduce sexual harassment, the movement would need to change *organizations* as much as individual behavior.

Backhouse and Cohen's ideas for how to reform organizations appeared in the form of their "action plan" for management, published in 1978.[33] The plan consisted, essentially, of a proposed model of legalized accountability aimed at generating deep change in the working routines of organizational employers.[34] It encompassed all the key components of what later became the dominant organizational model for addressing the problem. Foremost, Backhouse and Cohen's action plan favored (in its point number one) adoption by management of a "corporate blue letter"—a clear policy statement "condemning the practice of sexual harassment."[35] Such a policy statement should "define sexual harassment and clearly state that such behaviour is *unacceptable*."[36] Second, Backhouse and Cohen proposed that management policy should be clearly communicated to all employees in a variety of ways.[37] Management should post the policy widely throughout the premises, reprint it in in-house publications, and include it in official manuals. Additionally, the policy should be communicated through training sessions for all managers, covering all branches of the organization, and in orientation sessions for all new employees. Third, they proposed a multilevel oversight procedure aimed at assessing the extent of harassment within the organization and addressing any instances of harassment.[38] Their proposed oversight procedure encompassed a survey of employees and a procedure for carrying out investigations and administering discipline in response to individual complaints. Additionally, Backhouse and Cohen emphasized the need to protect complainants from reprisals.[39]

As activist pressure on employers increased, these employers and professional associations turned to Backhouse and Cohen's proposal. Word about it spread among personnel associations, and the two were asked to give talks and seminars widely.[40] Ultimately, Backhouse gave over two hundred such talks in business corporations and government agencies, commonly before hundreds of managers and employees. "There was a desire to hear this," Backhouse reported, "and the audiences were incredible."[41] "The women were so damn mad" about what they were going through. The men, by contrast, seemed stunned by the rapid change in gender relations. Some—Backhouse often learned that these were notorious harassers—would "spout off" with defensive and combative reactions. "The climate was electric," Backhouse reported, and human resources managers commonly told her they had brought her in specifically to push for organizational change.

A spin-off effect was connecting women with lawyers willing to bring sexual harassment lawsuits against employers. At many talks and seminars, Backhouse would hear from women who wanted to find a lawyer who would help file a suit. "We were very much in touch with lawyers, feeding information back and forth between women and lawyers. And we would regularly hear from women who wanted to sue, and we would refer them to lawyers who were taking these cases."[42]

Although MacKinnon's civil rights proposal and Backhouse and Cohen's managerial proposal eventually converged and came to dominate the field, until the early 1980s they were only two among many approaches, and it is instructive to survey the range of options in the earlier era. A number were conventional legal remedies. One was to encourage women to seek unemployment compensation after leaving a job over sexual harassment (in many jurisdictions this required changing the interpretation of state unemployment compensation laws to allow sexual harassment as a legitimate justification for leaving).[43] Although such a halfway remedy in retrospect was limited, since it acknowledged that harassment was impervious to reform, the proposal indicates the desperation many felt as they found many

work environments simply unacceptable. Another was to seek compensation under state-level human rights statutes, an approach pursued widely
in the late 1970s.[44] Another proposed remedy was criminal prosecution of
harassers (as perpetrating a form of assault), but those who pressed such
an alternative found little sympathy among prosecutors.[45] Still another alternative was ordinary tort (personal injury) lawsuits against harassers,
tried in several jurisdictions in the late 1970s.[46]

Some feminist activists, however, expressed deep misgivings about relying too heavily on the federal courts or, for that matter, any legal remedy.
The Alliance Against Sexual Coercion, the group Backhouse and Cohen
were affiliated with, observed that any of the available legal remedies (unemployment compensation, criminal sanctions, tort lawsuits, civil rights
lawsuits) took considerable time (often years), and imposed heavy legal
fees. The AASC therefore favored organized direct action against harassers, particularly "extralegal" actions, among them warning letters sent
directly to harassers; organized pressure on personnel departments and
workplace unions; leafleting women's bathrooms; surveying employees
about their experiences with harassment in order to pressure employers
for action; and picketing employers.[47] These grassroots efforts, the group
hoped, would force employers to adopt comprehensive policies and procedures to address the problem and, more broadly, would contribute to
cultural change. Similarly, the noted anthropologist Margaret Mead argued in 1978 that sexual harassment would be diminished only if its
cultural bases were eroded, and she therefore argued for a long-term effort aimed at establishing a cultural taboo against sex in the workplace.[48]
These remedies, in contrast to the court-based alternatives, left the levers
of influence in women's hands.

The EEOC, the Federal Courts, and the Consolidation of a Legalized Accountability Model

In 1980 the federal Equal Employment Opportunity Commission (EEOC)
issued guidelines addressing sexual harassment that combined the legal
remedy proposed by MacKinnon with the administrative policy proposed
by Backhouse and Cohen.[49] Although the EEOC has no statutory authority to issue legally binding regulations, its "guidelines" have often formed
the basis for judicial decisions, and so the EEOC's guidelines on sexual
harassment were widely considered to carry great weight.[50] In 1980 the
head of the EEOC was Eleanor Holmes Norton. Norton, as head of the
New York City Human Rights Commission, had supported the pioneering

group Working Women United in its earliest efforts on the sexual harassment issue.[51] Her connections to the women's movement against sexual harassment clearly informed the EEOC's official position.

Following MacKinnon's lead, the Guidelines defined sexual harassment as encompassing both quid pro quo harassment—essentially, demanding sexual favors in exchange for job benefits—and "hostile environment" harassment, or allowing the work environment to be permeated with hostility or offensiveness related to sex. The Guidelines interpreted Title 7 of the Civil Rights Act of 1964 as prohibiting both forms of sexual harassment. Additionally, and crucially, the Guidelines interpreted Title 7 as making organizational employers strictly liable for harassment by supervisors, and liable for hostile environment harassment and for harassment by line employees if supervisors knew or should have known of the harassment, unless the organization had taken affirmative steps to address the problem. Such an approach to employer liability provided a powerful incentive for employers to take proactive steps to minimize sexual harassment in their workplaces.

Following the lead of Backhouse and Cohen, the EEOC also recommended steps employers should take to address harassment. As Eleanor Holmes Norton later observed, the Guidelines announced to employers: "This is your burden. Chase it from the workplaces. If you don't, these guidelines will help a woman prove harassment."[52] The Guidelines declared that "prevention is the best tool for the elimination of sexual harassment."[53] They specifically observed that merely having a policy forbidding sexual harassment would not, in the view of the EEOC, be sufficient to shield the employer from liability: in the case of harassment by supervisors, employers would be "responsible" (thus legally liable) for harassment "whether the specific acts complained of were authorized or even forbidden by the employer."[54] Symbolic policy would not be enough. Instead, Title 7 demanded *prevention*: "Prevention is the best tool for the elimination of sexual harassment. An employer should take all steps necessary to prevent sexual harassment from occurring, such as affirmatively raising the subject, expressing strong disapproval, developing appropriate sanctions, informing employees of their right to raise and how to raise the issue of harassment under Title 7, and developing methods to sensitize all concerned."[55] The Guidelines declared that an employer is "responsible" in cases of harassment by either supervisors or fellow employees "unless it can show that it took immediate and appropriate corrective action."

In this brief but sweeping pronouncement, the EEOC Guidelines missed two elements of Backhouse and Cohen's action plan. The first was their call for proactive efforts by employers, among them surveys of employees, to ascertain the extent of harassment even in the absence of employee complaints. Backhouse and Cohen had observed that many women feared filing a complaint and therefore pressed employers to develop other ways to assess whether there was a problem in their workplace. The other was their demand for policies protecting complainants from reprisals. Each of these elements, as we shall see shortly, would ultimately be added to the model as it evolved in professional publications.

These Guidelines profoundly influenced federal legal policy. Shortly after the EEOC published them in preliminary form, a federal court cited them in ruling that Title 7 prohibited hostile environment harassment; and after the EEOC published the final guidelines several months later, the District of Columbia Circuit Court of Appeals ratified that interpretation.[56] Additionally, as Carrie Baker reports, several federal agencies modified their policies in response to the guidelines.[57]

The Reagan administration and its congressional allies, as Baker observes, responded with a full-scale attack on the EEOC Guidelines immediately on taking office in early 1981. Senator Orrin Hatch, chair of the Senate Committee on Labor and Human Resources, held hearings on the Guidelines in early 1981 and proposed to amend Title 7 with language that would override the EEOC's Guidelines and narrow the act's prohibition on sexual harassment.[58] Supporters of the Guidelines inundated the Committee with testimony documenting the severity of the harassment problem, and Hatch abandoned his effort. The Reagan administration then dramatically cut the EEOC's budget, appointed Clarence Thomas to chair the Commission, and appointed other commissioners who were opposed to vigorous enforcement of antidiscrimination rules. Additionally, Vice President George H. W. Bush headed up a task force to reduce regulations affecting business, and in August 1981 he announced that the task force would soon consider eliminating or narrowing the EEOC Guidelines on sexual harassment.[59] Supporters of the Guidelines mounted a broad effort to convince the administration to retain them. Ultimately, in August 1983, the EEOC voted to retain the Guidelines, citing widespread public and judicial support for them.[60]

But the effort to gut the EEOC Guidelines was not over. In 1986 *Meritor Savings Bank v. Vinson*, the first case testing the Guidelines' interpretation of Title 7 with regard to sexual harassment, reached the Supreme Court, and the EEOC, under the leadership of Clarence Thomas, filed an amicus brief on the side of the defendant bank. The Court, in an opinion written by conservative Chief Justice William Rehnquist, nonetheless handed down a decision that largely ratified the EEOC Guidelines and made them the authoritative interpretation of Title 7. The Court, following the EEOC, interpreted Title 7 to prohibit sexual harassment and accepted the EEOC's interpretation that sexual harassment encompassed both quid pro quo and hostile environment harassment. With regard to enforcement of the policy, the Court did two other significant things in *Meritor*. Following the EEOC Guidelines, it held that employers are strictly liable for quid pro quo harassment by a supervisor. Likewise, following the Guidelines, the Court held that employers are not strictly liable for hostile environment harassment, but it suggested that they are liable for such an environment unless they have taken clear preventive actions. The Court, however, left ambiguous what sorts of preventive actions would shield employers from liability. In light of the facts of the case, the Court's decision suggested that merely having a policy prohibiting discrimination is not sufficient to shield an employer from liability for sexual harassment by its supervisors (especially if the policy does not specifically prohibit sexual harassment). And the Court suggested that the employer's defense "might be substantially stronger if its procedures were better calculated to encourage victims of harassment to come forward." The Supreme Court's decision thus seemed to encourage employers to adopt policies specifically prohibiting sexual harassment and procedures specifically designed to encourage the filing of complaints through an internal organizational process. But the Court did not suggest a specific form or content for those policies and procedures.[61] The *Meritor* decision, in sum, effectively ended the Reagan administration's battle to gut the EEOC Guidelines on sexual harassment, but it left open the question of what employers should do to address the problem.

Other developments soon strengthened the emerging law on sexual harassment. The Civil Rights Act of 1991 expanded the tortlike characteristics of Title 7 by authorizing, in addition to the economic damages authorized by prior law, both compensatory and punitive damages. The change in the law increased the potential size of damage awards in sexual harassment cases.

Finally, in 1998, in *Faragher v. Boca Raton* and *Burlington Industries v. Ellerth*, the Court held that in sexual harassment cases in which the victim's tangible employment benefits are not affected, employers are shielded from liability only if their managers were unaware of the harassment; if the organization had in place a policy prohibiting sexual harassment along with grievance procedures that reasonably encouraged the filing of complaints; and only if the victim unreasonably declined to file a complaint.[62]

The *Faragher* decision thus provided incentives for employers to adopt basic sexual harassment policies and procedures. The decision, however, is narrow and formalist in that it does not appear to require employers to carry out searching efforts to ascertain whether employees are following the policy or even know of it.

The Personnel Administration Profession Responds

The personnel administration profession initially received feminists' complaints of sexual harassment coolly, and only later, as activist pressure increased, did members endorse the concern and move to address it. Ultimately, the profession accepted many of the feminists' policy recommendations and endorsed policies that reached significantly beyond the Supreme Court's narrow suggestions in *Faragher*.

After a brief summary of the development of the personnel administration profession, I trace the profession's changing perspective on the issue of sexual harassment through coverage in several practitioner journals over the period from 1975, when the term sexual harassment was coined, through 2000. These journals are the official voice of the American Society for Personnel Administration, titled *Personnel Administrator* (1956–89) and *HRMagazine* (1990–present); the official voice of the International Public Management Association for Human Resources, titled *Public Personnel Review* (1938–1972) and *Public Personnel Management* (1972-present); and an unaffiliated but prominent practitioner journal, *Personnel Journal* (circulation approximately 20,000).[63] Although my coverage of the personnel journals is not as broad as that of some studies, it has the advantage of focusing on the official voices of the key practitioner associations; these journals were marketed to practitioners and read by them, and they carried the legitimacy of endorsement by professional associations.[64]

The personnel administration profession's conflicted response to feminist activists grew from its divided identity, at once a voice for both management's prerogatives and employees' interests. This sense of professional mission, as Sanford Jacoby has shown, grew from reform impulses in the Progressive Era seeking to bring order and harmony to labor relations by addressing employees' needs and complaints managerially as an alternative to union organizing.[65] To this end, reformers sought to impose managerial control over workers but at the same time to improve their welfare and education and respond to their grievances.[66] Their diverse efforts on these issues consolidated into a common movement that became the personnel administration profession, complete with local, state, and national professional associations.[67] Personnel departments spread among firms gradually after the 1910s and then more rapidly in the late 1930s and 1940s, so that by 1946 almost 75 percent of firms employing 250 or more employees had these departments.[68]

The profession's mission has since remained divided. An early observer noted that the personnel manager was an intermediary between managers and workers: "He must always perform the functions of a mutual interpreter and often those of a peacemaker."[69] Playing such a role successfully, it was argued, required professional independence from each side and the capacity to represent the perspectives, needs, and interests of each to the other. Although a claim by managers to represent owners' interests was not surprising, the converse claim—that professional managers might seek to represent workers' interests—was a truly remarkable ideological development, and one that would ultimately shape the profession's reception of the women's movement against sexual harassment. After World War II, the profession's leaders sought to strengthen its mission as an intermediary between workers and management, one focused on both enhancing productivity and "present[ing] worker grievances to management."[70]

The major shifts in the economy in the 1970s and 1980s, particularly with the decline in union membership and later downsizing, as Jacoby observes, contributed to a crisis in the personnel administration profession.[71] Its members increasingly felt their role and influence in firms questioned or challenged, and they lost influence to a competing and rising profession—finance.[72] In this context, the growth of employee rights in the 1970s and 1980s, as Jacoby suggests, offered personnel administration a virtual lifeline, a new rationale for its existence and role.[73]

Still, personnel administrators were not by any means immediate converts to the feminist movement against sexual harassment, nor did they have their own ideas on how best to address harassment. Early activists in that movement described hostile receptions from personnel administrators. The Alliance Against Sexual Coercion observed later that in the 1970s "personnel [administrators] and management did very little except trivialize the complaints of those women who came forward."[74] The feminist authors Constance Backhouse and Leah Cohen interviewed a number of human resources managers in business firms and government agencies in the period before 1979 and concluded that "as things now stand, a woman who is being sexually harassed will not receive a particularly sympathetic audience with either personnel or management."[75] A number of personnel directors refused Backhouse and Cohen's requests for interviews on the subject, and the authors described those who agreed to be interviewed as extremely defensive, embarrassed, or hostile about the topic. Although female personnel administrators typically acknowledged that sexual harassment existed in their firms or agencies, all but one of the male personnel administrators declared categorically that it did not; and most insisted that if harassment existed, it occurred only because women invited such behavior or failed to make clear that they did not appreciate it.[76]

Two personnel managers who acknowledged the existence of sexual harassment in their workforces offered observations that are especially revealing. One, a man, observed: "I am not denying that it is a serious problem. But in today's world, it's a question of expectation. Men are conditioned to expect that men in power play around. Women, however, are still coping with a double standard that says, 'Nice girls don't do that.' So we have a situation where men generally wield enormous power over women and can coerce women into coming across sexually. . . . Men generally see sexual harassment as part of the work game."[77]

Another, a woman, when asked why female managers were more likely to acknowledge the existence of harassment, smiled and observed, "I suspect that most women managers have been victims of sexual harassment themselves." But she went on to acknowledge that little could be done to stop the problem if "senior management" offered no support.[78]

Although after 1975 the popular media devoted prominent attention to sexual harassment, the personnel journals remained completely silent on it until 1979. In the same period, the journals addressed sexual discrimination more generally only once when, in 1977, *Personnel Administrator* published an article on "sex bias," which focused on negative stereotypes of women in management settings and how to identify and overcome them.[79]

In 1979 the issue of sexual harassment began appearing in the public personnel journals, opening a three-year period from 1979 to 1982 when they devoted considerable attention to it and ultimately absorbed many elements of the feminist perspective. Nearly every article on sexual harassment published during this time characterized it as a very serious issue and urged personnel administrators to address it immediately. Thus, in April 1979 the first article on sexual harassment appearing in any of the personnel journals characterized it as the core discrimination problem confronting women in the workplace.[80] In support of this claim, the author cited the sorts of stories and survey results that were by then widely reported in the popular media. Some early articles struck a prophetic and almost plaintive tone, suggesting that although "harassment cannot be eliminated," as one put it, organizations must take strong steps to "give women the necessary support to take a stand."[81] Others expressed a tone of inevitability, predicting imminent broad changes in federal policy. Thus an article from 1980 reported that the chair of the EEOC, Eleanor Holmes Norton, had called the 1980s the "decade of the women" and stated that the agency would be working aggressively to attack sexual harassment.[82] Another declared simply that "sexual harassment will develop into one of the most controversial and complex issues that organizations will face in the next decade."[83] "Sexual harassment is now out of the closet," another author observed. "It's an issue of the 1980s" and "a powder-keg problem" likely to have greater impact on employers than the law on race discrimination.[84]

The tone of urgency reflected, in part, the growth of litigation and federal judicial decisions on the issue. Virtually every article on harassment in the initial three-year period from 1979 to 1981 highlighted plaintiff-friendly judicial decisions.[85] Thus the author who had predicted that the 1980s would be "the decade of the women" also observed that it would likely be "the decade of the seminar, in which prudent personnel professionals will scramble to catch up and keep up with revolutionary changes occurring in that area of discrimination law."[86] Similarly an article from 1980 on sexual harassment as "a form of sex discrimination" focused primarily on the leading legal precedents and their implications for organizational policies.[87]

Early articles on sexual harassment consistently argued that it imposed a range of unacceptable costs in addition to legal liability, among them absenteeism, turnover, damage to employee morale, loss of federal contracts, "a non-productive work atmosphere,"[88] and "adverse public relations."[89]

My survey confirms that personnel administrators in local governments share the view that liability's reputational costs outweigh its financial costs. Thus in my survey of the head of personnel in city governments in the year 2000, as illustrated in figure 8.1, respondents on average rated the costs to the agency's coverage in the media and public image at 7 on a scale from 1 to 10, with 10 being "major long-term damage," while they rated the budgetary costs at 5.3, just under the midpoint on the scale.

With regard to remedies, the early articles in personnel journals, like the early proposals from feminists and the early coverage in the popular press, suggested a relatively wide range of options. Some favored a version of the AASC's call for women to engage in organized self-help, declaring that they should confront alleged harassers, even to the exclusion of taking the issue to management.[90] Alternatively, an article from 1981 recommended mediation between complainants and alleged harassers so as to

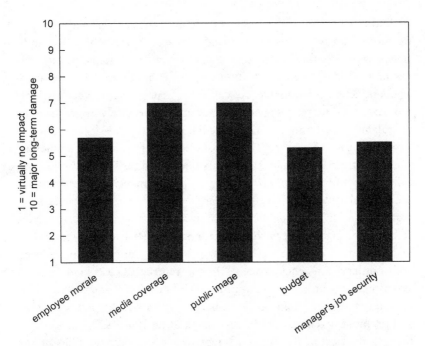

Figure 8.1. Perceived impact of a sexual harassment lawsuit on city government, by nature of impact. N = 428–38. Differences between the media coverage/public image measures and all others are significant below .001 (t > 13).

enable them "to understand each other's behavior."[91] By the 1990s, mediation was widely seen as a highly inappropriate response inasmuch as it implied that alleged harassment might grow out of "misunderstandings." By contrast, several early articles endorsed Margaret Mead's suggestion that the problem would never be solved without broad cultural change regarding sex roles, accompanied by a new "taboo" against sex at work.[92] Notably, early coverage recommended that personnel administrators contact the leading women's advocacy groups on sexual harassment, particularly the Alliance Against Sexual Coercion and the Working Women United Institute (the educational arm of WWU), to get advice regarding effective policies against sexual harassment.[93]

By 1981, however, most of these alternatives were being overtaken by an increasingly dominant legalized accountability model. The model, as in policing, had three main elements: formal employment policies prohibiting sexual harassment, communication of the policies to employees, and formalized internal oversight (particularly grievance procedures and remedies). Thus an article from early 1980—before publication of the preliminary version of the EEOC Guidelines—argued that federal court decisions increasingly were requiring that management have a written policy explicitly forbidding sexual harassment; take steps, particularly training sessions, to ensure that all employees are aware "that top management actively discourages sexual harassment"; have in place a widely known procedure for filing complaints; and immediately investigate any complaint and take appropriate remedial action.[94]

Shortly thereafter, the EEOC endorsed precisely such recommendations, and the personnel journals quickly reported the EEOC's action and called on employers to adopt rules against harassment, training on the issue, and grievance procedures.[95] An article from 1980, for instance, summarized the EEOC Guidelines, emphasized that they required employers to take "affirmative" steps to eliminate harassment from the workplace, and recommended adopting a written prohibition, grievance procedures, and training.[96] An article from 1981 reported the EEOC's guidelines on sexual harassment and summarized the Commission's recommendations for internal organizational policies, particularly a written policy defining and prohibiting sexual harassment; clear and easily accessible procedures for making a complaint of harassment; systematic investigations of any complaint; appropriate corrective actions; and steps to educate employees about the nature of the problem, the organization's policies against it, and the procedures for making a complaint.[97] Similarly, other articles from 1980 and 1981 typically summarized the EEOC Guidelines and suggested internal organizational reforms based on them.[98] Thus a 1981 article recommended "prevention and awareness of the problem. A company should develop a sexual harassment policy and grievance procedures. Meetings and/or training should be provided. . . . The message must be direct: that sexual harassment is serious and illegal and that managers must treat offenders firmly."[99] Similarly, another 1981 article observed that "a plethora of articles has already been written recommending model programs" but argued that not enough emphasis had been placed "on a mechanism for disseminating information. . . . A static and perfunctory training program" is insufficient.[100]

To be sure, some of these early articles equivocated on some elements of the emerging institutional model. Thus an article from 1981 recommended adopting a policy prohibiting sexual harassment but vacillated on grievance procedures, acknowledging that "each organization will differ in the type of grievance avenues offered."[101] Nonetheless, even by the early 1980s the professional journals had communicated an administrative model aimed at, in their words, eliminating sexual harassment. As one article declared, "If the organization sets a climate in which company policy forbids sexual harassment, and all employees realize that the organization seriously supports the policy, great strides will be made toward elimination of the problem."[102]

Some early articles in the personnel journals went beyond these initial elements of the policy model. An author in 1980, for instance, urged organizations to adopt rules, training, and grievance procedures but also recommended efforts aimed at discovering whether harassment exists even in the absence of complaints, among them exit interviews with all departing employees.[103]

And then, as suddenly as the sexual harassment issue appeared in the pages of the personnel profession's journals, it vanished almost entirely. As the Reagan administration pursued its campaign against the EEOC's sexual harassment guidelines, professional journals in the field abruptly dropped their coverage of the issue. Between 1982 and 1987, neither *Personnel Administrator* nor *Public Personnel Review* carried a single article on sexual harassment. *Personnel Journal*, the least prestigious of the three journals, carried only two articles on the subject during that five-year period.[104] The silence in the personnel journals is remarkable, especially in the wake of the earlier flurry of concern.[105]

The parallel with patterns in attention to legalized accountability in *Police Chief* magazine is striking. There too attention to abuses of authority waxed briefly (in the case of policing, in the late 1960s and early 1970s), but coverage of the problem was held in abeyance during the mid-1970s as police departments fought to avoid legalized accountability over frontline officers' discretionary uses of force. In the case of policing, the period of abeyance ended as fear of liability grew dramatically, propelling dramatic growth in attention to legalized accountability as a solution.

In 1987 the personnel journals, citing growing threats of liability, suddenly rejuvenated attention to legalized accountability in the area of sexual harassment. In January 1987 an article in *Personnel Administrator* revived many of the themes explored in the earlier discussions, suggesting that, in light of *Meritor Savings Bank vs. Vinson* (1987), "fortunately," grievance procedures "may insulate employers from liability for the acts of their supervisors."[106] The article went on to summarize four specific elements of a comprehensive policy that would both minimize harassment and insulate the organization from liability:

1) Publish a policy prohibiting sexual harassment . . . [encompassing both quid pro quo and hostile environment harassment]. 2) Develop procedures

whereby employees who feel they are victims of sexual harassment can state
their complaints in confidence. . . . 3) Educate both employees and supervisors
about sexual harassment and about the employer's policy and procedures to
combat it. 4) Take swift action against harassers. Get the word out that this
conduct will not be tolerated and back up the policy against sexual harassment with firm action.

Similarly, an article from 1988 provided a detailed discussion of the
Meritor decision, concluding that the Supreme Court had "given its general 'blessing'" to the EEOC's sexual harassment guidelines, indicating that
to minimize their exposure to liability employers should closely follow the
Guidelines in developing sexual harassment policies and procedures.[107]
Another article, observing that with "hundreds of sexual harassment cases"
pending in the federal courts, the issue "is one of the most critical issues
facing management," recommended adopting formal sexual harassment
policies and procedures.[108]

In the wake of *Meritor*, the recommendations regarding policies, procedures, and training became more specific and legally sophisticated.
Thus an article from 1990 recommended including in the policy on sexual
harassment "a broad list of examples" of prohibited conduct, complaint
procedures that allow multiple ways to make complaints (to allow a com-
plainant to bypass a superior if the superior is the alleged harasser), credible assurances of nonretaliation against complainants, and multifaceted
training on the policies and procedures.[109] The article concluded with a
remarkably strong reassurance that in hostile work environment cases, unless the employer knew of the offending conduct and did not adequately
address it, "a strongly worded and well-enforced policy, coupled with
the sensitivity training discussed above, should be a near absolute, if not
absolute, defense to employer liability."[110] A number of articles summarized these elements (clear policy; accessible complaint procedure; training and other efforts to communicate the policy; and fair investigations)
or expanded on one or another of them.[111] As the model gained a clear
and common institutional form, authors in the professional journals began providing increasingly detailed analyses of particular elements. For
another example, a 1998 article focused on selection of the investigator of
complaints, recommending that the more severe the alleged behavior or
the more the allegation implicated the organization's policies or culture,
the better it was to rely on external investigators with professional training in the law.[112] Similarly, some articles favored highly formalized policies

on "progressive discipline," carefully calibrating the level of discipline to the seriousness of the violation.[113] Others attempted to provide guidance in dealing with borderline issues, among them consensual romantic relationships, "risqué" humor, or rudeness.[114] Others observed that small but significant proportions of male employees responding to surveys reported experiencing sexual harassment and recommended adjusting policies and training to acknowledge this fact.[115] Same-sex harassment emerged as a significant theme in the wake of the Supreme Court's decision in *Oncale* (1998), extending the coverage of sexual harassment law to same-sex harassment.[116]

Warnings about the threat of liability increased in the 1990s, particularly following the confirmation hearing on the nomination of Clarence Thomas to the Supreme Court, in which Anita Hill's allegations of sexual harassment received prominent attention. Thus several articles in 1992 observed that harassment complaints had increased dramatically in the wake of the Thomas hearings, and one article encouraged employers to adopt policies that facilitated complaints.[117] In the mid-1990s Jonathan Segal, a lawyer and management consultant on sexual harassment policy, dated what he called a "sexual harassment litigation revolution" to the Thomas hearings.[118] Another observed, "In the wake of the Clarence Thomas and Anita Hill hearings, HR professionals are rethinking, revising, and reestablishing their companies' sexual harassment policies."[119] Similarly, authors increasingly warned of an explosion in sexual harassment litigation. The Society for Human Resources Management commissioned a survey of employers in which over half of respondents reported that their organizations had been sued and that sexual harassment claims constituted 14 percent of suits.[120] Another survey found that almost half of respondents had received a complaint of sexual harassment in 1996, that most resulted in discipline, but that only 5 percent of such complaints resulted in a lawsuit.[121] An author observed in 1996 (after extensively summarizing the elements of the now well-institutionalized model), "The courts have imposed a heavy burden on employers. . . . There is a lot employers can do, not only to avoid claims, but also to make the workplace more comfortable and, as such, profitable. It is as simple as paying now or paying later."[122]

Crucially, the personnel journals in the 1990s began to import additional elements of the feminists' policy recommendations. An article from 1997 emphasized the critical importance of protecting complainants from retaliation.[123] Additionally, a number of articles called on management to communicate the message that harassment will not be tolerated. "In essence," one observed, "an employer should take all necessary steps to see that harassment does not occur."[124] Another similarly observed that common defenses against harassment claims "have no merit," which "underscores the importance of preventive training in this area."[125] "An employer's best hope for avoiding sexual harassment liability," another observed, "is to prevent it in the first place," particularly through forceful training aimed at dispelling common myths about harassment.[126]

Recommendations for internal oversight, in particular, became more far-reaching. Several articles appearing after 1990 favored the use of proactive measures—surveys, telephone hotlines, or exit interviews—to assess the extent of harassment within the organization and make a response possible. Thus one article, observing that "ignorance is no defense," argued that employee surveys could help to identify "pockets of discontent," among them any possible perceptions that "the company tolerates harassment on account of sex."[127] An article from 1992 favored the use of internal surveys to learn about employees' perceptions of the extent of harassment, and telephone hotlines to inform employees about the employer's sexual harassment policies and procedures and how to file a complaint.[128] Another article from 1992 favored the use of formal "harassment audits," essentially surveys aimed at identifying the extent of sexual harassment in the organization.[129] A 1995 article encouraged using hotlines to field questions about sexual harassment.[130]

At the extreme, some writers began favoring "zero tolerance" policies, which authorize dismissing an employee on the first proven instance of harassment, no matter its severity, ostensibly to send a message that even the mildest and most borderline harassment would not be tolerated.[131] Although it has been claimed that such zero tolerance policies have become the norm, other articles in personnel journals at the same time favored deepening an organization's efforts short of firing, namely providing comprehensive counseling and retraining programs for violators.[132] Employers participating in one such program reported that it dramatically reduced the incidence of harassment by the participating employees.[133]

By the late 1990s, articles in the personnel journals interpreted judicial decisions as sending a clear message: take vigorous steps to stamp out the problem.[134] The message of *Faragher* and *Ellerth* (1998), as one put it, was "prevent now or pay later."[135] Another observed, "The message [from the courts] is clear: Companies can no longer afford to wait until an employee files a charge to confront the problem of harassment in the workplace. Proactive steps, including effective employee and supervisor training, must be taken to stop harassment before it starts."[136] But for employers whose policies had kept up with the now-institutionalized legalized accountability model, writers reported that the Court had also provided a reassurance. *Faragher* and *Ellerth*, declared the principal legal commentator for *HRMagazine*, "will make it easier for employees to sue" but also will protect employers from liability if they fully implement the now well-established institutional model of clear policy, accessible complaint procedures, thorough training and communication of the policy and procedures to employees, and "deliberate and decisive corrective action" in cases of harassment.[137]

To be sure, some recommendations in the professional journals ran counter to the more common recommendation to address sexual harassment by a multifaceted approach. Thus an article from 1992 emphasized the importance of legally defensible policies in employee handbooks, arguing that "incorporating a strong sexual harassment policy in employee manuals is one of the most effective ways for employers to avoid liability for charges of harassment."[138] "There is a fine line that separates legal protection from legal vulnerability," another observed. "That line is drawn by the content and wording of your EEO policies."[139] Still, these were rare exceptions to the multifaceted model favored by most writers in the personnel journals.

By 2000, in sum, with regard to sexual harassment, the field of personnel management had institutionalized a model of legalized accountability. The elements of the model combined MacKinnon's thesis that harassment is a violation of Title 7 of the Civil Rights Act of 1964 and encompasses both sexual demands and workplace culture ("hostile environment") with Backhouse and Cohen's thesis that remedies must include proactive organizational policies, training, and internal oversight. The EEOC in 1980 had drawn together these two lines of thinking. Not surprisingly, some discussions in professional human resources journals had sought to limit employer responsibility to merely the adoption of correct employee policy language, precisely the empty symbolism that Backhouse and Cohen had fought against. But these were rare expressions. By contrast, many discussions in professional journals pushed employer responsibility beyond what the EEOC had proposed in 1980, specifically by recommending such mechanisms of internal oversight as employee surveys and hotlines to discover problems not revealed by employee complaints. This model of legalized accountability parallels the policing model in its breadth and depth.

How Widely Have City Governments Adopted the Professional Recommendations?

To what extent have city governments adopted systems of legalized accountability for addressing sexual harassment? I address this question with data drawn from an original survey of city governments.

Agencies' antiharassment policies may range from limited and pro forma to elaborate, diverse, and proactive. Notably, feminist activists have consistently demanded broad-reaching programs, with the onus on the employer rather than the victims of harassment to identify problems and address them. Prior research reports that organizational employers have widely adopted two key elements of the legalized accountability model, training and grievance procedures, but scholars appropriately view these, at least if not accompanied by more searching efforts at eradicating harassment, as relatively limited steps.[140] It is worth noting, however, as observed above, that some authors in HR journals have recommended even less, merely the adoption of a carefully worded prohibition on harassment. Thus training and grievance procedures should be viewed as steps beyond mere written policy. Further, as Barbara Gutek, one of the leading scholars of sexual harassment and its prevention, has observed, the nature of agencies' sexual harassment training and communication programs may vary from limited and pro forma to elaborate and diverse.[141] Several surveys have found that about 40 to 50 percent of employed women are unaware of their employer's sexual harassment policy, suggesting that organizational employers vary considerably in their effort to educate their employees on the issue.[142] Some employers simply have a policy but provide no training or education on it. Others use a range of publicity methods, among them posters, giving written information to new employees, telephone hotlines, newsletters, and the like. Additionally, employers may provide focused sexual harassment prevention training, but these programs may vary considerably in their breadth and depth.[143] Some focus primarily on the legal definition of harassment, while others provide examples of various kinds of harassment and seek to sensitize employees to the problem. Some training programs are pro forma exercises in which employees simply watch an educational video. Others are far more elaborate, involving such things as lectures, role-playing, reading, and even homework and tests. Some training programs target only management, while others target all employees and may offer different types of training for different levels of organizational authority. Some programs are conducted only for entering employees, while others are done periodically for all employees. Finally, agencies' systems of internal oversight may vary considerably, taking one of three levels. They may make no effort to identify whether there is a harassment problem among employees; they may passively accept complaints through grievance procedures; or they may go beyond passive grievance procedures and use such oversight methods as telephone hotlines and employee surveys.

Beyond these administrative systems, agencies may vary considerably in how far they take action against individuals who harass. Cases of harassment may be swept under the rug, with the employer imposing no disciplinary action, counseling, or retraining; at the other extreme, employers may dismiss individuals guilty of harassment. A related question is whether the presence of such administrative systems contributes to taking actions against harassers or to avoiding such actions. Some have alleged that at least some elements of these programs are alternatives to, rather than elements of, real steps to address the problem of harassment.[144]

I designed my organizational survey specifically to assess how widely city governments have adopted the full range of possible administrative mechanisms described above, as well as whether they have taken a variety of disciplinary actions against people who engage in harassment. The survey was administered to a stratified random sample of city governments in the United States in 2000. There were 454 usable responses, representing a 54 percent response rate. Questions addressed each of the dimensions of the legalized accountability model discussed above, along with other matters to be discussed below. Readers interested in methodological issues may consult the book's appendix.

A simplified illustration of the variations among city governments on the basic administrative dimensions of the model appears in figure 8.2. The basic observation is that the least costly, least intrusive, and most visible dimensions are adopted the most widely; the most costly, intrusive, and, typically, most hidden dimensions are the least widely adopted.

Cities vary considerably on these dimensions of sexual harassment policy. By far the most widely adopted element of the common model is a written policy prohibiting harassment. Virtually all departments (98 percent) reported having adopted such a policy. Similarly, 77 percent of cities reported having a formal grievance procedure. Somewhat lower, but still large, proportions of cities report using a diverse array of training tools on the issue of sexual harassment, among them written materials (76 percent), oral presentations (74 percent), video presentations (54 percent), and role-playing (55 percent); two-thirds (66 percent) of cities report using three or more of these training tools. Just under half (46 percent)

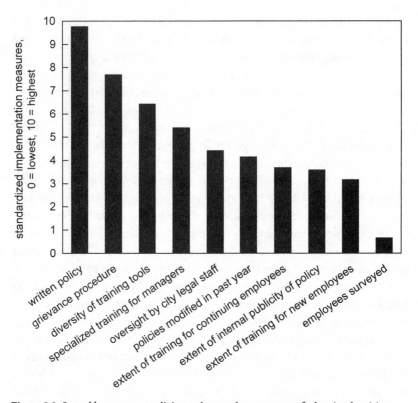

Figure 8.2. Sexual harassment policies and procedures, extent of adoption by cities.
$N = 414$–54. See accompanying text and methodological appendix for discussion.

report providing specialized sexual harassment training for managers. The
frequency of training for continuing employees varies considerably; on a
four-point scale from never to every six months or less, the average is
more than a year, just over the second point on the scale. Similarly, the
average extent of training for new and for continuing employees is rather
low compared with some other less intrusive sexual harassment policies.
Well over a third of cities report providing no sexual harassment training to new employees, and another quarter report providing only fifteen
minutes of training. As in my treatment of legalized accountability in policing, I include here a measure of internal legal oversight in the form of
how often personnel managers consult with city legal staff over the issue
of sexual harassment. On a five-point scale ranging from never or almost
never to communicating several times a week, the average is just under
half, roughly between "occasionally, a few times over the course of several
years," and "regularly, several times during a year"; this indicates, on aver-

age, relatively infrequent internal legal consultation on the issue. Finally, at the far low end of this comparative illustration is the most intrusive and constraining of these various procedures, the use of an employee survey to assess the extent of sexual harassment within the organization; only 7 percent of cities have carried out such a survey.

Finally, cities vary considerably on whether they took corrective actions against harassment in the year preceding the survey: 31 percent issued an oral reprimand, 37 percent issued a written reprimand, 42 percent required counseling or retraining, and 13 percent dismissed a person over sexual harassment. Still, most cities, 53 percent, took none of these steps, while 28 percent took three or more. Obviously, whether a city has taken one or more of these steps is likely to vary somewhat with the number of employees; still, city size has a very small influence on how widely cities have taken these actions (explaining less than 2 percent of the variance), leaving much of the variation to be explained by other factors, to be explored below.[145]

Why Do City Governments Vary in Their Level of Commitment to Legalized Accountability?

Why are some city governments more committed than others to legalizing accountability in the area of sexual harassment? Why have some taken corrective steps while many others have not? Are these variations haphazard or random? Or do they grow systematically from identifiable conditions? If they grow from identifiable conditions, are these influences mainly in the form of professional recommendations via personnel administration networks? Or have activists played a role as well?

To address these questions I employ a statistical model with the same structure as the model summarized in chapter 6 with regard to police policies. For the primary dependent variable, level of city commitment to legalizing accountability, I have combined the measures summarized in figure 8.2 into a single index that identifies how far each city in my database has adopted the various elements of a standard sexual harassment policy.[146] Some cities have adopted many of these policies and procedures while others have adopted few. For the dependent variable measuring city actions against harassment, I have combined the corrective steps listed previously (oral reprimand, written reprimand, counseling or retraining, and dismissal) into an additive index.

With two exceptions, the explanatory variables are identical to those described in chapter 6 with regard to the policing model, and here I will only briefly summarize the list of variables; readers interested in a more complete description should consult chapter 6 and the methodological appendix. One exception is that here I leave out the independent variable measuring the relative liberalism of state laws on soverign immunity because federal sex harassment law overrides these state laws. The other exception is that under organizational characteristics, I have added the proportion of city government employees who are women. Gutek has argued that harassment is more likely as contact between female and male employees increases; alternatively, we might expect that as female employment increases, women's influence over city policies may increase as well. In either case, we might expect that more cities are driven into adopting harassment policies the larger the proportion of women in their employ. Apart from this addition, the model is the same as for policing. In summary, the variables include the following:

1. Dependent variables
   a. Legalized accountability (the index above)
   b. Corrective actions (additive index of oral reprimand, written reprimand, requiring retraining or counseling, and dismissal)[147]
2. Independent variables
   a. Strength of the activist infrastructure of support
      (1) Report by the personnel director of the number of citizen groups and local attorneys that support sexual harassment or discrimination lawsuits
      (2) Independent, objective measure of the number of government liability attorneys in the local jurisdiction, obtained from the Martindale-Hubbell lawyer database at the time of the survey[148]
   b. Strength of personnel department connections to professional networks
      (1) Departmental policy changes are influenced by recommendations of professional associations
      (2) City employs a personnel director
      (3) City employs an EEO officer
   c. Organizational characteristics
      (1) Size
      (2) Reformed (council-manager) administrative structure
      (3) Employee unionization
      (4) Liability insurance coverage
      (5) Budgetary slack

    d. Formal legal environment
      (1) Federal appellate circuit court liberalism on civil rights
      (2) State supreme court liberalism on civil rights
    e. Political culture (state political preferences)
    f. Organizational experience with litigation (index of whether any
      lawsuits over sexual harassment have ever been filed against the city;
      whether the city settled any such lawsuit in the previous five years;
      whether the city lost any such lawsuit in court in the previous five
      years)
    g. Demographic context
      (1) Average income of local population
      (2) Education level of local population
      (3) Proximity to a major city

With regard to sexual harassment policies, among these possible influences, two factors primarily explain variations among cities: the relative strength of the local activist infrastructure for sexual harassment litigation and how closely city governments are connected to broader networks in the public personnel management profession. The stronger local support structures for sex harassment litigation, the more extensively city governments have adopted the elements of the legalized accountability model. Similarly, the more closely connected city governments are to broader networks in the personnel management profession, the more extensively have they adopted elements of the model. These two factors—support structures and professional networks—remain significant even when controlling for every other plausible influence. Their combined influence is especially powerful. Further, no other factor—size of city population, proximity to an urban area, partisan or other political attitudes of the local population, income, education level, or racial composition of the local population—influences how widely city governments have adopted the legalized accountability model as much as do these two primary factors.

These observations are illustrated by figure 8.3, which reports the extent of departmental adoption of the legalized accountability model to be expected for cities with weak and strong local support structures for sexual harassment litigation, weak and strong connections to broader professional networks, and low and high populations, controlling for other variables. The full statistical model these predictions are drawn from is presented in the appendix. The figure illustrates a basic observation: both the strength of local support structures and the strength of local governments'

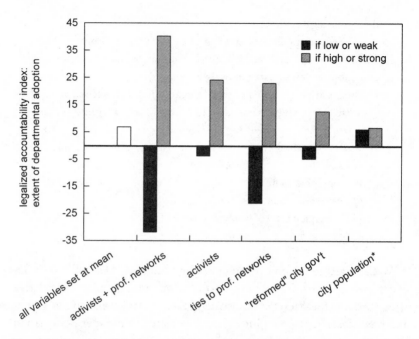

Figure 8.3. Factors explaining extent of city government adoption of legalized accountability in area of sexual harassment. *Indicates that relationship is not statistically significant; other insignificant variables not pictured. The figure's y-axis runs from the twenty-fifth to the eightieth percentile on the dependent variable (the legalized accountability index). Results obtained using Monte Carlo simulations derived from the Clarify application in Stata.

connections to professional networks contribute substantially to adoption of the legalized accountability model. Thus a shift in the strength of the local support structure from nonexistent (a very common status) to strong results in a shift in the level of adoption on the index from −.03 to .26.[149] A shift in strength of the city government's connections to professional networks in the human resources/personnel administration field from weak to strong yields an even more substantial shift in the level of adoption of the legalized accountability model from −.22 to .25.[150] A similar shift on both factors together has an even greater impact. By comparison, that a city has a "reformed" governing structure (a professional city manager rather than an elected mayor) yields a shift from −.05 to .13 on the index, and a shift in the city's population from the twenty-fifth to the seventy-fifth percentile yields no significant shift in the adoption of the model.

With regard to disciplinary actions, the most influential factors are how fully cities have adopted systems of legalized accountability and whether they employ a personnel director, an EEO officer, or both. Each of these contributes to carrying out disciplinary or corrective actions. Additionally, carrying out disciplinary actions increases with the female percentage of the workforce, providing support either for Gutek's "contact" hypothesis or simply the idea that the influence of women increases with their numbers. As in policing, the significant point is that systems of legalized accountability contribute to, rather than detract from, taking corrective actions.

Conclusion

The norm of legalized accountability with regard to sexual harassment grew rapidly in the 1980s, and by 2000 it had spread far and wide among city governments. According to one perspective, this sort of administrative legalization is an activist imposition on professional practitioners against their better judgment; according to another, it is practitioner-controlled, largely ceremonial, window dressing. I have shown, by contrast, that legalized accountability with regard to sexual harassment was a *joint* creation of activists and professional administrators; each was necessary to the development, but neither was sufficient alone.

Activists pressed the issue of sexual harassment onto the public agenda and framed the problem as an organizational responsibility. Activists, too, crafted the concrete proposal for what to do, organizationally, to eradicate harassment. This proposal, however, drew on two activists' extensive managerial experience and thus relied on several standard managerial tools: formal policies, employee training, and grievance procedures. Although these were standard tools, the activists proposed using them for a new project of fundamental institutional change aimed at eradicating support for sexual harassment within organizational culture.

Although professional personnel administrators initially were deaf to activists' complaints and proposals, under growing liability pressure they relatively quickly endorsed much of the activist agenda. Once the EEOC and the Supreme Court endorsed the feminists' claims, practitioners' support for that agenda increased considerably, and by the 1990s, at least in the area of public personnel administration, practitioner journals supported nearly every element of the activists' original program.

By 2000 the recommended administrative program—policies, training, grievance procedures, and methods of internal oversight—had spread widely among city governments, albeit in varying levels of completeness. Some cities had adopted all or nearly all of these elements, others only the most visible and least intrusive. And many cities acted to correct sexual harassment while many others did not. Those policies are more substantive and less ceremonial in cities that are under pressure from activist lawyers and citizen groups and that have robust connections to professional networks in the personnel administration field. Further, the more substantive a city's sexual harassment policies, the more likely the city is to discover instances of harassment and take corrective action.

The feminist campaign against sexual harassment, in sum, profoundly affected sexual harassment policy, even if it did not control it.

Playground Safety

If legalized accountability has grown and spread, is its reach limited to areas subject to federal law and "rights talk" (like policing and sexual harassment policy, the topics of earlier chapters) or has it extended into policy areas free of these pressures? To address this question I examine the response to liability in the area of playground management. Thirty years ago, by common assent, playgrounds in the United States were old, unimaginative, and dangerous. Children risked falling onto asphalt from ten-foot jungle gyms, being pulled under spinning open-centered merry-go-rounds, or getting hit on the head by heavy metal swings. Playground safety activists documented these dangers and the tens of thousands of injuries they caused, but when their efforts to establish mandatory federal playground safety rules failed, they began to despair of reforming the country's hundreds of thousands of playgrounds.

Yet playgrounds *were* reformed, as if overnight, by a remarkably common model of playground safety.[1] For critics of tort litigation, playground liability is the poster child of legalism run amok: an explosion of unreasonable lawsuits and jury verdicts has forced playground operators to adopt nonsense policies (like the supposedly widespread removal of diving boards from public swimming pools).[2] For liberal defenders of liability, this critique is baseless: there are extremely few such lawsuits.[3]

My central claim—missed by both sides of the debate—is that the growth of liability pressure led to a sudden flurry of playground safety reforms that quickly took a common form. The forces driving these changes, as in the other policy areas examined in this book, emerged out of an interaction between liability pressure and reformist practitioners. Further, variation among local areas in the strength of these forces helps explain why some parks agencies have adopted all or nearly all of the shared model's elements while others have adopted fewer. Finally, variation among local parks departments in adoption of the common model helps explain whether they have taken corrective steps against safety problems.

To support these claims I first analyze changes over time in the way liability and safety are discussed in the country's primary professional journal for parks administration. Then I analyze data drawn from an original survey of local parks departments that I conducted in 2000.

The Development of Playground Safety

Although playground safety is within the jurisdiction of parks and recreation administration, that profession showed little interest in the issue until the late 1980s. Safety advocates succeeded in getting the federal Consumer Product Safety Commission (CPSC) to issue playground safety guidelines in 1981, but these voluntary guidelines were largely ignored by the profession until liability lawyers, aided by safety advocates acting as expert witnesses, began employing them in personal injury lawsuits. In the late 1980s, under growing liability pressure, the parks administration profession suddenly awoke to the safety issue and quickly adopted a shared model for ensuring playground safety. Although based on the CPSC's 1981 guidelines, this shared model went beyond them in key ways, particularly in its attention to systematic safety training and auditing. In tracing these developments I rely especially on the evolving coverage of playground safety in *Parks and Recreation*, the official voice of the National Recreation and Parks Association and the leading practitioner journal in the field.

Playgrounds in the United States date to a Progressive Era "playground movement" seeking to offer city children opportunities for exercise.[4] Friedrich Froebel, the German creator of the kindergarten concept, was by the 1880s also advocating outdoor play areas for children to encourage mental and physical development. American reformers imported Froebel's playground idea, first with "sandgartens" in the Boston area in the 1880s and then with other playground forms. By the height of the Progressive Era in 1905–15, the playground movement was well under way, and playgrounds spread rapidly among American cities. In 1907 advocates formed the Playground Association of America, the precursor to the present-day

National Recreation and Parks Association (NRPA), the leading professional association for parks and playgrounds managers. By 1910 the Playground Association of America was fielding as many as fifty requests a day for advice, testament to a vibrant movement.[5] In 1905 there were 35 cities with playgrounds; in 1907 the number had grown to 90, in 1908 to 187, and in 1909 to 336.[6] In 1909 Massachusetts adopted a state law requiring all cities above 10,000 to have public playgrounds.[7] Although the movement collapsed when the country entered World War I, it left a lasting legacy throughout the United States, with public playgrounds in nearly every American city.

Although the playground idea represented a remarkable innovation, most early playgrounds were rudimentary and rather dangerous. Play equipment consisted mainly of sandboxes, digging tools, slides, swings, seesaws, sawhorses, merry-go-rounds, and such climbing devices as jungle gyms made of steel pipes.[8] Many of these types of equipment contributed to injuries.[9] Most merry-go-rounds had open centers, allowing children to slip and be pulled under the rapidly turning apparatus. Many swings and spring-based riding toys were made of metal and could strike children's heads with great force, leading to serious injuries. After an early phase of experimenting, by the 1950s many agencies in charge of playgrounds settled on concrete or asphalt as the ideal ground covering (since it avoided mud or dust under play equipment and needed little maintenance).[10] Asphalt remained the dominant ground covering on playgrounds well into the 1980s. Above the asphalt, many climbing devices reached extraordinary heights. In retrospect it is clear that concrete or asphalt under a fifteen-foot-high jungle gym or an open merry-go-round was a recipe for widespread injury and occasionally death.

The 1960s and 1970s proved a fertile period in playground design, as in so many other areas of American life. In the late 1950s a number of cities redesigned their playgrounds around such novelty themes as boating, the Wild West, and rocket ships.[11] Out of this ferment grew several alternative playground models. A participatory design movement favored community input in the design and construction of playgrounds, leading to a wide array of playground designs. An "adventure playground" movement, growing out of experimental urban playgrounds in postwar Europe, where it was found that children loved to play among the rubble and destruction of war, favored playgrounds designed to be sites of child-led experiment and adventure.[12]

A design-for-safety movement grew at roughly the same time. Its earliest advocates, however, unlike the activists who first generated interest in police abuse and workplace sex harassment, were associated with leading professional institutions. In 1969 the Committee for Accident Prevention of the American Academy of Pediatrics, with several other groups, began working to establish voluntary standards for safe playground equipment; but lacking data on playground injuries, they abandoned the effort.[13] The Nixon administration, building on the consumer safety initiatives of its predecessors, created the Consumer Product Safety Commission in 1972, and the Commission focused much of its early efforts on child safety. By 1973, using data from the newly established National Electronic Injury Survey System (which surveys a sample of the country's hospitals) and tests at a University of Iowa laboratory, proponents of playground safety could demonstrate that many injuries occurred on playgrounds.[14] Playground equipment was placed eighth on a Consumer Product Safety Commission list of the country's most dangerous products.[15] At the same time, playground equipment manufacturers and the National Recreation and Parks Association formed a task force to establish equipment safety standards.[16] In 1973, apparently acting prematurely, an equipment manufacturer took out a full-page advertisement in *Parks and Recreation* magazine claiming that its equipment had been certified as complying with the forthcoming standards.[17]

Irritated by this attempt to capitalize on the still-unfinished safety standards, Elayne Butwinick, a member of the safety task force, petitioned the CPSC, complaining that the task force process was dominated by manufacturing interests. She asked the commission to develop independent, mandatory playground safety standards.[18] An Ohio community PTA filed a similar petition, and Americans for Democratic Action and the Consumers Union endorsed the pair of petitions.[19]

On this basis the CPSC formally called for a proposal to develop a set of national playground safety standards and awarded the contract to the National Recreation and Parks Association. In 1976 the NRPA submitted its report, *Proposed Safety Standards for Playground Equipment*. The report "stimulated a great deal of controversy" but withered on the vine after manufacturers opposed the standards out of fear of costs and the CPSC raised questions about the study's testing methods.[20]

Under continued pressure from playground safety advocates, the CPSC then commissioned the National Bureau of Standards to conduct technical tests and make recommendations, and it published the reports in 1981 as voluntary playground safety guidelines.[21] The guidelines capped an unprecedented decade-long push by playground safety advocates for federal action on playground safety. They were the first prominent set of playground safety standards issued by any organization, and coming from the federal government, they sent a powerful message and constituted a symbolic resource for playground safety advocates. Although the guidelines were much criticized later for failing to recommend an alternative to asphalt as a ground covering, they framed future debates by recognizing playground injuries as a serious problem and identifying the most significant sources of those injuries as hard ground coverings and dangerous play equipment.[22]

Parks and Recreation magazine's coverage of playground safety and liability issues changed considerably from the late 1970s through the 1990s, evidence of the institutionalizing of legalized accountability. Although *Parks and Recreation* devoted attention to playground *management* before the late 1980s, playground *safety*—now a central concern of playground management—received virtually no attention until 1987. As the consumer safety movement gained energy in the early 1970s, a lone article appeared in 1971 calling for systematic data gathering on injuries and systematic safety audits, claiming that "existing facilities and areas are unusually hazardous" and that "our present attitude in respect to 'safety' tolerates too many injuries and deaths."[23] Still, until well into the 1980s advice on how to improve safety remained unfocused, limited to a general recommendation for reliance on "good professional judgment, adherence to current safety standards, reasonable inspections and repairs."[24]

Similarly, before the 1980s, *Parks and Recreation* published only a handful of articles on the risk of liability, and—as significant—they shared no common pattern. In 1977 an article characterized legal liability as a "black cloud" hanging over parks administrators.[25] But the message of concern about liability was muddied by conflicting signals. The 1977 article, for instance, was based on a survey that showed precisely the opposite, that "a majority of the respondents indicated that legal liability was not a great problem,"[26] and a 1979 article aimed to debunk the "myth" of an explosion in lawsuits, observing that "the number of cases annually which result in substantial damage awards is remarkably small."[27]

When the CPSC issued its long-awaited playground safety guidelines in 1981, *Parks and Recreation* gave them no coverage. Indeed, the magazine devoted no significant space to the guidelines for six years. Even as late as 1987, when the profession first began to awaken to the emerging issue of safety, the NRPA's legal director observed that only half of attendees at professional seminars reported having even heard of the CPSC guidelines, and "only a handful indicate that they have actually read the information contained therein."[28]

Plaintiffs' lawyers, however, recognized the significance of the CPSC playground safety guidelines. In 1980 the CPSC and the Association of Trial Lawyers of America, "recognizing their common aims," in the words of the agency's vice chairman, had begun cooperatively exchanging information about injurious products to "encourage and assist ATLA members to use the commission more effectively."[29] Upon publication of the playground safety guidelines, plaintiffs' lawyers began referring to them as a professional standard of care against which playgrounds could be measured.[30] By 1982, as in policing, plaintiffs' lawyers increasingly were relying on expert witnesses to build cases against municipalities, and parks managers were complaining of the "proliferation of negligence suits."[31] In this context, *Parks and Recreation* began carrying a monthly column titled "NRPA Law Review," focused primarily on liability issues, and in 1983 the association began publishing the *Recreation and Parks Law Reporter*. By 1985 the "Law Review" column observed that "personal injury lawsuits have become a familiar part of the leisure services landscape."[32]

Then, in the mid-1980s, the United States liability insurance market descended into a "hard" phase in its periodic cycle, marked by dramatic increases in insurance premiums.[33] As we saw in chapter 5, a similar hard phase of the cycle in the mid- to late 1970s drew police chiefs' attention to lawsuits against the police. In 1986 *Parks and Recreation* began to complain loudly about dramatic changes in the legal environment. The lead editorial for February 1986, for instance, titled "The Liability Crisis," complained of growing difficulties in obtaining liability insurance for playground injuries.[34] In January 1987 the magazine's cover focused on "The Liability Crisis" and pictured an insurance contract stamped "CANCELLED." A lead article, "How to Tame the Liability Monster," observed that "the liability insurance crisis is news to no one."[35]

As with policing, however, the parks profession's first reaction to the perceived crisis was to attribute blame anywhere but to itself. The crisis, some pointed out, reflected the liability insurance cycle, not an increase in liability lawsuits.[36] Thus, at the height of the mid-1980s crisis, the regular legal commentator for *Parks and Recreation* went so far as to call concerns about injuries and liability inaccurate "sensationalism." "The high cost or unavailability of insurance," he went on, "has little or nothing to do with the likelihood of recreational injury liability."[37] Equally prominently, many recreation professionals favored tort reform legislation aimed at making it more difficult for plaintiffs to prevail in cases over playground and parks injuries. One commentator even provided a "cut-and-paste" model for a state statute that would reduce liability for parks agencies.[38] A later commentary, made after attention had begun to shift toward the sources of playground injuries, observed that, early on, too many agency managers had "followed the lead of the media and blamed their situation on either changes in tort law or the insurance industry."[39]

Soon, however, *Parks and Recreation*—as in policing a decade earlier— began pointing the finger toward itself (and toward dangerous recreational conditions) and began encouraging parks managers to take specific steps to improve safety. These steps evolved in the late 1980s and early 1990s into an institutionalized model of playground safety administration. The model's basis was the long-dormant Consumer Product Safety Commission's *Playground Safety Handbook*. In 1987, as the profession began to respond to the perceived liability crisis, *Parks and Recreation* for the first time featured the CPSC playground safety guidelines.[40] At the same time, the journal solicited advice on safety from managers of three parks agencies who shared the view, as one put it, that "85% of all hazards are preventable."[41] The managers advised their professional audience to adopt a "policy statement committing their organization to hazard reduction" and to engage in active "risk management" aimed at minimizing injuries through careful planning, revision of playground equipment, training of staff, and ongoing inspections and maintenance, along with careful record-keeping on these efforts. Within a year, commercial publications on playground safety began appearing: *The Playground Safety Checker* and *Safety First Checklist*.[42] In October 1988 *Parks and Recreation* devoted its cover and two lead articles to playground safety and design, highlighting the CPSC guidelines throughout. By 1990 Frances Wallach, a prominent playground safety analyst, could observe that the existence of the CPSC guidelines had quickly become "common knowledge."[43]

It is clear that the engine driving professional acknowledgment of the playground safety issue was legal liability. As the NRPA's legal director at the time of the transformation observed, agency managers should know that if sued, "the reasonableness of your conduct, and that of your agency, will most likely be judged with reference to" the CPSC guidelines.[44] "I can assure you," he continued, "that a plaintiff's attorney (with assistance provided by a cadre of 'expert witnesses' . . .) will beat you over the head with this document during a playground injury lawsuit."[45] Another article put the matter succinctly: "The business of attorneys was considerably different [in the past], and the change is what forces today's playground designers to perform with greater care."[46] Similarly, as Frances Wallach observed at the time, "communities have begun to pay attention" to playground safety, mainly because of "rising insurance costs and reports of large awards and settlements due to injuries."[47] Later she noted that in the 1980s, "although some communities made a serious effort to provide safer playgrounds, the real impetus to do so came after an injury and lawsuit. . . . As the number of lawsuits increased, failure to meet the *Handbook* recommendations began to appear regularly in liability claims." After 1987, the close connection between liability reduction and safety remained a staple of *Parks and Recreation* reporting. Thus an author introduced an article on playground safety by inquiring, "Since litigation is a very real concern for recreation professionals, what can be done to reduce the number of accidents that occur on playgrounds?"[48] "Although these [CPSC and ASTM] documents are designed to be guidelines for voluntary compliance," another observed, "a court will likely rule that these standards should have been used by a 'reasonable and prudent' playground operator."[49]

As was the case in policing and personnel administration, lawsuits' reputational, rather than financial, cost seemed to matter most to parks administrators. A writer in *Parks and Recreation* in 1988, for instance, pointed out that managers increasingly feared lawsuits as "a personal affront to their individual and professional integrity."[50] This observation is consistent with responses to a survey of parks administrators that I conducted in 2000. When asked to rate the impact of a lawsuit on their agencies, parks administrators rated it as significantly greater in the areas of media coverage and public image than in the budget (see fig. 9.1).

The available evidence suggests that very few cities had addressed playground safety before 1987. For instance, Los Angeles, fearing growing liability for playground injuries, in that year introduced a systematic program to inspect and maintain playground equipment in its parks.[51] The Los Angeles program was reportedly the first such inspection program in the country.[52] Similarly, Ken Kutska, a leader of the NRPA playground safety initiatives, later observed that even he had not fully grasped the significance of the playground safety issue until 1988 when he joined the American Society for Testing and Materials (ASTM) subcommittee on playground safety standards, began to learn about the issue, and began giving advice to other practitioners—and then realized that his own parks agency, in Wheaton, Illinois, "wasn't practicing what I was preaching."[53] Kutska described reworking his agency's playground safety policies and practices from top to bottom during 1989, ultimately generating a "comprehensive public safety program."[54] But it was not until 1990 that Kutska's agency, a leader in the field, began a systematic program aimed at replacing outmoded and dangerous equipment and ground covering.[55]

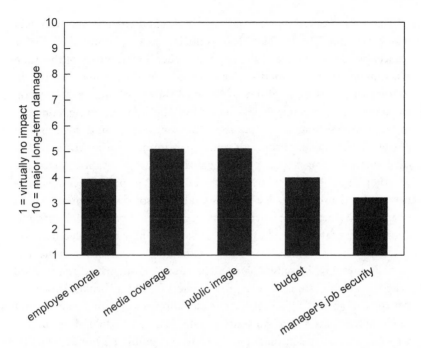

Figure 9.1. Impact of a playground injury lawsuit on parks agencies, as rated by parks administrators. $N = 220-25$. The differences between media coverage and public image and the other measures are significant below the .001 level ($t > 5.3$).

Shortly after the 1987 watershed, *Parks and Recreation* began providing specific advice on how to improve the safety of playgrounds, punctuated by threats that ignoring the advice would expose agencies to liability. Articles commonly included safety checklists or itemized key safety measures. One noted that "parks and recreation and law enforcement are two of the largest risks" for local governments and declared that the best way to address the problem is to "institute comprehensive risk management programs."[56] It went on to describe in detail the elements of a comprehensive program, among them replacement of unsafe equipment and ground covering, frequent inspections, staff training, and documentation of all such steps. Other articles similarly favored comprehensive risk management programs, and NRPA began offering a conference on risk management.[57] Similarly, an article on aquatic safety for children warned that "the area is ripe for continued and increased controversy and perhaps even expensive litigation if professionals neglect to take careful and appropriate steps." It went on to urge agencies to adopt a comprehensive risk management program encompassing dozens of bulleted elements.[58]

The level of detail in the magazine's newfound commitment to safety was remarkable. The 1987 article introducing the CPSC guidelines, for instance, provided an extraordinarily comprehensive summary of the main recommendations.[59] Similarly, an article on ground covering reported, in excruciating detail, the results of National Bureau of Standards tests on the impact performance of different types of ground covering, concluding that asphalt and concrete—the most common ground coverings in playgrounds—are inappropriate under playground equipment and that other materials, particularly wood chips or synthetic rubber mats, are greatly preferable.[60] That the new level of detail in policy recommendations marked a sharp change is indicated by the somewhat defensive tone of an article (focusing on specific distances required between playground equipment) that concluded: "Is the advice given here too far-fetched, too detailed? Not at all."[61] As time went on, the detail in safety recommendations, if anything, increased. An article from 1991 identified ten specific "safety inspection steps"; a "playground safety checklist" broken down under the categories of maintenance, leadership, and planning, each listing ten or more items; and a "preventive maintenance schedule," itemized by whether particular equipment and conditions should be inspected daily, weekly, monthly, or seasonally.[62] Regarding preventive maintenance, the article recommended daily inspection of S-hooks, anchor bolts, and guardrails, weekly inspection for exposed concrete footings and inadequate surfacing, and so on. Articles favoring comprehensive safety programs and making the link to tort liability continued to appear through the 1990s.[63]

By the early 1990s practitioners began expressing a new confidence in the maturation of playground safety as a professional field. In 1989 the NRPA had created the National Playground Safety Institute, a clearinghouse of information and training resources on playground safety, and it quickly became the institutional center of the emerging field.[64] In 1990 Frances Wallach, surveying the tumultuous changes of the past several years, confidently declared that the professional environment on playground safety had been transformed: playground equipment manufacturers had largely complied with the 1981 guidelines, "our watchdog and recording mechanisms have gotten stronger," a "body of knowledge" regarding playground safety had developed in the context of a raft of new books and training workshops, and "concern is spreading," as evinced by the packed rooms at playground safety workshops at national conferences.[65] Ken Kutska's "comprehensive public safety program," first begun in his parks agency in 1989, was revised in 1992 and published as the NRPA's leading official statement on playground safety, *Playground Safety Is No Accident.*[66]

Still, the leading playground safety advocates complained that many agencies were dragging their feet and had not brought themselves up to the new professional standards. Wallach observed that the conditions in most playgrounds were "poor," with hard ground surfaces and dangerous equipment. "There is no doubt," another article from 1990 observed, "that playgrounds all over the country need a serious evaluation."[67] Another 1990 article urged playground managers to rely on independent safety experts as consultants for upgrading their playgrounds, observing that such experts frequently appeared in court on behalf of plaintiffs and could provide invaluable advice to agencies.[68] Another, on ground coverings, argued that most agencies had not adequately replaced hard surfaces with impact-absorbing alternatives and urgently pressed for immediate action.[69]

Facing such recalcitrance, safety advocates relied heavily on the threat of liability as an inducement for playground reform.[70] Legal liability, and playground safety reforms as its remedy, was the "number one requested topic for information" from the National Recreation and Parks Association in 1992–93, and the organization responded by generating a number of informational products, ranging from written guides to videos.[71]

Just as the field began to gain institutional focus, in 1991 the Consumer Product Safety Commission published a greatly revised edition of the *Playground Safety Handbook*, and at the same time the American Society for Testing and Materials began extensive safety tests of equipment and ground covering in order to generate new, technically sophisticated standards, which were ultimately published in 1993. Both initiatives appear to have been generated by manufacturers' and parks agencies' concerns about rising liability pressures and ambiguities in the 1981 guidelines that left potential liability defendants exposed to uncertainties.[72]

After publication of the new standards in 1991 and 1993, it was only months before *Parks and Recreation* published major articles summarizing them, a stark contrast to the lag in covering the 1981 CPSC guidelines and an indication that safety was now a top priority. Thus a 1992 article on the 1991 CPSC guidelines addressed the interactive effects of height and ground covering in contributing to injuries, with a detailed technical report on the height above which a fall might lead to injuries with different types of ground covering.[73] Another article from early 1992 stressed the importance of the revised guidelines, calling them a "comprehensive package for the public."[74] An article from early 1993 provided another discussion of the revised guidelines, focusing particularly on a detailed discussion of recommendations for playground maintenance.[75] Similarly, shortly after the American Society of Testing and Materials released its playground safety standards in early 1993, *Parks and Recreation* announced the availability of NRPA publications, videos, and technical equipment for implementing the new standards.[76] In all, the quick and detailed discussion of the CPSC's revised guidelines in 1991 and the ASTM's standards in 1993 contrasted sharply with the nearly seven-year lag in acknowledging the first edition of the CPSC *Handbook*.

By the early 1990s much of the discussion in *Parks and Recreation* had begun to congeal around a shared legalized accountability model of playground safety centered on three principal components: formal policies, training and certification, and internal oversight. Thus, an article from 1991 argued that parks agencies had a new "legal duty to establish a safety program" consisting, the author observed, of several specific components (e.g., policy, employee manual, professional staff, inspection, maintenance, and the like).[77] Another, on playground safety generally, identified the key components of a comprehensive program as written policy (conforming to the CPSC and ASTM guidelines); appropriate selection and installation of playground equipment; "proactive" maintenance, particularly formal audits and repairs; and documentation.[78] Joe Frost, a leading scholar on matters of play and playground safety, contributed "Preventing Playground Injuries and Litigation," arguing that "the first step in preventing playground injuries and litigation is to develop a comprehensive playground safety program."[79] Frost, like other writers by the mid-1990s, distilled such a program, framed by the CPSC guidelines and the ASTM standards, into several discrete elements (for Frost and others, the key elements were "design, installation, maintenance, and supervision").[80]

In 1993 the National Playground Safety Institute (the NRPA's clearinghouse of information and training resources on playground safety) began providing professional certification for "certified playground safety inspectors," and these officials quickly became the central professional pillar of the consolidated playground safety model.[81] By 1996, articles in *Parks and Recreation* began to recommend having a certified playground safety inspector on staff, charged with conducting formal playground safety audits to assess whether playgrounds met the CPSC guidelines and ASTM standards.[82] As one such article observed, a third of playground injuries result from inadequate maintenance, and formal inspection by trained auditors is critical to identifying and addressing such problems.[83]

After the mid-1990s, coverage of playground safety and liability in *Parks and Recreation* generally continued themes established earlier, suggesting that the standard model had become institutionalized. There were articles on impact-absorbing ground covering (with detailed discussion of various surfaces);[84] detailed discussions of various safety issues related to formal safety audits and inspections;[85] and detailed discussions of the now well-institutionalized elements of the dominant playground safety model (characterized by one author as "planning/designing, construction/installing, inspecting/maintaining, and supervising").[86] Other articles emphasized the value of record-keeping to both liability reduction and safety improvement. Thus, as one advised, "Document, document, document! . . . You need to establish a checks and balances system that says, years down the road, I did what I said I would do and did so in a timely fashion. While this tends to be viewed as much as a risk reduction issue as it is a maintenance issue, my sense is that it is foolish to try to separate the two operations. Effective, challenging, functional well-maintained play sites are the goal; diligent care is the means to achieving that goal."[87]

By the 1990s an array of organizations and resources had developed in support of playground safety. In 1995 the Centers for Disease Control and Prevention provided funding for a National Program for Playground Safety, another center for research, and a clearinghouse for information and training on playground safety.[88] A number of guidebooks on playground safety have been published.[89] In 1996 manufacturers established the International Playground Equipment Manufacturers Association, and it quickly developed third-party testing of equipment for compliance with the ASTM standards.[90]

To What Extent Have Cities Adopted the Playground Safety Model?

Cities have widely adopted the playground safety model, and playgrounds have been transformed. Surveys of playgrounds report a massive change in typical playground equipment and surfaces, with asphalt and concrete being replaced by impact-absorbing ground coverings and heavy metal equipment replaced with impact-absorbing plastic.[91]

Little is known from these studies, however, about whether the change in playgrounds reflected changes in local governments' playground administration or simply innovations by manufacturers. Obviously some of each is at work. More particularly, to what extent have the *administrative systems* governing playgrounds changed, and if so why, and to what extent have these administrative changes contributed to the changes in playground design and safety? To address these questions, in 2000 I surveyed a stratified random sample of city parks and recreation departments; 233 departments responded, a 51 percent response rate.

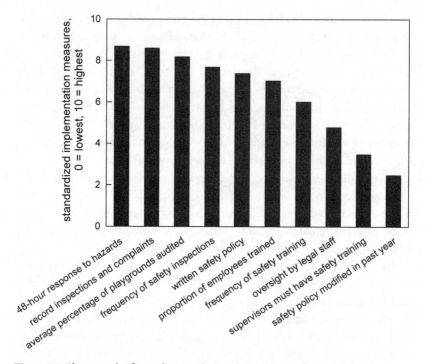

Figure 9.2. Playground safety policies and procedures, extent of adoption by city.
N = 216–32.

As in the other policy areas examined in this study, local parks departments have widely adopted many elements of the legalized accountability model with regard to playground safety but have less commonly adopted other elements (see fig. 9.2). Although written safety policies are widely adopted among cities, 26 percent of parks and recreation departments report having no written playground safety policy, a remarkable departure from the patterns in the other two policy areas. By contrast, very large proportions of parks departments report responding to complaints of playground safety hazards within twenty-four to forty-eight hours, report keeping records of such complaints and the response to them, and report having conducted a formal playground safety audit, all steps carrying significant costs. (I leave more detailed summaries of the data to the methodological appendix.)

With regard to corrective steps, very large majorities report removing equipment or ground covering that no longer meets Consumer Product Safety Commission safety standards (83 percent of cities) and modifying equipment or ground covering in the past year (81 percent). Nonetheless, only 45 percent of cities report that they have none of the common playground equipment that has been determined to be unsafe by the CPSC.

What explains how widely parks departments have adopted elements of the legalized accountability model with regard to playground safety? What explains how widely they have removed dangerous equipment from their playgrounds? Are these things related primarily to agencies' connections to professional networks and to professional association recommendations? Or does local support for legal pressure shape agency action here too? My survey was designed to address these questions. As in the other policy areas, I have controlled for every plausible influence on adoption of the model, among them size of city, region of the country, education and income levels of the local population, political attitudes (and other measures of political culture), and the like. The full list of control variables is found in the appendix.

As illustrated by figure 9.3, both the strength of local support structures for litigation on playground injuries and the strength of parks

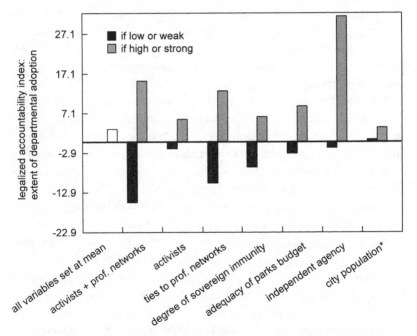

Figure 9.3. Factors explaining city government adoption of legalized accountability in area of playground safety. *Indicates relationship is not statistically significant. The figure's y-axis runs from the twenty-fifth to the seventy-fifth percentile on the dependent variable (the legalized accountability index). Results obtained using Monte Carlo simulations derived from the Clarify application in Stata.

department ties to professional networks (measured here by whether the department employs a certified playground safety inspector) significantly contribute to adoption of the legalized accountability model, and the two factors combined have an especially powerful influence. The figure's scale runs from the twenty-fifth to the seventy-fifth percentile on the index of departmental adoption of the legalized accountability model. Controlling for other factors, the strenght of ties to professional networks, measured by whether a department employs a certified playground safety inspector, contributes a shift from about −.08 to .11 on the legalized accountability index, a substantial shift. With regard to the local litigation support structure, again controlling for other factors, moving from having no local support structure (a very common condition) to the seventy-fifth percentile on my index of this factor contributes to a more modest but still substantial shift from about −.03 to .05 on the legalized accountability index.[92] Additionally, as the figure illustrates, both the sufficiency of departmental budgets (as reported by survey respondents) and the liberalism of state statutes on sovereign immunity also contribute substantially to adoption of the legalized accountability model. Purchasing, installing, and maintaining playground equipment and grounds is a substantial expense, and it would be surprising if the adequacy of departmental resources did not affect how extensively parks departments have implemented legalized accountability measures.

Additionally, adopting systems of legalized accountability, controlling for all other relevant factors, contributes to taking corrective actions (measured by an index of how far agencies have taken such actions).[93] The more an agency has adopted such things as playground safety audits, training, record-keeping and so on, the more likely it is to have taken actions in the past year to correct dangerous or risky playground conditions.

These statistical results are remarkably similar to my findings in the areas of policing and sexual harassment policy. How extensively agencies have adopted legalized accountability—whether they adopt only fine-sounding policies or make deeper administrative efforts to change actual practice—is shaped more by two factors than any other: the presence of local support for liability litigation and the strength of agency connections to professional networks. In comparison with these conditions, city size (or nearness to a big city), the tightness of the budget, or the liberalism of state laws or political culture—while somewhat influential—matters less. Further, these legalized administrative systems contribute to changes on the ground—literally—in such things as replacing asphalt with wood chips or rubber pellets, heavy metal swings with lighter rubber ones, towering jungle gyms with shorter but still challenging climbing equipment, and so on.

Conclusion

Although playgrounds in the United States date to the late nineteenth century and concerns about playground safety date at least to the 1930s, the conditions favoring a concerted, institutionalized effort to improve playground safety emerged only in the 1980s. After extended bureaucratic wrangling, safety entrepreneurs proposed a more-or-less clear model of playground safety, and it resulted in a set of voluntary playground safety guidelines published by the Consumer Product Safety Commission in 1981. The parks and recreation profession, however, largely ignored the issue of playground safety and the CPSC's guidelines for several years after publication of the proposed model.

Then, as in policing, the growth of tort lawsuits, combined with the shock imposed by a liability insurance crisis in the mid-1980s, generated a sudden and dramatic flurry of attention to the issue of playground safety. In policing, the perceived liability crisis of the late 1970s jump-started the administrative reforms. In playground safety, a similar liability crisis in the mid-1980s sparked the change. As in policing, the parks and recreation profession, under direct pressure from tort lawyers relying on the proposed model as a putative professional standard, were forced to begin respecting that model. Very quickly the CPSC proposal was incorporated into a rapidly institutionalizing model of safe playground management, which reached final form by the early 1990s and remains essentially unchanged today. As we have seen, its contours are roughly similar to those in policing, consisting of written policies, efforts at training and certifying staff in the policies, and ongoing internal oversight. By 2000, barely a decade after the acceleration of this developmental process, the main elements of the model had been widely adopted by United States cities, a remarkable reversal of past patterns.

Still, playground safety policy differs from similar policies in the police and sexual harassment areas in one significant way: it is more technocratic and less oriented to rights-based complaints. In both policing and sexual harassment a central concern is the individual complaint. Popular movements in these areas have framed these complaints in the potent language of rights. They have called on managers to address complaints fairly and to use the information gained from them as a basis for further policy reforms. Playground managers, to be sure, also rely on complaints to identify needed repairs. But the playground safety model gives no special attention to these complaints; the model focuses instead on technical certification for playground safety inspectors and on technical playground safety audits. Although law contributed to legalized reforms in each of these areas, rights-based movements gave a judicial cast to the version of legalism found in policing and sexual harassment policy.

The development of tort liability with regard to playground design and maintenance, in sum, strengthened the hand of safety advocates within parks administration. "By developing a sound program philosophy and implementing a comprehensive risk management program," as one author put it, "the playground operator will not only reduce the chances of litigation, but more importantly, reduce injuries to children."[94] The legalized accountability model in parks administration, as in policing and personnel management, thus grew from a synergy between legal mobilization and professional reform. Its form, however, is more technocratic than lawlike, more akin to engineering than to a judicial hearing.

Conclusion

10

Is seeking social change by lawsuit a hollow hope? Did the rights revolution create only empty symbolism, a "myth of rights" that makes big promises but never delivers?

Although most studies have found widespread bureaucratic evasion or merely symbolic compliance with new rights, they have commonly examined compliance in the short term. I have deliberately chosen a longer perspective, inspired by Stuart Scheingold's observation that although the rights revolution generated few immediate policy reforms it inspired a "politics of rights," a decades-long struggle over the practical meaning of its promises.[1] I have focused on these struggles and their products in three areas: police use of force, workplace sexual harassment, and playground safety. In this concluding chapter I will briefly summarize my main observations and then discuss their implications for debates over the nature and role of law in policy reform.

A Summary

My answer to the questions above has two sides. One is a story of dramatic change. I have documented the unexpected: the development in the past generation of fundamental, law-inspired institutional change. Where once bureaucratic agencies resisted external legal control, in the past generation a common policy model of legalized accountability has grown and consolidated; it focuses on bringing bureaucratic practice into conformity with evolving legal norms, and it does so by law-inspired administrative rules, training tailored to these rules, and systems of internal oversight aimed at assessing compliance with the rules and training. Ultimately, law-inspired administrative reform has remade the professional norms and identities of the managerial professions, shifting them decisively from a celebration of insulated discretionary expertise to a celebration of fidelity to legal norms.

The central features of this historical sea change are marked by its divided sources. It grew out of an interaction between bottom-up pressure, in the form of activist demands to give practical meaning to the rights revolution's promises, and top-down policymaking, in the form of professional administrators' managerial responses to these pressures. Activist pressure contributed a legal cast to the shared policy model; managerial responses channeled these pressures into administrative solutions. My analysis thus has much in common with perspectives that view law as emerging out of social relationships rather than imposed from above and, at the same time, with those that view law as emerging from elites' interests and power. Rather than seeing these alternatives as mutually exclusive, however, I have emphasized the contribution of both popular pressure and elite power, and particularly the role of conflict between these forces in shaping the course of legal development. Conflict among groups and their ideals played a key role at every stage, and judicial decisions gave an official imprimatur to particular viewpoints rather than others, often decisively shaping subsequent developments.

Activist movements played a critical role. I find, as scholars of social movements have long suggested, that activist movements offer radical critiques of reigning institutions but face the problem of sustaining this pressure over time.[2] In each policy area studied here, social movement activists inspired by the legal revolution of the 1960s—but equally frustrated by its limited impact—struggled to make its promises real. They were under no illusions about the difficulty of the task, believing that real reform required recognizing the organizational nature of modern society and thus changing bureaucratic cultures in tens of thousands of organizations scattered throughout the country under no central legal control. Although the activists believed strongly that true reform required fundamental institutional change, they were less clear about how to achieve this change administratively. They consistently demanded, at a minimum, mechanisms for exposing hidden administrative processes to the light. In policing, for instance, they sought to create citizen review boards to open police disciplinary processes to public accountability. Beyond more openness, however, they typically offered few concrete proposals.

Professional practitioners played a critical role too. The managerial professions, made up of the officials who managed the tens of thousands of local agencies targeted by the activists for reform, were the product of the Progressive Era, and they shared the Progressives' faith that bureaucratic insularity was a necessary condition for the exercise of professional expertise. Long into the 1970s they regarded the activists' complaints as exaggerated and the demand for public openness as partisan heresy. As organizational theory teaches us, practitioners initially resisted activists' calls for deep institutional reforms, preferring to carry on business as usual.[3]

Activists, their demands rebuffed, resorted to increasingly radical and confrontational tactics; professional practitioners circled their wagons and became defensive and indignant. Activists relied especially but not exclusively on liability lawsuits as a tactic. From the activist perspective, these lawsuits had three virtues: they generated publicity, they got the attention of practitioners, and sometimes they paid for themselves. Liability lawsuits thus enabled activist movements to overcome their chief limitation—their previously limited capacity to sustain pressure on dominant institutions over time. The news media, as suggested by scholarship on media coverage of the law, typically were drawn to the stories of these lawsuits by their graphic individual character—police shootings of fifteen-year-old burglars, lurid stories of workplace pressure for sex.[4] Although such individualized morality tales might ordinarily undercut any message favoring institutional reform, movement activists were able to emphasize recurring patterns in these cases, and over time media coverage came to reflect the activists' call for organizational changes rather than merely punishment of individuals. Liability-generated publicity thus amplified activists' demand for institutional reforms and swayed the sympathies of juries and judges. By the early 1980s, practitioners had lost the public relations battle.

A third group, policy experts with extensive practical experience inside the practicing professions but with their professional home in other fields, proposed concrete administrative reforms that were consolidated into the legalized accountability model. These policy experts typically were lawyers with extensive practical experience in administrative management, and they could draw on ideas from both law and management. Their reform proposals had the virtue of appearing to meet both the activists' demand for deep institutional reform and the practitioners' demand for continued managerial control. Thus the proposals' key elements—rules, training, and internal oversight—were *administrative* solutions, but they aimed to change administrative practice fundamentally by, for instance, eradicating abusive police force and employee sexual harassment. Although the policy experts' proposal for legalized accountability drew on standard administrative tools like rules and employee training, it is important to emphasize that these experts' loyalties lay as much or more with the activists as with the practitioners, and they viewed legalized accountability as an effective means of changing bureaucratic practice in keeping with legal norms. These proponents frankly and emphatically embraced the activists' demand for fundamental institutional reform and claimed their proposals would mark a break with the past. At the same time, however, they were sympathetic to the need for managerial professionalism as a means to carry out institutional reform. They recommended their proposals to practitioners as a contribution to managerial professionalism rather than a rejection. The resulting administrative model represented a sharp break with the past, an intrusion of legalized control over professional and managerial discretion. Some reformist practitioners accepted these ideas and broke from their professional mainstreams, adopting elements of legalized accountability in their own agencies, serving as expert witnesses in lawsuits against their fellow practitioners, and leading publicity campaigns on behalf of reform.

By 1980 administrative reformers and traditionalists had become consolidated into competing coalitions, and each watched anxiously for indications of judicial support for their cause. Judicial decisions were important less for what they required in precise legal terms than for which direction they pointed, which coalition they endorsed, and whether they exposed defendant organizations to liability. By the early 1980s, as the traditionalist practitioners began clearly losing the public relations battle, judges increasingly appeared to be siding with the reformist coalitions. In each policy area, leading practitioners read into judicial decisions a clear message requiring reform and turned to the nascent legalized accountability model as a solution, trumpeting it as a new paradigm of professional reform. Legalized accountability quickly took on the cast of a professional state of the art. Practitioners now acknowledged a need for fundamental institutional reform; they now supported rules, training, and oversight as means to that end; and they argued that this paradigm would enhance practitioners' professional legitimacy. Fueled by these dynamics, legalized accountability swept the practitioner professions, and by the 1990s it had become a dominant model of reform, widely endorsed by professional associations, textbooks, and federal agencies. My original survey data in each field demonstrate that virtually all local government agencies have adopted at least the symbolic trappings of the new model.

Viewed long term, legalized accountability contributed to a revision of the managerial professions' identity. Although the Progressive idea of insulated managerial professionalism gained widespread public support by the 1950s, by the late 1960s its reputation lay in tatters. In the 1970s and 1980s, in the wake of that crisis, the managerial professions effectively remade their identity and mission in the terms of public responsiveness ("community policing," "citizen engagement") and legalized accountability. Legalism is now at the heart of managerial professionalism: administrators are widely trained in the requirements of law and proudly champion their professions' legal bona fides.

The precise course of these developments, to be sure, differed among the three policy areas. Rights-based aspirations in the areas of policing and sexual harassment fueled more passionate citizen engagement than in the area of playground safety, where few activists framed the issue in the language of rights. The activist-practitioner conflict was hottest in policing, where activists alleged intentional abuse by practitioners and shared a strong sense that this was a violation of basic rights, and where practitioners shared an equally powerful professional ideology of insulation from partisan influence. The conflict was more moderate in playground safety, where it was not plausible to view injuries as intentionally caused by practitioners and where practitioners could use the threat of liability as a lever to get more resources from city governments. The delay between proposal of the administrative model and its embrace by practitioners was longest in policing, where practitioners dug in to fight activist-led reform and long enjoyed broad support from the white majority, and briefest in personnel management, where practitioners shared a professional ideology favoring responsiveness to employee complaints.

The nature of the resulting administrative model, too, differs somewhat among these areas. Although all three emphasize rules, training, and internal oversight, these things take different forms in different fields. Formal rules are more elaborate and extensive in policing than in the other two policy areas; likewise, policing dedicates vastly more time and attention to training than do the others. The nature of oversight also varies considerably. All rely to some degree on individual complaints as an indicator of problems. Thus playground safety leaders advocated making it easy for members of the public to report damaged equipment. In both policing and playground management, however, professional leaders forcefully advocated proactive internal oversight systems to catch early any problems not manifested in complaints. Thus the state of the art in policing is the elaborate early warning system relying on a variety of indicators of problems in officers' uses of force. By contrast, although some writers in personnel administration also recommended such proactive indicators of sexual harassment as employee surveys, others recommended only grievance procedures relying on individual complaints; and after the Supreme Court's narrow decision in *Faragher v. Boca Raton,* the latter have been adopted much more widely than the former. Still, even in sexual harassment policy the resulting administrative model bears the imprint of the activists' ideas.

If dramatic change is half of the story told here, however, the other half is widespread variation from place to place in the depth of the change or, to put the point more sharply, widespread evasion of legalized accountability. As I have shown, while some city agencies have adopted legalized accountability in full form, many others have adopted only its most visible, superficial elements, a finding consistent with Lauren Edelman's observation that many bureaucratic organizations adopt key innovations in symbolic form while leaving their underlying practices largely unchanged.[5] While virtually all cities, for instance, have rules governing use of force by their police officers and formal prohibitions on workplace sexual harassment, fewer carry out training tailored to these rules, and fewer still have formal administrative systems to assess employee compliance with the rules. Still, cities adopting only ceremonial commitments to legalized accountability are exposed to pressure to make good on those promises. Whether such pressures materialize, as I have shown, depends on how far the organization is exposed to the "stick" of pressure from local activists and the "carrot" of professional legitimacy via professional networks. In some places there are many citizen groups and lawyers willing to press agencies to do more, and some agencies are closely connected to professional networks; in other places there are few or none of these activists, and the agency is not connected to professional networks. Where these things are stronger, city agencies have adopted legalized accountability in fuller, more robust forms.

Do my observations apply beyond the relatively limited context of local governments? On the one hand, local governments may be characterized by denser professional networks and greater localized activist pressure than are business corporations or agencies of the federal government. On the other hand, it is undeniable that bureaucratic organizations generally are increasingly shaped by pressure from their legal environments and have adopted more legalized rules and procedures. Further, there is growing evidence that localized activist pressures affect not only government agencies but private businesses and other private organizations as well. Neil Gunningham, Robert Kagan, and Dorothy Thornton, for instance, have observed that business corporations "overcomply" with environmental regulations as a result of localized pressure from activists.[6] Similarly, some recent studies find that managerial innovations in general are more subject to social movement pressure—and strategic use of it by managerial innovators—than once thought.[7] Although these observations only sketch out possibilities, they suggest that my findings regarding the powerful influence of local activists (and their networks) may apply beyond local government. Future research might examine whether private corporations are as responsive to local pressures as these studies seem to indicate.

Future research might also examine why some professions "buy in" to legalistic reform while others do not. Each of the three professions examined here—policing, human resources, and parks administration—ultimately accepted legalism to such an extent that it has become a core part of its professional norms and missions. But this is by no means inevitable. The field of medicine has largely resisted legalism, carrying on a famous and long-running battle against medical malpractice lawyers. What explains the difference? It is not the depth of the legal challenge to core professional principles: police misconduct lawyers long alleged deliberate malfeasance and irresponsibility by the police, and yet the latter profession eventually acknowledged the point and made legalistic reform a key measure of police professionalism. Nor is it the unavailability of professionally accepted tools to comply with legal norms: as Tom Baker observes, we are starting to see the growth of a profession of hospital management that relies on systematic administration and record keeping regarding common sources of medical errors, and these tools seem, if anything, simply a systematization of good medical practice. And a similar development occurred a generation ago in the area of anesthesia, yielding a reduction in that profession's exposure to liability.[8] Instead, the explanation for the medical profession's resistance may be better explained in terms of its professional status. Compared with law, medicine is an older, more prestigious (and more lucrative) profession. By contrast, policing, personnel management, and parks administration are at best quasi professions, clearly subordinate to lawyers in training, prestige, and income. These quasi professions struggled through a crisis of legitimacy in the 1970s, and conversion to the model of law (particularly civil rights) offered the chance to regain legitimacy.

The medical profession has not suffered a similar crisis, nor have malpractice lawyers offered an attractive carrot like the civil rights model to accompany their stick of liability. But this status-oriented hypothesis is mere speculation, and why some professions accept legal accountability while others resist it seems a fertile area for research.

Broader Implications

The development of legalized accountability represents a shift from a model of insulated discretionary administration accountable mainly to bureaucratic (or legislative) superiors to one of legally checked, popularly accountable administration.[9] "Governments are now more aware that they can't do just anything," as a city official put it to me. "It is really . . . a change in attitude. It used to be that elected officials and also administrators felt that they were accountable to the public mainly through elections. 'If you don't like what we're doing, vote somebody else in at the next election, and evaluate us on our whole record over our term.' Now, however, we're much more responsive to complaints and concerns raised by citizens, apart from the election process, because we know in the back of our minds that the complaint might conceivably become a lawsuit." This shift gives individuals new levers of influence but also ironically empowers bureaucratic institutions.

To illustrate the nature of this shift I have chosen a hard case, one that at first seems to contradict my claim that accountability and authority relations have changed. It is the tragic story of Diane, a fifty-year-old African American woman living on the South Side of Chicago. A unit of Chicago police officers allegedly sadistically beat and harassed her with impunity in 2003 and 2004, as Craig Futterman describes, in ongoing incidents in which the officers forced her to take off her clothes, threatened her with a gun, pliers, and screwdriver, ransacked her home, beat her son and forced him to beat another man, and threatened to plant drugs on her and arrest her.[10] The Chicago police department did not sustain any of Diane's official complaints against the officers. Although many residents of Diane's South Side neighborhood claimed to have shared similar experiences at the hands of the same officers, known widely in the neighborhood as the "Skullcap Crew," the Chicago police department admitted no such knowledge. Unlike many leading police departments, the Chicago department allegedly did not inquire into its own internal records to determine which officers were "repeat offenders" and thus did not flag such officers for retraining or discipline.[11] In support of Diane's lawsuit, Futterman and his colleagues examined the Chicago department's own internal complaint and disciplinary files and found a higher rate of citizen complaints than the national average but a much lower rate of complaint confirmation (8 percent of complaints are sustained nationally, but only .48 percent in Chicago).[12] As is typical of police departments, less than 5 percent of Chicago officers receive over half of that department's citizen complaints: Futterman's analysis demonstrated that members of the police unit in question had racked up an unusually high record. The Chicago department, in the words of independent Chicago journalist Jamie Kalven, maintained "a regime of not knowing," sustained, as Futterman and his colleagues allege, by "a deep commitment to the machinery of denial."[13]

A key part of that machinery, it must be said, has been the Chicago department's claim that it has a state-of-the-art internal disciplinary system, complete with an early warning system. Chicago police spokespeople have defended the department's record specifically by claiming that it relies on its early warning system to monitor officers' behavior.[14] Although early warning systems were developed to better monitor officers' uses of force, how they work in practice is largely hidden from public view, opening the possibility for police departments, as in Chicago, to claim they have such a system but to let it languish. Chicago's early warning system thus has been used, ironically, to quell external critique.

Although some scholars may view the Chicago case as confirmation that law cannot reform bureaucracy and that nothing really has changed, it illustrates precisely the opposite.[15] Dominant models of what the law requires grow in part from activists' efforts to enforce legal norms; once in place, these models constrain the range of options available to regulated agencies and offer activists significant resources for challenging agencies' actions. Legalized accountability as an administrative model thus has changed the game. The Chicago department, like other police departments, adopted an internal system of oversight on the use of force in the context of growing pressure to address police misconduct. The early warning system, as I have observed, is a key component of the broader legalized accountability model, and it is becoming something like an industry standard, leaving big departments like Chicago's with little choice but to follow the dominant model. Although particular police departments have some latitude in how they implement early warning systems, data from a department's own system may be used to embarrass its officials, forcing greater reform. Thus, in Chicago litigation over police abuses exposed an alleged pattern of what amounts to sweeping abuses under the rug, and

Chicago police officials have been thoroughly embarrassed by continuing revelations from their own internal data demonstrating the sham nature of their system.

In all of these things, managers are sharply constrained by the dominant legalized accountability model. Thus, tellingly, as the scandal grew, no representative of the Chicago department has claimed that officers' uses of force should *not* be constrained by departmental rules; that the department should *not* gather and keep data on particular officers' uses of force and citizen complaints; that the department should *not* compare and examine these data and thereby identify and deal with officers having troublesome records. By contrast, before the ascendance of legalized accountability in the 1980s, spokesmen for the police made precisely such arguments. Today these earlier views are virtually unthinkable, or at least unspeakable in public, and the Chicago department's line of defense is now quite different: that there should be no public reporting of such data. But even here the Chicago department has given ground; where once the review of complaints against police officers was conducted by a branch of the police department, beginning in 2007 this is done by an independent city agency that is publicly reporting the number of complaints against particular officers (while maintaining the confidentiality of their names).[16] The development of legalized accountability as a policy model thus decisively shifted the conditions, giving activists new resources in their effort to check abuses of rights.

Still, although legalized accountability constrains administrative practitioners and empowers their activist critics, at the same time it has had the paradoxical effect of strengthening the administrative state and empowering the newly legalized managerial professions. Systems of legalized accountability are mainly internal to professionalized bureaucracies, and their operation is largely hidden. The model thus makes it far easier to adopt additional rules or adjustments in training or internal oversight than to implement mechanisms of popular accountability. These internal systems, in practice, rely almost exclusively on internal practitioners to track and analyze the relevant data. In the recent debates in Chicago, no one has suggested routinely overturning that premise. Critics simply ask for more faithful application of professional effort in tracking and analyzing data on official misconduct. Additionally, if activists want to acquire and independently analyze internal data held by agencies, this typically requires substantial investment in attorney time and expert consultation, and few aggrieved individuals have these resources. Further, agencies may prominently proclaim that they have state-of-the-art systems while allowing them to languish, and most observers will never know the difference. Thus, even though Chicago is home to some of the country's most sophisticated police misconduct lawyers, the facade was not disturbed until an independent journalist and a law professor began talking directly to people at the very bottom of the social order, people whose complaints had for years fallen on deaf ears.

Legalized accountability, in sum, is at its core a hybrid institution, part activist lever for reform and part managerial tool. Which of these potentials is cultivated depends significantly on local conditions, particularly the resource infrastructure of activists, the professional commitments of practitioners, and the course of public debate over rights versus managerial prerogatives.

A General Evaluation

Although my purpose in this book has been primarily to describe and analyze the development of legalized accountability and not to evaluate it, inevitably readers will find normative implications in my analysis, and therefore I want to make my own views clear by briefly assessing some common criticisms of legalized procedures.

The most common is that legalized rules and procedures undermine administrative efficiency while failing to achieve their ostensible purpose of increasing safety or protecting individual rights. This criticism is typically accompanied by the claim that safety and rights are better protected (meaning protected more efficiently and effectively) by other mechanisms, particularly systems of professional self-regulation. My before-and-after comparisons of legalized accountability and its alternative, insulated administrative professionalism, in both the United States and Britain have implications for these criticisms. In both countries, compared with insulated professional administration, legalized accountability, for all its limitations, does not look so bad.

To be sure, there is little doubt that practices at the front lines may elude even fully developed systems of legalized accountability, and thus reformers may have changed *administration* more than *practice*. Sexual harassment continues. Police officers still treat African Americans more harshly than whites: African Americans are stopped and searched at higher rates than whites and are more often the victims of egregious beatings or unjustified shootings. Careful evaluations of police practices by human rights and civil liberties organizations document widespread failings in systems for minimizing excessive use of force.[17] Ultimately, administrative systems, even systems that yield changes in professional cultures and practices, are incapable of fully eradicating these problems. Solutions require addressing underlying disparities of power, resources, and status. Women will remain vulnerable so long as their economic resources and cultural status are less than men's; African Americans will experience ill treatment at the hands of the police (and other officials) so long as urban poverty and the problems associated with it remain closely linked to race.

But these problems also persist because liability law makes it more difficult to sue municipalities than their employees, giving police departments and other local agencies too little incentive to carry out far-reaching reforms. Scholars as diverse in perspective as Peter Schuck, Samuel Walker and Morgan Macdonald, and Myriam Gilles have persuasively called for making it easier to sue municipalities over bureaucratic customs or patterns that contribute to misconduct.[18]

But acknowledging these points does not mean that legalized accountability has had no meaningful impact on the problems of harassment, abuse, and injury. Law-based reform has worked where virtually nothing else has. We risk losing these gains and failing to achieve still more if we do not recognize this.

At the narrowest level, has legalized accountability reduced abuses, harassment, and injuries compared with the legally insulated systems of professionalism in the earlier era? Probably it has. In the introduction I reported that local government officials had claimed to me that liability had made their agencies safer and more respectful of civil rights and liberties. Systematic studies seem to bear out their impressions, albeit with qualifications. With regard to the police use of force, as the new departmental rules governing shootings spread between 1970 and 1984, the number of police shootings in major cities declined by about a third, and the racial disparity in the rate of shooting whites and blacks was cut in half.[19] The changing patterns in shootings strongly suggest, as James Fyfe and Samuel Walker have observed, that rule-based reforms made the difference: shootings for reasons now considered least justified under the rules declined dramatically more than shootings for defense of life, and the reduced racial disparity suggests that officer discretion became increasingly focused on the legal justifications for shooting and less framed by legally unacceptable bases for suspicion (like race).[20] Observational studies of police behavior similarly suggest improvement beyond the limited area of shootings. In the late 1960s sociologists Donald Black and Albert Reiss, relying on a systematic observational study, reported that when faced with disrespect or defiance police officers widely exercised force, often excessively.[21] In the late 1990s Stephen Mastrofski and his colleagues carried out a systematic replication of that study, observing a significant reduction in police violence toward disrespectful citizens due, they believed, to the growing legalization of police departments.[22]

A similarly broad shift is evident in the area of sexual harassment. A growing number of studies demonstrate that administrative systems aimed at minimizing sexual harassment have a direct effect on the level of harassment in an organization. Particular organizational practices—essentially the components of the legalized accountability model—are key mechanisms for reducing harassment.[23] A recent comprehensive meta-analysis of data from forty-one studies of sexual harassment, comprising over 70,000 respondents, found that the relative presence of rules against sexual harassment, training, and organizational communications prohibiting sexual harassment, constituting what the authors called the "organizational climate" for sexual harassment, had the largest impact of any variable on the incidence of harassment.[24] Another study, focused on identifying which specific elements of administrative systems are most effective at minimizing sexual harassment, found that, among several common elements of sexual harassment programs, the frequency and comprehensiveness of employee training and specialized training for managers had the most substantial impact; additionally, and significantly, organizations that had model written *policies* but did not back them up with *training* had elevated levels of harassment.[25] Policies without training and oversight, as I have argued, are window dressing.

Ironically, there is less evidence of improvement where change has been most visible, in children's playgrounds. To be sure, playgrounds have been widely remade according to the new safety model. But whether these changes have reduced the number of playground injuries is debated. A Canadian study documented a dramatic reduction in children's playground injuries after Toronto elementary schools, complying with a new legal standard, removed hazardous equipment.[26] Children's playground injury rates in the United States, however, have remained relatively constant since 1996, although this may be because the most significant changes in playgrounds occurred earlier.[27]

A related criticism is that legalized accountability, as a bottom-up mechanism, varies considerably from place to place and therefore is an ineffective model for systemwide reform. Undoubtedly it is true that, unlike statutory or bureaucratic reforms imposed by national government, the pressures giving rise to legalized reforms—particularly local activist pressure—may lead to widely varied administrative implementation. As

I have shown, where these support structures are robust, administrative rights policies tend to be deep and effective; but where support structures are weak or absent, these policies tend to be shallow and merely symbolic. Nonetheless, the British policing system is vastly more centralized and more thoroughly managed by insulated professional mechanisms and norms than is the American system, yet it still suffers from many of the problems characteristic of American policing: widespread concern about racist abuse, racially discriminatory practices, and excessive use of force by frontline personnel. These problems have persisted through repeated waves of centralized reform. As my earlier analysis shows, the most significant reforms in Britain began only as tort litigation repeatedly brought the problems to public attention. In sum, although in theory a system of centralized, insulated professionalism has a greater capacity to engineer systemwide reform, in practice such systems rarely achieve such an ambitious goal. The relative success of administrative legalization in achieving it—far from perfect, but arguably greater even than in systems of insulated professionalism—suggests that, compared with the principal alternatives, legalized checks perform surprisingly well.

Why? What has enabled the fragmented, decentralized American system to generate such far-reaching administrative reforms? The standard answer is that litigation's financial sanction is the driving force. If my study is even partly persuasive, that answer is at least partly wrong. The engine of pressure is not, precisely speaking, litigation, and its inducement is not financial. The engine of pressure is *liability*—the amorphous legally framed risk associated with departure from popular legal norms—and its inducement is not money but damage to public legitimacy. All administrative systems, whether of the insulated professionalism or the legal oversight variety, are human systems shaped by patterns of socially based cognition and communication. All therefore are subject to substantial variation in their processes and behaviors based on variations in socially based models of knowledge and norms. All human systems seek to minimize embarrassment based on shared public norms. But systems of insulated professionalism have richly developed mechanisms for *protecting* members of the organization from embarrassment in the eyes of the public: individual complaints of wrongdoing typically are handled through secretive professionally controlled processes. The decentralized, court-centered system of oversight in the United States, by contrast, imposes the constant possibility of a fully public airing of individual complaints through the mechanism of the lawsuit, creating a powerful incentive for reform.

Still, legalized accountability imposes two significant costs. One is the heavy psychological burden on individual victims, who are effectively made responsible for identifying problems and driving reforms. It is well known that victims of harassment or abuse hesitate to file complaints, sometimes enduring great hardship rather than to take such a step.[28] There is a tragic irony in a legal-administrative system that makes administrative reform the responsibility of victims rather than organizations. But if we are concerned about the stresses individual claimants face under the legalized accountability model—and we should be—professionalism insulated from legal accountability does not offer an appealing alternative. Complaints from aggrieved individuals are often a necessary first step toward any meaningful reform even in systems of insulated professionalism. These complaints remain among the most important sources of information on where things have gone wrong, and a managerial system that does not rely on individual complaints would be subject to the criticism that it ignores the views of victims. But systems of legally insulated bureaucracy are far less attentive to individual grievances than are legalized administrative systems. Worse, these nonlegalized administrative systems have often actively discouraged individual grievances and have investigated them only informally or dismissively. In the insulated professionalism eras in the United States and Britain, victims of police abuse complained bitterly of haphazard or dismissive treatment. In both countries, insulated professionalism contributed to a tendency to tamp down and suppress oversight associated with individual grievances: far from seeing grievances as a potential resource or information source for professionally based reform, police managers seemed to see them as the opening wedge of expanded external oversight. Similarly, in the earlier era agency managers and personnel administrators ignored or belittled complaints of sexual harassment, and a key early goal of feminist activists was to get these officials to take these complaints seriously.

Second, legalized accountability undoubtedly contributes to administrative inefficiency. Legalized checks, as Bardach and Kagan observed long ago, make administrative processes slower, costlier, and more cumbersome and sometimes contribute to nonsensical outcomes.[29]

The ultimate question is whether the benefits of legalized accountability outweigh its obvious costs. In the end I cannot say, and I doubt that anybody can. It is worth noting, however, that complaints about cost and inefficiency and the burden imposed on individual claimants have not stalled its momentum. Administrative professionals and activists alike favor refinements in legalized procedures rather than their wholesale replacement. Administrative professionalism is now defined largely in relation to legal responsibility and fidelity to legal norms. As a consequence, legalized accountability has taken on a life of its own.

What conditions might encourage departure from the legalized accountability path? Nuclear power seemed unstoppable—until it was. In policing, unfettered officer discretion, even discretion to beat and harass people on the street, seemed to its critics a permanent feature of American life—until official discretion lost legitimacy as if overnight and was replaced by ruled-based regulation. In each case, the conditions for disruption of entrenched patterns lie in the conditions *for* those patterns, that is to say, the assumptions that make the reigning model "obviously" correct.

For years the primary argument against legalized accountability—that it is inefficient—has shown little sign of toppling it. This is principally so, I believe, because when in contest against the master argument in favor of legalized accountability—that those in institutional authority ultimately cannot be completely trusted with unfettered discretionary authority—the inefficiency argument carries little weight. What could possibly overcome Americans' deep-seated suspicion, prevailing since the 1970s, that those in institutional authority cannot be fully trusted without oversight? The assumption is that those in authority are not "us"—they are an "other." The only effective argument against this presumption, it seems to me, is one that shows they *can* be trusted, which is to say, that they *are* "us." White Americans shared such a view of the police through the 1950s and all the way through the long 1960s, abandoning it only as trust in institutions collapsed in the 1970s. Managers shared such a view of male prerogatives until increasing numbers of them were women. Since that era, Americans have not been persuaded by the claim that those in institutional authority deserve unfettered discretion except where they (we) perceive a foreign threat.

Precisely such a dynamic has unfolded, of course, in the racially coded war on drugs and the war on terrorism. In these areas the norms underlying legalized accountability have faced their most serious challenge. In a number of instances, systems of legalized accountability have fundamentally broken down in the face of a concerted willingness by those in authority to violate these legal norms and, it must be said, by a collective willingness to look the other way.

Still, although those in power can *violate* norms, they cannot on their own permanently remove or replace them.[30] Wholesale replacement depends on a collective process, and the networks and norms underlying the legalized accountability model seem surprisingly resilient. It appears that officials' claim to unfettered discretion, once on the march in the wake of the September 11 terrorist attacks, is now in retreat. Although the issue remains the subject of enormous conflict, it appears that we have not yet reached the point where those in authority regain implicit trust. Until then legalized accountability, although inefficient, is likely to seem eminently more sensible than the alternatives.

Methodological Appendix

The statistical analyses in this book are based on data drawn from original surveys of administrative managers of three city departments—personnel, parks and recreation, and policing—in several hundred cities, focusing on matters related to playground safety (for parks and recreation managers), sexual harassment (for personnel managers), and use of force (for police chiefs), supplemented by data from a variety of other sources.[1] In these particular policy areas, the three surveys asked managers a range of questions, with a particular focus, among other things, on the following matters:

- Their departments' policies, procedures, and working protocols
- Their perceptions of the threat of liability
- Their perceptions of the availability of attorneys and citizen groups that are known to support lawsuits on the topic
- Their departments' experience with being sued
- Their departments' size, resources, and extent of employee unionization, and whether they carry liability insurance

The data set used here contains survey responses from 838 police departments, 454 personnel departments, and 233 parks and recreation departments. For police departments, the population for the survey consisted of all United States cities with populations of 10,000 or greater; surveys were sent to a random sample of cities with populations ranging from 10,000 to 99,999, and to all cities with populations of 100,000 or greater.[2] The surveys used a combination of telephone and mail contacts in 2000 and early 2001; the response rate was 52% for police, 54% for personnel, and 51% for parks and recreation. In all cases the survey responses were completed either by the head of each department or by a senior official designated by that person.

My research design is cross-sectional rather than diachronic; it does not use event history analysis, as is now common in studies of policy diffusion. I adopted this cross-sectional design because data for the three concepts that are central to my theory—how widely departments have adopted the elements of the legalized accountability model, the extent of local support structures for litigation, and agency connections to professional networks—are for the most part impossible to gather for periods in the past. The cross-sectional design obviously represents a trade-off: it cannot capture the dynamics of policy diffusion over time, but it can assess the depth of legalized accountability procedures and the possible influence of factors for which time-based data cannot be gathered and that event history analysis thus cannot assess. I believe the trade-off is merited by the richness of the resulting data: my data on each of the three key factors are arguably richer than those obtained by any previous study.

The first section of this appendix summarizes the primary variables that constitute the legalized accountability model and variables associated with alternative explanations for adoption of that model. The second section reports the multivariate models that are the basis for the figures and interpretations in the substantive chapters. The third section reports the survey questions that are the basis for the variables used in the statistical models.

Primary Variables in the Analysis

The extent of departmental adoption of the elements of the legalized accountability model is measured by additive indexes of a number of variables. These variables, divided into the areas of formal policy, training, and oversight, are discussed in the substantive chapters, and I will not repeat the discussion here. The measures of the variables consist of original survey questions; the wording of these questions, the distribution of responses on them, and the like are reported in the final section of the appendix.

As reported in the substantive chapters, I have conducted multivariate tests of alternative possible explanations for adopting the legalized accountability model. The variables used in these analyses are drawn either from the original surveys or from other sources, as reported below. Table A.1 (see page 244) summarizes all variables, their expected relation to managerial perceptions of liability and departmental systems, and the sources for data on them.

Local Litigation Support Structures

Among the most important elements of the environment around local governments are infrastructures for support of civil rights and liberties, consisting of
civil rights lawyers and citizens' rights advocacy groups. Rights lawyers and
rights advocacy groups place pressure on administrative agencies to adopt
rights policies, oversee their implementation, and bring lawsuits, the ultimate
"hammer." But lawsuits are often a last resort, so ongoing pressure and oversight by these lawyers and groups, or simply their presence and the *possibility*
of pressure and oversight may be more significant than whether they regularly
support civil rights lawsuits against the city government.

   Localities vary considerably in these support structures for rights. In some
places citizens are organized and active in support of rights policies (in local
chapters of such national organizations as the ACLU and the NAACP, or in
more ad hoc local organizations). In some places there are many local attorneys who are both willing and able to bring rights-based lawsuits against local
governments or their officials. ("Able" is a key condition, since filing a lawsuit
against a government agency or official—at least in the areas of policing and
playground safety—requires a specialized knowledge of sovereign immunity
law that is beyond the competence of many garden-variety plaintiffs' attorneys.)[3] Yet many other localities have very few or, more commonly, no such
citizen groups or attorneys.

   I have developed two key measures of the vibrancy of local rights-advocacy
support structures. One is managers' reports of the number of local attorneys
and citizen groups who are willing to support lawsuits against the agency; this
is a measure of managers' *perceptions* of the strength of the local rights infrastructure. My other one is an objective measure of the number of attorneys in
each locality who specialize in lawsuits against government agencies.[4] There
is substantial variation among localities on these measures (see fig. A.1 for the
perceived number of attorneys by city who are willing to file lawsuits over
police misconduct, and fig. A.2 for perceptions of the presence of local rights-
advocacy groups). For instance, among the 838 localities represented in the
policing data set, just under 15% of police chiefs reported no local attorneys
who are known to file lawsuits against the police, more than a third reported
the presence of no citizen groups agitating on questions of police misconduct,
and just over 10% reported no such attorneys or groups; by contrast, 10% and
5%, respectively, reported "many" such attorneys and citizen groups. On the
other ("objective") measure, just over half (52%) of localities had no attorneys
specializing in government lawsuits, and only a little over 17% had more than
four such attorneys.[5]

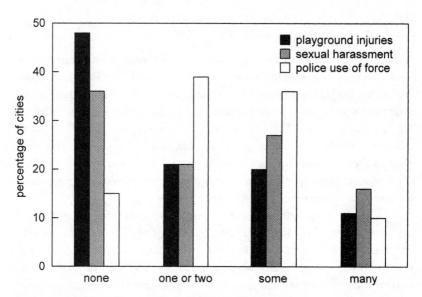

Figure A.1. Number of local attorneys willing to file lawsuits against city as perceived by chief administrators, by city and policy area. N = playgrounds, 211; sexual harassment, 432; policing, 828.

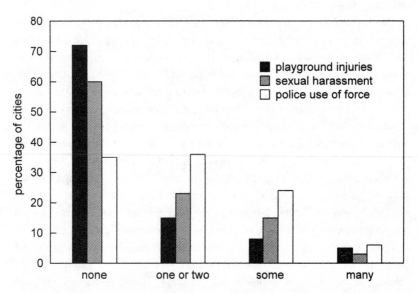

Figure A.2. Number of organized citizen groups that bring complaints, as perceived by chief administrators, by city and policy area. N = playgrounds, 220; sexual harassment, 435; policing, 828.

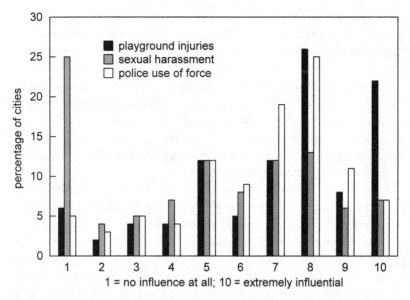

Figure A.3. Influence of professional associations on policies as reported by chief administrators, by city and policy area. *N* = playgrounds, 223; sexual harassment, 403; policing, 702.

Agency Connections to Professional Networks

If infrastructures of support for rights are a key element of city governments' environment, a second element is professional networks and the presence of particular administrative professionals within city governments. In the policy areas studied here, the leading professional associations are the International Association of Chiefs of Police, the International Public Management Association for Human Resources, and the National Recreation and Parks Association. Some city governments are very closely connected to the professional networks coordinated by these associations, others are largely unconnected to them.

As elaborated in the substantive chapters, we might expect that the more that local agencies are connected to professional networks—that is, connected to professional associations or to administrative professionals in other local agencies—the more likely they are to be attuned to the threat of legal liability and to adopt elements of the legalized accountability model.

Among cities in the legalization survey, chief administrators report widely varying influence by professional associations on their departments' policies (see fig. A.3). In the areas of playground safety and policing, chief administrators generally report that their departments are quite attentive to the advice of professional associations: on a ten-point scale, with ten representing the greatest influence by professional associations, the most common response in these areas was an eight, a remarkably high degree of influence. In playgrounds the second most common response was a ten. By contrast, in the area of sexual harassment policy the most common response by far was a one, representing no influence at all. Apart from these differences among policy areas, within each area chief administrators report widely varying influences by professional associations among cities: some cities seem to look heavily toward professional associations for advice while others do not.

A key path for influence by professional associations and professional networks is formal agency positions or offices associated with these networks. In the area of personnel policy (covering sexual harassment among many other things), many agencies employ human resources professionals to oversee the process; these officials participate in rich professional networks and attend professional conferences where they share information about law. In the area of policing, many departments employ lawyers charged with providing legal advice, defense, training, and so on. In the area of playgrounds, many departments employ officials who are "certified playground safety inspectors," certified by the National Recreation and Parks Association. Lauren Edelman aptly characterizes these organizational officials as "windows" between organizations and their legal environments. Among city departments participating in the survey, some employ such specialists and others do not.

Formal Legal Context

I have controlled for the relative liberalism of liability law. The measures consist of the relative liberalism of the appellate circuit courts on the issue of government immunity from lawsuits, by appellate circuit; the relative liberalism of the state supreme courts, by state; and the relative liberalism of the government immunity laws of the states, by state.

My measures of state law include a measure of the relative liberalism of state supreme courts and of state laws on government immunity from suit. I use here a measure of state supreme court liberalism developed by Brace, Langer, and Hall.[6] Scores on the judicial liberalism index increase with higher levels of judicial liberalism, so we should expect that the index will be positively associated with perceptions of liability and with the depth of administrative systems on rights. My measure of state sovereign immunity policies consists of an additive scale of several aspects of state statutes and judicial interpretations of them (coded by the author):[7]

- Monetary level (if any) of a cap on personal injury damages (three-point scale)
- Time limit or deadline for filing claims (three-point scale)
- Requirement to notify city of claim or delay of suit until response from city (three-point scale)
- Joint and several liability reforms (three-point scale)
- Comparative negligence reforms (three-point scale)

Higher values on the resulting index reflect more *conservative* sovereign immunity policies (i.e., greater restrictions on lawsuits and damages against government entities). Thus we should expect that the sovereign immunity scale will be negatively associated with perceptions of liability and with the depth of administrative rights policies, especially in the area of playground safety but possibly in the area of police use of force as well.

My measure of the relative liberalism of the federal appellate circuits consists of the mean liberalism score for each appellate circuit court of appeals in local government cases involving civil rights or torts.[8] On this measure the circuit courts of appeals vary considerably from the most liberal, the Ninth Circuit (covering the West Coast, Alaska, Hawaii, Arizona, Nevada, and Montana) to the most conservative, the Seventh Circuit (covering Indiana, Illinois, and Wisconsin), followed closely in conservatism by the Eleventh Circuit (covering Alabama, Florida, and Georgia).

Experience with Litigation

In addition to local support structures, particular lawsuits against cities, of course, are perhaps the most visible sort of localized liability pressure, but it is important not to overstate their significance. Even if a city has never been sued over excessive use of force by the police, for instance, its officials may justifiably perceive that such a suit is a real possibility (especially if they fall far below the standard set by professional norms). Moreover, not all lawsuits are equal—some are justifiably regarded as either frivolous or lacking sufficient backing to be carried far—while some forms of liability pressure such as a lawsuit threat from a city's leading civil rights litigator probably outweigh the impact of most ordinary lawsuits. In other words, we might expect that how widely agencies have adopted the legalized accountability model is shaped more by the relative availability of a local support structure than by whether the city has been sued or has lost a suit. Nonetheless, experience with being sued seems so closely associated with liability pressure that it obviously should be measured and tested. My survey pretests indicated that respondents were

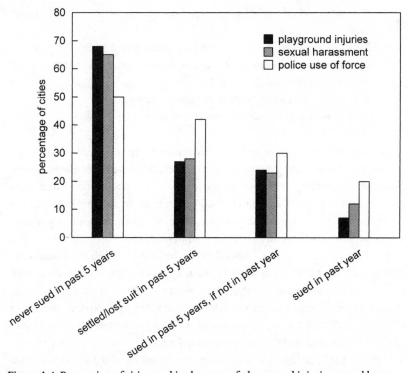

Figure A.4. Proportion of cities sued in the areas of playground injuries, sexual harassment, and police use of force. Number of cities: playground injuries, $N = 221$; sexual harassment, $N = 439$; police use of force, $N = 777$.

unable or unwilling to report the precise number of lawsuits per year filed against their departments. Thus I adopted a set of simpler indicators of organizational experience with litigation and summed them to form an "organizational experience with litigation index":

- Whether any lawsuits (in the respective areas of police misconduct, sexual harassment, or playground injuries) have ever been filed against the city
- Whether the city has settled any such lawsuit in the previous five years
- Whether the city has lost any such lawsuit in the previous five years

Cities vary considerably on this index as a measure of experience with litigation (see fig. A.4).

Organizational Characteristics

Undoubtedly a key set of possible influences on administrative policies consists of internal organizational characteristics. A general distinction is between cities that have a traditional political structure (mayor-council) and those that have a "reformed" structure, placing significant authority in the hands of a city manager. Traditional public administration research characterizes "reformed" cities as more professionally managed, which may contribute to more extensive adoption of elements of the legalized accountability model.

Another factor is likely to be the department's size. Organizations' size has a direct positive influence on their bureaucratization and rule-boundness,[9] either because larger organizations have greater needs for coordination or because larger size renders them more visible and more vulnerable to external pressure. I have measured department size as the number of full-time employees; we might expect size to be positively associated with the depth of administrative systems on rights. Because department size and the size of the local population are very closely correlated, and because in this matter population contributes to organization size rather than vice versa (and because data are obtained independently of the survey), I report results of models that include the population variable. The results do not differ appreciably if organization size is substituted for population.

In addition to organization size, employee unions may significantly affect organizational change.[10] In the area of policing, officers' unions often oppose intrusive external oversight of police departments, and they commonly have the resources necessary to fight the adoption of such policies.[11] Thus in the area of policing, unionization should be negatively associated with the adoption of intrusive policies. But in the area of personnel, employee unions may be associated with the adoption of more extensive sexual harassment policies (to protect members from harassment by managers). In the area of parks and recreation there is no past research on the effects of unionization, but it is plausible that unions may oppose onerous safety inspection rules and the like and thus that the measure of unionization will be negatively associated with the adoption of intrusive administrative policies. My measure of the extent of unionization is based on a survey question on the topic (for the wording, see the final section of this appendix).

Another possibly relevant organizational factor is insurance coverage. Insurance companies are known to press their organizational clients to adopt policies aimed at reducing their exposure to legal liability. Thus departments covered by liability insurance are likely to be more attentive to threats of legal liability than departments that are self-insured; insurance coverage should heighten the adoption of intrusive policies. Coverage is measured by a survey question (see below). Additionally, the more adequate the department's budget to its needs, the more likely it will be capable of adopting costly policies with minimal disruption;[12] well-funded departments are likely to feel less threatened by intrusive policies than departments that are constantly trying to stretch their resources. Thus the more adequate the departmental budget, the more likely is the adoption of costly, intrusive policies. The measure of relative budget adequacy is a survey question.

For reasons outlined in chapter 8, I also tested whether the proportion of women in the city's workforce—measured by a survey question—has an effect on either adoption of legalized accountability or corrective actions. It does on the latter but not the former and this is reported in table A.3.

Finally, in the area of playground safety, city parks and recreation departments differ: most are simply agencies of city government, but some are freestanding, independent agencies. Some observers believe that freestanding parks agencies are more responsive to professional norms than are city parks departments; others believe the opposite. I have coded the distinction as a dummy variable, with one representing independent parks agencies.

Political Culture

In addition to demographic factors, one of the oldest themes in law and society research is the idea that regional variations in the application of law may be shaped by variations in political culture. For instance, regionally variable cultural assumptions may lead to significant variations in how far city departments have developed administrative systems on rights. One conceptualization of political culture is the standard American political culture continuum between "conservative" and "liberal" political preferences. In contemporary American political discourse political conservatism favors insulating the police from external oversight to enhance organizational efficiency and officer morale, while political liberalism favors exposing them to external oversight to enhance individual rights and maintain organizational accountability. I use a standard state-level measure of political culture, the Erikson, Wright and McIver political liberalism score, updated through 2003.[13] As scores on the state liberalism index increase with liberalism, we should expect the variable to be positively associated with the depth of city administrative systems on rights.

Demographic Context

One could argue that the legalized accountability model is more likely to be adopted the larger the city's population, the wealthier its population, the larger the proportion of racial minorities in the population, the more educated the local population, whether the city is not in any of the states of the Confederacy (the "South"), and its distance from an urban area (defined as a city of 100,000 or greater population). Additionally, in the area of policing, adoption may be related to the crime rate, but the direction of this possible influence is not clear in advance of statistical tests. With the exception of whether a city is in the South and its distance from an urban area, these data have been gathered for each city from the U.S. Census for 2000. "South" and proximity to an urban area were coded by the author (the latter using mileage reported by Mapquest).

Multivariate Models

I have tested for these alternative possible influences using ordinary least squares regression with robust standard errors (clustered by state). The results are remarkably consistent across the three policy areas (see table A.3). Principally, the stronger local support structures for rights litigation, and the stronger agency connections to professional networks, the more widely local agencies adopt the legalized accountability model. Equally significant, the stronger departments' connections to professional networks, the greater is the depth of their administrative policies on rights. The only other factor that has at least a relatively consistent relation to administrative policies is whether city governments have adopted a "reformed" governing structure (replacing a politically elected mayor with a professional city manager): in cities with such a structure, the depth of administrative rights policies is greater than in "strong mayor" cities, and the relationship is significant in the areas of sexual harassment policy and policing. No other factor—the law, the extent of agencies' experience with litigation, the size of the population, per capita income, region of the country, budgetary slack, and so on—has a consistent significant association with the depth of administrative systems on rights.

The variable measuring state sovereign immunity laws is left out of the sexual harassment equation because federal employment civil rights laws override these state statutes and virtually all sexual harassment claims are brought under federal law. (Introducing the sovereign immunity variable has no significant effect on the results.)

Table A.1. Variables, Measures, Expected Relationships with Departmental Policies, and Data Sources

Variable	Expected relationship with policies or corrective actions	Data source
Dependent variables		
Legalized Accountability index		Administrative legalization survey
Extent of corrective actions (police, HR: employee discipline; playgrounds: correction of hazards)		Administrative legalization survey
Local support structure for litigation		
Support structure index (perceptions)	+	Administrative legalization survey
Number of local attorneys (objective measure)	+	*Martindale-Hubbell* lawyer index
Connection to professional networks		
Connection to professional associations	+	Administrative legalization survey
Police: presence of officer who is lawyer	+	Administrative legalization survey
HR: presence of human resources official	+	Administrative legalization survey
Playgrounds: presence of certified parks inspector	+	Administrative legalization survey
Control variables:		
Formal legal context		
State supreme court liberalism	+	Brace, Langer, and Hall[a]
Local gov't immunity (state law)	-	Statutes coded by author
Federal circuit liberalism	+	Songer database
Experience with litigation		
Index of lawsuits, judgments, and settlements	+	Administrative legalization survey
Organizational characteristics		
Extent of employee unionization	+	Administrative legalization survey
Adequacy of budget	+	Administrative legalization survey
Whether covered by insurance	+	Administrative legalization survey
"Reformed" city government	+	ICMA, 1999[b]
Parks agency is free-standing	+	Administrative legalization survey
Percentage of employees who are female	+ (HR discipline)	Administrative legalization survey

Table A.1. (*continued*)

Variable	Expected relationship with policies or corrective actions	Data source
Political culture		
Partisan conservatism index (by state)	-	Erikson, Wright, and McIver[c]
Local demographics		
Total population	+	U.S. 2000 Census
Income per capita	+	U.S. 2000 Census
South	-	Coded by author
Nearness to urban area	+	Gathered by author
Violent crime rate	+ (police)	U.S. Department of Justice

[a] Paul Brace, Laura Langer, and Melinda Gann Hall, "Measuring the Preferences of State Supreme Court Judges," *Journal of Politics* 62, 2 (2000): 387-413.

[b] International City/County Management Association, *Database of Local Governments* (Washington, DC: ICMA, 1999).

[c] Robert S. Erikson, Gerald C. Wright, and John P. McIver, "Public Opinion in the States: A Quarter Century of Change and Stability," in *Public Opinion in State Politics,* ed. Jeffrey Cohen (Stanford, CA: Stanford University Press, 2006).

Apart from the various alternative explanations tested in the previous analyses, one might argue that city policies are likely to vary in relation to the policies of neighboring cities through copying or information sharing. That is, one could argue that a city is likely to have a deeper administrative system on rights if many cities in the area have deeper administrative systems on rights. With advances in geographic information systems, it is possible to test this hypothesis directly. I use a standard technique and find no significant proximity-based similarity in local government policies.[14]

Finally, to test whether legalized accountability contributes to or detracts from making corrective actions (such as discipline or removal of playground hazards), I introduced the legalized accountability index as an independent variable in multivariate models explaining the extent of these corrective actions. The data for the dependent variables are ordinal, and therefore I have used ordered Probit as the method of analysis. For information on how I measured corrective actions, see the wording of the survey questions in the following section. Controlling for all relevant factors, the legalized accountability index is *positively* associated with the extent of corrective actions in each of the models, and the relationship is statistically significant in the areas of sexual harassment policy and playground safety, and it approaches statistical significance in the area of policing (see table A.3). These results should be treated

Table A.2. Explaining the Extent of Adoption of Legalized Accountability among Cities (OLS regression with robust standard errors, clustered by state)

	Police Coefficient (robust SE)	Sexual Harassment Coefficient (robust SE)	Playgrounds Coefficient (robust SE)
Local support structure for litigation			
Support structure index (perceptions)	3.16 (1.01)***	3.87 (1.62)**	3.85 (1.88)**
Number of local attorneys (objective measure)	4.60 (2.05)**	5.32 (2.48)**	-0.41 (2.39)
Connection to professional networks			
Connection to professional associations	1.33 (0.48)**	1.45 (0.68)**	0.98 (0.68)
Officer who is lawyer on staff	17.35 (5.33)***		
Human resources official on staff		17.90 (5.44)***	
Certified parks inspector on staff			5.75 (1.71)***
Control variables:			
Formal legal context			
State supreme court liberalism	0.19 (0.29)	0.23 (0.22)	0.55 (0.36)
Local gov't immunity (state law)	0.65 (1.32)		4.19 (1.97)**
Federal circuit liberalism	-10.56 (7.44)	1.79 (4.31)	-3.17 (6.30)
Experience with litigation			
Index of lawsuits, judgments, and settlements	-2.33 (2.79)	1.79 (4.31)	-3.17 (6.30)

Organizational characteristics			
Extent of employee unionization	−7.24 (4.30)*	5.19 (6.50)	−1.33 (4.13)
Adequacy of budget	1.54 (1.03)	1.10 (1.15)	4.00 (1.90)**
Whether covered by insurance	−9.04 (5.22)*	4.26 (5.84)	−9.61 (6.31)
"Reformed" city government	12.71 (6.13)**	17.42 (7.68)**	11.04 (6.50)*
Parks agency is free-standing			33.13 (12.80)**
Political culture			
Partisan conservatism index (by state)	−0.07 (0.50)	−0.32 (0.56)	−0.80 (0.58)
Local demographics			
Total population	0.024 (0.01)**	0.02 (0.03)	0.05 (0.02)**
Income per capita	−0.13 (0.39)	−0.39 (0.21)*	−0.27 (0.55)
South	−9.99 (6.92)	−1.40 (8.07)	6.33 (6.89)
Distance to urban area	−0.01 (0.04)	0.06 (0.04)***	0.09 (0.08)
Violent crime rate	0.07 (0.06)		
Constant	−22.56 (32.95)	−100.04 (30.11)***	−118.70 (44.51)**
R^2	.18****	.22****	.32****
N	391	250	154

*$p < .10$; **$p < .05$; ***$p < .01$; ****$p < .001$

Table A.3. Explaining the Extent of Corrective Actions (Discipline or Replacing Equipment) among Cities (ordered Probit with robust standard errors, clustered by state)

	Police Coefficient (robust SE)	Sexual Harassment Coefficient (robust SE)	Playgrounds Coefficient (robust SE)
Legalized accountability (index)	0.0035 (.0018)*	0.008 (.002)****	0.581 (0.274)**
Local support structure for litigation			
Support structure index (perceptions)	0.066 (0.035)*	0.090 (0.051)*	0.030 (0.064)
Number of local attorneys (objective measure)	0.150 (0.050)***	0.078 (0.092)	0.069 (0.073)
Connection to professional networks			
Connection to professional associations	−0.012 (0.016)	0.004 (0.016)	0.014 (0.026)
Officer who is lawyer on staff	0.091 (0.209)		
Human resources official on staff		0.334 (0.138)**	
Certified parks inspector on staff			−0.061 (0.046)
Control variables:			
Formal legal context			
State supreme court liberalism	−0.018 (0.005)****	−0.001 (0.007)	−0.015 (0.007)**
Local gov't immunity (state law)	−0.006 (0.049)		−0.201 (0.063)***
Federal circuit liberalism	−0.268 (90.207)	0.083 (0.190)	
Experience with litigation			
Index of lawsuits, judgments, and settlements	0.449 (0.082)****	0.428 (0.080)****	0.322 (0.215)
Organizational characteristics			
Extent of employee unionization	−0.197 (0.076)**	0.018 (0.122)	0.213 (0.158)

Adequacy of budget	−0.008 (0.033)	−0.016 (0.039)	0.00003 (0.051)
Whether covered by insurance	−0.062 (0.141)	−0.111 (0.201)	−0.097 (0.160)
"Reformed" city government	−0.008 (0.159)	−0.018 (0.168)	0.142 (0.198)
Percentage of employees who are women		0.010 (0.005)*	
Parks agency is free-standing			−0.955 (0.344)***
Political culture			
Partisan conservatism index (by state)	0.032 (0.012)***	−0.008 (0.012)	0.011 (0.012)
Local demographics			
Total population	0.0003 (0.0005)	0.0003 (0.001)	0.0001 (0.001)
Income per capita	−0.014 (0.007)*	−0.011 (0.009)	−0.034 (0.010)***
South	0.176 (0.127)	0.045 (0.155)	0.037 (0.237)
Distance to urban area	−0.0009 (−0.001)	−0.0002 (0.001)	0.004 (0.003)
Violent crime rate	0.0002 (0.001)		
Constant 1	−1.733 (0.976)	1.253 (0.755)	−4.358 (0.898)
Constant 2	−1.305 (0.986)	1.482 (0.754)	−2.819 (0.924)
Constant 3	−0.766 (1.002)	1.921 (0.753)	−1.517 (0.929)
Constant 3	0.403 (0.948)	2.794 (0.799)	−0.700 (0.963)
Constant 5			0.129 (0.935)
Constant 6			−0.953 (0.974)
R^2	.11****	.12****	.09****
X^2	402.2	522.5	191.8
N	377	240	148

*$p < .10$; **$p < .05$; ***$p < .01$; ****$p < .001$

with qualification, as I am unable to control for variations in the underlying extent of police misconduct, sexual harassment, and playground hazards. But I do control for factors that are arguably related to the relative incidence of these things, particularly population. The results suggest that systems of legalized accountability *contribute to rather than detract from* taking corrective actions against these problems.

Survey Question Wording

Police Policies, Procedures, and Protocols

Variables are discussed in the order of their appearance, from left to right, in figure 6.1.

Written Policy on Use of Force

Question: Which of the following best characterizes your department's policy on the use of nondeadly force?

No written policy	3 (0.4%)
A written policy that provides *general* rules on the proper use of force but *does not specifically* mention particular types of force, such as the use of a baton or a wristlock	148 (17.7%)
A written policy that *specifically mentions* particular types of force, such as the use of a baton or a wristlock	686 (82.0%)
Total	837 (100%)

Review Uses of Force

Departments vary widely in how much their superior officers review the uses of force by street-level officers.

Question: Does your department regularly review and investigate use-of-force reports by officers even if no citizen complaint or civil lawsuit has been filed?

Reports are generally not reviewed and investigated	57 (6.8%)
Selected reports are reviewed and investigated	136 (16.3%)
All reports are reviewed and investigated	642 (76.9%)
Total	835 (100%)

Require Reports on Uses of Force

Departments vary widely in when they require officers to file written reports on their uses of force. My measure of reporting requirements focuses on three common uses of force that appear at varying levels of the use-of-force continuum, one near the greatest force (use of a baton), one near the least force (use of a firm grip), and one between those extremes (use of a wristlock or twist lock, a common "pain compliance" technique). The responses, as expected, vary significantly.

Question: What is your department's policy on whether officers must report the following uses of force?

Use of a baton on a citizen:

No requirement to report	15 (1.8%)
Must report only in some circumstances, such as if injury results	37 (4.5%)
Must report all occurrences	774 (93.7%)
Total	826 (100%)

A twist lock or wristlock on a citizen:

No requirement to report	106 (13.0%)
Must report only in some circumstances, such as if injury results	239 (29.4%)
must report all occurrences	469 (57.6%)
Total	814 (100%)

Use of a "firm grip" on a citizen:

No requirement to report	222 (26.9%)
Must report only in some circumstances, such as if injury results	338 (41.0%)
Must report all occurrences	264 (32.0%)
Total	824 (100%)

Additive index of reporting requirements:

0	14 (1.8%)
1	13 (1.6%)
2	77 (9.7%)
3	67 (8.4%)
4	226 (28.4%)
5	147 (18.5%)
6	252 (31.7%)
Total	796 (100%)

Facilitation of Citizen Complaints

Although virtually all departments accept complaints from citizens against officers, they vary in how much they erect symbolic obstacles to filing complaints. Two such obstacles, which vary considerably in their burdensomeness, are a requirement to sign the complaint and a requirement to certify, notarize, or swear to the complaint.

> *Question:* Which of the following does your department require of persons who seek to file a complaint of police misconduct? (Please check any that apply.)
>
> *Sign the complaint:*
>
> | | |
> |---|---|
> | Yes | 529 (64.7%) |
> | No | 289 (35.3%) |
> | Total | 818 (100%) |
>
> *Certify, notarize, or swear to the complaint:*
>
> | | |
> |---|---|
> | Yes | 207 (25.8%) |
> | No | 597 (74.3%) |
> | Total | 804 (100%) |
>
> *Additive index* (with values ascending with
>   fewer obstacles to filing a complaint):
>
> | | | |
> |---|---|---|
> | | 0 | 150 (18.8%) |
> | | 1 | 418 (52.3%) |
> | | 2 | 232 (29.0%) |
> | | Total | 800 (100%) |

Type and Extent of Training

Departments vary widely in how much training their experienced officers receive in a range of topics.

> *Question:* How frequently does the typical experienced officer in your department receive in-service training in the following areas?
>
> *The proper use of a baton:*
>
> | | |
> |---|---|
> | No training | 66 (8.1%) |
> | Training every 13 months or more | 252 (30.7%) |
> | Training every 7 to 12 months | 394 (48.1%) |
> | Training every 0 to 6 months | 108 (13.2%) |
> | Total | 820 (100%) |
>
> *Role-play training in the proper use of force:*
>
> | | |
> |---|---|
> | No training | 105 (12.6%) |
> | Training every 13 months or more | 274 (32.9%) |
> | Training every 7 to 12 months | 322 (38.7%) |

Training every 0 to 6 months		131 (15.8%)
Total		832 (100%)

Cultural sensitivity training:

No training		80 (9.6%)
Training every 13 months or more		496 (59.6%)
Training every 7 to 12 months		226 (27.2%)
Training every 0 to 6 months		30 (3.6%)
Total		832 (100%)

Training in legal liability issues:

No training		49 (5.9%)
Training every 13 months or more		323 (38.9%)
Training every 7 to 12 months		326 (39.3%)
Training every 0 to 6 months		132 (15.9%)
Total		830 (100%)

Additive index of type and extent of training:

	0	8 (1.0%)
	1	11 (1.4%)
	2	30 (3.7%)
	3	51 (6.3%)
	4	127 (15.6%)
	5	93 (11.4%)
	6	108 (13.3%)
	7	139 (17.1%)
	8	144 (17.7%)
	9	41 (5.0%)
	10	35 (4.3%)
	11	17 (2.1%)
	12	11 (1.4%)
Total	13	815 (100%)

Early Warning System

Question: Does your department have a formal early warning or early identification system for identifying officers who receive a high rate of citizen complaints or exhibit other problematic performance?

No formal policy	371 (44.8%)
No policy in place, but one is planned	75 (9.1%)
Yes, a formal policy is in place	383 (46.2%)
Total	829 (100%)

Policies Modified in Past Year

More frequent modifications suggest ongoing attempts to improve policies and keep them up to date.

Question: Has your department modified your policy or training in the use of force in the past year?

No	423 (50.8%)
Yes	409 (49.2%)
Total	832 (100%)

Training by External Legal Experts

In some departments, training is provided not only by police officials but also by outside experts, among them lawyers.

Question: In your department, who provides in-service training to experienced officers?

A local prosecutor		527 (62.8% of 839)
A member of the city's legal staff		354 (42.2% of 838)
A law professor		168 (20.1% of 834)
Additive index:	0	272 (32.7%)
	1	211 (25.4%)
	2	223 (26.8%)
	3	126 (15.1%)
	Total	832 (100%)

Oversight by City Legal Staff

"Oversight by city legal staff" refers to how often command-level officers communicate with city attorneys and risk managers. More extensive communication provides the conditions for greater impact of law (as interpreted by lawyers) on police policies and procedures.

Question: How frequently do command-level officers in your department consult about issues related to the use of force with your city's risk management officials or legal staff other than prosecutors?

Continually (daily or weekly)	39 (4.7%)
Frequently (monthly)	64 (7.7%)
Regularly (several times a year)	237 (28.6%)
Occasionally (A few times over several years)	347 (41.2%)
Never or almost never	143 (17.2%)
Total	830 (100%)

Race of Stopped Drivers Reported

Question: For purposes of checking whether any officers are stopping members of some racial groups at higher rates than others, does your department require officers in traffic stops to record and report the race of the driver of the car being stopped?

No	572 (68.8%)
No such policy is in place, but one is planned	103 (12.4%)
Yes	157 (18.9%)

Citizen Review Board

Question: Does your jurisdiction have a citizen complaint review board or agency?

Yes	121 (14.5% of 835)

Question: In your jurisdiction, are citizens other than sworn officers involved in the citizen-complaint review process?

Yes		144 (17.9% of 804)
Additive index of two questions above:	0	621 (77.3%)
	1	102 (12.7%)
	2	80 (10.0%)
	Total	803 (100%)

Police Legalized Accountability Index

The measures above were combined into an index using Stata's alpha command, with the items standardized to a mean of O and a variance of I. Cronbach's alpha for the index is .59.

Corrective Actions against Police Misconduct

Question: In the year 1999, what actions, if any, were used by your city government in response to complaints of excessive use of force or concerns about legal liability for excessive use of force?

Dismissal of the accused officer?		102 of 802 (12.7%)
Counseling or retraining for the accused party?		355 of 798 (44.5%)
Written reprimand for the accused party?		275 of 790 (34.8%)
Oral reprimand for the accused party?		215 of 793 (27.1%)
Additive index (Cronbach's alpha = .95)	0	384 (49.2%)
	1	103 (13.2%)

2		107 (13.7%)
3		145 (18.6%)
4		42 (5.4%)
Total		781 (100%)

Sexual Harassment Policies, Procedures, and Protocols

Variables are discussed in the order of their appearance, from left to right, in figure 8.2.

Written Policy

Question: Does your city have a written policy prohibiting sexual harassment?

No	10 (2.2%)
Yes	444 (97.8%)
Total	454 (100%)

Grievance Procedure

Question: Does your city have a specific sexual harassment complaint procedure?

No	104 (22.9%)
Yes	350 (77.1%)
Total	454 (100%)

Diversity of Training Tools

This concept is measured by an index of several types of tools commonly used in sexual harassment training. Departments that use more of these tools provide richer and more complete training to their employees.

Question: Which of the following is included in the sexual harassment training for continuing employees?

Written information		320 of 421 (76%)
Oral presentations		313 of 421 (74.4%)
Examples or role-plays of prohibited behavior		228 of 415 (54.9%)
Video presentations		226 of 419 (53.9%)
Additive index:	0	88 (21.3%)
	1	16 (3.9%)
	2	38 (9.2%)
	3	113 (27.3%)
	4	159 (38.4%)
	Total	414 (100%)

Specialized Training for Managers

Question: Is there separate, specialized sexual harassment training for managers?

No	205 (45.9%)
Yes	242 (54.1%)
Total	447 (100%)

Oversight by City Legal Staff

"Oversight by city legal staff" refers to how much personnel managers communicate with city attorneys and risk managers. More extensive communication provides the conditions for greater impact of law (as interpreted by lawyers) on personnel policies and procedures.

Question: In your city, how frequently do personnel managers communicate about issues related to sexual harassment policy or procedures with your city's risk management officials or legal staff? (Check the ONE answer that best fits.)

Continually (daily or weekly)	50 (11.4%)
Frequently (monthly)	60 (13.6%)
Regularly (several times a year)	130 (29.6%)
Occasionally (a few times over several years)	137 (31.1%)
Never or almost never	63 (14.3%)
Total	440 (100%)

Policies Modified in Past Year

More frequent modifications suggest ongoing attempts to improve policies and keep them up to date.

Question: Has your city modified your sexual harassment policy or training in the past year?

No	264 (58.4%)
Yes	188 (41.6%)
Total	452 (100%)

Extent of Training for Continuing Employees

More frequent training may have a greater impact on organizational culture than less frequent training. *Question:* For the typical continuing employee, about how often is sexual harassment training provided?

Never	114 (25.4%)
Every thirteen months to four or more years, or irregularly	194 (43%)

Every seven to twelve months	119 (26.5%)
Every zero to six months	22 (4.9%)
Total	449 (100%)

Extent of Internal Publicity of Policy

Cities may use a variety of methods, or none, for communicating their sexual harassment policy to employees. The responses are summed to an index.

Question: In which of the following ways is your sexual harassment policy communicated to employees? (Check all that apply)

Included in periodic newsletters, e-mail messages or flyers	171 (39.3%)
Displayed in posters	235 (54.8%)
Telephone hotline	64 (15%)

Additive index:		
	0	112 (26.5%)
	1	92 (45.4%)
	2	92 (21.8%)
	3	27 (6.4%)
	Total	423 (100%)

Extent of Training for New Employees

For employees just entering the job, some cities provide training in their sexual harassment policy, while others do not. Additionally, the amount of training for new employees varies considerably.

Question: Is training regarding sexual harassment provided to the following employees? New employees, shortly after they are hired? For a typical new employee, about how much time is devoted to sexual harassment training? (Descriptive statistics combine responses from these two questions.)

None	158 (35.6%)
15 minutes	113 (25.5%)
30 minutes	57 (12.8%)
60 minutes	40 (9%)
90 minutes	20 (4.5%)
2 hours or more	56 (12.6%)
Total	444 (100%)

Employees Surveyed

Some cities have conducted a survey of their employees to assess their knowledge of the city's sexual harassment policy and the extent of perceived harassment in the organization.

Question: Has your city done a survey of employees on the issue of sexual harassment?

No	419 (93.3%)
Yes	30 (6.7%)
Total	449 (100%)

Sexual Harassment Legalized Accountability Index

The measures above were combined into an index using Stata's alpha command, with the items standardized to a mean of 0 and a variance of 1. Cronbach's alpha for the index is .72.

Corrective Actions against Harassment

Question: In the year 1999, what actions, if any, were used by your city government in response to complaints of sexual harassment or concerns about legal liability for sexual harassment?"

Dismissal of the accused party?	57 of 455 (12.5%)
Counseling or retraining for the accused party?	190 of 455 (41.8%)
Written reprimand for the accused party?	169 of 455 (37.1%)
Oral reprimand for the accused party?	140 of 455 (30.8%)

Additive index (Cronbach's alpha = .83):	0	243 (53.4%)
	1	32 (7%)
	2	52 (11.4%)
	3	92 (20.2%)
	4	36 (7.9%)
	Total	455 (100%)

Playground Safety Policy Variables

Variables are discussed in the order in which they appear in figure 9.2.

Quick Response to Hazards

Question: Does your department have a policy requiring that any hazard report is to be acted upon quickly, for example, in twenty-four to forty-eight hours?

No	30 (13.1%)
Yes	199 (86.9%)
Total	229 (100%)

Record Inspections and Complaints

Question: Does your department maintain the following kinds of records?

Inspection records indicating the date and/or nature of playground inspections	192 (83.5% of 230)
Logs of complaints or hazard reports by citizens	191 (83.1% of 229)
Accident or incident report records regarding any injuries	214 (92.6% of 231)

Additive index:

	0	4 (1.8%)
	1	16 (7.1%)
	2	47 (20.7%)
	3	160 (70.5%)
	Total	227 (100%)

Average Percentage of Playgrounds Audited

Question: How many of these playgrounds [referring to previous survey question—not reported here—asking how many playgrounds are managed or maintained by the responding department] have been given a formal playground audit to check for compliance with the most current Consumer Product Safety Commission's playground safety guidelines?

Percentage, ranging from 0 to 100, mean 81.6%; SD 36.5 ($N = 231$)

Frequency of Safety Inspections

Question: During seasons when playgrounds are in use, how frequently is each playground inspected to discover possible needed repairs on playground equipment?

Inspection is irregular	4 (1.7%)
About once every several years	2 (0.9%)
About twice a year	12 (5.2%)
About once a month	56 (24.2%)
About once a week	94 (40.7%)
Daily	63 (27.3%)
Total	231 (100%)

Written Safety Policy

Question: Does your department have a written safety policy that covers playground safety, such as requiring employees to report any safety hazards?

No	60 (26.0%)
Yes	171 (74.0%)
Total	231 (100%)

Proportion of Employees Trained

Question: Is training regarding playground safety provided to the following employees?

All new employees who work on playgrounds		79 (34.5% of 229)
All continuing employees who work on playgrounds		54 (23.6% of 229)
Additive index:	0	43 (19.0%)
	1	47 (20.8%)
	2	136 (60.2%)
	Total	226 (100%)

Frequency of Safety Training

Question: Regarding employees who work on playgrounds, how frequently does the typical employee receive training regarding playground safety?

No training	23 (10%)
Training every 13 months or more	21 (9%)
Training every 7 to 12 months	144 (66.7%)
Training every 0 to 6 months	28 (13.0%)
Total	216 (100%)

Oversight by Legal Staff

Question: How frequently do managers in your department consult about issues related to playground safety with your department's or city's risk management officials or legal staff?

Never or almost never	27 (12.1%)
Occasionally (a few times over several years)	47 (21.1%)
Regularly (several times a year)	88 (39.5%)
Frequently (monthly)	38 (17.0%)
Continually (daily or weekly)	23 (10.3%)
Total	223 (100%)

Supervisors Must Have Safety Training

Question: Does your department require that supervisors gain professional certification in playground safety?

No	151 (65.4%)
Yes	80 (34.6%)
Total	231 (100%)

Safety Policy Modified in Past Year

Question: Has your department modified your policy on playground safety in the past year?

No	171 (75.3%)
Yes	56 (24.7%)
Total	227 (100%)

Legalized Accountability Index for Playgrounds

The measures above were combined into an index using Stata's alpha command, with the items standardized to a mean of 0 and a variance of 1. Cronbach's alpha for the index is .54.

Corrective Actions with regard to Playground Hazards

Question: In playgrounds managed or maintained by your department, has anything mentioned above—hard ground surfaces, metal animal swings, swings for more than one person, seesaws, jungle gyms made from metal pipes—been removed in recent years?

No	38 (16.6%)
Yes	191 (83.4%)
Total	229 (100%)

Question: Has your department removed or replaced playground equipment in the past year?

No	43 (18.9%)
Yes	185 (81.1%)
Total	228 (100%)

Question: In playgrounds managed or maintained by your department, are there any of the following?

Hard surfaces under play areas	28 (12.1% of 232)
Metal animal swings	23 (10.0% of 230)

Swings designed for more than		
one person	17	(7.3% of 232)
Seesaws	53	(23.0% of 230)
Jungle gyms constructed		
with metal pipes	91	(39.2% of 232)

The measures above were combined into an index of corrective actions using Stata's alpha command, with the items standardized to a mean of 0 and a variance of 1. Cronbach's alpha for the index is .40.

Notes

Chapter One

1. Jeff Steffel and Donald Rossi. "Remarks: Psychological Aspects of Vicarious Liability," *Police Chief*, March 1983, 130–35, at 135.

2. Stuart Scheingold, *The Politics of Rights: Lawyers, Public Policy, and Political Change* (New Haven: Yale University Press, 1974), 95.

3. Gerald N. Rosenberg, *The Hollow Hope: Can Courts Bring about Social Change?* (Chicago: University of Chicago Press, 1991).

4. Max Weber, *The Protestant Ethic and the Spirit of Capitalism* (London: Allen and Unwin, 1958).

5. For a very valuable comparison of the place of government administration in the constitutional systems of the United States and Britain, see John A. Rohr, *Civil Servants and Their Constitutions* (Lawrence: University Press of Kansas, 2002).

6. See, e.g., Robert A. Kagan, *Adversarial Legalism: The American Way of Law* (Cambridge, MA: Harvard University Press. 2003), and Thomas Burke, *Lawyers, Lawsuits, and Legal Rights: The Battle over Litigation in America* (Berkeley: University of California Press, 2002).

7. Samuel Walker, *Taming the System: The Control of Discretion in Criminal Justice, 1950–1990* (New York: Oxford University Press, 1993).

8. Carrie N. Baker, *The Women's Movement against Sexual Harassment* (New York: Cambridge University Press, 2008), 177.

9. David H. Rosenbloom and Rosemary O'Leary, *Public Administration and Law*, 2nd ed. (New York: M. Dekker, 1997), 1.

10. Kagan, *Adversarial Legalism*; Barbara S. Romzek and Melvin J. Dubnick, "Accountability in the Public Sector: Lessons from the Challenger Tragedy," *Public Administration Review* 47 (1987): 227–38; Rosemary O'Leary, *Environmental Change: Federal Courts and the EPA* (Philadelphia: Temple University Press, 1987). For a simplistic version of this perspective see Walter Olson, *Litigation Explosion: What Happened When America Unleashed the Lawsuit* (New York: Dutton, 1991); see also Peter W. Huber,

Liability: The Legal Revolution and Its Consequences (New York: Basic Books, 1988), and Peter W. Huber and Robert E. Litan, *The Liability Maze: The Impact of Liability Law on Safety and Innovation* (Washington, DC: Brookings Institution, 1991).

11. Stuart Taylor Jr. and Evan Thomas, "Lawsuit Hell: How Fear of Litigation Is Paralyzing Our Professions," *Newsweek*, December 15, 2003. The *Newsweek* cover story is, of course, simply a handy example; many critics of tort liability have made similar claims See, e.g., George W. Bush, Remarks by the president at the Newspaper Association of America annual convention, Omni Shoreham Hotel, Washington, DC, April 21, 2004, and Philip K. Howard, *The Death of Common Sense: How Law Is Suffocating America* (New York: Random House, 1994).

12. These complaints are summarized in the *Newsweek* article.

13. Tom Baker, *The Medical Malpractice Myth* (Chicago: University of Chicago Press, 2005).

14. Kagan, *Adversarial Legalism*.

15. Lauren B. Edelman, "Legal Ambiguity and Symbolic Structures: Organizational Mediation of Civil Rights Law," *American Journal of Sociology* 97 (1992): 1531–76; see also Lauren Edelman and Marc C. Suchman, "The Legal Environments of Organizations," *Annual Review of Sociology* 23 (1997): 479.

16. The research supporting these propositions is too voluminous to note in its entirety; important contributions include Marc Galanter, "Reading the Landscape of Disputes: What We Know and Don't Know (and Think We Know) about Our Allegedly Contentious and Litigious Society," *UCLA Law Review* 31 (1983): 4–71; Marc Galanter, "Real World Torts: An Antidote to Anecdote," *Maryland Law Review* 55 (1996): 1093–1160; Richard E. Miller and Austin Sarat, "Grievances, Claims, and Disputes: Assessing the Adversary Culture," *Law and Society Review* 15 (1980–81): 525–66; Michael J. Saks, "Do We Really Know Anything about the Behavior of the Tort Litigation System—and Why Not?" *University of Pennsylvania Law Review* 140 (1992): 1147; Tom Baker, *The Medical Malpractice Myth* (Chicago: University of Chicago Press, 2005); Theodore Eisenberg and Stewart Schwab, "The Reality of Constitutional Tort Litigation," *Cornell Law Review* 72 (1987): 641–95; and Charles R. Epp, "Exploring the Costs of Administrative Legalization: City Expenditures on Legal Services, 1960–1995," *Law and Society Review* 34 (2000): 407.

17. Peter H. Schuck, *Suing Government: Citizen Remedies for Official Wrongs* (New Haven, CT: Yale University Press, 1983).

18. See, e.g., Gerald N. Rosenberg, *The Hollow Hope: Can Courts Bring about Social Change?* 2nd ed. (Chicago: University of Chicago Press, 2008).

19. See, e.g., Edelman, "Legal Ambiguity and Symbolic Structures," 1531–76; see also Edelman and Suchman, "Legal Environments of Organizations."

20. Jonathan Simon, *Governing through Crime* (New York: Oxford University Press, 2007); Doris Marie Provine, *Unequal under Law: Race in the War on Drugs* (Chicago: University of Chicago Press, 2007).

21. Frank Dobbin and Erin L. Kelly, "How to Stop Harassment: Professional Construction of Legal Compliance in Organizations," *American Journal of Sociology* 112, 4 (2007): 1203–43. See also Susan Bisom-Rapp, "Fixing Watches with Sledgehammers: The Questionable Embrace of Employee Sexual Harassment Training by the Legal Profession," *University of Arkansas at Little Rock Law Review* 24 (2001): 147–68; and Susan Bisom-Rapp, "An Ounce of Prevention Is a Poor Substitute for a Pound of Cure:

Confronting the Developing Jurisprudence of Education and Prevention in Employment Discrimination Law," *Berkeley Journal of Employment and Labor Law* 22 (2001): 1–46.

22. Desmond S. King and Rogers M. Smith, "Racial Orders in American Political Development," *American Political Science Review* 99, 1 (2005): 75–92.

23. Karen Orren, "Officers' Rights: Toward a Unified Field Theory of American Constitutional Development," *Law and Society Review* 34, 4 (2000): 873–909.

24. Marc Galanter, "Why the Haves Come Out Ahead: Speculations on the Limits of Legal Change," *Law and Society Review* 9, 2 (1974): 95–160.

25. These interviews are reported more fully in Charles R. Epp, "Litigation Stories: Official Perceptions of Lawsuits against Local Governments," paper presented at the 1998 annual meeting of the Law and Society Association, Snowmass, CO, on file with the author.

Chapter Two

1. Patrick V. Murphy, interview with the author, August 25, 2008; Tom Brady, interview with the author, August 20, 2008; James E. Adams, "Police Convention Closes with 'Deadly Force' Dispute," *St. Louis Post-Dispatch*, September 19, 1980, 13A.

2. Samuel Walker, *The New World of Police Accountability* (Thousand Oaks, CA: Sage, 2005).

3. Barbara A. Gutek, "Sexual Harassment Policy Initiatives," in *Sexual Harassment: Theory, Research, Treatment,* ed. William O'Donohue (New York: Allyn and Bacon, 1997), 185–98. See also chapter 8 of this book.

4. For evidence in support of this claim, see chapter 9.

5. Stuart Scheingold, *The Politics of Rights: Lawyers, Public Policy, and Political Change* (New Haven, CT: Yale University Press, 1974).

6. Robert A. Kagan, *Adversarial Legalism: The American Way of Law* (Cambridge, MA: Harvard University Press, 2003); Thomas Burke, *Lawyers, Lawsuits, and Legal Rights: The Battle over Litigation in America* (Berkeley: University of California Press, 2002).

7. William Haltom and Michael McCann, *Distorting the Law: Politics, Media, and the Litigation Crisis* (Chicago: University of Chicago Press, 2004).

8. Lauren B. Edelman, Christopher Uggen, and Howard S. Erlanger, "The Endogeneity of Legal Regulation: Grievance Procedures as Rational Myth," *American Journal of Sociology* 105, 2 (1999): 406–54; see also Edelman and Suchman, "Legal Environments of Organizations."

9. Malcolm M. Feeley and Edward L. Rubin, *Judicial Policy Making in the Modern State: How the Courts Reformed America's Prisons* (New York: Cambridge University Press, 1998); see also Jeb Barnes and Thomas F. Burke, "The Diffusion of Rights: From Law on the Books to Organizational Rights Practices," *Law and Society Review* 40, 3 (2006): 493–524.

10. Galanter, "Why the Haves Come out Ahead;" Austin Sarat and Stuart A. Scheingold, eds., *Cause Lawyering: Political Commitments and Professional Responsibilities* (New York: Oxford University Press, 1998); Austin Sarat and Stuart A. Scheingold, eds., *Cause Lawyers and Social Movements* (Stanford, CA: Stanford University Press, 2006). See also Joel F. Handler, Ellen Jane Hollingsworth, and Howard S. Erlanger, *Lawyers and the Pursuit of Legal Rights* (New York: Academic Press, 1978).

11. See, e.g., Doug McAdam, Sidney Tarrow, and Charles Tilly, *Dynamics of Contention* (New York: Cambridge University Press, 2001); Michael McCann, *Rights at Work: Pay Equity Reform and the Politics of Legal Mobilization* (Chicago: University of Chicago Press, 1994); Kathrin S. Zippel, *The Politics of Sexual Harassment: A Comparative Analysis of the U.S., the European Union, and Germany* (New York: Cambridge University Press, 2006); Joel F. Handler, *Social Movements and the Legal System: A Theory of Social Change* (New York: Academic Press, 1978); Helena Silverstein, *Unleashing Rights: Law, Meaning, and the Animal Rights Movement* (Ann Arbor: University of Michigan Press, 1996); Beth Harris, *Defending the Right to a Home: The Power of Anti-poverty Lawyers* (Burlington, VT: Ashgate 2004); David A. Snow and Robert D. Benford, "Ideology, Frame Resonance, and Participant Mobilization," in *From Structure to Action: Social Movement Participation across Cultures*, ed. Bert Klandermans, Hanspeter Kriesi, and Sidney Tarrow (Greenwich, CT: JAI Press, 1988); Robert D. Benford and David A. Snow, "Framing Processes and Social Movements: An Overview and Assessment," *Annual Review of Sociology* 26 (2000): 611–39; Steven Teles, *The Rise of the Conservative Legal Movement: The Battle for Control of the Law* (Princeton, NJ: Princeton University Press, 2008).

12. William L. Prosser, "The Fall of the Citadel (Strict Liability to the Consumer)," *Minnesota Law Review* 50 (1966): 791.

13. *Monroe v. Pape* 365 U.S. 167 (1961).

14. *Monell v. Department of Social Services* 436 U.S. 658 (1978).

15. 42 USC 1988.

16. On the importance of framing for social movement development, see Snow and Benford, "Ideology, Frame Resonance, and Participant Mobilization," and Benford and Snow, "Framing Processes and Social Movements."

17. William Haltom and Michael McCann, *Distorting the Law: Politics, Media, and the Litigation Crisis* (Chicago: University of Chicago Press, 2004).

18. See, e.g., Paul J. DiMaggio and Walter W. Powell, "The Iron Cage Revisited: Institutional Isomorphism and Collective Rationality in Organizational Fields," *American Sociological Review* 48, 2 (1983): 147–60.

19. Christopher Hood, *The Art of the State: Culture, Rhetoric, and Public Management* (Oxford: Oxford University Press, 1998); see also Colin Scott, "Accountability in the Regulatory State," *Journal of Law and Society* 27, 1 (2000): 38–60.

20. On institutional entrepreneurs, see Raghu Garud, Cynthia Hardy, and Steve Maguire. "Institutional Entrepreneurship as Embedded Agency: An Introduction to the Special Issue," *Organization Studies* 28 (2007): 957–69, and David Levy and Maureen Scully, "The Institutional Entrepreneur as Modern Prince: The Strategic Face of Power in Contested Fields," *Organization Studies* 28 (2007): 971–91. More generally, a growing body of neo-institutional scholarship has focused on dissent and on tensions among different institutional domains. See, e.g., Elisabeth S. Clemens and James M. Cook, "Politics and Institutionalism: Explaining Durability and Change," *Annual Review of Sociology* 25 (1999): 441–66; Kathleen Thelen, "How Institutions Evolve: Insights from Comparative Historical Analysis," in *Comparative Historical Analysis in the Social Sciences*, ed. James Mahoney and Dietrich Rueschemeyer (New York: Cambridge University Press, 2003); Timothy J. Hargrave and Andrew H. van de Ven, "A Collective Action Model of Institutional Innovation," *Academy of Management Review* 31, 4 (2006): 864–88.

21. See Thelen, "How Institutions Evolve"; Wayne Sandholtz, *Prohibiting Plunder: How Norms Change* (New York: Oxford University Press, 2007); and Karen Orren and Stephen Skowronek, *In Search of American Political Development* (New York: Cambridge University Press, 2004).

22. Nonetheless, unlike the classic professions, the administrative professions wholly lack control over who may practice their craft; there is, for instance, no administrative equivalent to the bar exam.

23. James Q. Wilson, *Varieties of Police Behavior: The Management of Law and Order in Eight Communities* (Cambridge, MA: Harvard University Press, 1968).

24. Jeffrey Legro, "The Transformation of Policy Ideas," *American Journal of Political Science* 44, 3 (2000): 425. See also Peter A. Hall, "Policy Paradigms, Social Learning, and the State: The Case of Economic Policymaking in Britain," *Comparative Politics* 25, 3 (1993): 275–96; Peter A. Hall, *Governing the Economy: The Politics of State Intervention in Britain and France* (New York: Oxford University Press, 1986); Peter A. Hall, "The Movement from Keynesianism to Monetarism: Institutional Analysis and British Economic Policy in the 1970s," in *Structuring Politics: Historical Institutionalism in Comparative Perspective*, ed. Sven Steinmo, Kathleen Thelen, and Frank Longstreth (Cambridge: Cambridge University Press, 1992), 90–113.

25. Clemens and Cook, "Politics and Institutionalism."

26. McAdam, Tarrow, and Tilly, *Dynamics of Contention.*

27. Lauren B. Edelman, Steven E. Abraham, and Howard S. Erlanger, "Professional Construction of the Law: The Inflated Threat of Wrongful Discharge," *Law and Society Review* 26 (1992): 47–84; Lynn Mather, "The Fired Football Coach (or How Trial Courts Make Policy)," in *Contemplating Courts,* ed. Lee Epstein (Washington, DC: CQ Press, 1995); Haltom and McCann, *Distorting the Law.* See also Dobbin and Kelly, "How to Stop Harassment."

28. Such a claim was common in my interviews with practicing administrators. In addition, a number of survey-based studies have observed that administrative professionals believe the threat of liability is significant. See, e.g., Charles R. Epp, "The Fear of Being Sued: Variations in Perceptions of Legal Threat among Managers in the United States," paper presented at the 2001 annual meeting of the Law and Society Association, Budapest, July 3–7, 2001; Arthur H. Garrison, "Law Enforcement Civil Liability under Federal Law and Attitudes toward Civil Liability: A Survey of University, Municipal and State Police Officers," *Police Studies* 18, 3–4 (1995): 19–37; Eric G. Lambert, Daniel E. Hall, and Lois Ventura, "Litigation Views among Jail Staff: An Exploratory and Descriptive Study," *Criminal Justice Review* 28, 1 (2003): 70–87; Susan A. MacManus, "The Impact of Litigation on Municipalities: Total Cost, Driving Factors, and Cost Containment Mechanisms," *Syracuse Law Review* 44 (1993): 833–60; Susan A. MacManus and Patricia A. Turner, "Litigation as a Budgetary Constraint: Problem Areas and Costs," *Public Administration Review* 53 (1993): 462–72; Forrest Scogin and Stanley L. Brodsky, "Fear of Litigation among Law Enforcement Officers," *American Journal of Police* 10, 1 (1991): 41–45; Michael S. Vaughn, Tab W. Cooper, and Rolando V. del Carmen, "Assessing Legal Liabilities in Law Enforcement: Police Chiefs' Views," *Crime and Delinquency* 47, 1 (2001): 3–27.

29. Haltom and McCann, *Distorting the Law.*

30. Lauren B. Edelman, "Legal Ambiguity and Symbolic Structures: Organizational Mediation of Civil Rights Law," *American Journal of Sociology* 97 (1992): 1531–76; Dobbin and Kelly, "How to Stop Harassment."

31. Mather, "Fired Football Coach."

32. DiMaggio and Powell, "Iron Cage Revisited"; Edelman, "Legal Ambiguity and Symbolic Structures"; Lauren Edelman and Marc C. Suchman, "The Legal Environments of Organizations," *Annual Review of Sociology* 23 (1997): 479.

33. Dobbin and Kelly, "How to Stop Harassment".

34. Dobbin and Kelly, "How to Stop Harassment," 1243.

35. James J. Fyfe, "Blind Justice: Police Shootings in Memphis," *Journal of Criminal Law and Criminology* 73, 2 (1982): 707–22.

36. Kenneth Culp Davis, *Discretionary Justice: A Preliminary Inquiry* (Urbana: University of Illinois Press, 1971); Samuel Walker, *Taming the System: The Control of Discretion in Criminal Justice* (New York: Oxford University Press, 1993).

37. Philip Selznick, *Law, Society, and Industrial Justice* (New York: Sage, 1969).

38. Hall, "Policy Paradigms," 279.

39. Legro, "Transformation of Policy Ideas," 420; Edelman, Uggen, and Erlanger, "Endogeneity of Legal Regulation," 407.

40. Malcolm Feeley and Edward S. Rubin, *Judicial Policy Making in the Modern State* (Berkeley: University of California Press, 1998); Edelman, "Legal Ambiguity and Symbolic Structures."

41. Regarding personnel administration, see, e.g., Sanford Jacoby, *Employing Bureaucracy: Managers, Unions, and the Transformation of Work in the 20th Century* (Mahwah, NJ: Lawrence Erlbaum, 2004). See also Herbert Kaufman, *The Forest Ranger: A Study in Administrative Behavior* (Baltimore: Johns Hopkins University Press, 1960); Samuel Walker, *A Critical History of Police Reform* (Lexington, MA: Lexington Books, 1977).

42. Walker, *Critical History of Police Reform.*

43. See, e.g., Lauren B. Edelman, "Legal Environments and Organizational Governance: The Expansion of Due Process in the American Workplace," *American Journal of Sociology* 95, 6 (1990): 1401–40; Edelman, "Legal Ambiguity and Symbolic Structures."

44. Christopher N. Osher, "Denver Police Department Training Remains Deficient, a Federal Lawsuit Says, Despite Calls for Change since 1983," *Denver Post*, April 24, 2007, A-1. The policing expert was James Fyfe.

45. William H. Rodgers Jr., "Negligence Reconsidered: The Role of Rationality in Tort Theory," *Southern California Law Review* 54 (1980): 1; John A. Siliciano, "Corporate Behavior and the Social Efficiency of Tort Law," *Michigan Law Review* 85 (1987): 1820; Stephen D. Sugarman, *Doing Away with Personal Injury Law: New Compensation Mechanisms for Victims, Consumers, and Business* (New York: Quorum, 1989); Eugene Bardach and Robert A. Kagan, "Liability," in *Going by the Book: The Problem of Regulatory Unreasonableness* (Philadelphia: Temple University Press, 1982); Alison L. Patton, "The Endless Cycle of Abuse: Why 42 U.S.C. § 1983 Is Ineffective in Deterring Police Brutality," *Hastings Law Review* 44 (1993): 753; Daryl J. Levinson, "Making Government Pay: Markets, Politics, and the Allocation of Constitutional Torts," *University of Chicago Law Review* 67 (2000): 345–420. These studies are a response to the now classic view that tort liability *does* deter negligence and abuse. See Guido Calabresi, *The Cost of Accidents: A Legal and Economic Analysis* (New Haven, CT: Yale University Press, 1970); Richard A. Posner, "A Theory of Negligence," *Journal of Legal Studies* 1

(1972): 29; William M. Landes and Richard A. Posner, *The Economic Structure of Tort Law* (Cambridge, MA: Harvard University Press, 1987); and Steven Shavell, *The Economic Analysis of Accident Law* (Cambridge, MA: Harvard University Press, 1987).

46. Michelle M. Mello and Troyen A. Brennan, "Deterrence of Medical Errors," *Texas Law* Review 80 (2002): 1595–1637; Michelle M. Mello, David M. Studdert, Eric J. Thomas, Catherine S. Yoon, and Troyen A. Brennan, "Who Pays for Medical Errors? An Analysis of Adverse Event Costs, the Medical Liability System, and Incentives for Patient Safety Improvement," *Journal of Empirical Legal Studies* 4, 4 (2007): 835–60; Daniel Kessler and Mark McClellan, "Do Doctors Practice Defensive Medicine?" *Quarterly Journal of Economics* 111, 2 (1996): 353–91; Frank A. Sloan, Katherine Whetten-Goldstein, Penny B. Githens, and Stephen P. Entman, "Effects of the Threat of Medical Malpractice Litigation and Other Factors on Birth Outcomes," *Medical Care* 33, 7 (1995): 700–714. See also Don Dewees, David Duff, and Michael Trebilcock, *Exploring the Domain of Accident Law: Taking the Facts* Seriously (New York: Oxford University Press, 1996); George Eads and Peter Reuter, *Designing Safer Products: Corporate Responses to Product Liability Law and Regulation* (Santa Monica, CA: Rand Institute for Civil Justice, 1983).

47. Michael J. Saks, "Do We Really Know Anything about the Behavior of the Tort Litigation System—and Why Not?" *University of Pennsylvania Law Review* 140 (1992): 1147; Theodore Eisenberg and Stewart Schwab, "The Reality of Constitutional Tort Litigation," *Cornell Law Review* 72 (1987): 641–95; Eads and Reuter, *Designing Safer Products.*

48. The quotation is from Stuart Taylor Jr. and Evan Thomas, "Lawsuit Hell," *Newsweek,* December 15, 2003. For a summary of the voluminous research supporting this generalization, see Saks, "Do We Really Know Anything?" See also Peter A. Bell and Jeffrey O'Connell, *Accidental Justice: The Dilemmas of Tort Law* (New Haven, CT: Yale University Press, 1997), 6–7.

49. Sugarman, *Doing Away with Personal Injury Law,* 10; see also Bell and O'Connell, *Accidental Justice,* 78–81.

50. Unlike auto insurance companies, liability insurers, it is said, seldom try to impose specific safety guidelines on the insured and do not vary their premiums in relation to clients' safety records. For a forceful statement of this position, see Sugarman, *Doing Away with Personal Injury Law,* 12–17. Julie Davies, "Federal Civil Rights Practice in the 1990's: The Dichotomy between Reality and Theory," *Hastings Law Journal* 48 (1997): 197; Levinson, "Making Government Pay." And since agencies typically indemnify frontline employees for the costs of being sued, these employees are said to care little about whether they might be sued. See Patton, "Endless Cycle of Abuse"; attorneys Patton interviewed believed that, in particular, individual officers who are the subject of damage judgments almost never bear the costs of defense or the judgment themselves, and cities' budgetary pockets are deep enough that damage judgments provide no meaningful economic incentive for reform. Bardach and Kagan, *Going by the Book;* Sugarman, *Doing Away with Personal Injury Law,* 7–8; Eads and Reuter, *Designing Safer Products.*

51. Craig B. Futterman, H. Melissa Mather, and Melanie Miles, "The Use of Statistical Evidence to Address Police Supervisory and Disciplinary Practices: The Chicago Police Department's Broken System." http://www.law.uchicago.edu/files/brokensystem-111407.pdf, 15–16 (accessed April 26, 2008).

Chapter Three

1. See, for instance, the classic analysis by David H. Bayley and Harold Mendelsohn, *Minorities and the Police* (New York: Free Press, 1969), and the equally thoughtful recent synthesis by Harlan Hahn and Judson L. Jeffries, *Urban America and Its Police: From the Postcolonial Era through the Turbulent 1960s* (Boulder: University of Colorado Press, 2003).

2. See, for example, the excellent discussion in Wesley Skogan and Kathleen Frydl, eds., *Fairness and Effectiveness in Policing: The Evidence* (Washington, DC: National Academies Press), especially chapter 3, "The Nature of Policing in the United States."

3. *Mapp v. Ohio* 367 U.S. 643 (1961); *Gideon v. Wainwright* 372 U.S. 335 (1963); and *Miranda v. Arizona* 384 U.S. 436 (1966).

4. See, e.g., Jerome Skolnick, *Justice without Trial: Law Enforcement in a Democratic Society* (New York: Wiley, 1966); Neal A. Milner, *The Court and Local Law Enforcement: The Impact of Miranda* (Beverly Hills, CA: Sage, 1971); Richard A. Leo, *Police Interrogation and American Justice* (Cambridge, MA: Harvard University Press, 2008).

5. See the discussion in Robert M. Fogelson, *Big-City Police* (Cambridge, MA: Harvard University Press, 1977).

6. Samuel Walker, *The New World of Police Accountability* (Thousand Oaks, CA: Sage, 2005).

7. For a perceptive analysis that parallels my own, see Candace McCoy, "How Civil Rights Lawsuits Improve American Policing," in *To Protect Life: Readings on Police Accountability*, ed. Candace McCoy (New York: Urban Institute Press, forthcoming).

8. Myron W. Orfield Jr. "The Exclusionary Rule and Deterrence: An Empirical Study of Chicago Narcotics Officers," *University of Chicago Law Review* 54 (1987): 1016-69; Samuel Walker, *Police Accountability: The Role of Citizen Oversight* (Belmont, CA: Wadsworth-Thompson, 2001).

9. 42 U.S.C. § 14141 (1994).

10. Walker, *New World*. Walker has recently proposed a model "pattern or practice" statute for states; see Samuel Walker and Morgan Macdonald, "An Alternative Remedy for Police Misconduct: A Model State 'Pattern or Practice' Statute," *George Mason University Civil Rights Law Journal* (forthcoming).

11. Egon Bittner. "The Rise and Fall of the Thin Blue Line," *American History*, September 1978, 421, quoted in George L. Kelling and Janice K. Stewart, "The Evolution of Contemporary Policing," in *Local Government Police Management*, ed. William A. Geller, 3rd ed. (Washington, DC: ICMA, 1991), 4. This section owes a considerable debt to Walker, *Critical History of Police Reform*, 8–31, and Fogelson, *Big-City Police*. See also Mark H. Haller, "Historical Roots of Police Behavior: Chicago, 1890–1925," *Law and Society Review* 10 (1976): 303–24.

12. Fogelson, *Big-City Police*, 13.

13. Walker, *Critical History of Police Reform*, 8.

14. Ibid., 24–26.

15. Ibid., 11–12.

16. Fogelson, *Big-City Police*, 18–19.

17. Walker, *Critical History of Police Reform*, 12–13.

18. Ibid., 15–16.

19. Raymond B. Fosdick, *European Police Systems* (New York: Century, 1915); Raymond B. Fosdick, *American Police Systems* (New York: Century, 1921), 379.

20. Fosdick, *European Police Systems* 39–60, at 44.

21. Ibid., 44 and 59.

22. Walker, *Critical History of Police Reform*, 56–61; Fogelson, *Big-City Police*, 75–84.

23. Walker, *Critical History of Police Reform*, 51–78; Fogelson, *Big-City Police*, 67–92.

24. Nelson A. Watson, "A Big Question: What Is Your Policy on the Use of Firearms?" *Police Chief*, July 1967, 12–13.

25. O. W. Wilson, *Police Administration* (New York: McGraw-Hill, 1950).

26. O. W. Wilson, *Police Administration*, 2nd ed. (New York: McGraw-Hill, 1963), 466–69.

27. Ibid.

28. Fogelson, *Big-City Police*, 97–101.

29. International City Managers' Association (ICMA), *Municipal Police Administration*, 4th ed. (Chicago: ICMA, 1954), 51, 52–54.

30. O. W. Wilson, "Can the State Help City Police Departments?" *Journal of Criminal Law, Criminology and Police Science* 45, 1 (1954): 102–9, at 105.

31. Wilson, *Police Administration*, 2nd ed., 161.

32. Wilson, "Can the State Help City Police Departments?" 105.

33. ICMA, *Municipal Police Administration*, 4th ed. 51, 52–54.

34. ICMA, *Municipal Police Administration*, 5th ed. (Chicago: ICMA, 1961), 438–39.

35. "IACP Critique of the Study," *Police Chief*, February 1964, 13; the study referred to was Note, "The Administration of Complaints by Civilians against the Police," *Harvard Law Review*, January 1964, 499–519.

36. "IACP Critique of the Study," 35.

37. ICMA, *Municipal Police Administration*, 4th ed., 467–69.

38. Samuel G. Chapman. "Police Policy on the Use of Firearms," *Police Chief*, July 1967, 16–37.

39. Michael Canlis, "The Police Position," *Police Chief*, December 1963, 29–31, at 31.

40. Quinn Tamm, "Police Professionalism and Civil Rights," *Police Chief*, September 1964, 28–32, at 30.

41. Tamm, "Police Professionalism and Civil Rights."

42. Ibid., citing "Police Brutality—or Smokescreen?" *Police Chief*, December 1963, 7.

43. Donald E. Clark, "Minority Group Rights and the Police," *Police Chief*, March 1965, 43–45, at 44.

44. Daniel S. C. Liu, "The President's Annual Message," *Police Chief*, December 1964, 50.

45. Homer Garrison Jr., "Local Problems Arising from the 1964 Act," *Police Chief*, September 1964, 22–25, at 23.

46. Tamm, "Police Professionalism and Civil Rights," 31.

47. Ibid., 31.

48. For excellent treatments of various aspects of these issues, see especially Bayley and Mendelsohn, *Minorities and the Police,* and the equally thoughtful recent synthesis by Hahn and Jeffries, *Urban America and Its Police.* See also Hubert Williams and Patrick V. Murphy, "The Evolving Strategy of Police: A Minority View," *Perspectives on Policing* 13 (1990): 1–15; Marilynn S. Johnson, *Street Justice: A History of Police*

Violence in New York City (Boston: Beacon Press, 2003); Dwight Watson, *Race and the Houston Police Department, 1930–1990: A Change Did Come* (College Station: Texas A&M University Press, 2005); Shannon King, "Home to Harlem: Community, Gender, and Working Class Politics in Harlem, 1916–1928" (PhD diss., SUNY-Binghamton, 2006); Edward J. Escobar, *Race, Police, and the Making of a Political Identity: Mexican Americans and the Los Angeles Police Department, 1900–1945* (Berkeley: University of California Press, 1999).

49. Walker, *Critical History of Police Reform*, 4; Williams and Murphy, "Evolving Strategy of Police, 1–15; Leon Litwack, *Trouble in Mind: Black Southerners in the Age of Jim Crow* (New York: Alfred A. Knopf, 1998), 263.

50. Johnson, *Street Justice.*

51. Watson, *Race and the Houston Police Department*, 32.

52. King, "Home to Harlem," 178.

53. King, "Home to Harlem"; William Tuttle, *Race Riot: Chicago in the Red Summer of 1919* (New York: Atheneum, 1970); Thomas J. Sugrue, *The Origins of the Urban Crisis: Race and Inequality in Postwar Detroit* (Princeton, NJ: Princeton University Press, 1996).

54. See, e.g., Tuttle, *Race Riot;* Elliot Rudwick, *Race Riot at East St. Louis, July 2, 1917* (Carbondale: Southern Illinois University Press, 1964); Cheryl Greenberg, "The Politics of Disorder: Reexamining Harlem's Riots of 1935 and 1943," *Journal of Urban History* 18, 4 (1992): 395–441.

55. Quoted in Allan H. Spear, *Black Chicago: The Making of a Negro Ghetto, 1890–1920* (Chicago: University of Chicago Press, 1967), 48.

56. Tuttle, *Race Riot*, 33; see also Spear, *Black Chicago*, 44.

57. See the thoughtful recent discussion in Hahn and Jeffries, *Urban America and Its Police;* Fogelson, *Big-City Police*, 247–64; see also Watson, *Race and the Houston Police Department*, 19.

58. Walker, *Critical History of Police Reform*, 10; Fogelson, *Big-City Police*, 247–64.

59. Escobar, *Race, Police, and the Making of a Political Identity*, 13.

60. Johnson, *Street Justice;* King, "Home to Harlem," 183–88; Eric W. Rise, "The NAACP's Legal Strategy against Police Brutality, 1920–1950," paper presented at the annual meeting of the Law and Society Association, St. Louis, MO, May 30, 1997.

61. See, e.g., Dan T. Carter, *Scottsboro: A Tragedy of the American South*, rev. ed. (Baton Rouge: Louisiana State University Press, 1979), 52–53.

62. Philip A. Klinkner, with Rogers M. Smith, *The Unsteady March: The Rise and Decline of Racial Equality in America* (Chicago: University of Chicago Press, 1999), 182; see also Patricia Sullivan, *Days of Hope: Race and Democracy in the New Deal Era* (Chapel Hill: University of North Carolina Press, 1996); John Egerton, *Speak Now against the Day: The Generation before the Civil Rights Movement in the South* (New York: Alfred A. Knopf, 1994); Roy Wilkins, "The Negro Wants Full Equality," in *What the Negro Wants*, ed. Rayford W. Logan (Chapel Hill: University of North Carolina Press, 1944), 115.

63. Klinkner and Smith, *Unsteady March*, 181–200.

64. 325 US 91 (1945).

65. *Chambers v. Florida* 309 U.S. 227 (1940).

66. Paul W. Tappan, "Official Homicide," *Lawyers Guild Review* 6 (1946): 400–405, at 404.

67. Jerome Hall, "Police and Law in a Democratic Society," *Indiana Law Journal* 28, 2 (1953): 133–77, at 152, 140.

68. Benjamin Davis and Marshall Horace, *Police Brutality: Lynching, Northern Style* (New York: Office of Councilman Benjamin Davis, 1947).

69. Adam Fairclough, *Better Day Coming: Blacks and Equality, 1890–2000* (New York: Viking, 2001), 188; Watson, *Race and the Houston Police Department*, 33.

70. According to the testimony of a patrol district commander; quoted in Sullivan, *Days of Hope*, 156.

71. Walter Francis White and Thurgood Marshall, *What Caused the Detroit Riot? An Analysis* (New York: NAACP, 1943).

72. Robert A. Hill, *The FBI's RACON: Racial Conditions in the United States during World War II* (Boston: Northeastern University Press, 1995).

73. Watson, *Race and the Houston Police Department*, 35, 157 n. 76; Sullivan, *Days of Hope*, 143; Mark V. Tushnet, *Making Civil Rights Law: Thurgood Marshall and the Supreme Court, 1936–61* (New York: Oxford University Press, 1994), 44–66.

74. Egerton, *Speak Now against the Day*, 362–63.

75. Johnson, *Street Justice*, 213.

76. Ann Fagan Ginger and Eugene M. Toobin, eds., *The National Lawyers Guild: From Roosevelt to Reagan* (Philadelphia: Temple University Press, 1988), 3–10.

77. William H. Hastie and Thurgood Marshall, "Negro Discrimination and the Need for Federal Action," *Lawyers Guild Review* 2 (1942): 21–23, at 21.

78. Resolution on Civil Liberties, *Lawyers Guild Review* 6, 2 (1946): 520–21; *Lawyers Guild Review* 11, 2 (1951): 98; see also *Lawyers Guild Review* 11, 3 (1951): 158; *Lawyers Guild Review* 11, 4 (1951): 180; *Lawyers Guild Review* 12, 3 (1952): 151; *Lawyers Guild Review* 12, 4 (1952): 181; *Lawyers Guild Review* 17, 1 (1957): 31–32. The 1957 resolution expressed the expectation that the American Bar Foundation's Comprehensive Survey of the Administration of Criminal Justice, to be discussed shortly, would provide systematic "factual information" documenting the need for reforms. "'Standing Room Only' Attendance," *Lawyers Guild Review* 11, 2 (1951): 98.

79. Samuel Walker, *In Defense of American Liberties: A History of the ACLU* (New York: Oxford University Press, 1990), 87–88, 110–11.

80. Ibid., 163–64.

81. Ibid., 247.

82. Ibid.

83. White and Marshall, *What Caused the Detroit Riot?*

84. John M. Coe, "Practices of Police and Prosecution prior to Trial," *Lawyers Guild Review* 17, 2 (1957): 62–66.

85. Walker, *In Defense of American Liberties*, 249.

86. Ibid., 249.

87. Key conference addresses were published in *Lawyers Guild Review* 19, 2 (1959).

88. James R. Akers, "Minority Groups and the Need for Criminal Law Reform," *Lawyers Guild Review* 19, 2 (1959): 61–63.

89. Ibid.

90. William A. Westley, "Violence and the Police," *American Journal of Sociology* 59, 1 (1953): 34–41.

91. Ibid., 40.

92. Note, "Philadelphia Police Practice and the Law of Arrest," *University of Pennsylvania Law Review* 100 (1952): 1182–1216.

93. Gerald D. Robin, "Justifiable Homicide by Police Officers," *Journal of Criminal Law, Criminology and Police Science* 54 (May-June 1963): 225–31.

94. My discussion relies on the work of Samuel Walker. See in particular Samuel Walker, "Origins of the Contemporary Criminal Justice Paradigm: The American Bar Foundation Survey, 1953–1969," *Justice Quarterly* 9 (1992): 50.

95. Samuel Walker, "Historical Roots of the Legal Control of Police Behavior," in *Police Innovation and Control of the Police: Problems of Law, Order, and Community,* ed. David Weisburd and Craig Uchida, with Lorraine Green (New York: Springer-Verlag, 1993), 38.

96. Ibid., 38.

97. These and other examples in this paragraph are taken from Walker, "Origins of the Contemporary Criminal Justice Paradigm," 57–58.

98. President's Commission on Law Enforcement and the Administration of Justice, Task Force on the Police, *Task Force Report: The Police* (Washington, DC: Government Printing Office, 1967), 189 (hereafter *Task Force Report*).

99. Walker, "Origins of the Contemporary Criminal Justice Paradigm," 58.

100. Ibid.

101. U.S. Commission on Civil Rights, *Report,* vol. 5, *Justice* (Washington, DC: Government Printing Office, 1961), 28.

102. Ibid., 5, 25.

103. For an excellent general discussion of the pattern, see Hahn and Jeffries, *Urban America and Its Police,* 133ff.

104. Joseph D. Lohman and Gordon E. Misner, *The Police and the Community* (Washington, DC: Government Printing Office, 1966), 1:127–34, cited in Hahn and Jeffries, *Urban America and Its Police,* 134.

105. Ibid.

106. United States, Kerner Commission, *Report of the National Advisory Commission on Civil Disorders* (Washington, DC: U.S. Government Printing Office, 1968), chap. 2.

107. Angus Campbell and Howard Schuman, "Racial Attitudes in Fifteen American Cities," in *Supplemental Studies for the National Advisory Commission on Civil Disorders* (Washington, DC: Government Printing Office, 1969), table 4.

108. Bayley and Mendelsohn, *Minorities and the Police.*

109. My summary is drawn from Hahn and Jeffries's excellent discussion (*Urban America and Its Police,* 134–35). On Newark, see Governor's Select Commission on Civil Disorder, State of New Jersey, *Report for Action* (Trenton: State of New Jersey, 1968), 22–37; on Detroit, see Harlan Hahn, "Ghetto Sentiments on Violence," *Science and Society* 33 (Spring 1969): 197–208; on Watts, see David O. Sears, "Black Attitudes toward the Political System in the Aftermath of the Watts Insurrection," *Midwest Journal of Political Science* 13 (1969): 524.

110. Skolnick, *Justice without Trial.*

111. For discussion, see Walker, "Historical Roots," 39, and Sheldon Krantz, Bernard Gilman, Charles G. Benda, Carol Rogoff Hallstrom, and Eric J. Nadworthy, *Police Policymaking: The Boston Experience* (Lexington, MA: D. C. Heath, 1979), 12–20.

112. *Task Force Report.* For much of the discussion in this section, I am indebted to the scholarship of Samuel Walker, especially the following sources: Walker, "Origins

of the Contemporary Criminal Justice Paradigm," 47–76; Walker, "Historical Roots"; Samuel Walker, *Taming the System: The Control of Discretion in Criminal Justice, 1950–1990* (New York: Oxford University Press, 1993); Walker, *Critical History of Police Reform*.

113. *Task Force Report*, 178.

114. Ibid., 180–81.

115. Ibid., 181–82.

116. Ibid., 147.

117. Ibid., 16.

118. Ibid., 18.

119. Ibid., 17.

120. Ibid., 19.

121. Ibid., 29.

122. Ibid., 189.

123. Ibid.

124. Ibid., 189–90.

125. Ibid., 20–21.

126. Ibid., 20.

127. Ibid.

128. Kerner Commission, *Report of the National Advisory Commission on Civil Disorders*, 313.

129. Ibid., 313–14.

130. Kenneth Culp Davis, *Discretionary Justice: A Preliminary Inquiry* (Baton Rouge: Louisiana State University Press, 1969); Kenneth Culp Davis, *Police Discretion* (St. Paul, MN: West, 1975).

131. Walker, "Historical Roots," 41.

132. American Bar Association Project on Standards for Criminal Justice, *Standards relating to the Urban Police Function* (New York: American Bar Association, 1973).

133. National Advisory Commission on Criminal Justice Standards and Goals, *Police* (Washington, DC: U.S. Government Printing Office, 1973).

134. *Model Penal Code* §§3.07–3.09 (1962).

135. Lawrence W. Sherman, "Restricting the License to Kill—Recent Developments in Police Use of Deadly Force," *Criminal Law Bulletin* 14 (1978): 577–83.

136. Nelson A. Watson, "The Fringes of Police-Community Relations: Extremism," *Police Chief*, August 1966, 8–9, 64–68.

137. Ibid., 68.

138. Watson, "Big Question," 12–13.

139. Chapman, "Police Policy on the Use of Firearms," 16–37.

140. Advertisement, *Police Chief*, July 1967, 14–15.

141. J. E. Weckler and Theo E. Hall, *The Police and Minority Groups: A Program to Prevent Disorder and to Improve Relations between Different Racial, Religious, and National Groups* (Chicago: ICMA, 1944) (ICMA archives, University of Kansas Spencer Research Library, box 48).

142. John P. Robinson, "Public Reaction to Political Protest: Chicago 1968," *Public Opinion Quarterly* 34, 1 (1970): 1.

143. Robinson, "Public Reaction to Political Protest"; "Poll Shows 71.4% Find Police Action Justified in Chicago," *New York Times*, August 31, 1968. See also *The Gallup Poll* (New York: Random House, 1972), 3:2160.

144. Quinn Tamm, "Apathy on the Decline?" *Police Chief*, March 1967, 6.

145. Quinn Tamm, "The Customer Isn't Always Right," *Police Chief*, June 1967, 6.

146. Ibid.

147. See, e.g., Jerry V. Wilson, "Deadly Force," *Police Chief*, December 1972, 44–46; Saadi Ferris, "Administrative Rulemaking: Police Discretion," *Police Chief*, June 1974, 70–71; Robert I. Macfarlane and Samuel Laudenslager, "Local Police/Bar Cooperation in the Standards/Goals Process," *Police Chief*, September 1974, 50.

148. Ralph E. Anderson, "Police Standards and Goals," *Police Chief*, September 1974, 28–31. See also Kenneth R. McCreedy and James L. Hague, "Administrative and Legal Aspects of a Policy to Limit the Use of Firearms by Police Officers," *Police Chief*, January 1975, 48–52.

149. Anderson, "Police Standards and Goals," 28; emphasis in original.

150. Sherman, "Restricting the License to Kill."

151. *Ashcroft v. Mattis*, 431 U.S. 171 (vacating a lower court ruling, on narrow grounds, holding that the fleeing felon rule violated the Constitution); *Wiley v. Memphis Police Department* 548 F.2d 1247 (6th Cir. 1977), *cert denied* by Supreme Court.

152. Catherine H. Milton, Jeanne Wahl Halleck, James Lardner, and Gary L. Albrecht, *Police Use of Deadly Force* (Washington, DC: Police Foundation, 1977); see also Gerald I. Uelman, "Varieties of Police Policy: A Study of Police Policies regarding the Use of Deadly Force in Los Angeles County," *Loyola Law Review* 6 (1973): 1.

153. Milton et al., *Police Use of Deadly Force*, 10 and 44.

154. Ibid., 46–48, quoted at 48; emphasis in original.

155. Ibid., 49–50.

156. Ibid., 56.

157. Ibid., 65–147.

158. Krantz et al., *Police Policymaking*, 212–13.

159. Ibid., 8, 215–17, 10, and 219–22.

160. Ibid., 219–22.

161. Ibid., 223.

162. Bruce Cory, "Deadly Force," *Police Magazine*, November 1978, 8–14.

163. Joseph E. Dominelli, "The Use of Force: A Time for Consideration," *Police Chief*, January 1980, 8; Joseph E. Dominelli, "Sources of Wisdom," *Police Chief*, February 1980, 8; Joseph E. Dominelli, letter to the IACP membership, headed "URGENT," dated August 27, 1980 (copy on file with the author). See also James E. Adams, "Police Chiefs Again Back Firing at Fleeing Felons," *St. Louis Post-Dispatch*, September 18, 1980, 11A.

164. Quoted in Adams, "Police Chiefs Again Back Firing."

165. Dominelli, letter to the IACP membership, 1.

166. James E. Adams, "Debate on 'Deadly Force' Splits Police Factions," *St. Louis Post-Dispatch*, September 19, 1980, 13A.

167. Ibid.

168. Ibid.

169. Resolution adopted July 15, 1980, copy on file with the author.

Chapter Four

1. See, e.g., Jerome Skolnick, *Justice without Trial: Law Enforcement in a Democratic Society* (New York: Wiley, 1966).

2. The studies that qualified the earlier pessimism were Myron Orfield, "The Exclusionary Rule and Deterrence: An Empirical Study of Chicago Narcotics Officers," *University of Chicago Law Review* 54 (1987): 1016–55, and Jerome Skolnick, *Justice without Trial*, 3rd ed. (New York: Macmillan, 1994), particularly the epilogue.

3. The story is well told in Stuart Speiser, *Lawsuit* (New York: Horizon, 1980), 142–44, at 299.

4. Thomas Lambert Jr. "The Jurisprudence of Hope," *Journal of the American Trial Lawyers Association* 31 (1965): 29–41, at 31.

5. Speiser, *Lawsuit,* 146–48.

6. The following discussion is based on Stuart Speiser, *Lawsuit,* 534ff., and John Fabian Witt, *Patriots and Cosmopolitans: Hidden Histories of American Law* (Cambridge, MA: Harvard University Press, 2007), 211–78.

7. Witt, *Patriots and Cosmopolitans,* 241; Speiser, *Lawsuit,* 266. The connection between the Guild and NACCA's founding is noted in the Guild's brief online history; http://www.nlg.org/about/aboutus.htm (accessed May 11, 2007). In a development resonant with symbolic significance, the association's journal, which from its inception had placed articles and summaries of cases on the topic of worker's compensation first in each issue, began placing articles on tort law first beginning in May 1958.

8. Melvin Belli, "The Adequate Award," *California Law Review* 39, 1 (1951): 1–41.

9. Melvin Belli, *Modern Trials* (Indianapolis: Bobbs-Merrill, 1954); Speiser, *Lawsuit,* 263.

10. Witt, *Patriots and Cosmopolitans,* 243–44.

11. Speiser, *Lawsuit,* 536.

12. Ann Fagan Ginger, interview with the author, December 14, 2006.

13. Ann Fagan Ginger and Eugene M. Tobin, *The National Lawyers Guild: From Roosevelt through Reagan* (Philadelphia: Temple University Press, 1988), 136.

14. Ann Fagan Ginger, interview with the author, December 14, 2006; Doris Brin Walker, interview with the author, January 26, 2007.

15. *Lawyers Guild Review* 13, 1 (1953) 38. See, e.g., "Report on Guild Activities," *Lawyers Guild Review* 20, 2 (1960): 58; *Lawyers Guild Review* 16, 1 (1956): 8, 29.

16. *Lawyers Guild Review* 16, 3 (1956): 131–34.

17. Doris Brin Walker, interview with the author, January 26, 2007.

18. Victor Rabinowitz, *Unrepentant Leftist: A Lawyer's Memoir* (Urbana: University of Illinois Press, 1996), 173–74.

19. Ann Fagan Ginger, interview with the author, December 14, 2006.

20. Rise, NAACP's Legal Strategy, 3–4.

21. Ibid., 25.

22. Marilynn Johnson, *Street Justice: A History of Police Violence in New York City* (Boston: Beacon Press, 2003), 205ff.

23. Ibid., 221–23.

24. Ibid.

25. Caleb Foote, "Tort Remedies for Police Violations of Individual Rights," *Minnesota Law Review* 39 (1954–55): 493–516.

26. Ibid., 509, 514–15.

27. U.S. Commission on Civil Rights, *Justice,* 69.

28. *Simmons v. Whitaker* 252 F.2d 758 (2d Cir. 1958); *Dye v. Cox* 125 F. Supp. 714 (E.D. VA 1954).

29. Ibid.

30. *Morgan v. Sylvester* 220 F.2d 758 (2d Cir. 1954); *Bottone v. Lindsley* 170 F.2d 705 (10th Cir. 1948); *Mackey v. Chandler* 152 F. Supp. 579 (W.D. SC 1957).

31. Brief for the petitioners, *Monroe v. Pape*, 41–42.

32. Quoted in "Constitutional Law: 'Under Color of' Law and the Civil Rights Act," *Duke Law Journal* 1961:452-59, at 458 n. 43.

33. *Monroe v. Pape* 365 U.S. 167 (1961).

34. Ibid., at 187.

35. Jack M. Beermann, "Municipal Responsibility for Constitutional Torts," *DePaul Law Review* 48 (1999): 627–68.

36. U.S. Commission on Civil Rights, *Justice*, 71.

37. "Recent Important Tort Cases: Civil Rights Act," *JATLA* 31 (1965): 218ff, at 222.

38. On Freedom Summer's impact generally, see Doug McAdam, *Freedom Summer* (New York: Oxford University Press, 1988).

39. McAdam, *Freedom Summer*, 154–57; Len Holt, *The Summer That Didn't End* (New York: William Morrow, 1965), 88.

40. Rabinowitz, *Unrepentant Leftist*, 179.

41. McAdam, *Freedom Summer*, 156.

42. Ann Fagan Ginger and Louis H. Bell, "Police Misconduct Litigation—Plaintiff's Remedies," *American Jurisprudence Trials* 15 (1968): 555–717.

43. Wayne Schmidt, interview with the author, December 8, 2006.

44. William Goodman, interview with the author, January 18, 2007.

45. David Rudovsky, interview with the author, October 20, 2006.

46. Ibid.

47. Michael Avery, interview with the author, November 6, 2007.

48. Ibid.

49. Ibid.

50. Michael Avery and David Rudovsky, eds., *Police Misconduct Litigation Manual* (Philadelphia: National Lawyers Guild, 1978).

51. Michael Avery, interview with the author, November 6, 2007.

52. See, e.g., Isidore Silver, *Police Civil Liability* (New York: M. Bender, 1986). In addition, there are many general guides to Section 1983 litigation, virtually all focusing in part on police civil liability. See, e.g, Sheldon H. Nahmod, *Civil Rights and Civil Liberties Litigation* (Colorado Springs, CO: Shepard's, 1979), and later editions; George C. Pratt and Martin A. Schwartz, *Section 1983 Civil Rights Litigation and Attorney's Fees* (New York: Practicing Law Institute, 1984), and subsequent years.

53. Quoted in Bruce Cory, "Deadly Force," *Police Magazine* 1, 5 (1978): 5–14, at 7.

54. Sean Farhang, *The Litigation State: Public Regulation and Private Lawsuits in the United States* (Princeton, NJ: Princeton University Press, forthcoming).

55. Michael Avery, interview with the author, November 6, 2007.

56. Marc Galanter, "Case Congregations and Their Careers," *Law and Society Review* 24, 2 (19990): 371–95.

57. *Kortum v. Alkire* (1977) 69 Cal. App. 3d 325 [138 Cal. Rptr. 26], at 31. The attorneys for the plaintiffs included Jacobs, Sills and Coblentz, Nicholas B. Waranoff, Amitai Schwartz, Charles Marson, Vilma S. Martinez, Sanford Jay Rosen, William Bennett Turner, Lowell Johnston, and Anthony G. Amsterdam.

58. *Mattis v. Schnarr*, 547 F.2d 1007 (8th Cir. 1976); see also *Mattis v. Schnarr*, 502 F.2d 588 (8th Cir. 1974).

59. *Wiley v. Memphis Police Department*, 548 F.2d 1247 (6th Cir. 1977); a discussion of the *Mattis* and *Wiley* cases may be found in Note, "Substantive Due Process and the Use of Deadly Force against the Fleeing Felon: *Wiley v. Memphis Police Department* and *Mattis v. Schnarr*," *Capital University Law Review* 7 (1978): 497.

60. *Ashcroft v. Mattis*, 431 U.S. 171 (1977).

61. *Landrum v. Moats*, 576 F.2d 1320 (8th Cir. 1978).

62. Note, "The Federal Injunction as a Remedy for Unconstitutional Police Conduct," *Yale Law Journal* 78 (1968): 143–55, at 144. See also Note, "Injunctive Relief for Violations of Constitutional Rights by the Police," *University of Colorado Law Review* 45 (1973): 91, at 95–96; and Malcolm M. Feeley and Edward L. Rubin, *Judicial Policymaking and the Modern State: How the Courts Reformed America's Prisons* (New York: Cambridge University Press, 1998).

63. *Allee v. Medrano* 416 U.S. 802 (1974).

64. Phillip J. Cooper, *Hard Judicial Choices: Federal District Courts and State and Local Officials* (New York: Oxford University Press, 1988), 297–327. The following discussion is based on Cooper.

65. Wayne W. Schmidt, "Recent Trends in Police Tort Litigation," *Urban Lawyer* 8 (1976): 682–92.

66. David Rudovsky, interview with the author, October 20, 2006.

67. *Bivens v. Six Unknown Federal Narcotics Agents*, 403 U.S. 388 (1971).

68. *Turpin v. Mailet* 579 F.2d 152 (2d Cir. 1978).

69. David Rudovsky, interview with author, October 20, 2006.

70. The story of the lawsuit is wonderfully told in Oscar G. Chase and Arlo Monell Chase, "*Monell*: The Story Behind the Landmark," *Urban Lawyer* 31 (1999): 491–503, at 491.

71. Chase and Chase, "*Monell*," 495–96. Neither Nancy Stearns nor Oscar Chase, the lead attorneys on the plaintiffs' brief, recalls any discussions about the possible implications for police misconduct litigation, and their brief did not address those implications or the possible financial impact of extending liability to cities; interviews with the author, January 22, 2007.

72. Ibid., 496–97.

73. Roger Wilkins, "Wide Application Seen for Ruling Opening Cities to Civil Rights Suits," *New York Times*, June 16, 1978, B32.

74. Michael Avery, interview with the author, November 6, 2007.

75. Candace McCoy, interview with the author, February 7, 2007.

76. Americans for Effective Law Enforcement, *Survey of Police Misconduct Litigation, 1967–1971* (Evanston, IL: Americans for Effective Law Enforcement, 1974), reported in Wayne W. Schmidt, "Recent Developments in Police Civil Liability," *Journal of Police Science and Administration* 4, 2 (1976): 197–202, at 197.

77. AELE, *Survey of Police Misconduct Litigation*, 9 and 14, respectively.

78. Ibid., 7.

79. Wayne Schmidt, interview with the author, December 8, 2006.

80. "Police Agencies Seek Ways to Avoid Citizens' Lawsuits," *New York Times*, November 3, 1985, 74.

81. *American Lawyer*, May 1994, 56.

82. Daniel Walker, "Rights in Conflict: The Violent Confrontation of Demonstrators and Police in the Parks and Streets of Chicago during the Week of the Democratic National Convention of 1968. A Report of the Chicago Study Team to the

National Commission on the Causes and Prevention of Violence," 1968. Later analyses have questioned that characterization, suggesting instead that the police were following orders traceable to Mayor Richard J. Daley to deal harshly with demonstrators; see Frank Kusch, *Battleground Chicago: The Police and the 1968 Democratic National Convention* (Westport, CT: Praeger, 2004).

83. David Farber, *Chicago '68*. (Chicago: University of Chicago Press, 1988), 255.

84. John P. Robinson, "Public Reaction to Political Protest: Chicago 1968," *Public Opinion Quarterly* 34, 1 (1970): 1. See also *The Gallup Poll* (New York: Random House, 1972), 3:2160.

85. Robinson, "Public Reaction to Political Protest," 3, table 1; the percentages believing that the police had used too much force were as follows: 82 percent of college-educated blacks and 63 percent of all blacks, 52 percent of people with a graduate degree, and 54 percent of all college-educated respondents below age thirty.

86. Todd Gitlin, *The Sixties: Years of Hope, Days of Rage* (New York: Bantam, 1987), 290.

87. See, e.g., "Panthers Upheld in Mt. Vernon Case," *New York Times*, March 21, 1971, 35; William E. Farrell, "Police in Chicago Sued over Spying," *New York Times*, December 8, 1975, 52; Reginald Stuart, "Michigan to Release Its Files about Political Surveillance," *New York Times*, December 27, 1980, 10; Angel Castillo, "After Long Court Fight, City Police Accept Political-Surveillance Curbs," *New York Times*, December 31, 1980, A1.

88. Bill Goodman, Wayne Schmidt, and Michael Avery, interviews with the author.

89. See, e.g., *New York Times*, April 26, 1971; October 5, 1971, 47; February 13, 1974, 18; May 25, 1974, 14; February 22, 1976, 40; November 27, 1976, 11.

90. Roy Wilkins and Ramsey Clark, *Search and Destroy: A Report by the Commission of Inquiry into the Black Panthers and the Police* (New York: Metropolitan Applied Research Center, 1973).

91. Jack Anderson columns, *Washington Post*, May 16, 1972; May 22, 1972; Peniel E. Joseph, *Waiting 'til the Midnight Hour: A Narrative History of Black Power in America* (New York: Henry Holt, 2006), 187–88; Yohuru Williams, "'A Red, Black and Green Liberation Jumpsuit': Roy Wilkins, the Black Panthers, and the Conundrum of Black Power," in *The Black Power Movement: Rethinking the Civil Rights–Black Power Era*, Peniel E. Joseph, (New York: Routledge, 2006), 179.

92. In 1979, after a federal trial court had dismissed the civil suit against Edward Hanrahan and the Chicago police, a federal appellate court ordered a new trial and excoriated the FBI and attorneys for the police for withholding documents and evidence. In the course of the litigation, it was revealed that one of the Panthers in the raided house was an FBI informer and had given police a detailed floor plan of the house, particularly the location of Hampton's bed. See *New York Times*, April 14, 1979, 16, and May 6, 1979, 20; "Settlement Near in a Panther Suit," *New York Times*, October 26, 1982, A18.

93. Lead editorial, "The Police and the Black Panthers," *Washington Post*, May 25, 1970, A22.

94. Excerpted in "The Grand Jury Report," *Washington Post*, May 25, 1970, A22.

95. Farrell, "Police in Chicago Sued over Spying," 52. See, e.g., Stuart, "Michigan to Release Its Files," 10; Castillo, "After Long Court Fight," A1.

96. "$3.3 Million Is Awarded Widow of Beating Victim," *New York Times*, June 10, 1978, 46.

97. "Drug Raids: Terror in the Night—in the U.S.," *New York Times*, July 1, 1973, 148; Alfonso A. Narvaez, "Brutal Melee in a Jersey Tavern Involves Policemen and Patrons," *New York Times*, March 12, 1977, 42.

98. "Beatings of 2 Blacks by Policemen Spur Calls for Miami Review Board," *New York Times*, March 3, 1979, 12; Wayne King, "Black Protest Is Monitored by Klan as a Mississippi Boycott Continues," *New York Times*, July 9, 1978, 26.

99. "$3.3 Million Is Awarded Widow of Beating Victim," 46; Juan Vasquez, "Killings of Chicanos by Police Protested," *New York Times*, October 12, 1977, A17; John M. Crewdson, "Houston Quiet after Violence Hospitalizes over 12," *New York Times*, May 9, 1978, 22; Robert Lindsey, "Los Angeles Police Scored on Shooting: Officers Called 'Trigger Happy' after Unarmed Chemist Is Slain," *New York Times*, August 15, 1977, 13.

100. Robert Lindsey, "Los Angeles Police Find Image of Efficiency Fades," *New York Times*, June 16, 1980, A16; David Johnston, "When L.A. Police Shoot, the D.A. 'Rolls Out,'" *Police Magazine*, March 1981, 17–20.

101. See, e.g., Martin Arnold, "Fatal Shooting of a Driver Stirs Up Flatbush District," *New York Times*, June 23, 1971, 37; "Policeman's Shot at Fleeing Driver Kills Bronx Woman," *New York Times*, May 22, 1972, 5; John Darnton, "S.I. Boy, 11, Killed by Police in Chase," *New York Times*, August 17, 1972, 1; "A Dead Boy, Community Outraged," *New York Times*, May 6, 1973, 241; Lee Dembart, "Shea Case Stirs Memories of Earlier Police Slaying," *New York Times*, June 30, 1974, 16; Mary Breasted, "Grand Jury to Get Report on Police Killing of Boy," *New York Times*, September 17, 1974, 1; Emanuel Perlmutter, "Brooklyn Man, 22, Is Shot in Apparent Police Error," *New York Times* September 23, 1974; Grace Lichtenstein, "500, at City Hall, Protest Reese Slaying," *New York Times*, September 26, 1974, 33; "Judge Assails Killing of Youth; Police Call Him 'Out of Order,'" *New York Times*, November 13, 1975, 22; "Killing by Police under Two Inquiries," *New York Times*, November 28, 1975; "Officer Shot Two in Back of Head," *New York Times*, December 27, 1975, 7.

102. E. R. Shipp, "Shootings by Indianapolis Police Lead to Outrage," *New York Times*, August 28, 1986, B11.

103. "Policeman in Fatal Raids Ousted," *New York Times*, June 13, 1981, 48.

104. "Alabama Prisoners Are Accusing Police of Using 60's Cattle Prods," *New York Times*, August 30, 1981, 55.

105. Fox Butterfield, "Boston Police Troubles Rise in Dispute over '75 Slaying," *New York Times*, September 15, 1983, A1.

106. Farrell, "Police in Chicago Sued over Spying," 52.

107. "Drug Raids: Terror in the Night," 148.

108. "Beatings of 2 Blacks by Policemen," 12.

109. Gary Orren, "Fall From Grace: The Public's Loss of Faith in Government," in *Why People Don't Trust Government*, ed. Joseph S. Nye Jr., Philip D. Zelikow, and David C. King (Cambridge, MA: Harvard University Press, 1997), 80.

110. Michael Avery, interview with author, November 6, 2007.

111. Wayne Schmidt, interview with the author; December 8, 2006.

112. "U.S. to Study Brutality Cases," *New York Times*, June 21, 1978, B20.

113. "Transcript of President's News Conference on Foreign and Domestic Matters," *New York Times*, July 21, 1978, A6.

114. Philip Taubman, "U.S. Plans Suit Assailing Police in Philadelphia: Calls Brutality Systematic against All Groups," *New York Times*, August 13, 1979, A1.

115. Taubman, "U.S. Plans Suit," A1. See also Edward Schumacher, "Rizzo Calls Suit on Police Abuse a Political Move," *New York Times,* August 14, 1979, A1; Philip Taubman, "U.S. Files Its Rights Suit Charging Philadelphia Police with Brutality," *New York Times,* August 14, 1979, D15; "Philadelphia Police: Toughest in the World," *Washington Post,* August 14, 1979; Edward Schumacher, "Rizzo's Stamp on Police Role: Law-and-Order Policies Are Deeply Ingrained," *New York Times,* August 16, 1979, A21; "Battered Prisoners' Photographs Asked in Philadelphia Police Suit," *New York Times,* August 19, 1979, 35.

116. Edward Schumacher, "For Mayor Frank Rizzo, One Issue Has Been Enough," *New York Times,* August 19, 1979, E4; Bruce Cory, "The New Politics of Deadly Force," *Police Magazine* March 1981, 7–11, at 10.

117. Cory, "New Politics of Deadly Force."

118. Ibid.

119. "Justice Department Battles against Conflicts between Police and Minorities," *New York Times,* November 13, 1983, 30; Philip Shenon, "More and More Communities Urge Police to Show Restraint," *New York Times,* April 8, 1984, E2.

120. Shenon, "More and More Communities."

121. Quoted in Shenon, "More and More Communities."

122. "Savannah Police Suit Settled," *New York Times,* July 7, 1987; "Police Agencies Seek Ways to Avoid Citizens' Lawsuits," *New York Times,* November 3, 1985, 74; "New Orleans to Settle Lawsuit on Police Abuse," *New York Times,* April 3, 1986, A16.

123. Shenon, "More and More Communities"; see also "Police Agencies Seek Ways to Avoid Citizens' Lawsuits."

124. Andrew H. Malcolm, "Police Brutality Cases, Once a Minority-Area Concern, Now Found Widely," *New York Times,* July 30, A19.

125. Ibid.

126. Ibid. On the New Orleans case, see also "Policeman in Fatal Raids Ousted."

127. Al Baker, "James Fyfe, 63, Criminologist and Police Training Director, Is Dead," *New York Times,* November 15, 2005.

128. Cory, "New Politics of Deadly Force," 9.

129. Ford Foundation, *Annual Report 1970,* 17 (accessed at http://www.fordfound .org/archives/item/1970). See also Police Foundation, http://www.policefoundation .org/.

130. Patrick V. Murphy and Thomas Plate, *Commissioner: A View from the Top of American Law Enforcement* (New York: Simon and Schuster, 1977), 256; emphasis added.

131. Patrick V. Murphy, interview with the author, August 25, 2008; Tom Brady, interview with the author, August 20, 2008; Candace McCoy, interview with the author, February 7, 2007.

132. Catherine H. Milton, Jeanne Wahl Halleck, James Lardner, and Gary L. Albrecht, *Police Use of Deadly Force* (Washington, DC: Police Foundation, 1977).

133. Ibid., 39–45.

134. Ibid., 40–41.

135. Ibid., 42–43.

136. Ibid., 43.

137. Ibid.

138. Ibid.

139. Ibid., 43–44.

140. Ibid., 65; emphasis added.

141. Ibid., 136–40.

142. Ibid.

143. James J. Fyfe, "Administrative Interventions on Police Shooting Discretion: An Empirical Examination," *Journal of Criminal Justice* 7 (1979): 309–24, at 322. This was a report of the principal findings of his dissertation, "Shots Fired: An Examination of New York City Police Firearms Discharges," PhD diss., State University of New York at Albany, 1978).

144. Albert J. Reiss Jr., "Controlling Police Use of Deadly Force," *Annals of the American Academy of Political and Social Science* 452 (November 1980): 126.

145. James J. Fyfe, "Deadly Force," *FBI Law Enforcement Bulletin*, December 1979, 7–9.

146. Ibid.

147. James J. Fyfe memo to "PVM" [Patrick V. Murphy], dated 12/31/84; copy on file with the author.

148. Quoted in Lance Gay, "Foundation Head Criticizes Police Use of Weapons," *Washington Post*, June 28, 1980.

149. John Herbers, "Murphy Is Accused by Police Chiefs," *New York Times,* July 8, 1982, A1; Francis X. Clines, "Urban Police Chief with a Scholastic Flair: Patrick Vincent Murphy," *New York Times* July 8, 1982, B15; "The Out-of-Touch Police," *New York Times,* July 9, 1982, A22.

150. "Blue Funk: Police Brass in Brouhaha," *Time,* July 26, 1982, 43; "Dissent Isn't Disloyalty," *Milwaukee Journal,* July 23, 1982; "Police Chiefs vs. Pat Murphy," *Stamford Advocate,* July 27, 1982.

151. Letter reproduced in *Crime Control Digest,* 16, 29 (July 19, 1982): 1–6.

152. "City Faces Bankruptcy over $3.5 Million Judgment," Associated Press, October 11, 1980.

153. John DeMers, "Police Chief Resigns under Fire," United Press International, November 25, 1980 (accessed on Lexis-Nexis).

154. "P.G. Police Told to Turn Over Internal Files," *Washington Post*, May 3, 1980, B4.

155. John Darnton, "S.I. Boy, 11, Killed by Police in Chase," *New York Times,* August 17, 1972, 1 (the age of the boy was initially misreported); Ronald Smothers, "Police Issue New Restrictions on Use of Firearms after the Shooting of 10-Year-Old Boy," *New York Times,* August 18, 1972, 62; Ronald Smothers, "Murphy Explains Gun-Rule Changes: Says Purpose Is to Protect Police and the Public," *New York Times,* August 19, 1972, 27.

156. "Gun Rules Tightened," *Los Angeles Times,* September 9, 1977, 1.

157. Bruce Cory, "Police on Trial in Houston," *Police Magazine,* July 1978, 33–40.

158. Garner v. City of Memphis 710 F.2d 240 (1983).

159. With the exception of nearly a year in 1972 for which data were not available. For discussion, see the analysis of the data in James J. Fyfe, "Blind Justice: Police Shootings in Memphis," *Journal of Criminal Law and Criminology* 73 (1982): 707–22.

160. James J. Fyfe, "Police Use of Deadly Force: Research and Reform," *Justice Quarterly* 5, 2 (1988): 165–205, at 194; Fyfe had earlier reported these in "Blind Justice."

161. Ibid., 194–95.

162. See, e.g., Kenneth J. Matulia, *A Balance of Forces* (Gaithersburg, MD: International Association of Chiefs of Police, 1982).

163. 471 U.S. 1, at 9-10.

164. Linda Greenhouse, "High Court Limits Rights of Police to Shoot to Kill," *New York Times*, March 28, 1985, A1.

165. John Whetsel, "Remarks," *Police Chief*, March 1986, 99–100.

166. James P. Manak, "Remarks," *Police Chief*, March 1986, 104–105.

167. Candace McCoy, interview with the author, February 7, 2007.

168. Ibid.

169. Michael Avery, interview with the author, November 6, 2007.

170. Candace McCoy, interview with the author, February 7, 2007.

171. James J. Fyfe, "Police Expert Witnesses," in *Expert Witnesses: Crimiologists in the Courtroom*, ed. Patrick R. Anderson and L. Thomas Winfree (Albany: SUNY Press, 1987), 100–118, at 100.

172. Ibid.

173. Ibid., 103.

174. Ibid., 102.

175. Ibid., 107.

176. Ibid., 108–12.

177. Ibid., 107.

178. Michael Avery, interview with author, November 6, 2007.

179. David Rudovsky, interview with author, October 20, 2006.

180. Susan Bandes, "The Emperor's New Clothes," *DePaul Law Review* 48 (1999): 619, at 624.

181. Michael Avery, interview with the author, November 6, 2007.

182. David Rudovsky, interview with the author, October 20, 2006.

183. Michael Avery, interview with author, November 6, 2007.

184. David Rudovsky, interview with the author, October 20, 2006.

185. *Oklahoma City v. Tuttle* 471 U.S. 808 (1985).

186. *Black's Law Dictionary* (St. Paul, MN: West, 1991). See, e.g., *Bergquist v. County of Cochise* 806 F.2d 1364 (9th Cir. 1986) and *Wierstak v. Heffernan* 789 F.2d 968 (1st Cir. 1986).

187. See, e.g., *Wellington v. Daniels* 717 F.2d 932 (4th Cir. 1983) and *Fiacco v. City of Rensselaer* 783 F.2d 319 (2d Cir. 1986).

188. *City of Springfield, Massachusetts v. Kibbe* 480 U.S. 257 (1987).

189. David Rudovsky, interview with the author, October 20, 2006.

190. Ibid.

191. Ibid.

192. James J. Fyfe memo to "PVM" [Patrick V. Murphy], dated 12/31/84; copy on file with the author.

Chapter Five

1. See, e.g., Wesley G. Skogan and Susan M. Hartnett, *Community Policing, Chicago Style* (New York: Oxford University Press, 1997); Wesley G. Skogan, ed., *Community Policing: Can It Work?* (Belmont, CA: Wadsworth/Thomson Learning, 2004); Steve Herbert, *Citizens, Cops, and Power* (Chicago: University of Chicago Press, 2006).

2. Samuel G. Chapman, "Police Policy on the Use of Firearms," *Police Chief*, July 1967, 16–37; Nelson A. Watson, "A Big Question: What Is Your Policy on the Use of

Firearms?" *Police Chief*, July 1967, 12–13; Richard H. Ichord, "A Legislative Proposal: Preventing the *Frivolous* Civil Rights Lawsuit against Police," *Police Chief*, July 1972, 34–35, at 34; Douglas M. Walters, "Civil Liability for Improper Police Training," *Police Chief*, November 1971, 28–36, at 28. Chapman and Watson mentioned liability only in passing.

3. Chapman, "Police Policy on the Use of Firearms," 20; the case was *McAndrew v. Mularchuk and Keansburg*, 33 N.J. 172, 88 A.L.R. (2d) 1313 (1960), imposing liability on a municipality for the negligent shooting of an innocent bystander; the latter quotation is from Watson, "Big Question," 12.

4. Francis B. Looney, "Improving the Accountability of Judges," *Police Chief*, December 1973, 8; Ichord, "Legislative Proposal," 34–35, at 34; AELE, *Survey of Police Misconduct Litigation*, 14.

5. John H. Burpo, "Advancing the Police Legal Advisor Concept," *Police Chief*, September 1969, 29–30. The legal adviser concept was first favored by the President's Commission on Law Enforcement and Administration of Justice, *The Challenge of Crime in a Free Society* (Washington, DC: Government Printing Office, 1967), 114; *Police Chief* authors supported the proposal in several articles: William L. Parker, "Training and Education: A Big 'Plus' for the Nashville Police Department," *Police Chief*, February 1973, 36–37; James T. O'Reilly, "Bridging the Gap: Law Enforcement and Legal Education," *Police Chief*, November 1973, 54–57; John W. Palmer, "The Police Paraprofessional: An Alternative to the Police Legal Advisor," *Police Chief*, December 1973, 56–57, at 56. Samuel Laudenslager, "Providing Legal Assistance to Small and Rural Law Enforcement Agencies: The Regional Legal Advisor," *Police Chief*, August 1974, 53–58.

6. Robert F. Thomas Jr., "Insurance for Police Agencies," *Police Chief*, January 16, 1979, 16.

7. "ICMA Agenda Communication No. 482," ICMA Archives, Spencer Research Library, University of Kansas, box 12, March 26–27, 1976.

8. There is now a substantial literature on the cycle and its sources. See, e.g., Baker, *Medical Malpractice Myth*; Ralph Winter, "The Liability Insurance Market," *Journal of Economic Perspectives* 5, 3 (1991): 115–36; Neil A. Doherty and James Garven, "Insurance Cycles: Interest Rates and the Capacity Constraint Model," *Journal of Business* 68 (1995): 383–404; Scott E. Harrington, "Cycles and Volatility," in *The Handbook of Insurance*, ed. G. Dionne (Boston: Kluwer, 2001).

9. Winter, "Liability Insurance Market," 115.

10. Thomas A. Hendrickson, "Local Governments May Be Sued for Civil Rights Violations: The *Monell* Decision," *Police Chief*, September 16, 1978.

11. Roy A. Tyler, "Insurance for Police Officers," *Police Chief*, January 1981, 18–19, at 18.

12. Karen Ayres Brophy, "Department Civil Liability for Officers' Off-Duty Acts," *Police Chief*, February 1982, 16–17, at 16.

13. William F. Quinn, "Training: A Critical Requirement," *Police Chief*, July 1981, 8.

14. Joseph E. Scuro Jr. and Lawrence J. Souza, "*Patsy v. Florida Board of Regents:* The Two-Edged Sword," *Police Chief*, December 1982, 18–19, at 18.

15. Jack Walsh, "Remarks," *Police Chief*, January 1982, 76.

16. George Sunderland, "Third-Party Suits: A Police Problem of the Future," *Police Chief*, March 1980, 50–51, at 51.

17. Joseph E. Scuro Jr., "Remarks: Police Discipline and Federal Liability," *Police Chief*, March 1983, 98.

18. Maurice A. Cawn, "Legal Implications in Handling Demonstrations," *Police Chief*, May 1981, 14–15, at 15.

19. An exception is Joseph E. Scuro Jr., "Recent Developments in Government Liability under 42 U.S.C. 1983," *Police Chief*, April 1982, 20–22, at 22.

20. Joseph E. Scuro Jr., "Remarks," *Police Chief*, March 1984, 57–58.

21. Carrington, "Avoiding Liability."

22. G. Patrick Gallagher, "Risk Management for Police Administrators," *Police Chief*, June 1990, 18–29, at 18.

23. R. Monte MacConnell, "Negligent Hiring and Retention: A Cause for Concern," *Police Chief*, July 1991, 12–15, at 12.

24. Diane M. Daane and James E. Hendricks, "Liability for Failure to Train," *Police Chief*, November 1991, 26–29, at 29.

25. Barbara E. Roberts, "Legal Issues in Use-of-Force Claims," *Police Chief*, February 1992, 16–29, at 16.

26. Kerry P. Steckowych, "Police Pursuit Liability Issues," *Police Chief*, October 1996, 8.

27. Rod Fick, "California's Police Pursuit Immunity Statute: Does it Work?" *Police Chief*, February 1997, 37–42, at 37.

28. Martin J. Mayer and Paul R. Coble, "Utilizing the Department's Legal Counsel at Major Incidents," *Police Chief*, May 1998, 8.

29. Victor E. Kappeler and Rolando V. del Carmen, "Avoiding Police Liability for Negligent Failure to Prevent Suicide," *Police Chief*, August 1991, 53–59.

30. Michael R. Santos, "Use of Force: *Tennessee v. Garner* Reviewed," *Police Chief*, October 1991, 13–16. See also Barbara E. Roberts, "Legal Issues in Use-of-Force Claims," *Police Chief*, February 1992, 16–29.

31. Diane M. Daane and James E. Hendricks, "Liability for Failure to Adequately Train," *Police Chief*, November 1991, 26–29.

32. James W. Hopper and William C. Summers, "Managing the Risks and Controlling the Losses," *Police Chief*, September 1989, 45–48; Bob Thomas and Randy Means, "*Canton v. Harris* Determines Standard for Training Liability Cases," *Police Chief*, June 1990, 37; Daane and Hendricks, "Liability for Failure to Adequately Train," 29; Milton Thurm, "The Need to Train: Constitutional Issues," *Police Chief*, April 1993, 16.

33. The threat was great enough that failing to carry liability insurance was "potential financial suicide," observed Tyler, "Insurance for Police Officers," 19. See also Frank Carrington, "Avoiding Liability for Police Failure to Protect," *Police Chief*, September 1989, 22–24, at 24.

34. G. Patrick Gallagher, "Risk Management for Police Administrators," *Police Chief*, June 1990, 18–29, at 18. See also Quinn, "Training," 8.

35. William A. Liquori, "Personal and Organizational Integrity: Maintaining Departmental Credibility," *Police Chief*, January 1992, 22.

36. William A. Liquori, "Maintaining Departmental Credibility," *Police Chief*, January 1992, 22; emphasis in original.

37. Quinn Tamm, "The Customer Isn't Always Right," *Police Chief*, June 1967, 6.

38. Lee P. Brown, "Law Enforcement and Police Brutality," *Police Chief*, May 1991, 6; emphasis in original.

39. Liquori, "Maintaining Departmental Credibility," 22; emphasis in original.

40. Jeff Steffel and Donald Rossi, "Remarks: Psychological Aspects of Vicarious Liability," *Police Chief*, March 1983, 130–35, at 135; emphasis added.

41. Robert F. Thomas Jr., "Remarks: The Contours of Municipal Liability under 42 U.S.C. §1983," *Police Chief*, March 1983, 82–84, at 84.

42. Steffel and Rossi, "Remarks," 134.

43. Lawrence M. Friedman, *Total Justice* (New York: Sage, 1985).

44. Robert W. Wennerholm, "Officer Survival Recommendations: New Civil Liability Concerns," *Police Chief*, June 1984, 59–62, at 60; emphasis added.

45. B. McAllister, "Spurred by Dramatic Rise in Lawsuits, Police Agencies Warm to Accreditation," *Washington Post*, March 17, 1987; see also Sheldon Greenberg, "Police Accreditation," in *Police and Policing: Contemporary Issues,* ed. Dennis Jay Kenney (Westport, CT: Praeger, 1989), 247–56, at 251.

46. Joseph E. Scuro Jr. and Lawrence J. Souza, "The Civil Liability Consequences of Departmental Rules and Regulations," *Police Chief*, October 1982, 18.

47. Leon R. Kutzke, "The Department Manual: An Organizational Necessity," *Police Chief*, December 1980, 46–47.

48. Kenneth J. Matulia, *A Balance of Forces* (Gaithersburg, MD: IACP, 1982).

49. Ibid., 160.

50. Ibid., 144–45.

51. Kenneth J. Matulia, "The Use of Deadly Force: A Need for Written Directives and Training," *Police Chief*, May 1983, 30–34, at 30; see also, e.g., Thomas, "Remarks," 84.

52. Advertisement for *A Balance of Forces, Police Chief*, May 1983, 33.

53. Ronald J. Greenalgh, "The Teachings of *Harlow v. Fitzgerald*," *Police Chief*, May 1983, 20.

54. "Deadly Force: Laws Vary," *New York Times*, March 28, 1985, D31.

55. "Models for Management: A Look at the Past; a Step towards the Future," *Police Chief*, August 1989, 16.

56. "Models for Management: Deadly Force," *Police Chief*, April 1987, 57.

57. "Models for Management: Response to Civil Litigation," *Police Chief*, March 1989, 65–67.

58. Philip Lynn, "Policy Problems? IACP's Policy Center Can Make a Difference," *Police Chief*, October 1990, 127–30, at 128.

59. Lynn, "Policy Problems?" 127.

60. See, e.g., James P. Manak, "New Constitutional Rule on Use of Deadly Force," *Police Chief*, September 1985, 12; William A. Geller, "Liability Issues—15 Shooting Reduction Techniques: Controlling the Use of Deadly Force by and against Officers," *Police Chief*, August 1985, 56–58; and Virginia Fazo, "Use of Deadly Force," *Police Chief*, August 1985, 54–55, at 54.

61. John C. Desmedt, "Use of Force Paradigm for Law Enforcement," *Journal of Police Science and Administration* 12, 2 (1984): 170–76; see also Bill Clede with Kevin Parsons, *Police Nonlethal Force Manual: Your Choices This Side of Deadly* (Harrisburg, PA.: Stackpole Books, 1987); Gregory J. Connor, "Use of Force Continuum: Phase 11," *Law and Order*, March 1991, 30–32; and Lawrence C. Trostle, "The Force Continuum: From Lethal to Less than Lethal Force," *Journal of Contemporary Criminal Justice* 6 (1990): 23–26.

62. Desmedt, "Use of Force Paradigm for Law Enforcement," 170.

63. Ibid., 175.

64. *Graham v. Connor* 490 U.S. 386 (1989).

65. John G. Peters and Michael A. Brave, "Force Continuums: Three Questions," *Police Chief,* January 2006, http://policechiefmagazine.org/magazine/index.cfm?fuseaction=display&article_id=791&issue_id=12006 (accessed April 17, 2009).

66. Confidential interview with the author, February 9, 2009.

67. Quinn, "Training," 8.

68. William C. Summers, "Police Chief Liability for Negligent Failure to Train," *Police Chief,* July 1981, 12–13, at 12.

69. Ibid., 13.

70. Ralph B. Strickland Jr., "*Stegald v. United States*: The Supreme Court adopts a Search Warrant Rule for Entries of Third-Party Residences," *Police Chief,* September 1981, 12–13, at 13.

71. Greenalgh, "Teachings of *Harlow v. Fitzgerald*," 20, quoting *Owen v. City of Independence* 100 S. Ct. 1398, at 1416 (1980).

72. Ibid., 20.

73. Angus J. Park, "Teaching the Constitution," *Police Chief,* July 1981, 60–63.

74. Michael L. Ciminelli, "A Positive, Procedural Approach to Legal Training for Police Officers," *Police Chief,* November 1986, 26–32, 62, at 27.

75. Ibid., 27.

76. Michael Avery, interview with the author, November 6, 2007.

77. "BJA Support Extended for Successful Deadly Force Training Project," *Police Chief,* May 1988, 11–12.

78. "Developing Better Law Enforcement Officers: Policing Executives Discuss Innovations in Education and Training," *Police Chief,* November 1987, 40–45, at 40; Ciminelli, "Positive, Procedural Approach," 26–32, 62; Michael A. Brave, "Liability Constraints on Human Restraints," *Police Chief,* March 1993, 28–35.

79. "Developing Better Law Enforcement Officers."

80. Daane and Hendricks. "Liability for Failure to Adequately Train," 26–29, at 26.

81. Michael P. Stone, "Developing a Policy on Use of Force: A Suggested Model," http://www.rcdsa.org/articles/force.htm (accessed December 28, 2008).

82. *Webster v. City of Houston* 689 F.2d 1220 (5th Cir. 1982).

83. Gerald S. Remey, "Defining the 'Policy or Custom' Requirement of *Monell*," *Police Chief,* August 1983, 17.

84. Ibid.; emphasis added.

85. Liquori, "Maintaining Departmental Credibility."

86. James W. Papst, "Basic Guidelines for Administrative Control," *Police Chief,* August 1993, 20–26.

87. Ibid.

88. Samuel Walker, Geoffrey P. Alpert, and Dennis J. Kenney, "Early Warning Systems for Police: Concept, History, and Issues," *Police Quarterly* 3, 2 (2000): 132–52.

89. Ibid., 133.

90. Ibid., 138–39.

91. U.S. Commission on Civil Rights, *Who Is Guarding the Guardians? A Report on Police Practices* (Washington, DC: U.S. Commission on Civil Rights, 1981).

92. Christopher Commission, *Report of the Independent Commission on the Los Angeles Police Department* (Los Angeles: City of Los Angeles, 1991).

93. Walker, Alpert, and Kenney, "Early Warning Systems for Police," 144.

94. J. C. Becker, "What's in Your Files?" *Police Chief,* December 1998, 12.

95. Robert F. Thomas Jr., "Remarks," *Police Chief* January 1982, 74–75, at 75.

96. M. M. Vines, "Remarks," *Police Chief,* January 1982, 73. See also Jack Walsh, "Remarks," 76.

97. Brave, "Liability Constraints on Human Restraints," 35.

98. Geller, "Liability Issues," 56–58.

99. G. Patrick Gallagher, "The Six-Layered Liability Protection System for Police," *Police Chief,* June 1990, 40–44, at 40.

100. Brown, "Law Enforcement and Police Brutality," 6; emphasis in original.

101. "IACP Addresses Police Brutality Concerns: 'Project Response' Underway," *Police Chief,* May 1991. 10.

102. Ibid. (The Center, not surprisingly, relied on data supplied by police departments, which showed, again not surprisingly, the vast majority of citizen complaints of misconduct to be "unfounded"—that is, without adequate supporting evidence. The first report of such data drew the equally unfounded conclusion that therefore the problem of police brutality is wildly exaggerated. See Mark Henriquez, "The IACP National Police Use-of-Force Database Project," *Police Chief,* October 1999, 154–59.)

103. Frank Dobbin and John R. Sutton, "The Strength of a Weak State: The Rights Revolution and the Rise of Human Resources Management Divisions," *American Journal of Sociology* 104, 2 (1998): 441. See also Lauren B. Edelman, "Legal Environments and Organizational Governance: The Expansion of Due Process in the American Workplace," *American Journal of Sociology* 95, 6 (1990): 1401–40, and Lauren B. Edelman, "Legal Ambiguity and Symbolic Structures: Organizational Mediation of Civil Rights Law," *American Journal of Sociology* 97 (1992): 1531–76.

104. G. Patrick Gallagher, "Risk Management for Police Administrators," *Police Chief,* June 1990, 18–29, at 18.

105. Ibid., 25.

106. Gallagher, "Six-Layered Liability Protection System for Police," 40.

107. Thomas H. Baynard and Bernard J. Giangiulio Jr., "Protecting Your Community from Lawsuits," *Police Chief,* November 1991, 19–25, at 25, 19.

108. Daane and Hendricks, "Liability for Failure to Adequately Train," 26.

109. Advertisement, *Police Chief,* February 1991, 32–33.

110. Advertisement, *Police Chief,* July 1991.

111. Samuel Walker, *The New World of Police Accountability* (Thousand Oaks, CA: Sage, 2005), 23.

112. O. W. Wilson and Roy Clinton McLaren, *Police Administration,* 4th ed. (New York: McGraw-Hill, 1977).

113. Ibid., 100.

114. Ibid., 431–32.

115. Ibid., 542–45.

116. James J. Fyfe, Jack R. Greene, William F. Walsh, O. W. Wilson, and Roy Clinton McLaren, *Police Administration,* 5th ed. (New York: McGraw-Hill, 1997).

117. Ibid., chaps. 1, 12, 13, 14, and 15.

118. Ibid., 451–56, 495–97, 529–34.

119. See, e.g., ibid., 48–49, 484–523.

120. Ibid., 489.

121. Ibid., 490.

122. Charles R. Swanson and Leonard Territo, *Police Administration: Structures, Processes, and Behavior* (New York: Macmillan, 1983) (2nd ed. 1988, 3rd ed. 1993, 4th ed. 1998).

123. Swanson and Territo, *Police Administration* (1st ed.), 296, 303–4.

124. Ibid., 319.

125. Charles R. Swanson, Leonard Territo, and Robert W. Taylor, *Police Administration: Structures, Processes, and Behavior*, 3rd ed. (New York: Macmillan, 1993), 401, 405–6, 432–34, 436; 4th ed. (1998), 408–13.

126. Edward A. Thibault, Lawrence M. Lynch, and R. Bruce McBride, *Proactive Police Management* (Englewood Cliffs, NJ, 1985) (2nd ed. 1990, 3rd ed. 1995, 4th ed. 1998, 5th ed. 2001, 6th ed. 2004).

127. Thibault, Lynch, and McBride (1st ed.), 250–51.

128. Thibault, Lynch, and McBride (2nd ed.), 345; emphasis in original.

129. Thibault, Lynch, and McBride (2nd ed.), 343–45, at 345; Thibault, Lynch, and McBride (3rd ed.), 302–5.

130. Paul M. Whisenand and R. Fred Ferguson, *The Managing of Police Organizations* (Upper Saddle River, NJ: Prentice-Hall, 1973) (2nd ed. 1978, 3rd ed. 1989, 4th ed. 1996, 5th ed. 2002).

131. Bennett E. Kaplan, G. Allen Dale, with Thomas Guinta, *Civil and Criminal Liability of Police Officers* (Washington, DC: Police Advocate, 1978).

132. Ibid., 39–40.

133. Ibid., 49 and 91, respectively.

134. Ibid., 105, 115–32.

135. Ibid., 129.

136. Ibid., 119.

137. Traffic Institute, *Civil Liability and the Police* (Evanston, IL: Traffic Institute, Northwestern University, 1982), 56.

138. Ibid.

139. Victor E. Kappeler, *Critical Issues in Civil Liability* (Prospect Heights, IL: Waveland Press, 1993), 3 (2nd ed. 1997, 3rd ed. 2001, 4th ed. 2006).

140. Kappeler, *Critical Issues in Civil Liability* (1st ed.), 182.

141. Samuel Walker, "The New Paradigm of Police Accountability: The U.S. Justice Department 'Pattern or Practice' Suits in Context," *St. Louis University Public Law Review* 22, 1 (2003): 3–52; Walker, "New Paradigm of Police Accountability."

142. Walker, "New Paradigm of Police Accountability."

143. Theodore Eisenberg and Stewart Schwab, "The Reality of Constitutional Tort Litigation," *Cornell Law Review* 72 (1987): 641–95. See also Epp, "Exploring the Costs of Administrative Legalization," 407.

144. Gary W. Buchanan, "Managing Police Use of Force," *Police Chief*, August 1993, 20.

145. Ibid.

Chapter Six

1. A number of other surveys cover some aspects of these issues, among them Antony M. Pate and Lorie A. Fridell with Edwin E. Hamilton, *Police Use of Force: Official Reports, Citizen Complaints, and Legal Consequences* (Washington, DC: Police Foundation, 1993); Samuel Walker, Geoffrey P. Alpert, and Dennis Kenney, *Early*

Warning Systems: Responding to the Problem Police Officer (Washington, DC: National Institute of Justice, 2001).

2. Some elements (for instance, the various components of training) have been combined into scales for greater ease in illustration.

3. Samuel Walker, *The New World of Police Accountability* (Thousand Oaks, CA: Sage, 2005).

4. In statistical terms, Middling is at the mean on the Legalized Accountability scale, Tradition is one standard deviation below the mean, and Legality is one standard deviation above the mean. The case IDs are Tradition, 1009, Middling, 693, and Legality, 342.

5. See, e.g., Joel Garner, John Buchanan, Tom Schade, and John Hepburn, *Understanding the Use of Force by and against the Police: Research in Brief* (Washington, DC: National Institute of Justice, 1996), accessed at http://www.ncjrs.gov/pdffiles/forcerib.pdf; and Joel H. Garner and Christopher D. Maxwell, "Understanding the Use of Force by and against the Police in Six Jurisdictions, Final Report" (Submitted to the National Institute of Justice Office of Justice Programs, U.S. Department of Justice, January 2002), accessed at http://www.ncjrs.gov/pdffiles1/nij/grants/196694.pdf; and William Terrill, *Police Coercion: Application of the Force Continuum* (New York: LFB Scholarly Publishing, 2001).

6. Garner et al., *Understanding the Use of Force*, 5.

7. Samuel Walker and Charles M. Katz, *The Police in America: An Introduction*, 5th ed. (Boston: McGraw-Hill, 2005), 140, citing the President's Commission on Law Enforcement and Administration of Justice, *Task Force Report*, 138.

8. Thomas M. Frost and Magnus J. Seng, "Police Entry Level Curriculum: A Thirty-Year Perspective," *Journal of Police Science and Administration* 12, 3 (1984): 251–59.

9. Ibid., 254.

10. N = 839, 838, and 834, respectively.

11. Walker, Alpert, and Kenney, *Early Warning Systems*.

12. Carol Archbold, "Managing the Bottom Line: Risk Management in Policing," *Policing* 28, 1 (2005): 30–48.

13. Pate, Fridell, and Hamilton, *Police Use of Force*.

14. Pearson's r = .18, sig. < .001 (N = 791).

15. N = 832.

16. Kenneth Culp Davis, *Police Discretion* (St. Paul, MN: West, 1975); Walker, *New World of Police Accountability*.

17. N = 835.

18. N = 818 and 804, respectively.

19. N = 829.

20. Walker, Alpert, and Kenney, *Early Warning Systems*.

21. See, e.g., Samuel Walker, *Police Accountability: The Role of Citizen Oversight* (Belmont, CA: Wadsworth/Thompson Learning, 2001).

22. N = 835 for citizen review boards, 804 for nonsworn officers involved in the complaint review process.

23. The first factor's eigenvalue is 1.43, with a difference of 1.11; the second factor's eigenvalue is only .32, with a difference of .23; χ^2 = 497.79, p < .0001 (n = 683).

24. Cronbach's alpha for the index is .95.

25. The measure consists of an index of attorneys specializing in each of the listed areas. The data source is the Martindale-Hubbell directory of attorneys, accessed at www.martindale.com at the time I administered the survey, and the data on attorneys by locality consisted of those who declared a specialty of "government." A typical attorney declaring this specialty, for instance, also specialized in "Plaintiff's Personal Injury Law; Medical Malpractice; Products Liability Law; Automobile Accident; Environmental Law; Qui Tam Litigation." Such attorneys are precisely the sort who are likely to have the knowledge and skills necessary to pursue a lawsuit against a local government. Almost all such attorneys are in private practice, not government employment. Both these measures—managers' perceptions of the strength of the rights infrastructure and the objective number of government-liability attorneys in the city—have some strengths and weaknesses. The perceptual measure captures the presence of both attorneys and citizen groups; the objective measure is an indication only of the number of attorneys. The perceptual measure reflects the usual biases associated with perceptions, but if the theory of this book is correct it is perceptions of the legal environment that matter. On the other hand, the senior manager answering the survey may not be as familiar with the true availability of attorneys as would a member of the department's policy planning staff, so the objective measure may in some respects provide a more accurate indicator of the local legal environment as experienced by departmental policymakers. Finally, the perceptual measure captures the relative presence of attorneys and citizen groups even if they are not within the city's jurisdiction; the objective measure captures only those attorneys whose offices are within that jurisdiction.

26. Peter M. Blau and Richard A. Schoenherr, *The Structure of Organizations* (New York: Basic Books, 1971); see also Lauren B. Edelman, "Legal Environments and Organizational Governance: The Expansion of Due Process in the American Workplace," *American Journal of Sociology* 95, 6 (1990): 1401–40, and Lauren B. Edelman, "Legal Ambiguity and Symbolic Structures: Organizational Mediation of Civil Rights Law," *American Journal of Sociology* 97 (1992): 1531–76.

27. Paul Brace, Laura Langer, and Melinda Gann Hall, "Measuring the Preferences of State Supreme Court Judges," *Journal of Politics* 62, 2 (2000): 387–413.

28. Robert S. Erikson, Gerald C. Wright, and John P. McIver, "Public Opinion in the States: A Quarter Century of Change and Stability," in *Public Opinion in State Politics*, ed. Jeffrey Cohen (Stanford, CA: Stanford University Press, 2006), accessed at http://mypage.iu.edu/~wright1/ewm_cohen.doc. An alternative is Robert Putnam's concept of "social capital," or the relative extent of cooperative nonstate organizations, trust in others, and cooperative, public-regarding actions and attitudes. See Robert Putnam, *Bowling Alone: The Collapse and Revival of American Community* (New York: Simon and Schuster, 2000). Putnam has shown that the level of social capital, by state, is strongly associated with state policies that contribute to general health, safety, and welfare. A plausible implication of his theory is that social capital is likely to be positively associated with the adoption of intrusive police departmental policies. Other alternatives for the policy areas of sexual harassment and playground safety are the Brace et al. state-level measures of liberalism on feminism and environmentalism. See Paul Brace, Kellie Sims-Butler, Kevin Arceneaux, and Martin Johnson, "Public Opinion in the States: New Perspectives Using National Survey Data," *American Journal of Political Science* 46, 1 (2002): 173. In my full statistical models, none of

these measures of state political opinion or culture is consistently related to the depth of city administrative systems on rights; in the tables here, I report the results for the Erikson, Wright, and McIver measure. Among the various measures, it has been the most widely used and is generalizable.

29. I have defined a "strong" support structure as the seventy-fifth percentile on several questions of chiefs' perceptions of the strength of the local support structure for police misconduct litigation and three (logged) government liability attorneys in the local jurisdiction, as listed in the Martindale-Hubbell national registry.

30. I have defined connections to professional networks as "weak" when departments have no internal legal adviser and score at the twenty-fifth percentile on a two-item index of connection to professional networks; I have defined these connections as "strong" when departments have an internal legal adviser and score at the seventy-fifth percentile on the index of connections to professional networks.

31. Candace McCoy, "How Civil Rights Lawsuits Improve American Policing," in *To Protect Life: Readings on Police Accountability*, ed. Candace McCoy (New York: Urban Institute Press, forthcoming).

32. The full model results are not reported but are available from the author on request.

33. Walker, *New World of Police Accountability*.

34. Additionally, state supreme court liberalism is negatively associated with taking corrective actions, an unexpected relationship.

35. John Darnton, "S.I. Boy, 11, Killed by Police in Chase," *New York Times*, August 17, 1972, 1 (the age of the boy was initially misreported); Ronald Smothers, "Police Issue New Restrictions on Use of Firearms after the Shooting of 10-Year-Old Boy," *New York Times*, August 18, 1972, 62; Ronald Smothers, "Murphy Explains Gun-Rule Changes: Says Purpose Is to Protect Police and the Public," *New York Times*, August 19, 1972, 27.

36. "Gun Rules Tightened," *Los Angeles Times*, September 9, 1977, 1; Bruce Cory, "Police on Trial in Houston," *Police Magazine*, July 1978, 33–40.

37. James W. Papst, "Basic Guidelines for Administrative Control," *Police Chief*, August 1993, 20–26, at 20.

Chapter Seven

1. David Rose, "Record Damages against Police," *Guardian* (London), December 6, 1989.

2. Ibid.

3. See, e.g., Robert A. Kagan, *Adversarial Legalism: The American Way of Law* (Cambridge, MA: Harvard University Press. 2003).

4. Robert Reiner, *The Politics of the Police*, 3rd ed. (Oxford: Oxford University Press, 2000), 62, 202.

5. Ibid., 59.

6. Ibid., 79; on the general issue of race and policing in Britain, see Ben Bowling and Coretta Phillips, *Racism, Crime and Justice* (New York: Longman, 2002); Satnam Choongh, *Policing as Social Discipline* (New York: Oxford University Press, 1997); Roger G. Hood and Graca Cordovil, *Race and Sentencing: A Study in the Crown Court, a Report for the Commission for Racial Equality* (New York: Oxford University Press, 1992).

7. Data are taken from Richard Skellington with Paulette Morris, *"Race" in Britain Today* (London: Sage, 1992), 37–38, and U.K. Office for National Statistics, http://www.statistics.gov.uk/StatBase/Expodata/Spreadsheets/D6205.xls (accessed January 9, 2007).

8. Ian K. McKenzie and G. Patrick Gallagher, *Behind the Uniform: Policing in Britain and America* (New York: St. Martin's Press, 1989), 84–85.

9. John Solomos, *Race and Racism in Britain*, 3rd ed. (New York: Palgrave Macmillan, 2003), 51–54; Zig Layton-Henry and Paul B. Rich, eds., *Race, Government and Politics in Britain* (Basingstoke, UK: Macmillan, 1986); Robin Cohen, *Frontiers of Identity: The British and the Others* (London: Longman, 1994).

10. Solomos, *Race and Racism in Britain*, 53, 54–55.

11. Quoted in ibid., 61.

12. John Solomos, *Black Youth, Racism and the State* (Cambridge: Cambridge University Press, 1988).

13. Gus John, *Race and the Inner City: A Report from Handsworth* (London: Runnymede Trust, 1970), quoted in Solomos, *Race and Racism in Britain*, 123.

14. Stuart Hall, Chas Critcher, Tony Jefferson, John Clarke, and Brian Roberts, *Policing the Crisis: Mugging, the State, and Law and Order* (New York: Holmes and Meier, 1978).

15. Ian K. McKenzie and G. Patrick Gallagher, *Behind the Uniform: Policing in Britain and America* (New York: St. Martin's Press, 1989), 134.

16. David J. Smith and Jeremy Gray, *Police and People in London: The PSI Report* (London: Gower, 1985). See also Bowling and Phillips, *Racism, Crime and Justice*; Choongh, *Policing as Social Discipline*; Andrew Sanders, "From Suspect to Trial," in *The Oxford Handbook of Criminology*, 2nd ed., ed. Mike Maguire, Rod Morgan, and Robert Reiner (Oxford: Clarendon Press, 1997), 1056–59.

17. Hall et al., *Policing the Crisis*, 337.

18. Reiner, *Politics of the Police*, 66; Clive Walker and Keir Starmer, eds., *Justice in Error* (London: Blackstone, 1993).

19. Reiner, *Politics of the Police*, 66.

20. Richard Clayton and Hugh Tomlinson, *Civil Actions against the Police*, 3rd ed. (London: Thomson/Sweet and Maxwell, 2004), 22–25.

21. The following discussion is based on McKenzie and Gallagher, *Behind the Uniform*, 125–26.

22. See, e.g., Reiner, *Politics of the Police*, 65.

23. Ibid., 65.

24. See, e.g., Robert Reiner, "Police Accountability: Principles, Patterns and Practices," in *Accountable Policing: Effectiveness, Empowerment and Equity*, ed. Robert Reiner and Sarah Spencer (London: Institute for Public Policy Research, 1993).

25. The following discussion is based on Reiner, *Politics of the Police*, 51ff.

26. In the area of criminal justice and policing, there have been several Royal Commissions or other official inquiries in the past half-century, notably the Royal Commission on the Police (1960), which led to the creation of the Police Act 1962; the Royal Commission on Criminal Procedure (1977, with final report in 1981) and the Inquiry on the Brixton Disorders (1981), which together led to the creation of the Police and Criminal Evidence (PACE) Act (1984); the Committee of Inquiry on the Police (1978) and the Inquiry into Police Responsibilities and Rewards (1993), each

of which led to changes in police salaries and promotion policies; and the Stephen Lawrence Inquiry (1997).

27. Robert Reiner, *Chief Constables: Bobbies, Bosses, or Bureaucrats?* (Oxford: Oxford University Press, 1991), 22–24.

28. Ibid.

29. Lord Scarman, *The Scarman Report: The Brixton Disorders* (London: Her Majesty's Stationery Office, 1981).

30. See, e.g., Reiner, *Politics of the Police*, 204–6.

31. Ben Bowling and Coretta Phillips, *Racism, Crime and Justice* (New York: Longman, 2002), 9–10.

32. Reiner, *Politics of the Police*, 205–6; Reiner, *Chief Constables*, chap. 6.

33. David Dixon, *Law in Policing: Legal Regulation and Police Practices* (Oxford: Oxford University Press, 1997).

34. Mike Maguire and Claire Corbett, *A Study of the Police Complaints System* (London: Her Majesty's Stationery Office, 1991). The PCA is statutorily precluded from investigating complaints about police policies above the level of the individual officer.

35. McKenzie and Gallagher, *Behind the Uniform*, 130.

36. Arthur Brown, *Police Governance in England and Wales* (London: Cavendish, 1998), 95–102; Stephen P. Savage, Sarah Charman, and Stephen Cope, *Policing and the Power of Persuasion: The Changing Role of the Association of Chief Police Officers* (London: Blackstone, 2000).

37. Hugh Alford, ACPO, London, interview with the author, May 20, 2004.

38. Clayton and Tomlinson, *Civil Actions against the Police*, 5.

39. William R. Smith, Donald Tomaskovic-Devey, Matthew T. Zingraff, H. Marcinda Mason, Patricia Y. Warren, and Cynthia Pfaff Wright, *The North Carolina Highway Traffic Study: Final Report to the Department of Justice*, http://www.ncjrs .gov/pdffiles1/nij/grants/204021.pdf (2004); Charles R. Epp, Steven Maynard-Moody, and Donald Haider-Markel, "Reconstructing Law on the Street: The Influence of Citizen Characteristics on Traffic Law Enforcement," paper presented at the annual meeting of the Law and Society Association, Chicago, May 27–30, 2004. (These studies rely on the driving population, rather than the general population, as the baseline.)

40. See, e.g., Metropolitan Police Authority, *Report of the MPA Scrutiny on MPS Stop and Search Practice* (London: Metropolitan Police Authority, Home Office, 2004), 5; Police Complaints Authority, *National Study on Stop and Search Complaints* (London: Police Complaints Authority. 2004). One study suggested that a significant portion of the racial disparities in stops and searches are due to the prevalence of young minority men on the street, an explanation that has done little to quell concerns about discriminatory policing; see Joel Miller, Paul Quinton, and Nick Bland, "Police Stops and Searches: Lessons from a Program of Research," Home Office Police Research Series Papers 127–32 (London: Home Office, Policing and Reducing Crime Unit, Home Office Research, Development and Statistics Directorate, 2000).

41. Reiner, *Politics of the Police*, 180; Sanders, "From Suspect to Trial," 1063–64; Mike McConville, Andrew Sanders, and Roger Leng, *The Case for the Prosecution* (London: Routledge, 1991); Sanders, "From Suspect to Trial," 1071; Maguire and Corbett, *Study of the Police Complaints System.*

42. Philip Scraton, "Denial, Neutralisation and Disqualification: The Royal Commission on Criminal Justice in Context," in *Criminal Justice in Crisis*, ed. Mike McConville and Lee Bridges (Aldershot, UK; Elgar, 1994), 102.

43. Sanders, "From Suspect to Trial," 1068.

44. Reiner, *Politics of the Police*, 182.

45. Scraton, "Denial, Neutralisation and Disqualification," 101, quoting the Legal Action Group.

46. Vicarious liability was one of the innovations of the 1964 Police Act. See Bill Dixon and Graham Smith, "Laying Down the Law: The Police, the Courts and Legal Accountability," *International Journal of the Sociology of Law* 26 (1998): 419–35, at 427.

47. Plaintiffs may request jury trials when alleging malicious prosecution and false imprisonment (which are typically combined into a single action with the third common claim, assault. See Section 69(1) of the Supreme Court Act 1981; Section 66(3) of the County Courts Act 1984 contains identical provisions. For discussion see Clayton and Tomlinson, *Civil Actions*, 107–8.

48. Graham Smith, lead organizer for the Hackney Community Defence Association, personal communication with the author, August 28, 2007.

49. Raju Bhatt, interview with the author, London, May 26, 2004.

50. Graham Smith, personal communication with the author, August 28, 2007.

51. John Harrison, *Police Misconduct: Legal Remedies* (London: Legal Action Group, 1987); Richard Clayton and Hugh Tomlinson, *Civil Actions against the Police* (London: Sweet and Maxwell, 1987); Richard Perks, *The Police in the Civil Courts* (London: LexisNexis, 2003); Patrick O'Connor, *Civil Actions against the Police* (Bristol: Jordans, 2004).

52. Graham Smith, interview with the author, Nottingham, England, June 4, 2004; Russell Miller, telephone interview with the author, June 2, 2004. See also Duncan Campbell, "Base Data," *Guardian* (London), March 28, 1995, features section, T12.

53. Sarah Ricca, convener of PALG, interview with the author, London, May 17, 2004.

54. The first reported damage judgment against the police in modern times was *White v. Commissioner of Police of the Metropolis; Times* (London), April 24, 1982. I am grateful to Graham Smith for the reference; see Graham Smith, "The Legacy of the Stoke Newington Scandal," *International Journal of Police Science and Management* 2, 2 (1999): 156–63; Seumas Milne, "Police to Pay £425,000 to 39 Arrested in Miners' Strike," *Guardian* (London), June 20, 1991; Stephen Goodwin, Malcolm Pithers, and Heather Mills, "Inquiry Is Urged into Policing of Miners' Strike," *Independent* (London), June 21, 1991, home news section, 3.

55. Robin Pauley "A Fuse Just Waiting to Be Lit . . . : Britain's Inner Cities," *Financial Times* (London), September 12, 1985, 14.

56. Shyama Perera, "Police Accuse Doctors over Brain Damage Case," *Guardian* (London), January 30, 1987, 8.

57. Cal McCrystal, "The Wrong Side of the Law," *Independent* (London), November 21, 1993, Sunday review section, 12. On the Roach case, see Peter Murtagh, "Doubts Still on Shotgun 'Suicide,'" *Guardian* (London), January 13, 1988; Pauley, "Fuse Just Waiting to Be Lit," 14. On the Monerville case, see Perera, "Police Accuse Doctors"; David Pallister, "'Victim of Police Attack' Is Cleared of Mugging," *Guardian* (London), August 10, 1988, 3.

58. Pauley, "Fuse Just Waiting to Be Lit," 14.

59. McCrystal, "Wrong Side of the Law," 12.

60. Duncan Campbell, "Spotlight/Guardian Libel Case: Fighting for Truth on the Front Line," *Guardian* (London), February 8, 1997, home section, 3.

61. Raju Bhatt, interview with the author, London, May 26, 2004.

62. Graham Smith, interview with the author, Nottingham, June 4, 2004.

63. Ibid.

64. Clare Dyer, "Police Agree to £20,000 Arrests Deal," *Guardian* (London), November 21, 1988.

65. David Pallister, "Woman Gets £8,000 Pounds after 'Rape' by PC," *Guardian* (London), August 1, 1989.

66. Rose, "Record Damages against Police." Although the case arose out of a west London neighborhood, it clearly shaped the legal climate in north and east London.

67. Terry Kirby, "Policing the Police: Elderly Couple 'Are Living in Fear after Attack by Officers,'" *Independent* (London), April 30, 1990, home news section, 3.

68. Kirby, "Policing the Police."

69. Graham Smith and Martin Walker, Letter, *Independent* (London), May 14, 1990, editorial page, 18.

70. Heather Mills and Rachel Borrill, "Closed Ranks on Both Sides; Not Guilty: The Tottenham Three's Triumph Has left Justice Tarnished and the Police in a Sombre Mood," *Independent* (London), December 1, 1991, inside story section, 19.

71. David Rose, "The Broadwater Farm Three: The Guilty of Scotland Yard," *Observer* (London), December 1, 1991, 22.

72. Heather Mills and David Connett, "Law Apologises for Blakelock Convictions," *Independent* (London), December 6, 1991, title page section, 1.

73. Robert Rice, "A Rapid Loss of Confidence," *Financial Times* (London), November 30, 1991, I6.

74. Duncan Campbell, "Drug Arrest Put Police in the Front Line," *Guardian* (London), July 11, 1992, home section, 3.

75. Smith, "Legacy of the Stoke Newington Scandal," 156–63.

76. Campbell, "Drug Arrest"; Terry Kirby, "Policeman 'Received £1,000 Drugs Wage,'" *Independent* (London), July 11, 1992, home news section, 2.

77. Duncan Campbell, "Police Suspected of Drugs Dealing," *Guardian* (London), January 31, 1992, home section, 1; Duncan Campbell, "Disquiet Dogs Community Police Station," *Guardian* (London), January 31, 1992, home news section, 2.

78. "Drugs, Denials, and the Ghosts Who Won't Go Away," *Evening Standard* (London), February 3, 1992, 14.

79. Duncan Campbell, "Thirty Officers Are Named as Group Seeks Judicial Inquiry into Policing," *Guardian* (London), February 8, 1992, home section, 2.

80. Ibid., 2.

81. Campbell, "Disquiet Dogs Community Police Station."

82. Campbell, "Thirty Officers," 1992.

83. Paul Myers and Duncan Campbell, "Woman, 73, Wins £50,000 against Met," *Guardian* (London), March 20, 1992, home section, 2.

84. Duncan Campbell, "Police Inquiry Plea to MP," *Guardian* (London), June 4, 1992, 6; Colin Brown, "Inquiry into Police 'May Affect Appeals,'" *Independent* (London), June 24, 1992, home section, 7.

85. Duncan Campbell, "Two Suspended after Police Inquiry," *Guardian* (London), June 24, 1992, home section, 2; Duncan Campbell, "Police Suspend Third Officer," *Guardian* (London), September 11, 1992, home section, 2.

86. Campell, "Drug Arrest."

87. McCrystal, "Wrong Side of the Law," 12.

88. Duncan Campbell, "Four Cleared of Police Drug 'Fit-Ups,'" *Guardian* (London), March 3, 1992, home section, 20.

89. Duncan Campbell, "DPP Gets New File on Police Station," *Guardian* (London), March 24, 1992, home section, 5.

90. McCrystal, "Wrong Side of the Law."

91. Campell, "Drug Arrest."

92. Duncan Campbell, "Police Station Cleared of Organized Drug-Dealing," *Guardian* (London), September 16, 1993, home section, 1.

93. Quoted in *Guardian* (London), November 8, 1993, home section, 2.

94. Quoted in Duncan Campbell, "Corruption Claims the 'Worst in 20 Years,'" *Guardian* (London), February 4, 1994, home section, 3.

95. "Police Could Face Criminal Charges after Drugs Inquiry," *Independent* (London), February 4, 1994, home section, 3.

96. Ibid.

97. Jason Bennetto, "Two Face Charges in Drugs Row Inquiry," *Independent* (London), July 27, 1994, home section, 4.

98. Smith, "Legacy of the Stoke Newington Scandal."

99. McCrystal, "Wrong Side of the Law."

100. Ibid.

101. Emily Barr, "Fair Cop?" *Guardian* (London), July 28, 1994, features section, T5.

102. Duncan Campbell, "Violent Arrest in Poll Tax Riot Costs Met £30,000," *Guardian* (London), January 13, 1995, home section, 8.

103. Ibid.

104. Ibid.

105. Tim Kelsey, "Shot Jogger Sues after 'Bungled Stake-Out,'" *Independent* (London), February 1, 1995, news section, 8.

106. See, e.g., "Police Pay £10,000 for 60p Arrest," *Times* (London), February 7, 1995; "£25,000 Pay-Out," *Independent* (London), February 28, 1995, home section, 4; "Limbo Dancer Wins Assault Damages," *Independent* (London), March 9, 1995, home section, 3.

107. Richard Ford, "Racial Arrest Victim Wins Police Damages," *Times* (London), March 17, home section.

108. Raju Bhatt, interview with the author, London, May 26, 2004.

109. See, e.g., Duncan Campbell, "Police to Pay for Drugs Lies: Victim of Fabricated Evidence and Malicious Prosecution Accepts £76,000," *Guardian* (London), December 12, 1995.

110. Raju Bhatt, interview with the author, London, May 26, 2004.

111. Heather Mills, "Complaints Cost Scotland Yard £1.5M to Settle," *Independent* (London), September 7, 1995, news section, 6.

112. Ibid.

113. Ibid.

114. Alan Travis, "Police 'Killed Woman with Gag,'" *Guardian* (London), May 16, 1995, home section, 3.

115. Will Bennett, "Officers Cleared of Gardner Killing," *Independent* (London), June 15, 1995, 1.

116. Alan Travis, "Joy Gardner Trio Escape Police Action," *Guardian* (London), July 13, 1995, home section, 2.

117. Ibid.

118. Jason Bennetto, "Verdict Opens Way for Action against Officers," *Independent* (London), November 11, 1995, news section, 7.

119. Heather Mills, "Police Chiefs 'Ignore Claims of Brutality,'" *Independent* (London), January 27, 1996, news section, 6.

120. Campbell, "Police to Pay for Drugs Lies," 9.

121. Ibid.

122. Jason Bennetto, "Met Chief Attacks Lawyers," *Independent* (London), August 2, 1994, title page, 1.

123. Ibid.

124. Ibid.

125. JoJo Moyes and Heather Mills, "Nigerian Killed Unlawfully by Police, Jury Says: A Force under Fire—Day of Shame for Scotland Yard as Inquest Finding Adds to Woe over Damages Defeat," *Independent* (London), January 26, 1996, news section, 2; Heather Mills, "Warnings about Neck Holds Failed to Prevent Death," *Independent* (London), January 26, 1996, news section, 2; Heather Mills, "Assault Case Settlement Costs £90,000," *Independent* (London), January 26, 1996, news section, 2.

126. Quoted in Mills, "Police Chiefs 'Ignore Claims of Brutality,'" 6.

127. Duncan Campbell, "Police Must Pay Record Damages," *Guardian* (London), March 29, 1996, home section, 5.

128. Ibid.

129. Quoted in ibid.

130. Heather Mills, "£220,000 Awarded to Police Assault Victim," *Independent* (London), March 29, 1996, news section, 11.

131. "Anger Grows at Soaring Cost of Police Assaults," *Independent* (London), March 30, 1996, news section, 6.

132. Ibid.

133. Quoted in ibid.

134. "Thuggery in Uniform," *Independent* (London), March 31, 1996, comment section, 20.

135. "Inquiry Call," *Sunday Times* (London), March 31, 1996, home section.

136. John Deane, "Civil Actions 'Will Not Deflect Police,'" *Press Association*, April 23, 1996, home news section.

137. Deane, "Civil Actions 'Will Not Deflect Police.'"

138. Richard Ford, "Policeman's Victim Awarded a Record £302,000 for Attack," *Times* (London), April 27, 1996, home news section. See also Jane Deighton and Sadiq Khan, "Brutal Cost of the Bill," *Guardian* (London), May 1, 1996, features section, 17.

139. Peter Victor, "Record Payout for Police Victim," *Independent* (London), April 27, 1996, 1.

140. Ibid.

141. "Police to Pay Man £108,000 Damages," *Independent* (London), April 30, 1996, news section, 7.

142. Deighton and Khan, "Brutal Cost of the Bill."

143. Sadiq Khan, "'Flawed' Inquiries into Police Conduct," *Times* (London), May 7, features section.

144. Nick Varley, "Victim of Beating by Police Wins £150,000," *Guardian* (London), June 5, 1996, home section, 5; Duncan Campbell, "Met Pays £150,000 after Assault on Kurd Refugees," *Guardian* (London), June 14, 1996, home section, 10; "Man Wins £27,500 after Police Assault," *Guardian* (London), July 12, 1996, home section, 4; Richard Ford, "Victim of Beating by Police Wins £125,000," *Times* (London), July 19, 1996, home news, 5; "Protester Gets £30,000," *Guardian* (London), July 25, 1996, home section, 6.

145. Paul Donovan, "Stoking the Fires of Resentment: There Is Concern at a 'Crisis of Accountability' over a Failure to Prosecute after Deaths in Police Custody," *Independent* (London), August 21, 1996, law section, 21.

146. Ibid.

147. Ibid.

148. Quoted in ibid.

149. Ibid.

150. "Yard Chief Warns against 'Stratospheric' Damages," *Press Association*, May 7, home news; see also Stewart Tendler, "Yard Wants Court to Set Limits on Damages Payouts," *Times* (London), May 7, 1996, home news section.

151. Duncan Campbell, "Court Claims Cut Police Strength," *Guardian* (London), June 3, 1996, home section, 5.

152. Quoted in Heather Mills, "Violence That Has Cost Scotland Yard £2M," *Observer* (London), July 21, 1996, news section, 8.

153. *Thompson and Hsu v. Commissioner of Police of the Metropolis* [1997] 2 *All England Reports* 762. The following discussion relies on Dixon and Smith, "Laying Down the Law."

154. See, e.g., Richard Ford, "Court Limits Exemplary Damages against Police," *Times* (London), February 20, home section; Patricia Wynn Davies, "Judges Curtail Juries' Ability to Punish Police Curbed by Court," *Independent* (London), February 20, news section, 9; Alan Travis, "Cap on Police Damages," *Guardian* (London), February 20, home section, 4.

155. Dixon and Smith, "Laying Down the Law."

156. Ibid.

157. *Thompson and Hsu v. Commissioner of Police of the Metropolis* [1997] 2 *All England Reports* 762, 777, quoted in Dixon and Smith, "Laying Down the Law," 429.

158. Mike Taylor and John Deane, "Mixed Reaction to Curb on Police Damages Awards," *Press Association*, February 19, home news.

159. Data on average awards obtained from the Metropolitan Police Force, on file with the author.

160. Clare Dyer, "Vicious Racism Costs Met £250,000: Respectable Family Man Abused, Assaulted and Falsely Accused," *Guardian* (London), February 1, 2003, home section, 6.

161. Her Majesty's Inspectorate of the Constabulary, *Winning the Race: Policing Plural Communities* (London: Her Majesty's Stationery Office, 1996–97), para. 2.9 and executive summary.

162. Clare Dyer, "Custody Deaths Provoke European Inquiry," *Guardian* (London), September 8, 1997, home section, 1; Clare Dyer, "DPP Loses Final Say on Deaths in Custody," *Guardian* (London), July 29, 1997, home section, 3.

163. Graham Smith, "Police Complaints and Criminal Prosecutions," *Modern Law Review* 65, 3 (2001): 372–92, at 382–85; "Up to 250 Yard Police 'Are Corrupt,'" *Times* (London), December 5, 1977, home news section.

164. William MacPherson, *The Stephen Lawrence Inquiry* (London: Her Majesty's Stationery Office, 1999).

165. Ibid., para. 6.34; the conclusion that British policing is subject to institutional racism was announced unequivocally in para. 6.39.

166. Ibid., para. 6.57.

167. Ibid., para. 45.12.

168. Ibid., para. 6.60.

169. Ibid., chap. 47.

170. A complete discussion of the agenda may be found in *Stephen Lawrence Inquiry—Home Secretary's Action Plan: First Annual Report on Progress* (London: Home Office, 2000); available at http://www.homeoffice.gov.uk/docs/slannrep.html.

171. For a valuable discussion of the implementation of the MacPherson Report, see Michael Rowe, *Policing, Race, and Racism* (Cullompton, Devon, UK: Willan Publishing, 2004).

172. "Guidance on Use of Handcuffs"; available at http://www.acpo.police.uk/asp/policies/Data/Guide_Use_Handcuffs_11x10x06.doc; and http://www.acpo.police.uk/asp/policies/Data/Guide_use_of_limb_restraints_11x10x06.doc (accessed February 19, 2008).

173. Nick Bland, Joel Miller, and Paul Quinton, "Managing the Use and Impact of Searches: A Review of Force Interventions," Police Research Series, paper 132, Home Office, esp. 9–19.

174. Her Majesty's Inspectorate of the Constabulary, *Winning the Race: Embracing Diversity* (HMIC Thematic Report) (London: HMIC, 2001), 2, quoted at 5.

175. Smith, "Legacy of the Stoke Newington Scandal."

176. "Halford Settles," *Guardian* (London), December 21, 1992, tabloid section, 4.

177. McCrystal, "Wrong Side of the Law."

178. John Beggs, interview with the author, London, May 26, 2004.

179. David Hamilton, head of legal services, Metropolitan Police, interview with the author, London, June 1, 2004

180. Ibid.

181. See, e.g., Tina Orr-Munro, "Safety Catch," *Police,* June 2005, 20–23.

182. Editorial, "What a Performance! Can Monitoring Deliver Better Policing?" *Police,* April 2003, 5.

183. Metropolitan Police Authority, *Report of the MPA Scrutiny on MPS Stop and Search Practice,* 5.

184. Ibid., 29–30.

185. Ibid., 35.

186. Ibid., 7, 43.

187. Commission for Racial Equality, *A Formal Investigation of the Police Service in England and Wales* (London: Commission for Racial Equality, 2004), 15.

188. "Let's Be Positive," *Police,* June 2003, 6–7 (reporting the remarks of Federation chair Jan Berry, defending the use of stops and searches and decrying the publication of statistics on racial disparities); Simon Reed, "Stop and Search: Facing Up to the Challenge of Our Strengths and Weaknesses," *Police,* January 2004, 6–7; and Simon Reed, "Stop and Search," *Police,* September 2004, 27.

189. Ray Powell, "Stop and Think," *Police*, September 2004, 26.

190. William Haltom and Michael McCann, *Distorting the Law: Politics, Media, and the Litigation Crisis* (Chicago: University of Chicago Press, 2004).

Chapter Eight

1. There are several excellent book-length studies of sexual harassment politics and policy, particularly the following: Carrie N. Baker, *The Women's Movement against Sexual Harassment* (New York: Cambridge University Press, 2008); Mia L. Cahill, *The Social Construction of Sexual Harassment Law: The Role of National, Organizational, and Individual Context* (Burlington, VT: Ashgate/Dartmouth, 2001); Abigail C. Saguy, *What Is Sexual Harassment? From Capitol Hill to the Sorbonne* (Berkeley: University of California Press, 2003); Vicki Schultz, "Reconceptualizing Sexual Harassment," *Yale Law Journal* 107 (1998): 1683–1805; Kathrin S. Zippel, *The Politics of Sexual Harassment: A Comparative Study of the United States, the European Union, and Germany* (New York: Cambridge University Press, 2006).

2. Walter K. Olson, *The Excuse Factory: How Employment Law Is Paralyzing the American Workplace* (New York: Martin Kessler/Free Press, 1997).

3. Frank Dobbin and Erin L. Kelly, "How to Stop Harassment: Professional Construction of Legal Compliance in Organizations," *American Journal of Sociology* 112, 4 (2007): 1203–43.

4. Baker, *Women's Movement against Sexual Harassment*. In addition, my discussion is indebted to a number of important analyses of the origins and institutional development of the sexual harassment concept and law, particularly Schultz, "Reconceptualizing Sexual Harassment," 1696ff., and Zippel, *Politics of Sexual Harassment*.

5. Lin Farley, *Sexual Shakedown* (New York: McGraw-Hill, 1978), xi–xiii; Susan Brownmiller, *In Our Time: Memoir of a Revolution* (New York: Dial Press, 1999), 281.

6. Farley, *Sexual Shakedown*, xi.

7. Baker, *Women's Movement against Sexual Harassment*, 32.

8. Ibid., 39–40.

9. Catharine MacKinnon, *Sexual Harassment of Working Women: A Case of Sex Discrimination* (New Haven, CT: Yale University Press, 1979), 248 n. 2; Farley, *Sexual Shakedown*, 70.

10. Alliance Against Sexual Coercion, *Fighting Sexual Harassment: An Advocacy Handbook* (Boston: Alyson Publications and Alliance Against Sexual Harassment, 1981).

11. Baker, *Women's Movement against Sexual Harassment*, 46.

12. In 1974, for instance, students at San Diego State University organized a workshop to speak out against sexual exploitation by professors; Farley, *Sexual Shakedown*, 70. In 1978 social service workers in the Minneapolis–St. Paul area formed the Coalition against Sexual Harassment, and about the same time, women sociology students at the University of California–Berkeley formed Women Organized against Sexual Harassment to press professors to stop using the "power of the grade" to gain sexual favors. James C. Renick, "Sexual Harassment at Work: Why It Happens, What to Do about It," *Personnel Journal*, August 1980, 659–62, at 652.

13. Deirdre Silverman, "Sexual Harassment: Working Women's Dilemma," *Quest: A Feminist Quarterly* 3 (1976–77): 15–24; Farley, *Sexual Shakedown*. See also Schultz, "Reconceptualizing Sexual Harassment," 1699.

14. Constance Backhouse and Leah Cohen, *The Secret Oppression: Sexual Harassment of Working Women* (Toronto: Macmillan, 1978). The book's copyright was 1978, but it was ultimately released in the spring of 1979, according to Baker, *Women's Movement against Sexual Harassment*, 195.

15. Alliance Against Sexual Coercion, *Fighting Sexual Harassment*.

16. See, generally, Elaine Lunsford Weeks, Jacqueline M. Boles, Albeno P. Garbin, and John Blount, "The Transformation of Sexual Harassment from a Private Trouble into a Public Issue," *Sociological Inquiry* 56 (1986): 432–55, at 433–34.

17. Enid Nemy, "Women Begin to Speak Out against Sexual Harassment at Work," *New York Times*, August 19, 1975, 38.

18. "Sex and the Legal Secretary," *Viva*, August 1976, 45; Claire Safran, "What Men Do to Women on the Job: A Shocking Look at Sexual Harassment," *Redbook*, November 1976, 19.

19. Karen Lindsey, "Sexual Harassment on the Job and How to Stop It," *Ms.* 6 (November 1977): 47–48, 50–51, 74–78; Mim Kelber, "Sexual Harassment . . . the UN's Dirty Little Secret," *Ms.* 6 (November 1977): 51, 79; Rochelle Lefkowitz, "Sexual Harassment on the Job: Help for the Sexually Harassed, a Grassroots Model," *Ms.* 6 (November 1977): 49; Letty Pogrebin, "Sex Harassment," *Ladies' Home Journal*, June 1977, 24, 28; Betty Harragan, *Games Mother Never Taught You* (New York: Warner Books, 1977), 366.

20. In 1978 *Ms.* reported excerpts from an outpouring of responses to its previous story about sexual harassment, and additional stories appeared in *Good Housekeeping*, *Redbook*, *Mother Jones*, *Chatelaine*, *McCall's*, and *Woman's Day*. See "Readers Tell What It's Like . . . and Lawyers Give Some Free Advice," *Ms.* 7 (July 1978): 86–88; Margaret Mead, "A Proposal: We Need Taboos on Sex at Work," *Redbook*, April 1978, 31–33; "My Boss Wanted More Than a Secretary," *Good Housekeeping* 186 (April 1978): 28; Caryl Rivers, "Sexual Harassment: The Executive's Alternative to Rape," *Mother Jones* 3 (June 1978): 21–24; Rhonda Rovan, "Sexual Harassment," *Chatelaine* 51 (August 1978): 16–18; M. Skrocki, "Sexual Pressure on the Job," *McCall's*, March 1978, 43; "Stop Apologizing When You say No," *Woman's Day* 23 (October 1978): 26.

21. Saguy, *What Is Sexual Harassment?* 186 n. 32.

22. Ibid.

23. *Williams v. Saxbe* 413 F. Supp. 654 (1976). See Weeks et al., "Transformation of Sexual Harassment," 434, 438. Another major decision, *Barnes v. Costle* 562 F. 2d 983 (1977), soon followed. See Schultz, "Reconceptualizing Sexual Harassment," 1703.

24. Weeks et al., "Transformation of Sexual Harassment," 438–39.

25. The House Committee on the Post Office and Civil Service held a hearing in 1979 titled "Sexual Harassment in the Federal Government" and carried the hearing over into the next year. The Senate Labor and Human Resources Committee held a hearing addressing sexual harassment in 1981. See Weeks et al., "Transformation of Sexual Harassment," 442–43.

26. Baker, *Women's Movement against Sexual Harassment*, 112–16.

27. Weeks et al., "Transformation of Sexual Harassment," 441.

28. MacKinnon, *Sexual Harassment of Working Women*.

29. Backhouse and Cohen, *Secret Oppression*.

30. Constance Backhouse, interview with the author, Montreal, May 31, 2008.

31. Ibid. (Cohen passed away several years ago).

32. The following material is drawn from the author's interview with Constance Backhouse in Montreal, Quebec, May 31, 2008.

33. Backhouse and Cohen, *Secret Oppression*.

34. Backhouse and Cohen, *Secret Oppression*, 184–93.

35. Ibid., 185–86.

36. Ibid.

37. Ibid., 186.

38. Ibid., 186–88.

39. Ibid., 186–87.

40. Constance Backhouse, interview with the author, Montreal, May 31, 2008.

41. Ibid.

42. Ibid.

43. See, e.g., Farley, *Sexual Shakedown*, 126–27; Alliance Against Sexual Coercion, *Fighting Sexual Harassment*.

44. See, e.g., Farley, *Sexual Shakedown*, 127–31.

45. Ibid., 3–10.

46. Farley, *Sexual Shakedown*, 131–33.

47. Alliance Against Sexual Coercion, *Fighting Sexual Harassment*, 46.

48. Mead, "Proposal," 31–33.

49. The EEOC published interim guidelines on April 11, 1980, and final guidelines on November 10, 1980. EEOC Guidelines on Sex Discrimination 29 C.F.R. 1604.11 (1980).

50. In 1977 the U.S. Department of Labor, in response to growing complaints from female construction workers, had adopted regulations requiring construction contractors to eliminate harassment, intimidation, and coercion at their work sites; reported in Backhouse and Cohen, *Secret Oppression*, 43.

51. Farley, *Sexual Shakedown*, xii.

52. Quoted in Joan Steinau Lester, *Eleanor Holmes Norton: Fire in My Soul* (New York: Atria, 2003), 208.

53. EEOC Guidelines, 29 C.F.R. 1604.11f.

54. The Guidelines stated that in cases of harassment by supervisors, employers are "responsible" (thus, possibly legally liable) "whether the specific acts complained of were authorized or even forbidden by the employer," 29 C.F.R. 1604.11.

55. EEOC Guidelines, 29 C.F.R. 1604.11.

56. *Brown v. City of Guthrie* 22 Fair Empl. Prac. Cas. (BNA) 1627 (W.D. Okla. 1980); *Bundy v. Jackson* 641 F.2d 934. See Baker, *Women's Movement against Sexual Harassment*, 120.

57. Baker, *Women's Movement against Sexual Harassment*, 120.

58. Ibid., 136–38.

59. Ibid., 138–39.

60. Ibid., 140.

61. The Court's sexual harassment decisions impose particular requirements on employers related to education and prevention of sexual harassment. In a key 1975 decision, the Court ruled that federal antidiscrimination law, much like tort law, has the dual purpose of compensating victims of discrimination and inducing employers to act proactively to minimize discrimination in their workplaces. In the Court's view, a key purpose of requiring employers to compensate employees who experienced discrimination resulting from employer action (or inaction) is deterrence, or

inducing reform of policies and practices. See *Albemarle Paper Co. vs. Moody* 422 U.S. 405 (1975).

62. *Faragher v. City of Boca Raton* 524 U.S. 775 (1998); *Burlington Industries v. Ellerth* 524 U.S. 742 (1998).

63. The International Public Management Association for Human Resources primarily serves personnel administrators in public agencies, and its official journal has a somewhat academic tone; the former serves both the private and public sectors, and its official journal has a more popular format similar to *Police Chief*.

64. For comparison, see Dobbin and Kelly, "How to Stop Harassment."

65. Jacoby, *Employing Bureaucracy*, 10–28.

66. Ibid., 15, 30–73, 86–122.

67. Ibid., 94–98.

68. Scholars disagree somewhat on the timing of this diffusion. Jacoby times the period of greatest growth to the late 1930s and attributes it to the influence of the Wagner Act and firms' attempts to use personnel management reforms to head off the growth of unions (*Employing Bureaucracy*, 166–204). By contrast, Baron, Dobbin, and Jennings date the fastest growth to the World War II years and attribute it to government pressure to rationalize production in the context of wartime needs. See James N. Baron, Frank R. Dobbin, and P. Devereaux Jennings, "War and Peace: The Evolution of Modern Personnel Administration in U.S. Industry," *American Journal of Sociology* 92, 2 (1986): 350–83; the 75 percent figure is from table 1, 354.

69. Quoted in Sanford Jacoby, *Employing Bureaucracy: Managers, Unions, and the Transformation of Work in the 20th Century* (Mahwah, NJ: Lawrence Erlbaum, 2004), 97.

70. Baron, Dobbin, and Jennings, "War and Peace," 375.

71. Jacoby, *Employing Bureaucracy*, 210–17.

72. Ibid., 211–12.

73. Ibid., 212.

74. Alliance Against Sexual Coercion, *Fighting Sexual Harassment*, 80.

75. Backhouse and Cohen, *Secret Oppression*, 90.

76. Ibid., 73–90.

77. Quoted in ibid., 82.

78. Quoted in ibid., 84.

79. Benson Rosen and Thomas H. Jerdee, "On-the-Job Sex Bias: Increasing Managerial Awareness," *Personnel Administrator*, January 1977, 15–18.

80. Patricia A. Somers and Judith Clementson-Mohr, "Sexual Extortion in the Workplace," *Personnel Administrator*, April 1979, 23–28, at 23, quoting management consultant Betty Harragan.

81. Renick, "Sexual Harassment at Work," 661.

82. Robert A. Holmes, "What's Ahead for Personnel Professionals in the '80s?" *Personnel Administrator*, June 1980, 33–37, 82–84.

83. Kathryn Thurston, "Sexual Harassment: An Organizational Perspective," *Personnel Administrator*, December 1980, 59–64.

84. George E. Biles, "A Program Guide for Preventing Sexual Harassment in the Workplace," *Personnel Administrator*, June 1981, 49–56.

85. See, e.g., Somers and Clementson-Mohr, "Sexual Extortion in the Workplace"; Renick, "Sexual Harassment at Work"; Holmes, "What's Ahead for Personnel Professionals?" Thurston, "Sexual Harassment"; and Paul S. Greenlaw and John P. Kohl,

"Sexual Harassment: Homosexuality, Bisexuality and Blackmail," *Personnel Administrator*, June 1981, 59–62.

86. Holmes, "What's Ahead for Personnel Professionals?"

87. Sandra Sawyer and Arthur A. Whatley, "Sexual Harassment: A Form of Sex Discrimination," *Personnel Administrator*, January 1980, 36–38.

88. Thurston, "Sexual Harassment," 59–64.

89. Kaleel Jamison, "Managing Sexual Attraction in the Workplace," *Personnel Administrator*, August 1983, 45–51.

90. Somers and Clementson-Mohr, "Sexual Extortion in the Workplace"; Jennifer James, "Sexual Harassment," *Public Personnel Management* 10, 4 (1981): 402–7.

91. Biles, "Program Guide for Preventing Sexual Harassment."

92. See, e.g., Somers and Clementson-Mohr 1979; Renick, "Sexual Harassment at Work."

93. Ibid., 23–28.

94. Sawyer and Whatley, "Sexual Harassment," 36–38.

95. See Holmes, "What's Ahead for Personnel Professionals?" 82–84; Thurston, "Sexual Harassment," 59–64; Renick, "Sexual Harassment at Work," 658–62; Michele Hoyman and Ronda Robinson, "Interpreting the New Sexual Harassment Guidelines," *Personnel Journal*, December 1980, 996–99.

96. Hoyman and Robinson, "Interpreting the New Sexual Harassment Guidelines."

97. Biles, "Program Guide for Preventing Sexual Harassment," 49–56.

98. James, "Sexual Harassment."

99. Ibid., 406.

100. George K. Kronenberger and David L. Bourke, "Effective Training and the Elimination of Sexual Harassment," *Personnel Journal*, November 1981, 879–83, at 879.

101. Jeanne Bossom Discoll, "Sexual Attraction and Harassment: Management's New Problems," *Personnel Journal*, January 1981, 33–36, 56, at 35.

102. Donald J. Petersen and Douglas Massengill, "Sexual Harassment: A Growing Problem in the Workplace," *Personnel Administrator*, October 1982, 799-89.

103. Thurston, "Sexual Harassment."

104. John F. Wymer, "Compensatory and Punitive Damages for Sexual Harassment," *Personnel Journal*, March 1983, 181–84, at 182, 184; Margaret S. Garvey, "The High Cost of Sexual Harassment Suits," *Personnel Journal*, January 1986, 75–80, at 75.

105. To be sure, there were some new sources of information on the topic, particularly a book: Kenneth C. Cooper, *Stop It Now: How Targets and Managers Can End Sexual Harassment* (St. Louis, MO: Total Communications Press, 1985).

106. David S. Bradshaw, "Sexual Harassment: Confronting the Troublesome Issues," *Personnel Administrator*, January 1987, 51–53.

107. Dawn Bennett-Alexander, "Sexual Harassment in the Office," *Personnel Administrator*, June 1988, 174–87.

108. David Terpstra, "Who Gets Sexually Harassed?" *Personnel Administrator*, March 1989, 84–88, 111.

109. Jonathan A. Segal, "Safe Sex: A Workplace Oxymoron?" *HRMagazine*, June 1990, 175–80; see also Robert C. Ford and Frank S. McLaughlin, "Should Cupid Come to the Workplace?" *Personnel Administrator*, October 1987, 100–110.

110. Segal, "Safe Sex."

111. See, e.g., Samuel J. Bresler and Rebecca Thacker, "Four-Point Plan Helps to Solve Harassment Problems," *HRMagazine*, May 1993, 117–21; Jonathan A. Segal, "Proceed Carefully, Objectively to Investigate Sexual Harassment Claims," *HRMagazine*, October 1993, 91–94; Gerald D. Bloch, "Avoiding Liability for Sexual Harassment," *HRMagazine*, April 1995, 91–95; Rebecca K. Spar, "Keeping Internal Investigations Confidential," *HRMagazine*, January 1996, 33–35; Jonathan A. Segal, "Where Are We Now?" *HRMagazine*, October 1996, 68–73; Anthony M. Townsend, Robert J. Aalberts, and Michael E. Whitman, "Danger on the Desktop," *HRMagazine*, January 1997, 82–85; Debbie Rodman Sandler, "Sexual Harassment Rulings: Less Than Meets the Eye," *HRMagazine*, October 1998, 137–42.

112. John Montoya, "Who Should Investigate Sexual Harassment Complaints?" *HRMagazine*, January 1998, 113–17.

113. Paul Falcone, "Adopt a Formal Approach to Progressive Discipline," *HRMagazine*, November 1998, 55–58.

114. See, e.g., Jonathan A. Segal, "Love: What's Work Got to Do with It?" *HRMagazine*, June 1993, 36–40; Lee A. Graf and Masoud Hemmsai, "Risqué Humor: How It Really Affects the Workplace," *HRMagazine*, November 1995, 65–68; Jonathan A. Segal, "The World May Welcome Lovers . . . ," *HRMagazine*, June 1996, 170–76; Gerald Skoning, "Explanations of Sexual Harassment: Are They Viable Defenses?" *HRMagazine*, July 1998, 130–34.

115. Anthony M. Townsend and Harsh K. Luthar, "How Do the Men Feel?" *HRMagazine*, May 1995, 92–95.

116. *Oncale v. Sundowner Offshore Services* (523 U.S. 75, 1998). Kenneth M. Jarin and Ellen K. Pomfret, "New Rules for Same Sex Harassment," *HRMagazine*, June 1998, 114–21.

117. Sybil Evans, "Conflict Can Be Positive," *HRMagazine*, May 1992, 49–51. Ann Meyer, "Getting to the Heart of Sexual Harassment," *HRMagazine*, July 1992, 82–84, encouraged making complaints easier.

118. Segal, "Where are We Now?"

119. Charlene Marmer Solomon, "Sexual Harassment after the Thomas Hearings," *Personnel Journal*, December 1991, 32–37.

120. Maureen Minehan, "Employment Litigation an Ongoing Concern," *HRMagazine*, August 1997, 144.

121. Elaine McShulskis, "Sexual Harassment Complaints on the Rise," *HRMagazine*, February 1998, 28.

122. Segal, "Where Are We Now?" 73.

123. Jonathan A. Segal, "The Catch-22s of Remedying Sexual Harassment Complaints," *HRMagazine*, October 1997, 111–17.

124. Paul J. Champagne, R. Bruce McAfee, and Phillip B. Moberg, "A Workplace of Mutual Respect," *HRMagazine*, October 1992, 78–80.

125. Jonathan A. Segal, "The Defenselessness of Sexual Harassment," *HRMagazine*, May 1994, 31–35.

126. Theresa Donahue Egler, "Five Myths about Sexual Harassment," *HRMagazine*, January 1995, 27–30.

127. Jonathan A. Segal, "Ignorance Is No Defense," *HRMagazine*, April 1990, 93–94. For another example, which did not address sexual harassment directly, see Stephen L. Guinn, "Surveys Capture Untold Story," *HRMagazine*, September 1990, 64–66.

128. Meyer, "Getting to the Heart of Sexual Harassment."

129. Champagne, McAfee, and Moberg, "Workplace of Mutual Respect," 78–80.

130. Kate Walter, "Ethics Hot Lines Tap into More Than Wrongdoing," *HRMagazine*, September 1995, 79–83.

131. Tony Cornish, ed., *Zero Tolerance: An Employer's Guide to Preventing Sexual Harassment and Healing the Workplace* (Washington, DC: Bureau of National Affairs Communication, 1997).

132. Gloria G. Harris and David A. Tansey, "Relearning Relationships," *HRMagazine*, September 1997, 116–18.

133. Ibid.

134. Thus, see Jarin and Pomfret, "New Rules for Same Sex Harassment"; Paul Gibson, "The Future of Sexual Harassment Suits," *HRMagazine*, October 1998, 142–43; and Sandler, "Sexual Harassment Rulings," 137–42.

135. Jonathan A. Segal, "Prevent Now or Pay Later," *HRMagazine*, October 1998, 145–48.

136. Marjorie A. Johnson, "Use Anti-harassment Training to Shelter Yourself from Suits," *HRMagazine*, October 1999, 76–80.

137. Segal, "Prevent Now or Pay Later."

138. Cecily A. Waterman, "Update Handbooks to Avoid Risk," *HRMagazine*, November 1992, 97–99. See also Jonathan Segal, "Is Your Employee Handbook a Time Bomb?" *HRMagazine*, August 1993, 95–99.

139. Jonathan Segal, "EEO Policies: Walking a Razor's Edge," *HRMagazine*, December 1997, 109–13, at 109.

140. Dobbin and Kelly, "How to Stop Harassment."

141. This discussion draws on Gutek, "Sexual Harassment Policy Initiatives," 189–90.

142. Ibid., 189; Ellen R. Peirce, Benson Rosen, and Tammy Bunn Hiller, "Breaking the Silence: Creating User-Friendly Sexual Harassment Policies," *Employee Responsibilities and Rights Journal* 10, 3 (1997): 225–42, at 239.

143. See Gutek, "Sexual Harassment Policy Initiatives," 193–95.

144. See, e.g., Susan Bisom-Rapp, "An Ounce of Prevention Is a Poor Substitute for a Pound of Cure: Confronting the Developing Jurisprudence of Education and Prevention in Employment Discrimination Law," *Berkeley Journal of Employment and Labor Law* 22 (2001): 1–46.

145. Using either ordered logit or ordered probit, pseudo R^2 is .018 for a model employing the total number of employees to explain variation in the disciplinary action index.

146. The index contains observations for 357 cases (cases with missing data on any item are dropped from the index) and has a Cronbach's alpha of .72. Factor analysis using the principal factors method confirms that the index has one primary dimension; the eigenvalue for the first factor is 2.18, while the eigenvalue for the second factor is .23 and that for the third is .03. These tests confirm the value of the index as a measure of a common underlying, shared pattern among cities in adoption of the elements of the legalized accountability model.

147. Cronbach's alpha for the index is .83.

148. The measure consists of an index of attorneys specializing in each of the listed areas. The data source is the Martindale-Hubbell directory of attorneys, accessed at www.martindale.com at the time I administered the survey, and the data on attorneys

by locality consisted of those who declared a specialty of "government." A typical attorney declaring this specialty, for instance, also specialized in "Plaintiff's Personal Injury Law; Medical Malpractice; Products Liability Law; Automobile Accident; Environmental Law; Qui Tam Litigation." Such attorneys are precisely the sort who are likely to have the knowledge and skills necessary to pursue a lawsuit against a local government. Almost all such attorneys are in private practice, not government employment. Both these measures—managers' perceptions of the strength of the rights infrastructure and the objective number of government-liability attorneys in the city—have some strengths and weaknesses. The perceptual measure captures the presence of both attorneys and citizen groups; the objective measure is an indication only of the number of attorneys. The perceptual measure reflects the usual biases associated with perceptions, but if the theory of this book is correct it is perceptions of the legal environment that matter. On the other hand, the senior manager answering the survey may not be as familiar with the true availability of attorneys as would a member of the department's policy planning staff, and so the objective measure may in some respects provide a more accurate indicator of the local legal environment as experienced by departmental policymakers. Finally, the perceptual measure captures the relative presence of attorneys and citizen groups even if they are not within the city's jurisdiction; the objective measure captures only those attorneys whose offices are within that jurisdiction.

149. Here I have defined a "strong" local support structure as being at the seventy-fifth percentile on managers' perceptions of the availability of local attorneys and citizen groups who support sexual harassment lawsuits, and three local attorneys (logged scale) who list a specialty in government law in the Martindale-Hubbell lawyer registry.

150. I have defined "weak" connections to professional networks as having no human resources department or official and no equal employment opportunity office or official (a common scenario) and as being at the twenty-fifth percentile on my measure of the strength of connections to external professional HR/personnel administration associations. I have defined "strong" connections as having both a human resources department and an equal employment opportunity office or official and as being at the seventy-fifth percentile on my measure of the strength of connections to professional associations.

Chapter Nine

1. Benjamin H. Barton, "Tort Reform, Innovation, and Playground Design," *Florida Law Review* 58 (2006): 265–302.

2. Phillip K. Howard, "Lawsuits Are Drowning America," *USA Today Magazine*, March 1, 2003, 20; Susan Levine, "The Fall of the High Dive: Liability Concerns Prompt Pools to Scrap the Beloved Three-Meter Board," *Washington Post*, July 13, 2002, B1.

3. Carl T. Bogus, "Fear-Mongering Torts and the Exaggerated Death of Diving," *Harvard Journal of Law and Public Policy* 28 (2004): 17–37.

4. Joe L. Frost, *Play and Playscapes* (Albany, NY: Delmar, 1992), 112–14.

5. Ibid., 122.

6. Ibid.

7. Ibid., 120–22.

8. Ibid., 117–20.

9. Ibid., 122–25, 192–94.

10. Ibid., 198–200.

11. Ibid., 125–28.

12. Arvid Bengtsson, *Adventure Playgrounds* (London: Crosby Lockwood Staples, 1972).

13. Frost, *Play and Playscapes,* 201.

14. Ibid.

15. Ibid.

16. Ibid., 202.

17. Advertisement for Game Time play equipment by Toro, *Parks and Recreation,* December 1973, back cover.

18. Frost, *Play and Playscapes,* 202–3.

19. Ibid.

20. National Recreation and Parks Association, *Proposed Safety Standard for Public Playground Equipment* (Arlington, VA: Consumer Product Safety Commission, 1976). The quotation is from Frost, *Play and Playscapes,* 203.

21. Consumer Product Safety Commission, *A Handbook for Public Playground Safety*: vol. 1, *General Guidelines for New and Existing Playgrounds,* vol. 2, *Technical Guidelines for Equipment and Surfacing* (Washington, DC: U.S. Government Printing Office, 1981). See Frost, *Play and Playscapes,* 203.

22. Frances Wallach, "Playground Safety: The Long Trail," *Parks and Recreation,* April 1995, 61–67.

23. Ray Hall, "Security, Safety: Two Sides of the Coin," *Parks and Recreation,* December 1971, 22, 45–48, at 46.

24. Arthur Frakt, "Putting Recreation Programming and Liability in Perspective," *Parks and Recreation,* December 1979, 43–47, at 46. See also Janna Rankin, "Legal Risks and Bold Programming," *Parks and Recreation,* July 1977, 47–48, 67–69; George F. Nickolaus, "Liability in Parks and Recreation," *Parks and Recreation,* February 1980, 46, 52–56; and Betty Van Der Smissen, "Where Is Legal Liability Heading?" *Parks and Recreation,* May 1980, 50–52, 81.

25. Rankin, "Legal Risks and Bold Programming," 47–48, 67–69; see also "Lightning: The Enemy Above," *Parks and Recreation,* July 1978, 22, and Albert M. Farina, "Accident Liability: What Is Your Legal Responsibility?" *Parks and Recreation,* March 1979, 28–31, 50–51, at 28.

26. Diana R. Dunn and John M. Gulbis, "The Risk Revolution," *Parks and Recreation,* August 1976, 12–17, at 16.

27. Frakt, "Putting Recreation Programming and Liability in Perspective," 44.

28. James C. Kozlowski, "Are You Familiar with the Public Playground Safety Guidelines?" *Parks and Recreation,* September 1987, 16–22.

29. Stuart M. Statler, "CPCS: Only a Beginning," *Trial,* November 1980, 77–81, at 77.

30. Frances Wallach, "An Update on the Playground Safety Movement," *Parks and Recreation,* April 1996, 47–52, at 48.

31. See, e.g., Neil J. Dougherty, "Legal Liability: The Role of the Expert Witness," *Parks and Recreation,* January 1982, 68–69.

32. James L. Kozlowski, "NRPA Law Review," *Parks and Recreation,* January 1985, 28.

33. Ralph A. Winter, "The Liability Insurance Market," *Journal of Economic Perspectives* 5, 3 (1991): 115–36.

34. Editorial, "The Liability Crisis," *Parks and Recreation*, February 1986, 32.

35. Amanda Tiffany, "How to Tame the Liability Monster," *Parks and Recreation*, January 1987, 64–69, 103.

36. Bonnie Direnfeld-Michael and David R. Michael, "Everything You Ought to Know about the Liability Insurance Crisis but Didn't Know How to Ask," *Parks and Recreation*, January 1987, 74–79.

37. James C. Kozlowski, "A Common Sense View of Liability," *Parks and Recreation*, September 1988, 56–59, at 56 and 58.

38. See, e.g., Tiffany, "How to Tame the Liability Monster"; James C. Kozlowski, "A 'Cut and Paste' of Model Rec Use Law to Include Public," *Parks and Recreation*, March 1987, 22–28.

39. Bonnie Direnfeld-Michael, "A Risk Management Primer for Recreators," *Parks and Recreation*, March 1989, 40–45, at 40.

40. Kozlowski, "Are You Familiar with the Public Playground Safety Guidelines?" 16. I found one earlier reference to the CPSC standards, also in 1987, in Tiffany, "How to Tame the Liability Monster," 66, in the context of new efforts at liability reduction.

41. "Case Studies: Three from the Field," *Parks and Recreation*, January 1987, 69–72, at 71.

42. Paul Hogan, *The Playground Safety Checker: A Checklist Approach to Risk Management* (Phoenixville, PA: Playground Press, 1988); Sally McIntyre, Susan M. Goltsman, and Lowell Kline, *Safety First Checklist: The Site Inspection System for Play Equipment* (Berkeley, CA: MIG Communications, 1989).

43. Frances Wallach, "Playground Safety Update," *Parks and Recreation*, August 1990, 46–50, at 50.

44. Kozlowski, "Are You Familiar with the Public Playground Safety Guidelines?"

45. Ibid., 16.

46. William J. Burke, "Designing Safer Playgrounds," *Parks and Recreation*, September 1987, 38–43, 73, at 42.

47. Frances Wallach, "Are We Teaching Playground Abuse?" *Parks and Recreation*, October 1988, 34–36.

48. Travis L. Teague, "Playgrounds: Managing Your Risk," *Parks and Recreation*, April 1996, 55–60, at 55.

49. Ibid.

50. Kozlowski, "Common Sense View of Liability," 56.

51. Al Goldfarb, "These Doctors Make House Calls," *Parks and Recreation*, October 1987, 44–46, 63.

52. Ibid.

53. Ken Kutska, "Public Playground Safety: Paradigm or Paradox?" *Parks and Recreation*, April 1994, 47–52, at 49.

54. Ibid., 49–51.

55. Ibid., 51.

56. Direnfeld-Michael, "Risk Management Primer for Recreators," 40.

57. See, e.g., "Risk Management: The Defensive Game Plan," *Parks and Recreation*, September 1988, 53–55; full-page advertisement for the "NRPA Pacific Risk Management School," *Parks and Recreation*, August 1996, 3; Teague, "Playgrounds."

58. Stephen Langendorfer, Dianna P. Gray, and Lawrence D. Bruya, "Children's Aquatics: Managing the Risk," *Parks and Recreation,* February 1989, 20–24.

59. Kozlowski, "Are You Familiar with the Public Playground Safety Guidelines?"

60. James P. Donovan, "Playground Surfacing: What Are Your Choices?" *Parks and Recreation,* September 1987, 34–37.

61. Burke, "Designing Safer Playgrounds," 43.

62. Seymour Gold, "The New Experts on Safety," *Parks and Recreation,* November 1991, 50–53.

63. See, e.g., Kutska, "Public Playground Safety," and Joe L. Frost, "Preventing Playground Injuries and Litigation," *Parks and Recreation,* April 1994, 53–60.

64. Wallach, "Playground Safety: The Long Trail"; Kenneth F. Kutska and Thomas M. Kalousek, "A Vision for the Future: Working toward Safer Playgrounds," *Parks and Recreation,* April 2000, 92–95.

65. Frances Wallach, "Playground Safety Update," *Parks and Recreation,* August 1990, 46–50, at 50.

66. Kutska, "Public Playground Safety," 51.

67. Jensen Mogens, "Playground Safety: Is It Child's Play?" *Parks and Recreation,* August 1990, 36–38, at 37.

68. Gold, "New Experts on Safety," 50–53.

69. Frances Wallach, "Answers to Your Playground Surface," *Parks and Recreation,* March 1989, 34–38.

70. See, e.g., Frost, "Preventing Playground Injuries and Litigation."

71. Kutska, "Public Playground Safety," 47.

72. Frances Wallach, "Old Playgrounds, New Problems," *Parks and Recreation,* April 1993, 46–50, 91; Wallach, "Playground Safety: The Long Trail," 61–67.

73. James A. Peterson, "Playground Safety and Height: The Real Issue?" *Parks and Recreation,* April 1992, 32–39.

74. Frances Wallach, "Playground Safety: What Did We Do Wrong?" *Parks and Recreation,* April 1992, 52–57, 83, at 56.

75. James C. Kozlowski, "Playground Safety Maintenance Guidelines: The Next Generation," *Parks and Recreation,* April 1993, 30–35, 90.

76. Frances Wallach, "Playgrounds and Standards," *Parks and Recreation,* April 1994, 44–45.

77. Seymour M. Gold, "Inspecting Playgrounds for Hazards," *Parks and Recreation,* August 1991, 32–35.

78. Teague, "Playgrounds."

79. Frost, "Preventing Playground Injuries and Litigation," 57.

80. Ibid., 53; for a similar analysis, see Monty Christiansen, "An Evaluation of Playground Management," *Parks and Recreation,* April 1999, 74–82.

81. Wallach, "Playground Safety: The Long Trail"; Monty L. Christiansen, "Certification for Safety Inspectors, Not Playgrounds," *Parks and Recreation,* April 1994, 62–65; Wallach, "Update on the Playground Safety Movement," 51; Teresa B. Hendy, "National Playground Safety Institute Certified Playground Safety Inspectors: Who Are They and Where Did They Come From?" *Parks and Recreation,* April 1998, 33–37; Kutska and Kalousek, "Vision for the Future," 92–95.

82. Wallach, "Update on the Playground Safety Movement," 51; Hendy, "National Playground Safety Institute Certified Playground Safety Inspectors," 33–37.

83. Steve King, "Prevent Playground Injuries with Professional Inspection," *Parks and Recreation*, April 1996, 62–67.

84. Walter Henderson, "Catching Kids When they Fall: Guidelines to Choosing a Playground Surface," *Parks and Recreation*, April 1997, 84–92.

85. Hendy, "National Playground Safety Institute Certified Playground Safety Inspectors; Dave Parker, "Checkin' It Twice: Playground Maintenance Is Crucial for Safe Areas for Child's Play," *Parks and Recreation*, April 2000, 96–99.

86. Christiansen, "Evaluation of Playground Management," 74–82.

87. Parker, "Checkin' It Twice," 99.

88. Susan D. Hudson, Donna Thompson, and Mick Mack, "America's Playgrounds: Make Them Safe!" *Parks and Recreation*, April 1997, 69–72.

89. Arlene Brett, Robin C. Moore, and Eugene F. Provenzo, *The Complete Playground Book* (Syracuse, NY: Syracuse University Press, 1993); Frost, *Play and Playscapes*; Robin C. Moore, Susan M. Goltsman, and Daniel S. Iacofano, *Play for All Guidelines: Planning, Design, and Management of Outdoor Play Settings for All Children* (Berkeley, CA: MIG Communications, 1987); Leonard E. Phillips, *Parks: Design and Management* (New York: McGraw-Hill, 1996).

90. Monty Christiansen, "International Perspectives of Playground Safety," *Parks and Recreation*, April 1997, 100–101.

91. Susan D. Hudson, Mick Mack, and Donna Thompson, *How Safe Are America's Playgrounds? A National Profile of Childcare, School and Park Playgrounds* (Cedar Falls, IA: Program for Playground Safety, University of Northern Iowa, School of Health, Physical Education, and Leisure Services, 2000).

92. Unlike policing and personnel management, however, in the area of playground safety the availability of government liability attorneys, as measured by their listings locally in the Martindale-Hubbell lawyer registry, is not significantly associated with adoption of the legalized accountability model.

93. The index consists of removing play equipment or ground covering that is proscribed by the CPSC guidelines and of how far playgrounds managed by the agency have conditions proscribed by the guidelines. Results are reported in the methodological appendix. The relationship approaches statistical significance ($p < .1$).

94. Teague, "Playgrounds," 60.

Chapter Ten

1. Stuart Scheingold, *The Politics of Rights: Lawyers, Public Policy, and Political Change* (New Haven, CT: Yale University Press, 1974).

2. See, e.g., Doug McAdam, Sidney Tarrow, and Charles Tilly, *Dynamics of Contention* (New York: Cambridge University Press, 2001).

3. Frank Dobbin and Erin L. Kelly, "How to Stop Harassment: Professional Construction of Legal Compliance in Organizations," *American Journal of Sociology* 112, 4 (2007): 1203–43; Lauren B. Edelman, Christopher Uggen, and Howard S. Erlanger, "The Endogeneity of Legal Regulation: Grievance Procedures as Rational Myth," *American Journal of Sociology* 105, 2 (1999): 406–54; see also Lauren Edelman and Marc C. Suchman, "The Legal Environments of Organizations," *Annual Review of Sociology* 23 (1997): 479.

4. William Haltom and Michael McCann, *Distorting the Law: Politics, Media, and the Litigation Crisis* (Chicago: University of Chicago Press, 2004).

5. Lauren B. Edelman, "Legal Ambiguity and Symbolic Structures: Organizational Mediation of Civil Rights Law," *American Journal of Sociology* 97 (1992): 1531–76; Lauren B. Edelman, "Legal Environments and Organizational Governance: The Expansion of Due Process in the American Workplace," *American Journal of* Sociology 95, 6 (1990): 1401–40.

6. Neil Gunningham, Robert A. Kagan, and Dorothy Thornton, "Social License and Environmental Protection: Why Businesses Go Beyond Compliance," *Law and Social Inquiry* 29, 2 (2004): 307.

7. See, e.g., Michael Lounsbury, Marc Ventresca, and Paul M. Hirsch, "Social Movements, Field Frames, and Industry Emergence: A Cultural-Political Perspective on U.S. Recycling," *Socio-economic Review* 1, 1 (2003): 71–104; David Levy and Maureen Scully, "The Institutional Entrepreneur as Modern Prince: The Strategic Face of Power in Contested Fields," *Organization Studies* 28 (2007): 971–91.

8. Tom Baker, *The Medical Malpractice Myth* (Chicago: University of Chicago Press, 2005), 106–10.

9. See Karen Orren, "Officers' Rights: Toward a Unified Field Theory of American Constitutional Development," *Law and Society Review* 34, 4 (2000): 873–909.

10. Craig B. Futterman, H. Melissa Mather, and Melanie Miles, "The Use of Statistical Evidence to Address Police Supervisory and Disciplinary Practices: The Chicago Police Department's Broken System"; available at http://www.law.uchicago.edu/files/brokensystem-111407.pdf, 2008, 15–16 (accessed April 26, 2008).

11. Futterman, Mather, and Miles, "Use of Statistical Evidence," 21–23.

12. Ibid., 15–16.

13. Ibid., 32.

14. Jamie Kalven, "Kicking the Pigeon," http://www.viewfromtheground.com/wp-content/media/ktp/kicking_the_pigeon.pdf (accessed April 16, 2009). See also Kari Lydersen, "Chicago's Police Problem: Despite a Long History of Scandals and Abuse, the City Has Yet to Discipline and Reform Its Police Department," *Free Library* (May 1, 2007), http://www.thefreelibrary.com/Chicago's police problem: despite a long history of scandals, -a0163530704 (accessed April 16, 2009).

15. This line of scholarship is admirably summarized and analyzed in Bradley C. Canon and Charles A. Johnson, *Judicial Policies: Implementation and Impact*, 2nd ed. (Washington, DC: CQ Press, 1999). See also, e.g., Michael Wald et al., "Interrogations in New Haven: The Impact of Miranda," *Yale Law Journal* 76 (1967): 1519–1748; Richard A. Leo Jr., "Miranda's Revenge: Police Interrogation as a Confidence Game," *Law and Society Review* 30 (1996): 259–88. Stephen L. Wasby, for instance, while observing that small town police officers had become more willing over time to adapt to Warren Court requirements, nonetheless observed that overall the police were "not highly knowledgeable about the law" and lacked sufficient training in it to become so. Stephen L. Wasby, *Small Town Police and the Supreme Court: Hearing the Word* (Lexington, MA: Lexington Books, 1976), 220.

16. See, for instance, the April 15, 2008, quarterly report of the Independent Police Review Authority.

17. See, e.g., Human Rights Watch, Shielded from Justice: Police Brutality and Accountability in the United States (New York: Human Rights Watch, 1998); New York Civil Liberties Union, Mission Failure: Civilian Review of Policing in New York City, 1994–2006 (New York: New York Civil Liberties Union, 2007).

18. Peter H. Schuck, *Suing Government: Citizen Remedies for Official Wrongs* (New Haven, CT: Yale University Press, 1983); Samuel Walker and Morgan Macdonald, "An Alternative Remedy for Police Misconduct: A Model State 'Pattern or Practice' Statute," *George Mason University Civil Rights Law Journal* (forthcoming); Myriam E. Gilles, "Breaking the Code of Silence: Rediscovering "Custom" in Section 1983 Municipal Liability," *Boston University Law Review* 80 (1999): 17–92.

19. Lawrence W. Sherman and Ellen G. Cohn, *Citizens Killed by Big City Police, 1970–1984* (Washington, DC: Crime Control Institute, 1986).

20. For an excellent discussion, see Samuel Walker, *Taming the System: The Control of Discretion in Criminal Justice, 1950–1990* (New York: Oxford University Press, 1993), 30–32. Particular studies include James J. Fyfe, "Administrative Interventions on Police Shooting Discretion: An Empirical Examination," *Journal of Criminal Justice* 7 (1979): 309–23; James J. Fyfe, "Blind Justice: Police Shootings in Memphis," *Journal of Criminal Law and Criminology* 73, 2 (1982): 707–22.

21. Albert J. Reiss Jr., *The Police and the Public* (New Haven, CT: Yale University Press, 1971).

22. Stephen D. Mastrofski, Michael D. Reisig, and John D. McCluskey, "Police Disrespect toward the Public: An Encounter-Based Analysis," *Criminology* 40, 3 (2002): 519–51, at 541.

23. These are written rules prohibiting harassment; procedures for filing grievances and carrying out investigations; and comprehensive training programs and mechanisms for communicating the policy to employees. See J. H. Williams, Louise F. Fitzgerald, and Fritz Drasgow, "The Effects of Organizational Practices on Sexual Harassment and Individual Outcomes in the Military," *Military Psychology* 11 (1999): 303–28; Louise F. Fitzgerald, Fritz Drasgow, C. L. Hulin, M. J. Gelfand, and V. J. Magley, "Antecedents and Consequences of Sexual Harassment in Organizations: A Test of an Integrated Model," *Journal of Applied Psychology* 82 (1997): 578–89.

24. Chelsea R. Willness, Piers Steel, and Kibeom Lee, "A Meta-analysis of the Antecedents and Consequences of Workplace Sexual Harassment," *Personnel Psychology* 60 (2007): 127–62.

25. Laura A. Reese and Karen E. Lindenberg, "The Importance of Training on Sexual Harassment Policy Outcomes," *Review of Public Personnel Administration* 23, 3 (2003): 175–91.

26. Andrew H. Howard, Colin MacArthur, Andrew Willan, Linda Rothman, Alexandra Moses-McKeag, and Alison K. MacPherson, "The Effect of Safer Play Equipment on Playground Injury Rates among School Children," *Canadian Medical Association Journal* 172, 11 (2005): 1443.

27. David Vollman, Rachel Witsaman, R. Dawn Comstock, and Gary A. Smith, "Epidemiology of Playground Equipment-Related Injuries to Children in the United States, 1996–2005," *Clinical Pediatrics;* http://cpj.sagepub.com/cgi/rapidpdf/0009922808321898v1.pdf (2008).

28. Kristin Bumiller, *The Civil Rights Society: The Social Construction of Victims* (Baltimore: Johns Hopkins University Press, 1988); Jennie Kihnley, "Unraveling the Ivory Fabric: Institutional Obstacles to the Handling of Sexual Harassment Complaints," *Law and Social Inquiry* 25 (2000): 69–90; Anna-Maria Marshall, "Idle Rights: Employees' Rights Consciousness and the Construction of Sexual Harassment Policies," *Law and Society Review* 39, 1 (2005): 83–123; Laura A. Reese and Karen E. Lindenberg,

Implementing Sexual Harassment Policy: Challenges for the Public Sector Workplace (Thousand Oaks, CA: Sage, 1999).

29. Eugene Bardach and Robert A. Kagan, *Going by the Book: The Problem of Regulatory Unreasonableness* (Philadelphia: Temple University Press, 1982).

30. Wayne Sandholtz, *Prohibiting Plunder: How Norms Change* (New York: Oxford University Press, 2007).

Methodological Appendix

1. For suggestions and comments on the survey instruments, I am very grateful to Mia Cahill, Lauren Edelman, Lori Fridell, Bert Kritzer, and Samuel Walker.

2. For personnel departments, the population consisted of all cities responding to the police survey; for parks departments, the population consisted of all cities responding to the personnel survey.

3. See, e.g., Julie Davies, "Federal Civil Rights Practice in the 1990's: The Dichotomy between Reality and Theory," *Hastings Law Journal* 48 (1997): 197.

4. The measure consists of an index of attorneys specializing in each of the listed areas. The data source is the Martindale-Hubbell directory of attorneys, accessed at www.martindale.com at the time I administered the survey, and the data on attorneys by locality consisted of those who declared a specialty in "government." A typical attorney declaring this specialty, for instance, also specialized in "Plaintiff's Personal Injury Law; Medical Malpractice; Products Liability Law; Automobile Accident; Environmental Law; Qui Tam Litigation." Such attorneys are precisely the sort who are likely to have the knowledge and skills necessary to pursue a lawsuit against a local government. Almost all such attorneys are in private practice, not government employment. These two measures—managers' perceptions of the strength of the rights infrastructure and the objective number of government-liability attorneys in the city—both have some strengths and weaknesses. The perceptual measure captures the presence of both attorneys and citizen groups; the objective measure is an indication only of the number of attorneys. The perceptual measure reflects the usual biases associated with perceptions, but if the theory of this book is correct, it is perceptions of the legal environment that matter. On the other hand, the senior manager answering the survey may not be as familiar with the true availability of attorneys as would a member of the department's policy planning staff, and so the objective measure may in some respects provide a more accurate indicator of the local legal environment as experienced by departmental policymakers. Finally, the perceptual measure captures the relative presence of attorneys and citizen groups even if they are not within the city's jurisdiction; the objective measure captures only those attorneys whose offices are within that jurisdiction.

5. Yet 5% had more than 30 government-law attorneys, and the city with the most had 254. This highly skewed distribution suggests the value of expressing the measure as the natural log of the number of government-law attorneys, and that is therefore the measure used in the following analysis.

6. Paul Brace, Laura Langer, and Melinda Gann Hall, "Measuring the Preferences of State Supreme Court Judges," *Journal of Politics* 62, 2 (2000): 387–413.

7. I coded the data on damage caps, deadline for filing of claims, and requirement to notify of claims from the original statutes and judicial interpretations; the joint and several liability reforms and comparative negligence reforms were coded from sum-

maries of these statutes produced by the American Tort Reform Association (on file with the author).

8. Speaking precisely, the cases included a sample of all cases decided from 1990 to 1996 (before the survey conducted here) in which a primary party was a local government and the primary issue was civil rights or torts. The source for the data is the United States Courts of Appeals Data Base, Principal Investigator Donald R. Songer. I also tried a second, broader measure of appellate court liberalism, the mean liberalism score in civil rights cases for those years, but the results were similar to those for the narrower and arguably more appropriate measure in which local governments were primary parties.

9. Peter M. Blau and Richard A. Schoenherr, *The Structure of Organizations* (New York: Basic Books, 1971).

10. Lauren B. Edelman, "Legal Ambiguity and Symbolic Structures: Organizational Mediation of Civil Rights Law," *American Journal of Sociology* 97 (1992): 1531–76.

11. Samuel Walker, "Origins of the Contemporary Criminal Justice Paradigm: The American Bar Foundation Survey, 1953–1969," *Justice Quarterly* 9, 1 (1992): 47–76.

12. See, e.g., Bradley C. Canon and Charles A. Johnson, *Judicial Policies: Implementation and Impact,* 2nd ed. (Washington, DC: CQ Press, 1999), 82.

13. Robert S. Erikson, Gerald C. Wright, and John P. McIver, "Public Opinion in the States: A Quarter Century of Change and Stability," in Public Opinion in State Politics, ed. Jeffrey Cohen (Stanford, CA: Stanford University Press, 2006); accessed at http://mypage.iu.edu/~wright1/ewm_cohen.doc. An alternative is Robert Putnam's concept of "social capital," or the relative extent of cooperative nonstate organizations, trust in others, and cooperative, publicly regarding actions and attitudes. See Robert Putnam, Bowling Alone: The Collapse and Revival of American Community (New York: Simon and Schuster, 2000). Putnam has shown that the level of social capital, by state, is strongly associated with the adoption of state policies that contribute to general health, safety, and welfare. A plausible implication of his theory is that social capital, measured by state, is likely to be positively associated with the adoption of intrusive police departmental policies. Other alternatives for the policy areas of sexual harassment and playground safety are the Brace et al. state-level measures of liberalism on feminism and environmentalism. See Paul Brace, Kellie Sims-Butler, Kevin Arceneaux, and Martin Johnson, "Public Opinion in the States: New Perspectives Using National Survey Data," American Journal of Political Science 46, 1 (2002): 173. In my full statistical models, none of these measures of state political opinion or culture is consistently related to the depth of city administrative systems on rights; in the tables here, I report the results for the Erikson, Wright, and McIver measure among the various measures, since it has been the most widely used and is the generalizable measure.

14. The technique involves calculating for each city the Moran's I-score, a measure of how much the city's level on the dependent variable differs from the levels of surrounding cities, and then comparing the distribution of z-scores to a normal distribution; if the distribution of z-scores differs significantly from a normal (random) distribution, then we cannot reject the hypothesis that city values on the dependent variable are not spatially dependent. In the present data set, there is no evidence that the dependent variable is spatially dependent.

Bibliography

Adams, James E. "Debate on 'Deadly Force' Splits Police Factions." *St. Louis Post-Dispatch*, September 19, 1980, 13A.
———. "Police Chiefs Again Back Firing at Fleeing Felons." *St. Louis Post-Dispatch*, September 18, 1980, 11A.
———. "Police Convention Closes with 'Deadly Force' Dispute." *St. Louis Post-Dispatch*, September 19, 1980, 13A.
Akers, James R. "Minority Groups and the Need for Criminal Law Reform." *Lawyers Guild Review* 19, 2 (1959): 61–63.
Alliance Against Sexual Coercion. *Fighting Sexual Harassment*. Boston: Alliance Against Sexual Coercion, 1979.
———. *Fighting Sexual Harassment: An Advocacy Handbook*. Boston: Alyson Publications and Alliance Against Sexual Harassment, 1981.
American Bar Association Project on Standards for Criminal Justice. *Standards relating to the Urban Police Function*. New York: American Bar Association, 1973.
Americans for Effective Law Enforcement. *Survey of Police Misconduct Litigation, 1967–1971*. Evanston, IL: Americans for Effective Law Enforcement, 1974.
Anderson, Ralph E. "Police Standards and Goals." *Police Chief*, September 1974, 28–31.
"Anger Grows at Soaring Cost of Police Assaults." *Independent* (London), March 30, 1996, news section, 6.
Arsenault, Raymond. *Freedom Riders: 1961 and the Struggle for Justice*. New York: Oxford University Press, 2006.
Austin, Curtis J. *Up against the Wall: Violence in the Making and Unmaking of the Black Panther Party*. Fayetteville: University of Arkansas Press, 2006.
Backhouse, Constance, and Leah Cohen. *The Secret Oppression: Sexual Harassment of Working Women*. Toronto: Macmillan, 1978.
Baker, Carrie N. *The Women's Movement against Sexual Harassment*. New York: Cambridge University Press, 2008.

Baker, Tom. *The Medical Malpractice Myth.* Chicago: University of Chicago Press, 2005.

Bardach, Eugene, and Robert A. Kagan. *Going by the Book: The Problem of Regulatory Unreasonableness.* Philadelphia: Temple University Press, 1982.

———. "Liability." In *Going by the Book: The Problem of Regulatory Unreasonableness.* Philadelphia: Temple University Press, 1982.

Barnes, Jeb, and Thomas F. Burke. "The Diffusion of Rights." *Law and Society Review* 40 (2006): 493–523.

Baron, James N., Frank R. Dobbin, and P. Devereaux Jennings. "War and Peace: The Evolution of Modern Personnel Administration in U.S. Industry." *American Journal of Sociology* 92, 2 (1986): 350–83.

Barr, Emily. "Fair Cop?" *Guardian* (London), July 28, 1994, features section, T5.

Baumgartner, Frank R., and Bryan D. Jones. *Agendas and Instability in American Politics.* Chicago: University of Chicago Press, 1993.

Bayley, David H., and Harold Mendelsohn. *Minorities and the Police.* New York: Free Press, 1969.

Baynard, Thomas H., and Bernard J. Giangiulio Jr. "Protecting Your Community From Lawsuits." *Police Chief,* November 1991, 19–25.

Becker, J. C. "What's in Your Files?" *Police Chief,* December 1998, 12.

Bell, Peter A., and Jeffrey O'Connell. *Accidental Justice: The Dilemmas of Tort Law.* New Haven, CT: Yale University Press, 1997.

Belli, Melvin. "The Adequate Award." *California Law Review* 39 (1951): 1.

Benford, Robert D., and David A. Snow. "Framing Processes and Social Movements: An Overview and Assessment." *Annual Review of Sociology* 26 (2000): 611–39.

Bennett, Will. "Officers Cleared of Gardner Killing." *Independent* (London), June 15, 1995, 1.

Bennett-Alexander, Dawn. "Sexual Harassment in the Office." *Personnel Administrator,* June 1988, 174–87.

Bennetto, Jason. "Met Chief Attacks Lawyers." *Independent* (London), August 2, 1994, title page, 1.

———. "Two Face Charges in Drugs Row Inquiry." *Independent* (London), July 27, 1994, home news section, 4.

———. "Verdict Opens Way for Action against Officers." *Independent* (London), November 11, 1995, news section, 7.

Biles, George E. "A Program Guide for Preventing Sexual Harassment in the Workplace." *Personnel Administrator* (June 1981): 49–56.

Bittner, Egon. "The Rise and Fall of the Thin Blue Line," quoted In *Local Government Police Management,* ed. William A. Geller, 3rd ed. Washington, DC: ICMA, 1991.

"BJA Support Extended for Successful Deadly Force Training Project." *Police Chief,* May 1988, 11–12.

Bland, Nick, Joel Miller, and Paul Quinton. "Managing the Use and Impact of Searches: A Review of Force Interventions." Police Research Series, paper 132. Home Office, 2000.

Blau, Peter M., and Richard A. Schoenherr. *The Structure of Organizations.* New York: Basic Books, 1971.

Bloch, Gerald D. "Avoiding Liability for Sexual Harassment." *HRMagazine,* April 1995, 91–95.

Bowling, Ben, and Coretta Phillips. *Racism, Crime and Justice.* New York: Longman, 2002.

Brace, Paul, Laura Langer, and Melinda Gann Hall. "Measuring the Preferences of
State Supreme Court Judges." *Journal of Politics* 62, 2 (2000): 387–413.

Brace, Paul, Kellie Sims-Butler, Kevin Arceneaux, and Martin Johnson. "Public Opinion in the States: New Perspectives Using National Survey Data." *American Journal
of Political Science* 46, 1 (2002): 173.

Bradshaw, David S. "Sexual Harassment: Confronting the Troublesome Issues." *Personnel Administrator,* January 1987, 51–52.

Brave, Michael A. "Liability Constraints on Human Restraints." *Police Chief,* March
1993, 28–35.

Breitel, Charles D. "Controls in Criminal Law Enforcement." *University of Chicago
Law Review* 27 (1960): 427–35.

Bresler, Samuel J., and Rebecca Thacker. "Four-Point Plan Helps to Solve Harassment
Problems." *HRMagazine,* May 1993, 117–21.

Brophy, Karen Ayres. "Department Civil Liability for Officer's Off-Duty Acts." *Police
Chief,* February 1982, 16–17.

Brown, Arthur. *Police Governance in England and Wales.* London: Cavendish, 1998.

Brown, Colin. "Inquiry into Police 'May Affect Appeals.'" *Independent* (London),
June 24, 1992, home news section, 7.

Brown, Lee P. "Law Enforcement and Police Brutality." *Police Chief,* May 1991, 6.

Brownmiller, Susan. *In Our Time: Memoir of a Revolution.* New York: Dial Press, 1999.

Buchanan, Gary W. "Managing Police Use of Force." *Police Chief,* August 1993, 20.

Bumiller, Kristin. *The Civil Rights Society: The Social Construction of Victims.* Baltimore:
Johns Hopkins University Press, 1988.

Burke, Thomas. *Lawyers, Lawsuits, and Legal Rights: The Battle over Litigation in
America.* Berkeley: University of California Press, 2002.

Burke, William J. "Designing Safer Playgrounds." *Parks and Recreation,* September
1987, 38–43, 73.

Burpo, John H. "Advancing the Police Legal Advisor Concept." *Police Chief,* September 1969, 29–30.

Cahill, Mia L. *The Social Construction of Sexual Harassment Law: The Role of National,
Organizational, and Individual Context.* Burlington, VT: Ashgate/Dartmouth, 2001.

Calabresi, Guido. *The Cost of Accidents: A Legal and Economic Analysis.* New Haven:
Yale University Press, 1970.

Campbell, Angus, and Howard Schuman. "Racial Attitudes in Fifteen American Cities." In *Supplemental Studies for the National Advisory Commission on Civil Disorders.*
Washington, DC: U.S. Government Printing Office, 1969.

Campbell, Duncan. "Base Data." *Guardian* (London), March 28, 1995, features section, T12.

Campbell, Duncan. "Corruption Claims the 'Worst in 20 Years.'" *Guardian* (London),
February 4, 1994, home section, 3.

———. "Court Claims Cut Police Strength." *Guardian* (London), June 3, 1996, home
section, 5.

———. "Disquiet Dogs Community Police Station." *Guardian* (London), January 31,
1992.

———. "DPP Gets New File on Police Station." *Guardian* (London), March 24, 1992,
home section, 5.

———. "Drug Arrest Puts Police in the Front Line." *Guardian* (London), July 11, 1992,
home section, 3.

———. "Four Cleared of Police Drug 'Fit-Ups.'" *Guardian* (London), March 3, 1992, home section, 20.

———. "Met Pays £150,000 after Assault on Kurd Refugees." *Guardian* (London), June 14, 1996, home section, 10.

———. "Police Inquiry Plea to MP." *Guardian* (London), June 4, 1992, 6.

———. "Police Must Pay Record Damages." *Guardian* (London), March 29, 1996, home section, 5.

———. "Police Station Cleared of Organized Drug-Dealing." *Guardian* (London), September 16, 1993, home section, 1.

———. "Police Suspected of Drugs Dealing." *Guardian* (London), January 31, 1992, home section, 1.

———. "Police Suspend Third Officer." *Guardian* (London), September 11, 1992, home section, 2.

———. "Police to Pay for Drugs Lies." *Guardian* (London), December 12, 1995, home section, 9.

———. "Spotlight/Guardian Libel Case: Fighting for Truth on the Front Line." *Guardian* (London), February 8, 1997, home section, 3.

———. "Thirty Officers Are Named as Group Seeks Judicial Inquiry into Policing." *Guardian* (London), February 8, 1992, home section, 2.

———. "Two Suspended after Police Inquiry." *Guardian* (London), June 24, 1992, home section, 2.

———. "Violent Arrest in Poll Tax Riot Costs Met £30,000." *Guardian* (London), January 13, 1995, home section, 8.

Canlis, Michael. "The Police Position." *Police Chief*, December 1963, 29–31.

Canon, Bradley C., and Charles A. Johnson, *Judicial Policies: Implementation and Impact*. 2nd ed. Washington, DC: CQ Press, 1999.

Carrington, Frank. "Avoiding Liability for Police Failure to Protect." *Police Chief*, September 1989, 22–24.

Carson, Clayborne. *In Struggle: SNCC and the Black Awakening of the 1960s*. Cambridge, MA: Harvard University Press, 1981.

Carter, Dan T. *Scottsboro: A Tragedy of the American South*. Rev. ed. Baton Rouge: Louisiana State University Press, 1979.

"Case Studies: Three from the Field." *Parks and Recreation*, January 1987, 69–72.

Cawn, Maurice A. "Legal Implications in Handling Demonstrations." *Police Chief*, May 1981, 14–15.

"The Central Point." *Time*, March 19, 1965, 15.

Chapman, Samuel G. "Police Policy on the Use of Firearms." *Police Chief*, July 1967, 16–37.

Christiansen, Monty. "An Evaluation of Playground Management." *Parks and Recreation*, April 1999, 74–82.

———. "Certification for Safety Inspectors, Not Playgrounds." *Parks and Recreation* April 1994, 62–65.

———. "An Evaluation of Playground Management." *Parks and Recreation*, April 1999, 74–82.

———. "International Perspectives of Playground Safety." *Parks and Recreation*, April 1997, 100–101.

Christopher Commission. *Report of the Independent Commission on the Los Angeles Police Department*. Los Angeles: City of Los Angeles, 1991.

Ciminelli, Michael L. "A Positive, Procedural Approach to Legal Training for Police Officers." *Police Chief,* November 1986, 26–32, 62.

Clark, Donald E. "Minority Group Rights and the Police." *Police Chief,* March 1965, 43–45.

Clayton, Richard, and Hugh Tomlinson. *Civil Actions against the Police.* London: Sweet and Maxwell, 1987.

Clemens, Elisabeth S. and James M. Cook, "Politics and Institutionalism: Explaining Durability and Change," *Annual Review of Sociology* 25 (1999): 441–466.

Coe, John M. "Practices of Police and Prosecution prior to Trial." *Lawyers Guild Review* 17, 2 (1957): 62–66.

Cohen, Robin. *Frontiers of Identity: The British and the Others.* London: Longman, 1994.

Commission on Racial Equality (CRE). *A Formal Investigation of the Police Service in England and Wales.* London: Commission for Racial Equality, 2004, 2004.

Conot, Robert. *Rivers of Blood, Years of Darkness.* New York: Bantam, 1967.

"Constitutional Law: 'Under Color of' Law and the Civil Rights Act." *Duke Law Journal* 1961:452–59.

Consumer Product Safety Commission. *A Handbook for Public Playground Safety,* vol. 1, *General Guidelines for New and Existing Playgrounds,* and vol. 2, *Technical Guidelines for Equipment and Surfacing.* Washington, DC: U.S. Government Printing Office, 1981.

Cooper, Kenneth C. *Stop It Now: How Targets and Managers Can End Sexual Harassment.* St. Louis, MO: Total Communications Press, 1985.

Cory, Bruce. "Police on Trial in Houston." *Police Magazine,* July 1978, 33–40.

Daane, Diane M., and James E. Hendricks. "Liability for Failure to Adequately Train." *Police Chief,* November 1991, 26–29.

Darnton, John. "S.I. Boy, 11, Killed by Police in Chase." *New York Times,* August 17, 1972, 1.

Davies, Julie. "Federal Civil Rights Practice in the 1990's: The Dichotomy between Reality and Theory." *Hastings Law Journal* 48 (1997): 197.

Davies, Patricia Wynn. "Judges Curtail Juries' Ability to Punish Police Curbed by Court." *Independent* (London), February 20, 1997, news section, 9.

Davis, Benjamin, and Marshall Horace. *Police Brutality: Lynching, Northern Style.* New York: Office of Councilman Benjamin Davis, 1947.

Davis, Kenneth Culp. *Discretionary Justice: A Preliminary Inquiry.* Baton Rouge: Louisiana State University Press, 1969.

———. *Police Discretion.* St. Paul, MN: West, 1975.

"Deadly Force: Laws Vary." *New York Times,* March 28, 1985, D31.

Deane, John. "Civil Actions 'Will Not Deflect Police.'" *Press Association,* April 23, 1996, home news section.

Deighton, Jane, and Sadiq Khan. "Brutal Cost of the Bill." *Guardian* (London), May 1, 1996, features section, 17.

Desmedt, John C. "Use of Force Paradigm for Law Enforcement." *Journal of Police Science and Administration* 12, 2 (1984): 170–76.

"Developing Better Law Enforcement Officers: Policing Executives Discuss Innovations in Education and Training." *Police Chief.* November 1987. 40ff.

DiMaggio, Paul J., and Walter W. Powell. "The Iron Cage Revisited: Institutional Isomorphism and Collective Rationality in Organizational Fields." *American Sociological Review* 48, 2 (1983): 147–60.

Direnfeld-Michael, Bonnie. "A Risk Management Primer for Recreators." *Parks and Recreation,* March 1989, 40–45.

Direnfeld-Michael, Bonnie, and David R. Michael. "Everything You Ought to Know about the Liability Insurance Crisis but Didn't Know How to Ask." *Parks and Recreation,* January 1987, 74–79.

Discoll, Jeanne Bossom. "Sexual Attraction and Harassment: Management's New Problems." *Personnel Journal,* January 1981, 33–36, 56.

Dittmer, John. *Local People: The Struggle for Civil Rights in Mississippi.* Urbana: University of Illinois Press, 1994.

Dixon, Bill, and Graham Smith. "Laying Down the Law: The Police, the Courts and Legal Accountability." *International Journal of the Sociology of Law* 26 (1998): 419–35.

Dixon, David. *Law in Policing: Legal Regulation and Police Practices.* Oxford: Oxford University Press, 1997.

Dobbin, Frank, and Erin L. Kelly, "How to Stop Harassment: Professional Construction of Legal Compliance in Organizations." *American Journal of Sociology* 112, 4 (2007): 1203–43.

Dobbin, Frank, and John R. Sutton. "The Strength of a Weak State: The Rights Revolution and the Rise of Human Resources Management Divisions." *American Journal of Sociology* 104, 2 (1998): 441.

Doherty, Neil A., and James Garven. "Insurance Cycles: Interest Rates and the Capacity Constraint Model." *Journal of Business* 68 (1995): 383–404.

Dominelli, Joseph E. "Sources of Wisdom." *Police Chief,* February 1980, 8.

———. "The Use of Force: A Time for Consideration." *Police Chief,* January 1980, 8.

Donovan, Paul. "Stoking the Fires of Resentment: There Is Concern at a 'Crisis of Accountability' over a Failure to Prosecute after Deaths in Police Custody." *Independent* (London), August 21, 1996, law section, 21.

Dougherty, Neil J. "Legal Liability: The Role of the Expert Witness." *Parks and Recreation,* January 1982, 68–69.

"Drugs, Denials, and the Ghosts Who Won't Go Away." *Evening Standard* (London), February 3, 1992, 14.

Dudziak, Mary L. *Cold War Civil Rights: Race and the Image of American Democracy.* Princeton, NJ: Princeton University Press, 2000.

Dunn, Diana R., and John M. Gulbis. "The Risk Revolution." *Parks and Recreation,* August 1976: 12–17.

Dyer, Clare. "Custody Deaths Provoke European Inquiry." *Guardian* (London), September 8, 1997, home section, 1.

———. "DPP Loses Final Say on Deaths in Custody." *Guardian* (London), July 29, 1997, home section, 3.

———. "Police Agree to £20,000 Arrests Deal." *Guardian* (London), November 21, 1988.

———. "Vicious Racism Costs Met £250,000: Respectable Family Man Abused, Assaulted and Falsely Accused." *Guardian* (London), February 1, 2003, home section, 6.

Eads, George, and Peter Reuter. *Designing Safer Products: Corporate Responses to Product Liability Law and Regulation.* Santa Monica, CA: Rand Institute for Civil Justice, 1983.

Edelman, Lauren B. "Legal Ambiguity and Symbolic Structures: Organizational Mediation of Civil Rights Law." *American Journal of Sociology* 97 (1992): 1531–76.

Edelman, Lauren B., Steven E. Abraham, and Howard S. Erlanger. "Professional Construction of Law: The Inflated Threat of Wrongful Discharge." *Law and Society Review* 26 (1992): 47–84.

Edelman, Lauren, and Marc C. Suchman. "The Legal Environments of Organizations." *Annual Review of Sociology* 23 (1997): 479.

Edelman, Lauren B., Christopher Uggen, and Howard S. Erlanger. "The Endogeneity of Legal Regulation: Grievance Procedures as Rational Myth." *American Journal of Sociology* 105, 2 (1999): 406–54.

Egerton, John. *Speak Now against the Day: The Generation before the Civil Rights Movement in the South.* New York: Alfred A. Knopf, 1994.

Eisenberg, Theodore, and Stewart Schwab. "The Reality of Constitutional Tort Litigation." *Cornell Law Review* 72 (1987): 641–95.

Epp, Charles R. "Exploring the Costs of Administrative Legalization: City Expenditures on Legal Services, 1960–1995." *Law and Society Review* 34 (2000): 407.

———. "The Fear of Being Sued: Variations in Perceptions of Legal Threat among Managers in the United States." Paper presented at the annual meeting of the Law and Society Association, Budapest, Hungary, July 3–7, 2001.

Erikson, Robert S., Gerald C. Wright, and John P. McIver. "Public Opinion in the States: A Quarter Century of Change and Stability." In *Public Opinion in State Politics*, ed. Jeffrey Cohen. Stanford, CA: Stanford University Press, 2006.

Escobar, Edward J. *Race, Police, and the Making of a Political Identity: Mexican Americans and the Los Angeles Police Department, 1900–1945.* Berkeley: University of California Press, 1999.

Eskew, Glenn. *But for Birmingham: The Local and National Movements in the Civil Rights Struggle.* Chapel Hill: University of North Carolina Press, 1997.

Evans, Sybil. "Conflict Can Be Positive." *HRMagazine*, May 1992, 49–51.

Fairclough, Adam. *Better Day Coming: Blacks and Equality, 1890–2000.* New York: Viking, 2001.

Falcone, Paul "Adopt a Formal Approach to Progressive Discipline." *HRMagazine*, November 1998, 55–58.

Farina, Albert M. "Accident Liability: What Is Your Legal Responsibility?" *Parks and Recreation*, March 1979, 28–31, 50–51.

Farley, Lin. *Sexual Shakedown: The Sexual Harassment of Women on the Job.* New York: McGraw-Hill, 1978.

Fazo, Virginia. "Use of Deadly Force." *Police Chief*, August 1985, 54–55.

Feeley, Malcolm, and Edward S. Rubin. *Judicial Policy Making in the Modern State.* Berkeley: University of California Press, 1998.

Feeley, Malcolm M., and Austin Sarat. *The Policy Dilemma: Federal Crime Policy and the Law Enforcement Assistance Administration.* Minneapolis: University of Minnesota Press, 1980.

Ferris, Saadi. "Administrative Rulemaking: Police Discretion." *Police Chief*, June 1974, 70–71.

Finney, Martha I. "A Game of Skill or Chance?" *Personnel Administrator*, March 1988, 38–43.

Fitzgerald, Louise F., Fritz Drasgow, C. L. Hulin, M. J. Gelfand, and V. J. Magley. "Antecedents and Consequences of Sexual Harassment in Organizations: A Test of an Integrated Model." *Journal of Applied Psychology* 82 (1997): 578–89.

Fogelson, Robert M. *Big-City Police.* Cambridge, MA: Harvard University Press, 1977.

Foote, Caleb. "Tort Remedies for Police Violations of Individual Rights." *Minnesota Law Review* 39 (1954–55): 493–516.

Ford, Richard. "Court Limits Exemplary Damages against Police." *Times* (London), February 20, 1997, home news section.

———. "Policeman's Victim Awarded a Record £302,000 for Attack." *Times* (London), April 27, 1996, home news section.

———. "Racial Arrest Victim Wins Police Damages." *Times,* (London), March 17, 1995, home news section.

———. "Victim of Beating by Police Wins £125,000." *Times* (London), July 19, 1996, home news section, 5.

Ford, Robert C., and Frank S. McLaughlin. "Should Cupid Come to the Workplace?" *Personnel Administrator,* October 1987, 100–110.

Fosdick, Raymond B. *American Police Systems.* New York: Century, 1921.

———. *European Police Systems.* New York: Century, 1915.

Frakt, Arthur. "Putting Recreation Programming and Liability in Perspective." *Parks and Recreation,* December 1979. 43–47.

Friedman, Lawrence M. *Total Justice.* New York: Sage, 1985.

Frost, Joe L. *Play and Playscapes.* Albany, NY: Delmar, 1992.

———. "Preventing Playground Injuries and Litigation." *Parks and Recreation,* April 1994, 53–60.

Frost, Thomas M., and Magnus J. Seng. "Police Entry Level Curriculum: A Thirty-Year Perspective." *Journal of Police Science and Administration* 12, 3 (1984): 251–59.

Futterman, Craig B., H. Melissa Mather, and Melanie Miles. "The Use of Statistical Evidence to Address Police Supervisory and Disciplinary Practices: The Chicago Police Department's Broken System." http://www.law.uchicago.edu/files/broken-system-111407.pdf, 15–16.

Fyfe, James J. "Administrative Interventions on Police Shooting Discretion: An Empirical Examination." *Journal of Criminal Justice* 7 (1979): 309–23.

———. "Blind Justice: Police Shootings in Memphis." *Journal of Criminal Law and Criminology* 73, 2 (1982): 707–22.

Galanter, Marc. "Reading the Landscape of Disputes: What We Know and Don't Know (and Think We Know) about Our Allegedly Contentious and Litigious Society." *UCLA Law Review* 31 (1983): 4–71.

———. "Real World Torts: An Antidote to Anecdote." *Maryland Law Review* 55 (1996): 1093–1160.

———. "Why the Haves Come Out Ahead: Speculations on the Limits of Legal Change." *Law and Society Review* 9, 2 (1974): 95–160.

Gallagher, G. Patrick. "Risk Management for Police Administrators." *Police Chief,* June 1990, 18–29.

———. "The Six-Layered Liability Protection System for Police." *Police Chief,* June 1990, 40–44.

Garner, Joel, John Buchanan, Tom Schade, and John Hepburn. *Understanding the Use of Force by and against the Police, Research in Brief.* National Institute of Justice, 1996. http://www.ncjrs.gov/pdffiles/forcerib.pdf.

Garner, Joel H. and Christopher D. Maxwell, *Understanding the Use of Force by and against the Police in Six Jurisdictions, Final Report* Submitted to the National Institute of Justice Office of Justice Programs U.S. Department of Justice, January 2002. http://www.ncjrs.gov/pdffiles1/nij/grants/196694.pdf.

Garrison, Arthur H. "Law Enforcement Civil Liability under Federal Law and Attitudes toward Civil Liability: A Survey of University, Municipal and State Police Officers." *Police Studies* 18, 3–4 (1995): 19–37.

Garrison, Homer, Jr. "Local Problems Arising from the 1964 Act." *Police Chief*, September 1964, 22–25.

Garrow, David J. *Protest at Selma: Martin Luther King, Jr., and the Voting Rights Act of 1965.* New Haven, CT: Yale University Press, 1978.

Garud, Raghu, Cynthia Hardy, and Steve Maguire. "Institutional Entrepreneurship as Embedded Agency: An Introduction to the Special Issue." *Organization Studies* 28 (2007): 957–69.

Garvey, Margaret S. "The High Cost of Sexual Harassment Suits." *Personnel Journal,* January 1986, 75–80.

Geller, William A. "Liability Issues—15 Shooting Reduction Techniques: Controlling the Use of Deadly Force by and against Officers." *Police Chief*, August 1985, 56–58.

Gillman, Howard. *The Constitution Besieged: The Rise and Demise of Lochner-Era Police Powers Jurisprudence.* Durham, NC: Duke University Press, 1993.

Ginger, Ann Fagan, and Eugene M. Tobin, eds. *The National Lawyers Guild: From Roosevelt to Reagan.* Philadelphia: Temple University Press, 1988.

Gitlin, Todd. *The Sixties: Years of Hope, Days of Rage.* New York: Bantam, 1987.

Gold, Seymour M. "Inspecting Playgrounds for Hazards." *Parks and Recreation,* August 1991, 32–35.

———. "The New Experts on Safety." *Parks and Recreation,* November 1991, 50–53.

Goldfarb, Al. "These Doctors Make House Calls." *Parks and Recreation,* October 1987, 44–46, 63.

Goldstein, Herman. "Administrative Problems in Controlling the Exercise of Police Authority." *Journal of Criminal Law, Criminology, and Police Science* 58 (1967): 160–72.

———. "Police Discretion: The Ideal versus the Real." *Public Administration Review* 23 (1963): 148–56.

———. "Police Policy Formulation: A Proposal for Improving Police Performance." *Michigan Law Review* 65 (1967): 1123–46.

Goodwin, Stephen, Malcolm Pithers, and Heather Mills. "Inquiry Is Urged into Policing of Miners' Strike." *Independent* (London), June 21, 1991, home news section, 3.

Graf, Lee A., and Masoud Hemmsai. "Risque Humor: How It Really Affects the Workplace." *HRMagazine,* November 1995, 65–68.

Greenalgh. Ronald J. "The Teachings of *Harlow v. Fitzgerald.*" *Police Chief*, May 1983, 20.

Greenberg, Cheryl. "The Politics of Disorder: Reexamining Harlem's Riots of 1935 and 1943." *Journal of Urban History* 18, 4 (1992): 395–441.

Greenlaw, Paul S., and John P. Kohl. "Sexual Harassment: Homosexuality, Bisexuality and Blackmail." *Personnel Administrator,* June 1981, 59–62.

"Gun Rules Tightened." *Los Angeles Times,* September 9, 1977, 1.

Gutek, Barbara A. "Sexual Harassment Policy Initiatives." In *Sexual Harassment: Theory, Research, Treatment,* ed. William O'Donohue, 185–98. New York: Allyn and Bacon, 1997.

Hahn, Harlan, and Judson L. Jeffries. *Urban America and Its Police: From the Postcolonial Era through the Turbulent 1960s.* Boulder: University of Colorado Press, 2003.

"Halford Settles." *Guardian* (London), December 21, 1992, tabloid section, 4.

Hall, Jerome. "Police and Law in a Democratic Society." *Indiana Law Journal* 28, 2 (1953): 133–77.

Hall, Peter A. *Governing the Economy: The Politics of State Intervention in Britain and France.* New York: Oxford University Press, 1986.

———. "The Movement from Keynesianism to Monetarism: Institutional Analysis and British Economic Policy in the 1970s." In *Structuring Politics: Historical Institutionalism in Comparative Perspective,* ed. Sven Steinmo, Kathleen Thelen, and Frank Longstreth, 90–113. Cambridge: Cambridge University Press, 1992.

———. "Policy Paradigms, Social Learning, and the State: The Case of Economic Policymaking in Britain." *Comparative Politics* 25, 3 (1993): 275–96.

Hall, Ray. "Security, Safety: Two Sides of the Coin." *Parks and Recreation,* December 1971, 22, 45–48.

Hall, Stuart, Chas Critcher, Tony Jefferson, John Clarke, and Brian Roberts. *Policing the Crisis: Mugging, the State, and Law and Order.* New York: Holmes and Meier, 1978.

Haller, Mark H. "Historical Roots of Police Behavior: Chicago, 1890–1925." *Law and Society Review* 10 (1976): 303–24.

Haltom, William, and Michael McCann. *Distorting the Law: Politics, Media, and the Litigation Crisis.* Chicago: University of Chicago Press, 2004.

Hargrave, Timothy J., and Andrew H. van de Ven. 2006. "A Collective Action Model of Institutional Innovation," *Academy of Management Review* 31, 4 (2006): 864–88.

Harragan, Betty. *Games Mother Never Taught You.* New York: Warner Books, 1977.

Harrington, Scott E. "Cycles and Volatility." In *The Handbook of Insurance,* ed. Georges Dionne. Boston: Kluwer Academic, 2000.

Harris, Beth. *Defending the Right to a Home: The Power of Anti-poverty Lawyers.* Burlington, VT: Ashgate, 2004.

Harrison, John. *Police Misconduct: Legal Remedies.* London: Legal Action Group, 1987.

Harvey, Steve. "Don't Try This at Home: Wacky Warnings Gone Wild." *Los Angeles Times,* January 13, 2005, part B, 3.

Hastie, William H., and Thurgood Marshall. "Negro Discrimination and the Need for Federal Action." *Lawyers Guild Review* 2 (1942): 21–23.

Henderson, Walter. "Catching Kids When They Fall: Guidelines to Choosing a Playground Surface." *Parks and Recreation,* April 1997, 84–92.

Hendrickson, Thomas A. "Local Governments May Be Sued for Civil Rights Violations: The Monell Decision." *Police Chief,* September 16, 1978.

Hendy, Teresa B. "National Playground Safety Institute Certified Playground Safety Inspectors: Who Are They and Where Did They Come From?" *Parks and Recreation,* April 1998, 33–37.

Henriquez, Mark. "The IACP National Police Use-of-Force Database Project." *Police Chief,* October 1999, 154–59.

Herbert, Steve. *Citizens, Cops, and Power.* Chicago: University of Chicago Press, 2006.

Her Majesty's Inspectorate of the Constabulary. *Winning the Race: Policing Plural Communities.* London: Her Majesty's Stationery Office, 1996–97.

Hill, Robert A. *The FBI's RACON: Racial Conditions in the United States during World War II.* Boston: Northeastern University Press, 1995.

Hochschild, Jennifer L. *Facing Up to the American Dream: Race, Class, and the Soul of the Nation.* Princeton, NJ: Princeton University Press, 1995.

Hogan, Paul. *The Playground Safety Checker: A Checklist Approach to Risk Management.* Phoenixville, PA: Playground Press, 1988.

Holmes, Robert A. "What's Ahead for Personnel Professionals in the '80s?" *Personnel Administrator,* June 1980, 33–37, 82–84.

Howard, Philip K. *The Death of Common Sense: How Law Is Suffocating America.* New York: Random House, 1994.

Hoyman, Michele, and Ronda Robinson. "Interpreting the New Sexual Harassment Guidelines." *Personnel Journal,* December 1980, 996–99.

Huber, Peter W. *Liability: The Legal Revolution and Its Consequences.* New York: Basic Books, 1988.

Huber, Peter W., and Robert E. Litan. *The Liability Maze: The Impact of Liability Law on Safety and Innovation.* Washington, DC: Brookings Institution, 1991.

Hudson, Susan D., Donna Thompson, and Mick Mack. "America's Playgrounds: Make Them Safe!" *Parks and Recreation,* April 1997, 69–72.

"IACP Addresses Police Brutality Concerns: 'Project Response' Underway.'" *Police Chief,* May 1991, 10.

"IACP Critique of the Study." *Police Chief,* February 1964, 13.

"The IACP Police Legal Center." *Police Chief,* December 1970, 48–49.

International City Managers' Association. *Municipal Police Administration.* 4th ed. Chicago: ICMA, 1954.

———. *Municipal Police Administration.* 5th ed. Chicago: ICMA, 1961.

"Inquiry Call." *Sunday Times* (London), March 31, 1996, home section.

Jacoby, Sanford. *Employing Bureaucracy: Managers, Unions, and the Transformation of Work in the 20th Century.* Mahwah, NJ: Lawrence Erlbaum, 2004.

James, Jennifer. "Sexual Harassment." *Public Personnel Management* 10, 4 (1981): 402–7.

Jamison, Kaleel. "Managing Sexual Attraction in the Workplace." *Personnel Administrator,* August 1983, 45–51.

Jarin, Kenneth M., and Ellen K. Pomfret. "New Rules for Same Sex Harassment." *HRMagazine,* June 1998, 114–21.

John, Gus. *Race and the Inner City: A Report from Handsworth.* London: Runnymede Trust, 1970.

Johnson, Marilynn. *Street Justice: A History of Police Violence in New York City.* Boston: Beacon Press, 2003.

Joseph Peniel E. *Waiting 'til the Midnight Hour: A Narrative History of Black Power in America.* New York: Henry Holt, 2006.

Kagan, Robert A. *Adversarial Legalism: The American Way of Law.* Cambridge, MA: Harvard University Press, 2003.

———. "Liability." In *Going by the Book: The Problem of Regulatory Unreasonableness,* ed. Eugene Bardach and Robert A. Kagan. Philadelphia: Temple University Press, 1982.

Kalven, Jamie. "'97 Blueprint for Reining in Rogue Cops Gathering Dust Today." *Chicago Sun Times,* January 1, 2007, 23.

Kappeler, Victor E., and Rolando V. del Carmen. "Avoiding Police Liability for Negligent Failure to Prevent Suicide." *Police Chief,* August 1991, 53–59.

———. "Police Conduct at Accident Scenes: Avoiding Liability for Negligent Service." *Police Chief,* September 1989, 25–30.

Kaufman, Herbert. *The Forest Ranger: A Study in Administrative Behavior.* Baltimore: Johns Hopkins University Press, 1960.

Kelber, Mim. "Sexual Harassment . . . the UN's Dirty Little Secret." *Ms.* 6 (November 1977): 47–48.

Kelsey, Tim. "Shot Jogger Sues after 'Bungled Stake-Out.'" *Independent* (London), February 1, 1995, news section, 8.

Kerner Commission. *Report of the National Advisory Commission on Civil Disorders.* Washington, DC: U.S. Government Printing Office, 1968.

Kessler, Daniel, and Mark McClellan. "Do Doctors Practice Defensive Medicine?" *Quarterly Journal of Economics* 111, 2 (1996): 353–91.

Khan, Sadiq. "'Flawed' Inquiries Into Police Conduct." *Times* (London), May 7, 1996, features section.

King, Desmond S., and Rogers M. Smith. "Racial Orders in American Political Development." *American Political Science Review* 99, 1 (2005): 75–92.

King, Shannon. "Home to Harlem: Community, Gender, and Working Class Politics in Harlem, 1916-1928." PhD diss., SUNY-Binghamton, 2006.

King, Steve. "Prevent Playground Injuries with Professional Inspection." *Parks and Recreation,* April 1996, 62–67.

Kinoy, Arthur. *Rights on Trial: The Odyssey of a People's Lawyer.* Cambridge, MA: Harvard University Press, 1983.

Kirby, Terry. "Policing the Police: Elderly Couple Are Living in Fear after Attack by Officers.'" *Independent* (London), April 30, 1990, home news section, 3.

———. "Policeman 'Received £1,000 Drugs Wage.'" *Independent* (London), July 11, 1992, home news section, 2.

Klinkner, Philip A., and Rogers M. Smith. *The Unsteady March: The Rise and Decline of Racial Equality in America.* Chicago: University of Chicago Press, 1999.

Kozlowski, James C. "Are You Familiar with the Public Playground Safety Guidelines?" *Parks and Recreation,* September 1987, 16–22.

———. "A Common Sense View of Liability." *Parks and Recreation,* September 1988, 56–59.

———. "A 'Cut and Paste' of Model Rec Use Law to Include Public." *Parks and Recreation,* March 1987, 22–28.

———. "NRPA Law Review." *Parks and Recreation,* January 1985, 28.

———. "Playground Safety Maintenance Guidelines: The Next Generation." *Parks and Recreation,* April 1993, 30–35, 90.

Krantz, Sheldon, Bernard Gilman, Charles G. Benda, Carol Rogoff Hallstrom, and Eric J. Nadworthy. *Police Policymaking: The Boston Experience.* Lexington, MA: D. C. Heath, 1979.

Kronenberger, George K., and David L. Bourke. "Effective Training and the Elimination of Sexual Harassment." *Personnel Journal,* November 1981, 879–83.

Kutska, Ken. "Public Playground Safety: Paradigm or Paradox?" *Parks and Recreation,* April 1994, 47–52.

Kutska, Kenneth F., and Thomas M. Kalousek. "A Vision for the Future: Working toward Safer Playgrounds." *Parks and Recreation,* April 2000, 92–95.

LaFave, Wayne R. "The Police and Non-enforcement of the Law." *Wisconsin Law Review* 1962: 104–37, 179–239.

Lambert, Eric G., Daniel E. Hall, and Lois Ventura. "Litigation Views among Jail Staff: An Exploratory and Descriptive Study." *Criminal Justice Review* 28, 1 (2003): 70–87.

Lambert, Thomas, Jr. "The Jurisprudence of Hope." *Journal of the American Trial Lawyers Association* 31 (1965): 29–41.

Landes, William M., and Richard A. Posner. *The Economic Structure of Tort Law.* Cambridge, MA: Harvard University Press, 1987.

Langendorfer, Stephen, Dianna P. Gray, and Lawrence D. Bruya. "Children's Aquatics: Managing the Risk." *Parks and Recreation,* February 1989, 20–24.

Layton-Henry, Zig, and Paul B. Rich, eds. *Race, Government and Politics in Britain.* Basingstoke, UK: Macmillan, 1986.

Lefkowitz, Rochelle. "Sexual Harassment on the Job: Help for the Sexually Harassed, a Grassroots Model." *Ms.* 6 (November 1977): 49.

Legro, Jeffrey. "The Transformation of Policy Ideas." *American Journal of Political Science* 44, 3 (2000): 419–32.

Leo, Richard A. "Miranda's Revenge: Police Interrogation as a Confidence Game." *Law and Society Review* 30 (1996): 259–88.

———. *Police Interrogation and American Justice.* Cambridge, MA: Harvard University Press, 2008.

Lester, Joan Steinau. *Eleanor Holmes Norton: Fire in My Soul.* New York: Atria, 2003.

"Let's Be Positive." *Police,* June 2003, 6–7.

Levinson, Daryl J. "Making Government Pay: Markets, Politics, and the Allocation of Constitutional Torts." *University of Chicago Law Review* 67 (2000): 345–420.

Levy, David, and Maureen Scully. "The Institutional Entrepreneur as Modern Prince: The Strategic Face of Power in Contested Fields." *Organization Studies* 28 (2007): 971–91.

"Limbo Dancer Wins Assault Damages." *Independent* (London), March 9, 1995, home section, 3.

Lindsey, Karen. "Sexual Harassment on the Job and How to Stop It." *Ms.* 6 (November 1977): 47–48.

Liquori, William A. "Personal and Organizational Integrity: Maintaining Departmental Credibility." *Police Chief,* January 1992, 22.

Litwack, Leon. *Trouble in Mind: Black Southerners in the Age of Jim Crow.* New York: Alfred A. Knopf, 1998.

Liu, Daniel S. C. "The President's Annual Message." *Police Chief,* December 1964, 50.

Looney, Francis B. "Improving the Accountability of Judges." *Police Chief,* December 1973, 8.

Lynn, Philip. "Policy Problems? IACP's Policy Center Can Make a Difference." *Police Chief,* October 1990, 127–30.

Macfarlane, Robert I., and Samuel Laudenslager. "Local Police/Bar Cooperation in the Standards/Goals Process." *Police Chief,* September 1974, 50–54.

MacKinnon, Catharine. *Sexual Harassment of Working Women: A Case of Sex Discrimination.* New Haven, CT: Yale University Press, 1979.

MacManus, Susan A. "The Impact of Litigation on Municipalities: Total Cost, Driving Factors, and Cost Containment Mechanisms." *Syracuse Law Review* 44 (1993): 833–60.

MacManus, Susan A., and Patricia A. Turner. "Litigation as a Budgetary Constraint: Problem Areas and Costs." *Public Administration Review* 53 (1993): 462–72.

MacPherson, William. *The Stephen Lawrence Inquiry.* London: Her Majesty's Stationery Office, 1999.

Maguire, Mike, and Claire Corbett. *A Study of the Police Complaints System*. London: Her Majesty's Stationery Office, 1991.

"Man Wins £27,500 after Police Assault." *Guardian* (London), July 12, 1996, home section, 4.

Marshall, Anna-Maria. "Idle Rights: Employees' Rights Consciousness and the Construction of Sexual Harassment Policies." *Law and Society Review* 39, 1 (2005): 83–123.

Mastrofski, Stephen D., Michael D. Reisig, and John D. McCluskey. "Police Disrespect toward the Public: An Encounter-Based Analysis." *Criminology* 40, 3 (2002): 519–51.

McAdam, Doug. *Freedom Summer*. New York: Oxford University Press, 1988.

McAllister, B. "Spurred by Dramatic Rise in Lawsuits, Police Agencies Warm to Accreditation." *Washington Post*, March 17, 1987.

McCann, Michael. *Rights at Work: Pay Equity Reform and the Politics of Legal Mobilization*. Chicago: University of Chicago Press, 1994.

McCarthy, Ron. "Real Issues and Answers on Police Use of Deadly Force." *Police Chief*, October 1988, 33–37.

McConville, Mike, A. Sanders, and R. Leng. *The Case for the Prosecution*. London: Routledge, 1991.

McCreedy, Kenneth R., and James L. Hague. "Administrative and Legal Aspects of a Policy to Limit the Use of Firearms by Police Officers." *Police Chief*, January 1975, 48–52.

McCrystal, Cal. "The Wrong Side of the Law." *Independent* (London), November 21, 1993, Sunday review section, 12.

McIntyre, Sally, Susan M. Goltsman, and Lowell Kline. *Safety First Checklist: The Site Inspection System for Play Equipment*. Berkeley, CA: MIG Communications, 1989.

McKenzie, Ian K., and G. Patrick Gallagher. *Behind the Uniform: Policing in Britain and America*. New York: St. Martin's Press, 1989.

McShulskis, Elaine. "Sexual Harassment Complaints on the Rise." *HRMagazine*, February 1998, 28.

Mead, Margaret. "A Proposal: We Need Taboos on Sex at Work." *Redbook*, April 1978, 31–33.

Metropolitan Police Authority. *Report of the MPA Scrutiny on MPS Stop and Search Practice*. London: Metropolitan Police Authority, 2004.

Miller, Joel, Paul Quinton, and Nick Bland. "Police Stops and Searches: Lessons from a Program of Research." Home Office Police Research Series Papers 127–32. London: Home Office, 2000.

Miller, Richard E., and Austin Sarat. "Grievances, Claims, and Disputes: Assessing the Adversary Culture." *Law and Society Review* 15 (1980–81): 525–66.

Mills, Heather. "Assault Case Settlement Costs £90,000." *Independent* (London), January 26, 1996, news section, 2.

———. "Complaints Cost Scotland Yard £1.5M to Settle." *Independent* (London), September 7, 1995, news section, 6.

———. "Police Chiefs 'Ignore Claims of Brutality.'" *Independent* (London), January 27, 1996, news section, 6.

———. "£220,000 Awarded to Police Assault Victim." *Independent* (London), March 29, 1996, news section, 11.

———. "Warnings about Neck Holds Failed to Prevent Death." *Independent* (London), January 26, 1996, news section, 2.

———. "Violence That Has Cost Scotland Yard £2M." *Observer* (London), July 21, 1996, news section, 8.

Mills, Heather, and Rachel Borrill. "Closed Ranks on Both Sides; Not Guilty: The Tottenham Three's Triumph Has left Justice Tarnished and the Police in a Sombre Mood." *Independent* (London), December 1, 1991, inside story section, 19.

Mills, Heather, and David Connett. "Law Apologises for Blakelock Convictions." *Independent* (London), December 6, 1991, title page section, 1.

Milne, Seumas. "Police to Pay £425,000 to 39 arrested in Miners' Strike." *Guardian* (London), June 20, 1991.

Milner, Neal A. *The Court and Local Law Enforcement: The Impact of Miranda.* Beverly Hills, CA: Sage, 1971.

Milton, Catherine H., Jeanne Wahl Halleck, James Lardner, and Gary L. Albrecht. *Police Use of Deadly Force.* Washington, DC: Police Foundation, 1977.

Minehan, Maureen. "Employment Litigation an Ongoing Concern." *HRMagazine,* August 1997, 144.

"Miranda's Revenge: Police Interrogation as a Confidence Game." *Law and Society Review* 30 (1967): 259–88.

"Models for Management: A Look at the Past, a Step towards the Future." *Police Chief,* August 1989, 16.

"Models for Management: Deadly Force." *Police Chief,* April 1987, 57.

"Models for Management: Response to Civil Litigation." *Police Chief,* March 1989, 65–67.

Mogens, Jensen. "Playground Safety: Is It Child's Play?" *Parks and Recreation,* August 1990: 36–38.

Montoya, John. "Who Should Investigate Sexual Harassment Complaints?" *HRMagazine,* January 1998, 113–17.

Moyes, JoJo, and Heather Mills. "Nigerian Killed Unlawfully by Police, Jury Says: A Force under Fire—Day of Shame for Scotland Yard as Inquest Finding Adds to Woe over Damages Defeat." *Independent* (London), January 26, 1996, news section, 2.

Murtagh, Peter. "Doubts Still on Shotgun 'Suicide.'" *Guardian* (London), January 13, 1988.

"My Boss Wanted More Than a Secretary." *Good Housekeeping* 186 (April 1978): 28.

Myers, Paul, and Duncan Campbell. "Woman, 73, Wins £50,000 against Met." *Guardian* (London), March 20, 1992, home section, 2.

National Advisory Commission on Criminal Justice Standards and Goals. *Police.* Washington, DC: U.S. Government Printing Office, 1973.

National Commission on Law Observance and Enforcement. *Report on Lawlessness in Law Enforcement.* Washington, DC: U.S. Government Printing Office, 1980.

National Recreation and Parks Association. *Proposed Safety Standard for Public Playground Equipment.* Arlington, VA: Consumer Product Safety Commission, 1976.

Nemy, Enid. "Women Begin to Speak Out against Sexual Harassment at Work." *New York Times,* August 19, 1975, 38.

Nickolaus, George F. "Liability in Parks and Recreation." *Parks and Recreation,* February 1980. 46, 52–56.

"NRPA Pacific Risk Management School." *Parks and Recreation,* August 1996, 3.

O'Connor, Patrick. *Civil Actions against the Police.* Bristol, UK: Jordans, 2004.

Olson, Walter. *Litigation Explosion: What Happened When America Unleashed the Lawsuit.* New York: Dutton, 1991.

O'Reilly, James T. "Bridging the Gap: Law Enforcement and Legal Education." *Police Chief,* November 1973, 54–57.

Orr-Munro, Tina. "Safety Catch." *Police,* June 2005, 20–23.

Orren, Karen. "Officers' Rights: Toward a Unified Field Theory of American Constitutional Development." *Law and Society Review* 34, 4 (2000): 873–909.

Orren, Karen, and Stephen Skowronek, *In Search of American Political Development.* New York: Cambridge University Press, 2004.

Osher, Christopher N. "Denver Police Department Training Remains Deficient, a Federal Lawsuit Says, Despite Calls for Change since 1983." *Denver Post,* April 24, 2007, A-1.

Pallister, David. "'Victim of Police Attack' Is Cleared of Mugging." *Guardian* (London), August 10, 1988, 3.

———. "Woman Gets £8,000 after 'Rape' by PC." *Guardian* (London), August 1, 1989.

Palmer, John W. "The Police Paraprofessional: An Alternative to the Police Legal Advisor." *Police Chief,* December 1973, 56–57.

P and R Editorial. "The Liability Crisis." *Parks and Recreation,* February 1986, 32.

Papst, James W. "Basic Guidelines for Administrative Control." *Police Chief,* August 1993, 20–26.

Park, Angus J. "Teaching the Constitution," *Police Chief,* July 1981, 60–63.

Parker, Dave. "Checkin' It Twice: Playground Maintenance Is Crucial for Safe Areas for Child's Play." *Parks and Recreation,* April 2000, 96–99.

Parker, William L. "Training and Education: A Big 'Plus' for the Nashville Police Department." *Police Chief,* February 1973, 36–37.

Pate, Antony M., and Lorie A. Fridell, with Edwin E. Hamilton. *Police Use of Force: Official Reports, Citizen Complaints, and Legal Consequences.* Washington, DC: Police Foundation, 1993.

Patton, Alison L. "The Endless Cycle of Abuse: Why 42 U.S.C. § 1983 Is Ineffective in Deterring Police Brutality." *Hastings Law Review* 44 (1993): 753.

Pauley, Robin. "A Fuse Just Waiting to Be Lit . . . : Britain's Inner Cities." *Financial Times* (London), September 12, 1985, 14.

Perera, Shyama. "Police Accuse Doctors over Brain Damage Case." *Guardian* (London), January 30, 1987, 8.

Perks, Richard. *The Police in the Civil Courts.* London: LexisNexis, 2003.

Peterson, James A. "Playground Safety and Height: The Real Issue?" *Parks and Recreation,* April 1992, 32–39.

"Philadelphia Police Practice and the Law of Arrest." *University of Pennsylvania Law Review* 100 (1952): 1182–1216.

Pilant, Lois. "Less-Than-Lethal Devices." *Police Chief,* September 1996, 49–51.

Pogrebin, Letty. "Sex Harassment." *Ladies' Home Journal,* June 1977, 24, 28.

Police Complaints Authority. *National Study on Stop and Search Complaints.* London: Police Complaints Authority, 2004.

"Police Could Face Criminal Charges after Drugs Inquiry." *Independent* (London), February 4, 1994, home news section, 3.

"Police Pay £10,000 for 60p Arrest." *Times* (London), February 7, 1995.

"Police to Pay Man £108,000 Damages." *Independent* (London), April 30, 1996, news section, 7.

Porter, Bruce D., and Marvin Dunn. *The Miami Riot of 1980: Crossing the Bounds.* Lexington, MA: Lexington Books, 1984.

Posner, Richard A. "A Theory of Negligence." *Journal of Legal Studies* 1 (1972): 29.

Powe, L. A. Scot. *The Warren Court and American Politics.* Cambridge, MA: Harvard University Press, 2000.

Powell, Ray. "Stop and Think." *Police,* September 2004, 26.

President's Commission on Law Enforcement and the Administration of Justice, Task Force on the Police. *Task Force Report: The Police.* Washington, DC: U.S. Government Printing Office, 1967.

"Protester Gets £30,000." *Guardian* (London), July 25, 1996, home section, 6.

Provine, Doris Marie. *Unequal under Law: Race in the War on Drugs.* Chicago: University of Chicago Press, 2007.

Putnam, Robert. *Bowling Alone: The Collapse and Revival of American Community.* New York: Simon and Schuster, 2000.

Quinn, William F. "Training: A Critical Requirement." *Police Chief,* July 1981, 8.

Rabinowitz, Victor. *Unrepentant Leftist: A Lawyer's Memoir.* Urbana, IL: University of Illinois Press, 1996.

Rankin, Janna. "Legal Risks and Bold Programming." *Parks and Recreation,* July 1977, 47–48, 67–69.

———. "Lightning: The Enemy Above." *Parks and Recreation,* July 1978, 22.

"Readers Tell What It's Like . . . and Lawyers Give Some Free Advice." *Ms.* 7 (July 1978): 86–88.

Reak, Kevin P. "Reporting the Use of Force." *Police Chief,* May 1996, 10.

"Recent Important Tort Cases: Civil Rights Act," *JATLA* 31:218ff.

Reed, Simon. "Stop and Search." *Police,* September 2004, 27.

———. "Stop and Search: Facing Up to the Challenge of Our Strengths and Weaknesses." *Police,* January 2004, 6–7.

Reese, Laura A., and Karen E. Lindenberg. *Implementing Sexual Harassment Policy: Challenges for the Public Sector Workplace.* Thousand Oaks, CA: Sage, 1999.

———. "The Importance of Training on Sexual Harassment Policy Outcomes." *Review of Public Personnel Administration* 23, 3 (2003): 175–91.

Reiner, Robert. *Chief Constables: Bobbies, Bosses, or Bureaucrats?* Oxford: Oxford University Press, 1991.

Reiner, Robert. "Police Accountability: Principles, Patterns and Practices." In *Accountable Policing: Effectiveness, Empowerment and Equity,* ed. Robert Reiner and Sarah Spencer. London: Institute for Public Policy Research, 1993.

———. *The Politics of the Police.* 3rd ed. Oxford: Oxford University Press, 2000.

Reiss, Albert J., Jr. *The Police and the Public.* New Haven, CT: Yale University Press, 1971.

Remey, Gerald S. "Defining the 'Policy or Custom' Requirement of *Monell.*" *Police Chief,* August 1983, 17.

Remington, Frank J., and Victor J. Rosenblum. "Criminal Law and the Legislative Process." *University of Illinois Law Forum* 1960:481–99.

Renick, James C. "Sexual Harassment at Work: Why It Happens, What to Do about It." *Personnel Journal,* August 1980, 659–62.

"Report on Guild Activities." *Lawyers Guild Review* 20, 2 (1960): 58.

Report of the National Advisory Commission on Civil Disorders. New York: E. P. Dutton, 1968.

Rice, Robert. "A Rapid Loss of Confidence." *Financial Times* (London), November 30, 1991, 16.

Rise, Eric W. "The NAACP's Legal Strategy against Police Brutality, 1920–1950." Paper presented at the annual meeting of the Law and Society Association, St. Louis, MO, May 30, 1997.

"Risk Management: The Defensive Game Plan." *Parks and Recreation,* September 1988, 53–55.

Rivers, Caryl. "Sexual Harassment: The Executive's Alternative to Rape." *Mother Jones* 3 (June 1978): 21–24.

Roberts, Barbara E. "Legal Issues in Use-of-Force Claims." *Police Chief,* February 1992, 16–29.

Robin, G. "Justifiable Homicide by Police." *Journal of Criminal Law, Criminology and Police Science,* May-June, 225–31.

Rodgers, William H., Jr. "Negligence Reconsidered: The Role of Rationality in Tort Theory." *Southern California Law Review* 54 (1980): 1.

Rose, David. "The Broadwater Farm Three: The Guilty of Scotland Yard." *Observer,* December 1, 1991, 22.

——. "Record Damages against the Police." *Guardian* (London), December 6, 1989.

Rosenberg, Gerald N. *The Hollow Hope: Can Courts Bring about Social Change?* 2nd ed. Chicago: University of Chicago Press, 2008.

Rovan, Rhonda. "Sexual Harassment." *Chatelaine* 51 (August 1978): 16–18.

Rudwick, Elliot. *Race Riot at East St. Louis, July 2, 1917.* Carbondale: Southern Illinois University Press, 1964.

Safran, Claire. "What Men Do to Women on the Job: A Shocking Look at Sexual Harassment." *Redbook,* November 1976, 149.

Saguy, Abigail C. *What Is Sexual Harassment? From Capitol Hill to the Sorbonne.* Berkeley: University of California Press, 2003.

Saks, Michael J. "Do We Really Know Anything about the Behavior of the Tort Litigation System—and Why Not?" *University of Pennsylvania Law Review* 140 (1992): 1147–1292.

Sanders, Andrew. "From Suspect to Trial." In *The Oxford Handbook of Criminology,* 2nd ed., ed. Mike Maguire, Rod Morgan, and Robert Reiner. Oxford: Clarendon Press, 1997.

Sandholtz, Wayne. *Prohibiting Plunder: How Norms Change.* New York: Oxford University Press, 2007.

Sandler, Debbie Rodman. "Sexual Harassment Rulings: Less Than Meets the Eye." *HRMagazine,* October 1998, 137–42.

Santos, Michael R. "Use of Force: *Tennessee v. Garner* Reviewed." *Police Chief,* October 1991, 13–16.

Savage, Stephen P., Sarah Charman, and Stephen Cope. *Policing and the Power of Persuasion: The Changing Role of the Association of Chief Police Officers.* London: Blackstone, 2000.

Sawyer, Sandra, and Arthur A. Whatley. "Sexual Harassment: A Form of Sex Discrimination." *Personnel Administrator,* January 1980, 36–38.

Scarman, Lord. *The Scarman Report: The Brixton Disorders.* London: Her Majesty's Stationery Office, 1981.

Schmidt, Wayne W. "Recent Developments in Police Civil Liability." *Journal of Police Science and Administration* 4, 2 (1976): 197–202.

Schultz, Vicki. "Reconceptualizing Sexual Harassment." *Yale Law Journal* 107 (1998): 1683–1805.

Scogin, Forrest, and Stanley L. Brodsky. "Fear of Litigation among Law Enforcement Officers." *American Journal of Police* 10, 1 (1991): 41–45.

Scott, Colin. "Accountability in the Regulatory State." *Journal of Law and Society* 27, 1 (2000): 38–60.

Scraton, Philip. "Denial, Neutralisation and Disqualification: The Royal Commission on Criminal Justice in Context." In *Criminal Justice in Crisis,* ed. Mike McConville and Lee Bridges. Aldershot, UK: Elgar, 1994.

Scuro, Joseph E., Jr. "Recent Developments in Government Liability under 42 U.S.C. 1983." *Police Chief,* April 1982, 20–22.

———. "Remarks: Police Discipline and Federal Liability." *Police Chief,* March 1983, 98.

Scuro, Joseph E., Jr., and Lawrence J. Souza. "The Civil Liability Consequences of Departmental Rules and Regulations." *Police Chief,* October 1982, 12.

———. "*Patsy v. Florida Board of Regents:* The Two-Edged Sword." *Police Chief,* December 1982, 18–19.

Segal, Jonathan A. "Love: What's Work Got to Do with It?" *HRMagazine,* June 1993, 36–40.

———. "Proceed Carefully, Objectively to Investigate Sexual Harassment Claims." *HRMagazine,* October 1993, 91–94.

———. "Safe Sex: A Workplace Oxymoron?" *HRMagazine,* June 1990, 175–80.

———. "Where Are We Now?" *HRMagazine,* October 1996. 68–73.

———. "The World May Welcome Lovers . . ." *HRMagazine,* June 1996, 170–76.

"Sex and the Legal Secretary." *Viva,* August 1976, 45.

Shavell, Steven. *The Economic Analysis of Accident Law.* Cambridge, MA: Harvard University Press, 1987.

Sherman, Lawrence W. "Restricting the License to Kill—Recent Developments in Police Use of Deadly Force." *Criminal Law Bulletin* 14 (1978): 577–83.

Sherman, Lawrence W., and Ellen G. Cohn. *Citizens Killed by Big City Police, 1970–1984.* Washington, DC: Crime Control Institute, 1986.

Siliciano, John A. "Corporate Behavior and the Social Efficiency of Tort Law." *Michigan Law Review* 85 (1987): 1820.

Silverman, Dierdre. "Sexual Harassment: Working Women's Dilemma." *Quest: A Feminist Quarterly* 3 (1976–77): 15–24.

Silverstein, Helena. *Unleashing Rights: Law, Meaning, and the Animal Rights Movement.* Ann Arbor: University of Michigan Press, 1996.

Simon, Jonathan. *Governing through Crime.* New York: Oxford University Press, 2007.

Skellington, Richard, with Paulette Morris. *"Race" in Britain Today.* London: Sage, 1992.

Skogan, Wesley G., ed. *Community Policing: Can It Work?* Belmont, CA: Wadsworth/Thomson Learning, 2004.

Skogan, Wesley G., and Susan M. Hartnett. *Community Policing, Chicago Style.* New York: Oxford University Press, 1997.

Skolnick, Jerome. *Justice without Trial: Law Enforcement in Democratic Society*. New York: Wiley, 1966.

———. *Justice without Trial: Law Enforcement in Democratic Society*. 3rd ed. New York: Macmillan, 1994.

Skolnick, Jerome H., and James J. Fyfe. *Above the Law: Police and Excessive Use of Force*. New York: Free Press, 1993.

Skoning, Gerald. "Explanations of Sexual Harassment: Are They Viable Defenses?" *HRMagazine*, July 1998, 130–34.

Skrocki, M. "Sexual Pressure on the Job." *McCall's*, March 1978, 43.

Sloan, Frank A., Katherine Whetten-Goldstein, Penny B. Githens, and Stephen P. Entman. "Effects of the Threat of Medical Malpractice Litigation and Other Factors on Birth Outcomes." *Medical Care* 33, 7 (1995): 700–714.

Smith, David J., and Jeremy Gray. *Police and People in London: The PSI Report*. London: Gower, 1985.

Smith, Graham. "The Legacy of the Stoke Newington Scandal." *International Journal of Police Science and Management* 2, 2 (1999): 156–63.

Smith, Graham, and Martin Walker. Letter. *Independent* (London), May 14, 1990, editorial page, 18.

Smothers, Ronald. "Murphy Explains Gun-Rule Changes: Says Purpose Is to Protect Police and the Public." *New York Times*, August 19, 1972, 27.

———. "Police Issue New Restrictions on Use of Firearms after the Shooting of 10-Year-Old Boy." *New York Times*, August 18, 1972, 62.

Snow, David A., and Robert D. Benford. "Ideology, Frame Resonance, and Participant Mobilization." In *From Structure to Action: Social Movement Participation across Cultures*, ed. Bert Klandermans, Hanspeter Kriesi, and Sidney Tarrow. Greenwich, CT: JAI Press, 1988.

Solomon, Charlene Marmer. "Sexual Harassment after the Thomas Hearings." *Personnel Journal*, December 1991, 32–37.

Solomos, John. *Black Youth, Racism and the State*. Cambridge: Cambridge University Press, 1988.

———. *Race and Racism in Britain*. 3rd ed. New York: Palgrave Macmillan, 2003.

Somers, Patricia A., and Judith Clementson-Mohr. "Sexual Extortion in the Workplace." *Personnel Administrator*, April 1979, 23–28.

Spar, Rebecca K. "Keeping Internal Investigations Confidential." *HRMagazine*, January 1996, 33–35.

Spear, Allan H. *Black Chicago: The Making of a Negro Ghetto, 1890–1920*. Chicago: University of Chicago Press, 1967.

Spector, Elliott B. "Police Brutality Hysteria." *Police Chief*, October 1992, 13.

Speiser, Stuart. *Lawsuit*. New York: Horizon Press, 1980.

Steffel, Jeff, and Donald Rossi. "Remarks: Psychological Aspects of Vicarious Liability." *Police Chief*, March 1983, 130–35.

Stephen Lawrence Inquiry—Home Secretary's Action Plan: First Annual Report on Progress. London: Home Office, 2000. Available at: http://www.homeoffice.gov.uk/docs/slannrep.html.

Steward, Barbara. "Adventure Goes Out of Style: Deemed Unsafe, 60's Playgrounds Are Being Replaced." *New York Times*, May 20, 1999, B1.

"Stop Apologizing When You Say No." *Woman's Day* 23 (October 1978): 26.

Strickland, Ralph B., Jr. *"Stegald v. United States*: The Supreme Court Adopts a Search Warrant Rule for Entries of Third-Party Residences." *Police Chief*, September 1981, 12–13.

Sugarman, Stephen D. *Doing Away with Personal Injury Law: New Compensation Mechanisms for Victims, Consumers, and Business*. New York: Quorum, 1989.

Sullivan, Patricia. *Days of Hope: Race and Democracy in the New Deal Era*. Chapel Hill: University of North Carolina Press, 1996.

Summers, William C. "Police Chief Liability for Negligent Failure to Train." *Police Chief*, July 1981, 12–13.

Sunderland, George. "Third-Party Suits: A Police Problem of the Future." *Police Chief*, March 1980, 50–51.

Symposium. "Developing Better Law Enforcement Officers: Policing Executives Discuss Innovations in Education and Training." *Police Chief*, November 1987, 40–45.

Tamm, Quinn. "Apathy on the Decline?" *Police Chief*, March 1967, 6.

———. "The Customer Isn't Always Right." *Police Chief*, June 1967, 6.

———. "Police Brutality—or Smokescreen?" *Police Chief*, December 1963, 7.

———. "Police Professionalism and Civil Rights." *Police Chief*, September 1964, 28–32.

Taylor, Mike, and John Deane. "Mixed Reaction to Curb on Police Damages Awards." *Press Association*, February 19, 1997, home news.

Taylor, Stuart, Jr., and Evan Thomas. "Lawsuit Hell: How Fear of Litigation Is Paralyzing Our Professions." *Newsweek*, December 15, 2003.

Teague, Travis L. "Playgrounds: Managing Your Risk." *Parks and Recreation*, April 1996, 55–60.

Teles, Steven. *The Rise of the Conservative Legal Movement: The Battle for Control of the Law*. Princeton, NJ: Princeton University Press, 2008.

Tendler, Stewart, "Yard Wants Court to Set Limits on Damages Payouts." *Times* (London), May 7, 1996, home news section.

Tennenbaum, Abraham N. "The Influence of the 'Garner' Decision on Police Use of Deadly Force." *Journal of Criminal Law and Criminology* 85, 1 (1994): 241–60.

Terpstra, David. "Who Gets Sexually Harassed?" *Personnel Administrator*, March 1989, 84–88, 111.

Terrill, William. *Police Coercion: Application of the Force Continuum*. New York: LFB Scholarly Publishing, 2001.

Thelen, Kathleen. "How Institutions Evolve: Insights from Comparative Historical Analysis." In *Comparative Historical Analysis in the Social Sciences*, ed. James Mahoney and Dietrich Rueschemeyer. New York: Cambridge University Press, 2003.

Thomas, Bob, and Randy Means. "*Canton v. Harris* Determines Standard for Training Liability Cases." *Police Chief*, June 1990, 37.

Thomas, Robert F., Jr. "Insurance for Police Agencies." *Police Chief*, January 1979, 16.

———. "Remarks." *Police Chief*, January 1982, 74–75.

———. "Remarks: The Contours of Municipal Liability under 42 U.S.C. §1983." *Police Chief*, March 1983, 82–84.

"Thuggery in Uniform." *Independent* (London), 1996, comment section, 20.

Thurm, Milton. "The Need to Train: Constitutional Issues." *Police Chief*, April 1993, 16.

Thurston, Kathryn. "Sexual Harassment: An Organizational Perspective." *Personnel Administrator*, December 1980, 59–64.

Tiffany, Amanda. "How to Tame the Liability Monster." *Parks and Recreation*, January 1987, 64–69, 103.

Townsend, Anthony M., Robert J. Aalberts, and Michael E. Whitman. "Danger on the Desktop." *HRMagazine*, January 1997, 82–85.

Townsend, Anthony M., and Harsh K. Luthar. "How Do the Men Feel?" *HRMagazine*, May 1995, 92–95.

Travis, Alan. "Cap on Police Damages." *Guardian* (London), February 20, 1997, home section, 4.

———. "Joy Gardner Trio Escape Police Action." *Guardian* (London), July 13, 1995, home section, 2.

———. "Police 'Killed Woman with Gag.'" *Guardian* (London), May 16, 1995, home section, 3.

Tuttle, William. *Race Riot: Chicago in the Red Summer of 1919*. New York: Atheneum, 1970.

"£25,000 Pay-Out," *Independent* (London), February 28, 1995, home section, 4.

Tyler, Roy A. "Insurance for Police Officers." *Police Chief*, January 1981, 18–19.

"Up to 250 Yard Police 'Are Corrupt.'" *Times* (London), December 5, 1977, home news section.

U.S. Commission on Civil Rights. *Report*, vol. 5, *Justice*. Washington, DC: U.S. Government Printing Office, 1961.

U.S. Commission on Civil Rights. *Who Is Guarding the Guardians? A Report on Police Practices*. Washington, DC: U.S. Commission on Civil Rights, 1981.

Van Der Smissen, Betty. "Where Is Legal Liability Heading?" *Parks and Recreation*, May 1980, 50–52, 81.

Varley, Nick. "Victim of Beating by Police Wins £150,000." *Guardian* (London), June 5, 1996, home section, 5.

Vaughn, Michael S., Tab W. Cooper, and Rolando V. del Carmen. "Assessing Legal Liabilities in Law Enforcement: Police Chiefs' Views." *Crime and Delinquency* 47, 1 (2001): 3–27.

Victor, Peter, "Record Payout for Police Victim." *Independent* (London), April 27, 1996, 1.

Vines, M. M. "Remarks." *Police Chief*, January 1982, 73. Wald, Michael, et al. "Interrogations in New Haven: The Impact of *Miranda*." *Yale Law Journal* 76 (1967): 1519–1748.

Walker, Clive, and Keir Starmer, eds. *Justice in Error*. London: Blackstone, 1993.

Walker, Samuel. *A Critical History of Police Reform*. Lexington, MA: Lexington Books, 1977.

———. "Historical Roots of the Legal Control of Police Behavior." In *Police Innovation and Control of the Police: Problems of Law, Order, and Community*, ed. David Weisburd and Craig Uchida, with Lorraine Green. New York: Springer-Verlag, 1993.

———. *In Defense of American Liberties: A History of the ACLU*. New York: Oxford University Press, 1990.

———. *The New World of Police Accountability*. Thousand Oaks, CA: Sage, 2005.

———. "Origins of the Contemporary Criminal Justice Paradigm: The American Bar Foundation Survey, 1953–1969." *Justice Quarterly* 9, 1 (1992): 47–76.

———. *Police Accountability: The Role of Citizen Oversight*. Belmont, CA: Wadsworth/ Thompson Learning, 2001.

——. *Popular Justice: A History of American Criminal Justice*. New York: Oxford University Press, 1980.

——. *Taming the System: The Control of Discretion in Criminal Justice, 1950–1990*. New York: Oxford University Press, 1993.

Walker, Samuel, Geoffrey P. Alpert, and Dennis J. Kenney. "Early Warning Systems for Police: Concept, History, and Issues." *Police Quarterly* 3, 2 (2000): 132–52.

——. *Early Warning Systems: Responding to the Problem Police Officer*. Washington, DC: National Institute of Justice, 2001.

Walker, Samuel, and Lorie Fridell. "Forces of Change in Police Policy: The Impact of *Tennessee v. Garner* on Deadly Force Policy." *American Journal of Police* 11, 3 (1993): 97–112.

Walker, Samuel, and Charles M. Katz. *The Police in America: An Introduction*. 5th ed. Boston: McGraw-Hill, 2005.

Wallach, Frances. "Answers to Your Playground Surface." *Parks and Recreation*, March 1989, 34–38.

——. "Are We Teaching Playground Abuse?" *Parks and Recreation*, October 1988, 34–36.

——. "Old Playgrounds, New Problems." *Parks and Recreation*, April 1993, 46–50, 91.

——. "Playground Safety: The Long Trail." *Parks and Recreation*, April 1995, 61–67.

——. "Playground Safety Update." *Parks and Recreation*, August 1990, 46–50.

——. "Playground Safety: What Did We Do Wrong?" *Parks and Recreation*, April 1992, 52–57, 83.

——. "Playgrounds and Standards." *Parks and Recreation*, April 1994, 44–45.

——. "An Update on the Playground Safety Movement." *Parks and Recreation*, April 1996, 47–52.

Walsh, Jack. "Remarks." *Police Chief*, January 1982, 76.

Wasby, Stephen L. *Small Town Police and the Supreme Court: Hearing the Word*. Lexington, MA: Lexington Books, 1976.

Watson, Dwight. *Race and the Houston Police Department, 1930–1990: A Change Did Come*. College Station: Texas A&M University Press, 2005.

Watson, Nelson A. "A Big Question: What Is Your Policy on the Use of Firearms?" *Police Chief*, July 1967, 12–13.

——. "The Fringes of Police-Community Relations: Extremism." *Police Chief*, August 1966, 8–9, 64–68.

Weckler, J. E., and Theo E. Hall. *The Police and Minority Groups: A Program to Prevent Disorder and to Improve Relations between Different Racial, Religious, and National Groups*. Chicago: ICMA, 1944. (ICMA Archives, University of Kansas Spencer Research Library, box 48.)

Weeks, Elaine Lunsford, Jacqueline M. Boles, Albeno P. Garbin, and John Blount. "The Transformation of Sexual Harassment from a Private Trouble into a Public Issue." *Sociological Inquiry* 56 (1986): 432–55.

Wennerholm, Robert W. "Officer Survival Recommendations: New Civil Liability Concerns." *Police Chief*, June 1984, 59–62.

Westley, William A. "Violence and the Police," *American Journal of Sociology* 59, 1 (1953): 34–41.

"What a Performance! Can Monitoring Deliver Better Policing?" *Police*, April 2003, 5.

White, Walter Francis, and Thurgood Marshall. *What Caused the Detroit Riot? An Analysis*. New York: NAACP, 1943.

Wilkins, Roy. "The Negro Wants Full Equality." In *What the Negro Wants,* ed. Rayford W. Logan. Chapel Hill: University of North Carolina Press, 1944.

Williams, Hubert, and Patrick V. Murphy. "The Evolving Strategy of Police: A Minority View." *Perspectives on Policing.* Washington, DC: National Institute of Justice, 1990.

Williams, J. H., Louise F. Fitzgerald, and Fritz Drasgow. "The Effects of Organizational Practices on Sexual Harassment and Individual Outcomes in the Military." *Military Psychology* 11 (1999): 303–28.

Willness, Chelsea R., Piers Steel, and Kibeom Lee. "A Meta-analysis of the Antecedents and Consequences of Workplace Sexual Harassment." *Personnel Psychology* 60 (2007): 127–62.

Wilson, Jerry V. "Deadly Force." *Police Chief,* December 1972, 44–46.

Wilson, O. W. "Can the State Help City Police Departments?" *Journal of Criminal Law, Criminology and Police Science* 45, 1 (1954): 102–9.

———. *Police Administration.* New York: McGraw-Hill, 1950.

———. *Police Administration,* 2nd ed. New York: McGraw-Hill, 1963.

Winter, Ralph A. "The Liability Insurance Market." *Journal of Economic Perspectives* 5, 3 (1991): 115–36.

Witt, John Fabian. 2007. *Patriots and Cosmopolitans: Hidden Histories of American Law.* Cambridge, MA: Harvard University Press.

Wymer, John F. "Compensatory and Punitive Damages for Sexual Harassment." *Personnel Journal,* March 1983, 181–84.

"Yard Chief Warns against 'Stratospheric' Damages." *Press Association,* May 7, 1996, home news.

Zippel, Kathrin S. *The Politics of Sexual Harassment: A Comparative Analysis of the U.S., the European Union, and Germany.* New York: Cambridge University Press, 2006.

activists: liability pressure by, 3–4, 14, 15, 28, 217; and professional practitioners, 3–4, 18–21, 24, 28; role of, summarized, 1–4, 13–18, 29–30, 216–18; and social movements, 15–18; source of professional reforms, 23–24

activists (British policing): and academic research, 142; critique by, 142, 146–48, 149–50, 155; influence on police, 160–61; and infrastructure of support for litigation, 146–48; liability pressure by, 147–57; and media coverage, 147–57; reform proposals of, 148, 158; role of, summarized, 162–64. *See also* infrastructure of support for liability pressure (Britain)

activists (playground safety): critique by, 197, 199–201; liability pressure by, 202; reform proposals of, 200–201; role of, summarized, 213. *See also* infrastructure of support for liability pressure (playground safety)

activists (sexual harassment): critique by, 167–68; influence of, 166, 174–75, 195–96, 306n50; and infrastructure of support, 167–68, 304n12; liability pressure by, 169; and media coverage, 168–69; and personnel professional journals, 166, 178–79; reform proposals of, 166, 170–73; role of, summarized, 195–96. *See also* infrastructure of support for liability pressure (sexual harassment)

activists (United States policing): and academic research, 40–41, 45–47, 48; and civilian review boards, 117, 126; critique by, 32, 38, 40–47, 90–91; and infrastructure of support for litigation, 60–72, 116; liability pressure by, 61–72, 90–91; and media coverage, 75–77, 90–91; and reform proposals, 47–52; role of, summarized, 135–37. *See also* infrastructure of support for liability pressure (United States police)

adventure playgrounds. *See* playgrounds

adversarial legalism, 14

African Americans: activism against police abuse, 42, 43–44, 73–75; jury (white) skepticism of, 63; migration to urban areas, 41; police discrimination (and brutality) against, 30, 33, 38, 40–47, 48–49, 145, 222–23, 225; police shootings of, 13, 24, 73, 82, 90, 136; view of police, 72, 73, 74; and riots, 46–47; and war on drugs, 9

Alliance Against Sexual Coercion (AASC), 168, 171, 173, 180

Alpert, Geoffrey, 107
American Academy of Pediatrics Committee for Accident Prevention, 200
American Bar Foundation, study of police practices, 46
American Civil Liberties Union (ACLU): Chicago chapter, 45, 64; Committee on Police Practices, 44; and fleeing felon rule, 68–69; and infrastructure of support for litigation, 27, 235; New York chapter, 44; and police abuses, 44, 45. See also *Monroe v. Pape*
American Law Institute, 78
American political development, 7, 10
Americans for Democratic Action, 200
Americans for Effective Law Enforcement (AELE), 66, 69, 71. *See also* Schmidt, Wayne
American Society for Testing and Materials, 204, 209
Appellate Committee of the House of Lords, 152
asphalt. *See under* playground ground covering
Association of Chief Police Officers (ACPO), 145, 160
Association of Trial Lawyers of America (ATLA), 61, 65, 85, 202
Audit Commission (Britain), 145
Avery, Michael: on jury sympathies, 75; lawsuits against New Haven police, 67; litigation manual, 67–68; and *Monell v. Dep't of Social Services*, 71; on police experts, 85–86; police misconduct litigation seminars, 67; and police training, 87–88, 105, 136; and *Turpin v. Mailet*, 70

Backhouse, Constance: and AASC, 171; "action plan" for management, 171; book on sexual harassment, 168; influence on EEOC guidelines, 173–75; influence on legalized accountability model, 187; managerial experience, 171; on personnel administrators' views, 171, 178–79; reform proposal by, 170–71
Baker, Carrie, 8, 168, 175

Baker, Tom, 9, 221
Baldwin, James, 31
Bardach, Eugene, 229
baton (police), 123–24
Bayley, David H., 47
Beggs, John, 161
Bell, Griffin, 75
Belli, Melvin, 61–62
Bhatt, Raju, 146, 147–48, 151–52, 153
Birnberg's (firm of solicitors), 146
Bittner, Egon, 35
Bivens v. Six Unknown Federal Narcotics Officers, 69
Black, Donald, 226
Black, Hugo, 43
Black Panthers, 73–74
blacks (Britain), 141–43
Blakelock, Keith, 148–49
Brace, Paul, 131, 238
Britain: admired by Progressives, 37–38; centralized reform in, 144–45; immigration to, 141; Labour government, 158–59; and racial minorities, 141–42; selected as case, 7, 140; summary of case of, 162–64. *See also* activists (British policing); infrastructure of support for liability pressure (Britain); police (Britain); professional networks (British policing)
Brixton riots, 142–43, 144
Broadwater Farm riot, 149
Brown, Lee, 108
Brownell, Herbert, 62
budgetary slack, 130, 192, 212
bureaucracy: accountability of, 1–4, 14, 15, 215–25; insularity of, 1–4, 215; professional networks and, 18–20; professional orthodoxies and, 18–19; resistance to legal control, 1–4, 9–10, 23, 215–17; theories of, 15, 18–20. *See also* professional networks; symbolic policies
bureaucratic culture. *See* organizational culture
Burke, Marie, 149
Burlington Industries v. Ellerth, 176, 186–87
Bush, George H. W., 175
Butwinick, Elayne, 200

Canton v. Harris, 88–89, 91
Carter, Dan, 42
Carter, Jimmy, 75
case congregation, 68
cause lawyers, 15
Center for Constitutional Rights, 70
Center on Police Use of Force and Misconduct, 108
Centers for Disease Control and Prevention, 209
Certified Playground Safety Inspector (CPSI), 208, 212, 238
Chapman, Samuel, 39, 281n71
Chase, Oscar, 70
Chicago. *See* police departments (U.S.)
Christopher Commission, 107
citizen review boards, 5, 34, 35, 117, 126, 128, 216, 255
city governments, 2, 4–5, 33. *See also* liability, civil; police departments (U.S.)
Civil Liberties Docket (National Lawyers Guild), 63
civil rights, 2, 5, 8, 9, 14; case reporter on, 63; as legal norm, 19, 24, 29; legal remedies for, 63–65, 70–71; and sexual harassment, 169–70; and WWI, 42. *See also* police (Britain): racial discrimination by
Civil Rights Act of 1871, 17, 63–64, 66
Civil Rights Act of 1964. *See* Title 7, Civil Rights Act of 1964
Civil Rights Act of 1991, 176
Civil Rights Attorneys Fees Awards Act, 17, 68
Civil Rights Commission. *See* Commission on Civil Rights, United States
civil rights movement, 2, 5, 16; critique of police by, 35; and National Lawyers Guild, 65–66; targeted by police, 46, 75
Clark, Tom C., 45
Cochran, Johnnie, 68, 72
Codes of Practice, 145, 159
Cohen, Leah: and AASC, 171; "action plan" for management, 171; book on sexual harassment, 168; influence on EEOC guidelines, 173–75; influence on legalized accountability model, 187; managerial experience, 171; on

personnel administrators' views, 171, 178–79; reform proposal by, 170–71
Commission for Racial Equality (British), 162
Commission on Civil Rights, United States, 46, 107
Commission on Law Enforcement Accreditation, 90
Committee for Accident Prevention, 200
Committee on Labor and Human Resources (U.S. Senate), 175
Committee to End the Murder of Black People, 73–74
complaint procedures: element of legalized accountability, 219–20, 222–24, 228; element of legalized accountability (policing), 123, 125, 126; element of legalized accountability (sexual harassment), 172, 176, 178, 182, 184, 185, 189; regarding playground safety, 210; regarding policing (Britain), 143, 144, 146, 152–56; regarding sexual harassment, 14, 23; survey question wording, 252. *See also* complaints (filed by individuals); grievance procedures
complaints (filed by individuals): against British police, 143, 150; psychological costs of filing, 229; regarding playground safety, 213–14; regarding sexual harassment, 185; against U.S. police, 82, 86, 106, 107, 125, 222–24. *See also* complaint procedures
Condon, Sir Paul, 153–54, 156
Congress, United States: authorizes Justice Department lawsuits against police departments, 35; authorizes liability, 14, 17; hearings on sexual harassment, 169; members on police brutality, 75; members on sexual harassment, 175; and municipal liability, 65; sex scandals of members, 170
consent decrees, 35
Conservative Party (Britain). *See* Tory Party
constitutional torts: and activists, 17; emergence of, 63–64; litigation to develop, 69–70, 90; police leaders on, 99, 102; policing text on, 111

Consumer Product Safety Commission
(CPSC): cooperation with ATLA,
202; formed, 200; and playground
safety standards, 198, 200–201. *See
also* playground safety guidelines
Consumers Union, 200
corrective actions (playground safety),
210–11, 212; survey question wording, 262
corrective actions (sexual harassment):
recommended, 174, 182, 187; survey
question wording, 259; variations
among city governments, 191–92, 195
corrective actions (U.S. police), 86,
126–28, 129, 134–35; survey question
wording, 255
council-manager form of government.
See reformed governmental structure
(council-manager form of government)
Court of Appeal (British), 149, 152, 156
crime rates: Britain, 142; United States,
5, 132, 243
Crown Prosecution Service: created,
144–45; credibility of, 158; and police
misconduct, 149–51, 153; and Stoke
Newington scandal, 149–51
culture, political: British, 141; generally,
3, 242; and playground safety, 211,
212; and policing, 33, 131, 134; and
sexual harassment, 167, 193

Davis, Kenneth Culp, 25, 51
defense attorneys (civil): Britain, 140,
149, 161; U.S., 66, 95, 96, 107, 134,
238
defense attorneys (criminal): British,
149; U.S., 34, 65–66
defense of life rule, 50–51, 55, 84, 102,
226. *See also* fleeing felon rule
"defensive medicine," 9
Deighton, Jane, 155, 156, 157
Democratic National Convention, 1968,
53, 72–73
Desmedt, John, 103–4
direct action (against sexual harassment),
173
disciplinary actions. *See* corrective actions (sexual harassment); corrective
actions (U.S. police)

discretion, checks on. *See* legalized
accountability
discretion, professional: and British police, 143, 145, 151; ideology of, 19,
23, 24, 29, 216, 222; and use of force
(U.S. police), 39, 46, 48–55, 79, 84,
102, 117, 183
diving boards, 197
Dobbin, Frank, 109
Dominelli, Joseph, 55
Douglas, William O., 45, 65

early warning systems (United States
policing): British reforms compared
to, 160; example of, 223–24; Justice
Department on, 113; significance
of, 14, 30, 107; survey question
wording, 253; variation among U.S.
departments, 119, 123, 125–26,
128
Edelman, Lauren, 14, 22, 26, 220, 238,
318n1
efficiency. *See* legalized accountability:
evaluation
Emerson, Thomas I., 67
environmental regulation, 221
Equal Employment Opportunities
Commission (EEOC) (U.S.): personnel administration journals on, 182,
187, 195; and Reagan administration, 175–76, 183; sexual harassment
guidelines by, 168, 170, 173–76
Erikson, Robert, 131, 242
Ernst, Morris, 65
European Committee for the Prevention
of Torture, 158
exclusionary rule, 61
exemplary damages (Britain), 139–40,
154, 155, 156
expert witnesses: and development of
legalized accountability, 21, 24, 218;
NACCA's list, 61; regarding playground safety, 198, 202, 203; regarding police misconduct, 85–86, 89, 91,
96, 136

Faragher v. Boca Raton, 176–77, 186–87,
220
Farhang, Sean, 68
Farley, Lin, 167

Federal Bureau of Investigation (FBI): and African Americans, 43, 74; and Black Panthers, 73–74; and Fred Hampton, 73–74; *Law Enforcement Bulletin* of, 80

Feeley, Malcolm, 15, 26

fee shifting: in Britain, 146; in United States (*see* Civil Rights Attorneys Fees Awards Act)

Ferguson, R. Fred, 111–12

firm grip, 123–24

fleeing felon rule: as anachronism, 50; IACP reverses and supports, 102–3; IACP staff opposes, 103; IACP supports, 81; litigation to strike down, 68–69; *Police Chief* authors condemn, 51–52, 102, 110; *Tennessee v. Garner* on, 83–84, 91, 102. *See also* defense of life rule

Fogelson, Robert, 36

Foote, Caleb, 63–64

Ford Foundation, 46, 78

Forest Service, U.S., 26

Fosdick, Raymond, 36–37

framing, issue or problem: activists and the media, 16–18; in British policing, 142, 158–59, 162–64; in U.S. policing, 75, 90

Freedom of Information Act (Britain), 159

Freedom Summer project, 65–66

Friedman, Lawrence, 100

Froebel, Friedrich, 198

Futterman, Craig, 222–23

Fyfe, James: as expert witness, 86; as police reformer, 77–78, 80–81, 89–90; on police shootings, 24, 83–84; policing text by, 110; on rules restricting shootings, 80, 226; and *Tennessee v. Garner*, 84

Galanter, Marc, 15, 68

Games Mother Never Taught You, 169

Gardner, Joy, 152–53

Garner, Edward, 13

gays, 46

Geller, William, 108

Gilles, Myriam, 226

Ginger, Ann Fagan, 62–63, 66, 68

Ginger, Ray, 62

Gitlin, Todd, 73

Goldstein, Herman, 21, 48

Goodman, Bill, 66

Graham v. Connor, 104

Greater London Council, 147

grievance procedures: adoption by city governments, 189–90; as component of legalized accountability, 14, 166, 188–89; recommended by activists, 172; recommended by EEOC, 182; recommended by personnel administration journals, 181–84; summary, 220; Supreme Court on, 176–77; survey question wording, 256; as a symbolic policy, 23, 166

Gunningham, Neil, 221

Gutek, Barbara, 188, 192

Hackney Community Defence Association (London): critique by, 148, 149–50; lawsuits against police by, 147, 148, 149, 150; MacPherson Report and, 158; organized, 147; and police reforms, 161

Hahn, Harlan, 46

Hall, Melinda Gann, 131, 238

Hall, Peter (British barrister), 160–61

Hall, Peter (political scientist), 26

Hall, Stuart, 142

Haltom, William, 15, 17, 22, 163

Hampton, Fred, 73–74, 75

Hanley, James, 169

Harlow v. Fitzgerald, 104

Harragan, Betty, 169

Hatch, Orrin, 175

Hayes, Brian, 154

Her Majesty's Inspectorate of the Constabulary, 145, 158

Hill, Anita, 185

"hollow hope," 2, 215

Home Office (British), 144–45, 159, 160, 162

Home Secretary, 145

Hood, Christopher, 18

Horovitz, Sam, 61

hotline (telephone), 186, 187, 188, 189, 258

House of Lords. *See* Appellate Committee of the House of Lords

House of Representatives (U.S.), 169

Hsu, Kenneth, 154. See also *Thompson and Hsu v. Commissioner of Police*
Human Rights Commission (New York City), 173

If You are Arrested, 44
infrastructure of support for liability pressure: concept introduced, 15–17, 27; concluding illustration, 222–25; survey measurement of, 235–37
infrastructure of support for liability pressure (Britain), 146–47
infrastructure of support for liability pressure (playground safety), 211–13
infrastructure of support for liability pressure (sexual harassment), 192–96
infrastructure of support for liability pressure (United States police): as condition for legalized accountability, 84, 116, 128, 131, 132–35; development of, 60, 61–72, 89, 90; measures of, 129, 235–37, 294n25
injunctions, 69
inquest juries (Britain), 153, 155
institutional entrepreneurs, 19
institutional norms. *See* professional norms or standards
institutional racism, 158–59
insurance (for liability): impact of, 28; regarding police misconduct, 95, 130, 134; regarding sexual harassment, 192; variable in statistical models, 241–42. *See also* insurance cycle
insurance cycle, 95, 202–3
International Association of Chiefs of Police (IACP): censure of Patrick Murphy, 81; on citizen review boards, 39; compared to British police associations, 160; and internal oversight, 123; on legalized accountability, acceptance of, 86, 87, 90, 98–114, 137; on legalized accountability, resistance to, 13, 39–40, 53, 55, 78, 81; on legalized accountability, tentative steps toward, 51–52; Models for Management by, 102–4; and professionalism, 31; professional standards, evolution of, 93–114; survey of police training by, 120; in survey question on organization's influence, 129

International City/County Management Association (ICMA), 38, 52, 81, 130
International Playground Equipment Manufacturers Association, 209
Irish Republican Army (IRA), 143

Jackson, Robert, 46
Jacoby, Sanford, 177–78
Jeffries, Judson, 46
Johnson, Lyndon, 46–47
Johnson, Marilynn, 41
Judges' Rules, 143
judicial liberalism, 131, 134, 193, 238
jungle gyms. *See* playground equipment
juries: and British police, 139–40, 146, 151, 153–57, 163–64; generally, 21, 22; and U.S. police, 34, 63, 73–77, 79, 89, 111
Justice, Department of, United States: authority to investigate police departments, 35, 113; Community Relations Service, 77; Law Enforcement Assistance Administration, 77; lawsuits against Philadelphia and Memphis police, 75–76; prosecution of police brutality, 42

Kagan, Robert, 9, 14, 221, 229
Kalven, Jamie, 223
Kappeler, 113
Kaufman, Herbert, 26
Kelly, Ace, 148
Kenney, Dennis, 107
Kerner Commission. *See* National Advisory Commission on Civil Disorders (Kerner Commission)
Khan, Sadiq, 154, 155
King, Desmond, 10
King, Rodney, 107, 108
Kutska, Ken, 204

Labour Party, 158
Lambert, Thomas, 61
Langer, Laura, 131, 238
Law Enforcement Assistance Administration, 77
Lawrence, Stephen, 158
lawyers: generally, role characterized, 3–4, 15–18, 217–18; measures of presence, 235–36; and playground safety,

202; and police misconduct (Britain), 146–57; and police misconduct (U.S.), 43–45, 48, 60–72; and sexual harassment, 167–68, 169
Lawyers' Committee for Civil Rights Under Law, 70
legal aid (Britain), 146
legalistic rules, controversy over, 9, 10
legalized accountability: concept introduced, 2–4, 8, 24–26; concluding illustration, 222–25; character of, 29–30, 222–25; development of, 3–4, 15–24, 28, 29, 215–20; evaluation of, 225–29; and fear of liability, 4, 20–21; variations, by policy area, 219–20; variations, geographical, 4, 8, 26–27, 220. *See also* oversight, internal; rules; training
legalized accountability (British police), 7, 140, 157–62, 228
legalized accountability (playground safety): adoption of, by parks agencies, 210–13; development of, 201–9; evaluation of, 227; measurement of, 210, 259–62; *Parks and Recreation*'s endorsement of, 208–9; statistical model explaining variations in, 211–13, 244–50; summarized, 213–14, 215–20
legalized accountability (sexual harassment): adoption of, 188–91; development of, 170–73; evaluation of, 227; measurement of, 256–59, 310n146; professional journals' endorsement of, 181–87; statistical model explaining variations in, 191–95, 244–50; summarized, 195–96, 215–20
legalized accountability (United States police): adoption of, by police departments, 115–29; development of, 47–52, 77–91; evaluation of, 225–27; measurement of, 129, 250–55, 293n23; *Police Chief*'s endorsement of, 101–9, 114; police textbooks' endorsement of, 110–13; statistical model explaining variations in, 129–35, 244–50; summarized, 135–37, 215–20, 222–25
Legro, Jeffrey, 20, 25
liability, civil: activists' use of, 3–4, 14–18, 21–22, 217; constitutional

tort, 17, 69–71; debates about, 8–10; economic theories of, 27–28; expansion of, 2; fear of, 3, 4, 9, 20–24, 217, 228; financial cost of, 3, 11; judicial decisions on, 17, 218; and legalized accountability, 3–4, 20–25; local officials' views of, 11, 226; and media coverage, 17–18, 22–23, 217, 228; and medical malpractice, 221–22; municipal, 17, 69–71, 226; and professional reputation, 3, 22–23, 217, 228
liability, civil (British police): activists' use of, 146–57; expansion of, 139–40, 146–56; fear of, 154–55, 156, 163–64; judicial decisions on, 152, 156–57; and legalized accountability, 157–62; and media coverage, 151–57, 163–64; and professional reputation, 163–64; summarized, 7, 228
liability, civil (playgrounds): activists' use of, 202; expansion of, 202–3; fear of, 202–4; and insurance cycle, 202–3; and legalized accountability, 204–9; and professional reputation, 203–4
liability, civil (sexual harassment): activists' use of, 172–73; expansion of, 169, 172–73, 175–77; fear of, 180, 183–87; judicial decisions on, 169, 175–77; and legalized accountability, 181–87; and professional reputation, 180
liability, civil (U.S. police): activists' use of, 60–72, 90–91, 116; expansion of, 64–65, 68–72, 83–84, 87–89; fear of, 94–98, 101–2, 104–5, 107, 108–10; judicial decisions on, 64–65, 68–71, 83–84, 87–89; and legalized accountability, 77–91, 101–9, 114; media coverage of, 72–77; and professional reputation, 97–98, 137
liability, fear of, 3, 4, 20–24, 28; administrative reform and, 22–23; professional reputation and, 22, 24. *See also under* liability, civil (British police); liability, civil (playgrounds); liability, civil (sexual harassment); liability, civil (U.S. police)
liability, respondeat superior, 70
liability, vicarious, 146. *See also* liability, respondeat superior

litigation: against cities (sexual harassment), measured, 193; rates, 9; survey measurement of, generally, 239–40; against U.S. police departments, measured, 131–32. *See also* liability, civil (British police); liability, civil (playgrounds); liability, civil (sexual harassment); liability, civil (U.S. police)
litigation manuals: Britain, 146–47; U.S., 66, 67–68, 87
London: Greater London Council, 147; police department of, 140, 147–57; police misconduct litigation in, 139, 147–57; riots, 141, 142–43
Love, Eula, 74
Lynch, Lawrence, 111–12
"lynching, northern style," 43

MacDonald, Morgan, 226
MacKinnon, Catharine, 168, 170, 173–74, 187
MacPherson, Sir William, 158–59
Mastrofski, Stephen, 227
Mather, Lynn, 22
Mattis v. Schnarr, 68
Matulia, Kenneth, 102
McBride, R. Bruce, 111–12
McCann, Michael, 15, 17, 22, 163
McCarthyism, 62–63, 65
McClaren, Roy, 110
McCoy, Candace, 71, 85, 134
McIver, John, 131, 242
Mead, Margaret, 173, 181
media coverage: and activist liability pressure, 3–4, 7, 15, 16, 17–18; role of, summarized, 217. *See also* framing, issue or problem; juries
media coverage (police misconduct, Britain): compared to U.S., 163–64; of police abuse, 139–40, 152–57; of police misconduct litigation, 152–57
media coverage (police misconduct, U.S.): compared to Britain, 163–64; of police abuse, 40, 60, 72–77; of police misconduct litigation, 72–77
media coverage (sexual harassment), 168–69
Mendelsohn, Harold, 47
Meritor Savings Bank v. Vinson, 175–76, 183–84

Merit Systems Protection Board (U.S.), 169
merry-go-rounds. *See under* playground equipment
Metropolitan Police Authority (London), 162
Metropolitan Police Force (London), 148; alleged brutality by officers of, 152–56; investigation of Stoke Newington allegations, 150–51; jury awards against, 152–57; racially disparate stops and searches by, 162. *See also* Condon, Sir Paul
Miller, Russell, 147, 153
minorities (Britain): litigation by, 139, 146–57; police abuse of, 139–40, 145, 147–56, 158–59; police reforms regarding, 158–60; police stops of, 142–43, 145, 162; population growth of, 140, 141–42; and riots, 142–43, 144; segregation of, 141–42
minorities (U.S.). *See* African Americans
model, administrative, 25–26. *See also* legalized accountability
Model Penal Code, 78
Monell v. Department of Social Services, 17, 70–71, 83, 85, 87
Monerville, Trevor, 147, 148, 149
Monroe v. Pape, 17, 64–65, 69–70
Moore, Donald Page, 64
moral panic, 142
Mullin, Chris, 152, 153–54, 158
municipal liability. *See under* liability, civil
Murphy, Patrick: and New York City shootings policy, 136; and police shootings reform, 13, 19, 55; reform campaign by, 20, 21, 24, 77–81, 89–90

NAACP-Legal Defense Fund, 68, 70, 84
National Advisory Commission on Civil Disorders (Kerner Commission), 46–47, 50–51
National Advisory Commission on Criminal Justice Standards and Goals, 51
National Association for the Advancement of Colored People (NAACP): and McCarthyism, 63; New York Chapter of, 44; on police brutality,

42, 43–44, 45; and Police Founda-
tion, 55; and police misconduct litigation, 63
National Association of Claims Compensation Attorneys (NACCA), 61–62.
See also Association of Trial Lawyers
of America (ATLA)
National Black Police Association (Brit-
ain), 162
National Bureau of Standards, 200, 206
National Commission on Reform of Fed-
eral Criminal Laws, 51
National Commission on the Causes and
Prevention of Violence, 73
National Electronic Injury Survey Sys-
tem, 200
National Lawyers Guild: and McCarthy-
ism, 62–63; and NACCA, 61; origins
of, 44; police brutality, campaign
against, 44, 45; and Student Nonvio-
lent Coordinating Committee, 65–66.
See also Avery, Michael; Ginger, Ann
Fagan; *Police Misconduct Litigation
Manual*; Rudovsky, David
National League of Cities, 81
National Organization of Black Law En-
forcement Executives (NOBLE), 78
National Playground Safety Institute,
206
National Program for Playground Safety,
209
National Recreation and Parks Associa-
tion, 198, 200
National Union of Miners (Britain), 147
Nazis, 43, 73, 75
neck hold, 153
Newsweek, 9
New York Human Rights Commission,
167
Nixon administration, 200
norms, 59–60. *See also* professional norms
or standards
Norton, Eleanor Holmes, 167, 173, 180

O'Leary, Rosemary, 9
Oncale v. Sundowner Offshore Services,
185
Operation Jackpot, 149, 153
Operation Swamp, 142–43
Orfield, Myron, 35

organizational culture: legalized reform
of, 24–25, 26–27, 216–17; need for
reform of, 6, 14, 16, 18
organizational culture (British police),
158–59
organizational culture (sexual harassment), 171–72, 195
organizational culture (U.S. police):
legalized reform of, 104–9, 115; need
for reform of, 32, 56, 61, 71, 85
organizational size, hypothesis regarding:
generally, 241; police policies, 130,
134; sexual harassment policies, 192
Orren, Karen, 10
oversight, internal, 8, 14, 25, 217–20
oversight, internal (British police),
159–61
oversight, internal (playground safety):
audits, 198, 201, 208–10, 212, 214,
260; inspections, 203, 204–6, 208–10,
260; by legal staff, 210, 261; policies
modified, 210, 262; recommended by
professional journal, 208–10; record-
keeping, 209, 210, 260; response to
hazards, 210, 259; variations among
agencies, 210. *See also* corrective actions (playground safety)
oversight, internal (sexual harassment):
grievance procedures, 14, 23, 166,
172, 176–77, 182, 181–84, 189–90,
256; by legal staff, 190–91, 257;
policies modified, 190, 257; recommended by professional journals, 183,
186–87; survey of employees, 166,
169, 172, 175, 186, 187, 189, 191, 258;
variation among city governments,
188–91. *See also* corrective actions
(sexual harassment)
oversight, internal (U.S. police): citizen
review board, 5, 34, 35, 117, 126,
128, 216, 255; complaint procedures,
118, 123, 125, 252; by legal staff, 126,
254; policies modified, 118, 254;
proposals for, 48–50, 79, 85; reporting
requirements, 118, 123–25, 251, 255;
review uses of force, 125, 250; variation among departments, 116–19,
123–28. *See also* corrective actions
(U.S. police)
Owen v. City of Independence, 102

parks agencies, freestanding versus nonfreestanding, 242
Parks and Recreation (journal): ignores safety issue, 201–2; on insurance cycle, 202–3; on legalized accountability, 208–9; on legal liability, 203–9; on safety reforms, 203–9
personnel administration journals: compared to policing journals, 183; described, 177; on sexual harassment, 179–87. *See also* personnel administration profession
personnel administration profession: as case study, 5, 13–14; divided mission of, 178; origins of, 177–78, 307n68; on sexual harassment, 177–87. *See also* personnel administration journals
playground administration journal. See *Parks and Recreation* (journal)
playground administration profession: as case study, 5, 13–14; on legal liability, 201–9; origins of, 198–99. See also *Parks and Recreation* (journal)
Playground Association of America, 198–99
playground equipment: jungle gyms, 197, 199; merry-go-rounds, 197, 199; nature of, 1910–60, 199; reform of, 201–9; swings, 197
playground ground covering: asphalt, 197, 199; concrete, 199; impact-absorbing, 206, 207, 209
playground injuries, 197, 199, 200, 227
playgrounds: different styles, 199–200; growth of, 198–99; and infrastructure of support for litigation, 211–13; and professional networks, 211–13; reform of, 199–209; variations in, 209–11. *See also* legalized accountability (playground safety)
Playground Safety Checker, 203
Playground Safety Checklist, 203
playground safety guidelines: as basis for reforms, 213–14; compliance with, 210–11; and plaintiff lawyers, 202; and playground administration profession, 201, 203, 206–9; published, 200; revised, 207
Playground Safety Handbook. See playground safety guidelines

police (Britain): compared to U.S. police, 5, 7, 140, 162–63; constabulary independence, 143; judicial oversight of, favored, 145; MacPherson report on, 158–59; racial composition of, 141; racial discrimination by, 141–43, 144, 147–56, 158–59; regulated nationally, 144–45; shielded from liability, 140; shielded from judicial oversight, 143. *See also* Association of Chief Police Officers (ACPO); legalized accountability (British police); liability, civil (British police); media coverage (police misconduct, Britain); Metropolitan Police Force (London); oversight, internal (British police); Police Federation (Britain); rules (British police); training (British police)
police (U.S.): abuse by, 31–32, 36, 38–47, 72–77; accountability of, 33–35; ACLU on, 44–45; activist critique of, 31–32, 40–47, 90–91; activist critique of, response to, 38–40; Commission on Civil Rights on, 46; constitutional checks on, 33–34, 35; gays, harassment of, 46; NAACP on, 42, 43–44, 45, 55, 63; National Lawyers Guild on, 44, 45, 65–66; Progressive reform of, 35–40; prosecution of, 34, 42; public opinion of, 53, 59, 73; uniform of, 26, 36, 37; unions, 55. *See also* defense of life rule; fleeing felon rule; International Association of Chiefs of Police (IACP); legalized accountability (United States police); liability, civil (U.S. police); media coverage (police misconduct, U.S.); oversight, internal (U.S. police); *Police Chief*; rules (United States police); training (United States police)
police abuses (Britain), 7, 139, 142–43, 144, 147–56, 158–59
police abuses (U.S.): activists' critique of, 40–47; concluding illustration, 222–25; controversies over, 53; IACP on, 39–40, 51, 53; lawsuits over, 17, 60–72; media coverage of, 72–77; O. W. Wilson on, 38, 110; *Task Force Report* on, 48–49; as widespread

problem, 5, 32–33. *See also* police shootings (U.S.)

Police Action Lawyers Group (PALG), 147

Police and Criminal Evidence Act of 1984 (PACE), 144–45

police brutality. *See* police abuses (Britain); police abuses (U.S.)

Police Chief: advertisements in, 109–10; on criticisms of police in 1960s, 39; described, 94; on internal oversight, 106–7; on liability, 94–109; on rules, 101–4; on training, 104–5

Police Complaints Authority, 144, 150, 152, 153, 154, 155

police departments (U.S.): Bessemer, AL, 75; Boston, 75; Chicago, 41–42, 73–74, 75, 222–25; Choctaw, OK, 84; Concordia Parish, LA, 76; Cook County, IL, 73–74; Gary, IN, 45; Georgia Highway Patrol, 43; Houston, 82; Los Angeles, 42, 74, 80, 82; Memphis, 24, 76; Miami, 75, 107; Milwaukee, 46; Montgomery County, MD, 55; New Haven, CT, 67; New Orleans, 74, 76, 77, 82; New York City, 41, 74, 80, 82; Ohio Highway Patrol, 96; Philadelphia, 45, 67, 76; Pontiac, MI, 46; Prince Georges County, MD, 82; Richmond, CA, 76; San Diego, 46; San Jose, CA, 55; Saugus, MA, 76; Savannah, GA, 76; South Tucson, AZ, 76, 82; Troy, MI, 76

Police Executive Research Forum (PERF), 78

Police Federation (Britain), 161–62

Police Foundation: *Garner* amicus brief by, 84, 102–3, 114; reform campaign by, 55, 78–81, 82, 89–90, 94, 114; studies by, 54

police misconduct. *See* police abuses (Britain); police abuses (U.S.)

Police Misconduct Litigation Manual, 67–68

police shootings (Britain), 151

police shootings (U.S.): controversies over, 27, 73–75; IACP on, 13, 55, 102–3; lawsuits over, 68–69, 72, 73–75, 82–84; *Police Chief* on, 51–52, 94–95, 110; racial discrimination in,

27, 45–46; reform movements and, 8, 13, 78–81, 108, 114; *Tennessee v. Garner* and, 82–84, 102–3. *See also* defense of life rule; fleeing felon rule

political culture, measures of, 242, 294n28

political party machines, 19, 36

Post Office and Civil Service Committee (U.S. House of Representatives), 169

Pound, Roscoe, 61

Powell, Enoch, 141–42

Powell, Ray, 162

practitioner journals. *See* professional journals

President's Commission on Law Enforcement and the Administration of Justice, 48

preventive patrol, 42

professionalism, 9, 10, 20

professional journals, 22–23. See also *Parks and Recreation* (journal); personnel administration journals; *Police Chief*

professional judgment, 9, 10. *See also* discretion, professional

professional networks: role of, 3, 18–20, 27, 28, 216–18; survey measurement of, 237–38

professional networks (British policing), 159–62

professional networks (personnel administration): activists' influence on, 172; influence of, 193–96; survey measurement of, 192

professional networks (playground safety), 211–13

professional networks (U.S. policing): activists' influence on, 82–90; development of, 35–40; influence of, 132–35; survey measures of, 129

professional norms or standards: in British policing, 160, 161–62; and legalized accountability, 21–22, 23, 216; in personnel administration, 177–88; in playground administration, 201–9; summary of changes in, 217–19, 221, 222–25; in U.S. policing, 59–60, 82–83, 86–87, 98–99, 108–13

professional reputation, as incentive: in British policing, 163–64; generally, 3, 22, 28, 221–22; in personnel management, 180–81; in playground safety, 204–5; in U.S. policing, 97–98
professions, administrative: characterized, 19–20, 221–22; interactions with activists, 20–21, 28; reform campaigns in, 13, 14, 28. See also professional journals; professional networks; professional norms or standards
Progressive Era: and administrative professionalism, 7, 19, 26, 217; and personnel administration, 177–78; and playgrounds, 198–99; and police professionalism, 35–38, 56, 135–36
prosecution, criminal: regarding police misconduct, 34, 42; regarding sexual harassment, 173
Provine, Doris Marie, 9
punitive damages, 176
Putnam, Robert, 131

Rabinowitz, Victor, 63
race of drivers reported (U.S. police): as measure of internal oversight, 124–25; survey question wording, 255
Race Relations (Amendment) Act (Britain), 159
racial discrimination. See police abuses (Britain); police abuses (U.S.)
racial profiling, 124–25, 145, 225
Reagan administration, 175, 183
reformed governmental structure (council-manager form of government): regarding police misconduct, 130, 134; regarding sexual harassment, 192, 194; survey measurement, 241–42
Rehnquist, William, 175–76
Reiner, Robert, 141, 144, 145
Reiss, Albert, 226
Remington, Frank, 21, 48, 51
reports on uses of force. See oversight, internal (U.S. police)
resource mobilization, 15–16
respondeat superior liability. See liability, respondeat superior
review uses of force (police). See oversight, internal (U.S. police)

rights, politics of, 1, 14, 215
rights revolution, 2, 5, 14, 165, 215, 216
riots, urban: Britain, 141–43, 149; United States, 5, 41, 43, 46–47, 145
risk management, 109, 123, 203, 205, 214
Rizzo, Frank, 67, 76
Rizzo v. Goode, 69
Roach, Colin, 147, 148
Roach Family Support Committee, 147
Rosenberg, Gerald, 2
Rosenbloom, David, 9
royal commissions, 144, 296n26
Rubin, Edward, 14, 26
Rudovsky, David, 66–67, 69, 70, 71, 87–89, 136
rules (British police), 159–61
rules (playground safety): Parks and Recreation on, 208; survey question wording, 261; variations among agencies, 210
rules (sexual harassment): activists on, 171; EEOC guidelines on, 174; personnel administration journals on, 181–87; survey question wording, 256; variation among city governments, 189
rules (United States police): adoption by departments, 78, 80, 82, 84–85; Police Chief on, 101–4; police reformers on, 49, 79; survey question wording, 250; variation among departments, 116–20
rules, 14, 25, 26, 217–20
R v. Chief Constable ex parte Wiley, 152

Sanders, Andrew, 145
Sarat, Austin, 15
Scarman, Lord, 144
Scarman Report, 144, 158
Scheingold, Stuart, 2, 15, 215
Schmidt, Wayne, 66, 69, 75. See also Americans for Effective Law Enforcement (AELE)
Schuck, Peter, 226
Scotland Yard. See Metropolitan Police Force (London)
Scraton, Philip, 145
Screws v. United States, 42, 64
search and seizure, 104
Secret Detention by the Chicago Police, 45, 64

Secret Service (U.S.), 103
Section 1983 of the Civil Rights Act of 1871, 17, 63–64, 66
Selznick, Philip, 25
Senate (U.S.). *See* Committee on Labor and Human Resources (U.S. Senate)
sexual harassment: activists on, 166, 167–68; as case study, 6; hostile environment, 174–75; liability for, 165–66, 169, 174–75; remedies for, 170–73; surveys on, 169. *See also* legalized accountability (sexual harassment); sexual harassment law
sexual harassment, movement against. *See* activists (sexual harassment)
sexual harassment law: appellate court decisions on, 169–70; EEOC and, 175; MacKinnon on, 170; personnel administration journals on, 180–87; Supreme Court decisions on, 175–77. *See also* Equal Employment Opportunities Commission (EEOC) (U.S.); *Meritor Savings Bank v. Vinson*; Title 7, Civil Rights Act of 1964
Sexual Harassment of Working Women, 168
sexual harassment policies. *See* legalized accountability (sexual harassment)
Silverman, Deirdre, 168
Simon, Jonathan, 9
Skolnick, Jerome, 47
Skullcap Crew, 222–23
Smith, Graham: and database of abusive officers, 147; and Hackney Community Defence Association, 148; on Operation Jackpot, 150; on Stoke Newington scandal, 149. *See also* Hackney Community Defence Association (London)
Smith, Rogers, 10
Society for Human Resources Management, 185
Songer, Donald, 131
sovereign immunity, 9, 28, 131, 192, 212, 235, 238
speak-out (on sexual harassment), 167, 168
Speiser, Stuart, 61–62
Standards Relating to the Urban Police Function (American Bar Association), 51

Stearns, Nancy, 70, 281n71
Stoke Newington police station (London), 147, 148, 149–51, 160–61
stop and frisk (U.S. police), 46, 48
stop and search (British police), 142, 144, 145, 160, 162
Student Nonviolent Coordinating Committee (SNCC), 65–66
support structure for legal mobilization. *See* infrastructure of support for liability pressure
Supreme Court: and constitutional torts, 64–65; and failure to train, 88, 104, 137; and fleeing felon rule, 53–54, 69; and municipal liability, 64–65, 69–71, 88–89, 137; and official liability, 42, 64–65; and police practices generally, 5, 33–34, 42; and rights revolution, 2; on sexual harassment, 175–76, 195; and use of force, 104, 137; as viewed by police, 96; Warren Court, 2, 64–65
surveys: of employees regarding sexual harassment, 14, 186, 190–91, 220; of population regarding police abuse, 47, 53; of population regarding sexual harassment, 169
surveys (as basis for this book): described, 7–8; methodological summary, 233–34; personnel departments, 189; playground administration, 209; police departments (U.S.), 116–17; question responses, 250–63; question wording, 250–63;
Sutton, John, 109
Swanson, Charles, 107
symbolic policies: as distinct from deep reform, 3, 9, 10, 23, 26, 215–16, 220; in policing, 116; regarding sexual harassment, 171, 174, 187

taboo against sexual harassment, 173, 181
Tamm, Quinn, 39–40, 53, 98
Task Force Report, 48–52
Taylor, Lord, 150
Taylor, Robert, 107
technological progress, 100
Tennessee v. Garner: decision in, 84, 91; impact of, 84–85, 87–88, 102–3, 105, 114; litigation of, 24, 83–84, 90

Territo, Leonard, 107
Thames Valley Police, 161
Thibault, Edward, 111–12
Thomas, Clarence, 175–76, 185
Thompson and Hsu v. Commissioner of Police, 156
Thornton, Dorothy, 221
Title 7, Civil Rights Act of 1964, 6, 169, 170, 174–75, 187
tort liability. *See* liability, civil
tort reform, 202–3
Tory Party, 141–42
Traffic Institute (Northwestern University), 113
training, 8, 14, 25, 217–20
training (British police), 153, 159–61
training (playground safety): recommended, 208–9; variations among agencies, 210; survey question wording, 261, 262
training (sexual harassment): activists, recommended by, 171–72; EEOC, endorsed by, 174; personnel administration journals, endorsed by, 181–87; survey question wording, 256–58; variation among city governments, 188–91
training (United States police): endorsed by IACP, 104–5; liability for failure, 85–88, 104–5; reformers, recommended by, 49, 79; survey question wording, 252–53, 254; variations among departments, 116–19, 120–22
Trevor Monerville Campaign, 147
Turpin v. Mailet, 70
Tuttle, William, 41–42

unions: and personnel administration, 177–78, 192; and police departments, 55, 130, 134; survey measurement, 241; and tort bar, 61–62
University of Delaware Commission on the Status of Women, 168

U.S. Conference of Mayors, 81
use of force continuum, 103–4

Walker, Martin, 148, 149
Walker, Samuel: on liability, 134, 226; on O. W. Wilson, 110; on police abuses, 36, 46; on police accountability, 8, 14, 34, 35, 107, 113, 117; on police professionalism, 26, 36; on rules, 25; on *Task Force Report*, 51
Wallace, George, 73
Wallach, Frances, 203, 206
Watergate scandal, 75
Watson, Nelson A., 31, 51
Weber, Max, 4
Webster v. City of Houston, 106
Welles, Orson, 43
Westley, William, 45
West Midlands Serious Crime Squad, 143
Whisenhand, Paul, 111–12
whites: opinions on police misconduct, 72–73, 76, 77; racial discrimination by, 41–42; riots against African Americans, 41
Wickersham Commission, 44
Wiley v. Memphis Police Department, 69
Williams, John, 67
Williams v. Saxbe, 169
Wilkins, Roger, 71
Wilson, James Q., 19
Wilson, O. W., 37, 38, 48, 110
window dressing. *See* symbolic policies
Winning the Race, 158
Winter, Steven L., 84
Woolf, Lord, 156
Working Women United, 168, 174, 181
Working Women United Institute, 181
Wright, Gerald, 131, 242
wristlock, 123–24

zero tolerance policies: regarding excessive force, 99, 106; regarding sexual harassment, 186

THE CHICAGO SERIES IN LAW AND SOCIETY

Edited by John M. Conley and Lynn Mather

Series titles, continued from frontmatter:

The Common Place of Law: Stories from Everyday Life
by Patricia Ewick and Susan S. Silbey

The Struggle for Water: Politics, Rationality, and Identity in the American Southwest
by Wendy Nelson Espeland

Dealing in Virtue: International Commercial Arbitration and the Construction of a
Transnational Legal Order
by Yves Dezalay and Bryant G. Garth

Rights at Work: Pay Equity Reform and the Politics of Legal Mobilization
by Michael W. McCann

The Language of Judges
by Lawrence M. Solan

Reproducing Rape: Domination through Talk in the Courtroom
by Gregory M. Matoesian

Getting Justice and Getting Even: Legal Consciousness among Working-Class Americans
by Sally Engle Merry

Rules versus Relationships: The Ethnography of Legal Discourse
by John M. Conley and William M. O'Barr